D1312248

Addison-Wesley Mathematics

Robert E. Eicholz
Phares G. O'Daffer
Charles R. Fleenor

Randall I. Charles
Sharon Young
Carne S. Barnett

Addison-Wesley Publishing Company

Menlo Park, California • Reading, Massachusetts • Don Mills, Ontario • Wokingham, England
Amsterdam • Sydney • Singapore • Tokyo • Madrid • Bogotá • Santiago • San Juan

Illustration Acknowledgments

Frank Ansley 6–7, 20–21, 32, 72–73, 134–135, 190, 240, 242, 326–327

Sherry Balestra 8–9, 30–31, 40–41, 51, 114, 117, 136–137, 160–161, 177, 184, 199, 218–219, 250–251, 302–303, 318–319, 336–337, 355

Ellen Blonder 50, 84, 116, 147, 148, 176, 196, 221, 222, 244, 264, 289, 290, 310, 330–331, 339, 340, 354

Cindy Brodie 19, 53, 75, 76, 85, 122–123 (clock faces), 124–125 (clock faces), 130–131, 140–141, 149, 151, 184–185, 202–203, 212, 265, 272, 276–277, 280–281, 284–285, 306–307, 320–321, 341, 348–349

Kirk Caldwell 10–11, 44, 97, 104–105, 124–125, 154–155, 170, 182–183, 197, 216–217, 229 (lower right), 232–233, 308–309, 322–323, 350–351, 357

Liz Callen 27, 46–47, 52, 68–69, 78, 93, 112–113, 132, 158–159, 203, 208–209, 224, 234–235, 245, 256–257, 262–263, 270–271, 304–305, 311, 328–329, 334, 346–347, 356, 360–365, 367

Maxie Chambliss 4–5, 18, 22, 38–39, 43, 54–55, 100–101, 118, 123, 139, 144, 164–165, 179, 186, 198–199, 206–207, 231, 252–253, 260–261, 266–267, 296–297, 332–333, 342, 352–353

Randy Chewning 12, 65, 70–71, 102–103, 162–163, 169, 171, 189, 195, 241, 254, 273

Myron Grossman 48–49

Roberta Holmes 36–37, 115, 343

Glenn Iwasaki 34–35, 95, 106–107, 168, 172–173, 214–215, 258–259

Susan Jaekel 59, 86, 166–167, 178, 194, 246, 312

Jane McCreary 14–15, 23, 26, 42, 58, 60–61, 62, 74, 90, 92, 94, 96, 110–111, 126–127, 130 (upper right), 133, 138, 142–143, 166, 183 (lower right), 188, 191, 205, 210, 228–229, 236–237, 255, 274–275, 278–279, 286–287, 300–301, 313, 316–317, 324–325

Yoshi Miyake 1, 25, 57, 89, 121, 153, 181, 201, 227, 249, 269, 295, 315, 345, 359

Deborah Morse (money) 33, 34–35, 36–37, 51, 155, 167

Susan Nelson 156–157, 174–175, 230, 298–299

Dennis Nolan 66, 185, 187

Valerie Randall 64, 78 (graph), 82–83, 128, 145, 192–193, 243, 282–283, 291, 375–378

Frank Remkiewicz 46–47, 182–183

Judy Sakaguchi 16, 247

Ed Taber 2–3, 80–81, 98–99, 108–109, 238–239

Cover Photograph
© **Kim Taylor/Bruce Coleman Inc.**

ISBN 0-201-26300-9

EFGHIJKL-DO-8987

Contents

CHAPTER 1 ADDITION AND SUBTRACTION FACTS, 1

CHAPTER 2 PLACE VALUE, 25

CHAPTER 3 ADDITION, 57

CHAPTER 4 SUBTRACTION, 89

CHAPTER 5 MEASUREMENT: Metric Units, 121

CHAPTER 6 MULTIPLICATION FACTS, 153

CHAPTER 7 MORE MULTIPLICATION FACTS, 181

CHAPTER 8 GEOMETRY AND GRAPHING, 201

CHAPTER 9 DIVISION FACTS, 227

CHAPTER 10 MORE DIVISION FACTS, 249

CHAPTER 11 MULTIPLICATION, 269

CHAPTER 12 DIVISION, 295

CHAPTER 13 FRACTIONS AND DECIMALS, 315

CHAPTER 14 MEASUREMENT: Customary Units, 345

TECHNOLOGY RESOURCE BANK

APPENDIX

1 ADDITION AND SUBTRACTION FACTS

Julie belongs to the 4-H Club. 4-H stands for head, hands, heart, and health. Julie has many 4-H projects. One project is to train guide-dog puppies. She teaches puppies how to be "eyes" for blind people. Julie trains the puppies to be good in stores. She teaches them to ride on buses. Julie has trained 4 German shepherds. She has also trained 3 golden retrievers.

Sums Through 10

How many bugs are there in all?

$2 + 3 = 5$

↑ Addend ↑ Addend ↑ Sum

$$\begin{array}{r} 2 \leftarrow \text{Addend} \\ +\,3 \leftarrow \text{Addend} \\ \hline 5 \leftarrow \text{Sum} \end{array}$$

There are 5 bugs in all.

Warm Up Add.

1. $\begin{array}{r} 4 \\ +\,2 \\ \hline \end{array}$

2. $\begin{array}{r} 3 \\ +\,3 \\ \hline \end{array}$

3. $\begin{array}{r} 3 \\ +\,1 \\ \hline \end{array}$

Read each number sentence aloud and give the sum.

Example We read $5 + 4 = 9$ as **"Five plus four equals nine."**

4. 2 + 6 = ____	**5.** 2 + 8 = ____	**6.** 5 + 3 = ____	**7.** 2 + 2 = ____
8. 1 + 7 = ____	**9.** 4 + 3 = ____	**10.** 7 + 0 = ____	**11.** 1 + 8 = ____
12. 1 + 6 = ____	**13.** 2 + 4 = ____	**14.** 3 + 6 = ____	**15.** 4 + 6 = ____
16. 4 + 1 = ____	**17.** 7 + 2 = ____	**18.** 1 + 2 = ____	**19.** 2 + 5 = ____
20. 3 + 4 = ____	**21.** 0 + 9 = ____	**22.** 6 + 2 = ____	**23.** 3 + 3 = ____

Practice Add.

1. $\begin{array}{r}6\\+\ 2\\\hline\end{array}$	**2.** $\begin{array}{r}3\\+\ 7\\\hline\end{array}$	**3.** $\begin{array}{r}4\\+\ 2\\\hline\end{array}$	**4.** $\begin{array}{r}5\\+\ 4\\\hline\end{array}$	**5.** $\begin{array}{r}5\\+\ 2\\\hline\end{array}$	**6.** $\begin{array}{r}9\\+\ 1\\\hline\end{array}$	**7.** $\begin{array}{r}2\\+\ 7\\\hline\end{array}$
8. $\begin{array}{r}3\\+\ 2\\\hline\end{array}$	**9.** $\begin{array}{r}8\\+\ 2\\\hline\end{array}$	**10.** $\begin{array}{r}1\\+\ 2\\\hline\end{array}$	**11.** $\begin{array}{r}0\\+\ 9\\\hline\end{array}$	**12.** $\begin{array}{r}2\\+\ 2\\\hline\end{array}$	**13.** $\begin{array}{r}4\\+\ 1\\\hline\end{array}$	**14.** $\begin{array}{r}6\\+\ 1\\\hline\end{array}$
15. $\begin{array}{r}4\\+\ 6\\\hline\end{array}$	**16.** $\begin{array}{r}3\\+\ 4\\\hline\end{array}$	**17.** $\begin{array}{r}5\\+\ 3\\\hline\end{array}$	**18.** $\begin{array}{r}2\\+\ 4\\\hline\end{array}$	**19.** $\begin{array}{r}2\\+\ 8\\\hline\end{array}$	**20.** $\begin{array}{r}4\\+\ 5\\\hline\end{array}$	**21.** $\begin{array}{r}6\\+\ 3\\\hline\end{array}$
22. $\begin{array}{r}3\\+\ 3\\\hline\end{array}$	**23.** $\begin{array}{r}8\\+\ 0\\\hline\end{array}$	**24.** $\begin{array}{r}7\\+\ 1\\\hline\end{array}$	**25.** $\begin{array}{r}5\\+\ 5\\\hline\end{array}$	**26.** $\begin{array}{r}4\\+\ 3\\\hline\end{array}$	**27.** $\begin{array}{r}1\\+\ 5\\\hline\end{array}$	**28.** $\begin{array}{r}7\\+\ 3\\\hline\end{array}$

29. 7 + 2 **30.** 5 + 1 **31.** 2 + 5 **32.** 3 + 6

33. 2 + 3 **34.** 2 + 6 **35.** 1 + 3 **36.** 4 + 4

Find the sum for each pair of addends.

37. **38.**

39. **40.**

THINK

Patterns

Write as many more sums as you can.

Sums of 8

$\begin{array}{r}0\\+\ 8\\\hline 8\end{array}$ $\begin{array}{r}1\\+\ 7\\\hline 8\end{array}$ $\begin{array}{r}2\\+\ 6\\\hline 8\end{array}$ $\begin{array}{r}3\\+\ 5\\\hline 8\end{array}$ . . .

Sums of 9

$\begin{array}{r}0\\+\ 9\\\hline 9\end{array}$ $\begin{array}{r}1\\+\ 8\\\hline 9\end{array}$ $\begin{array}{r}2\\+\ 7\\\hline 9\end{array}$ $\begin{array}{r}3\\+\ 6\\\hline 9\end{array}$ . . .

MATH

More Practice, page 379, Set A

Differences Through 10

How many carrots are left?

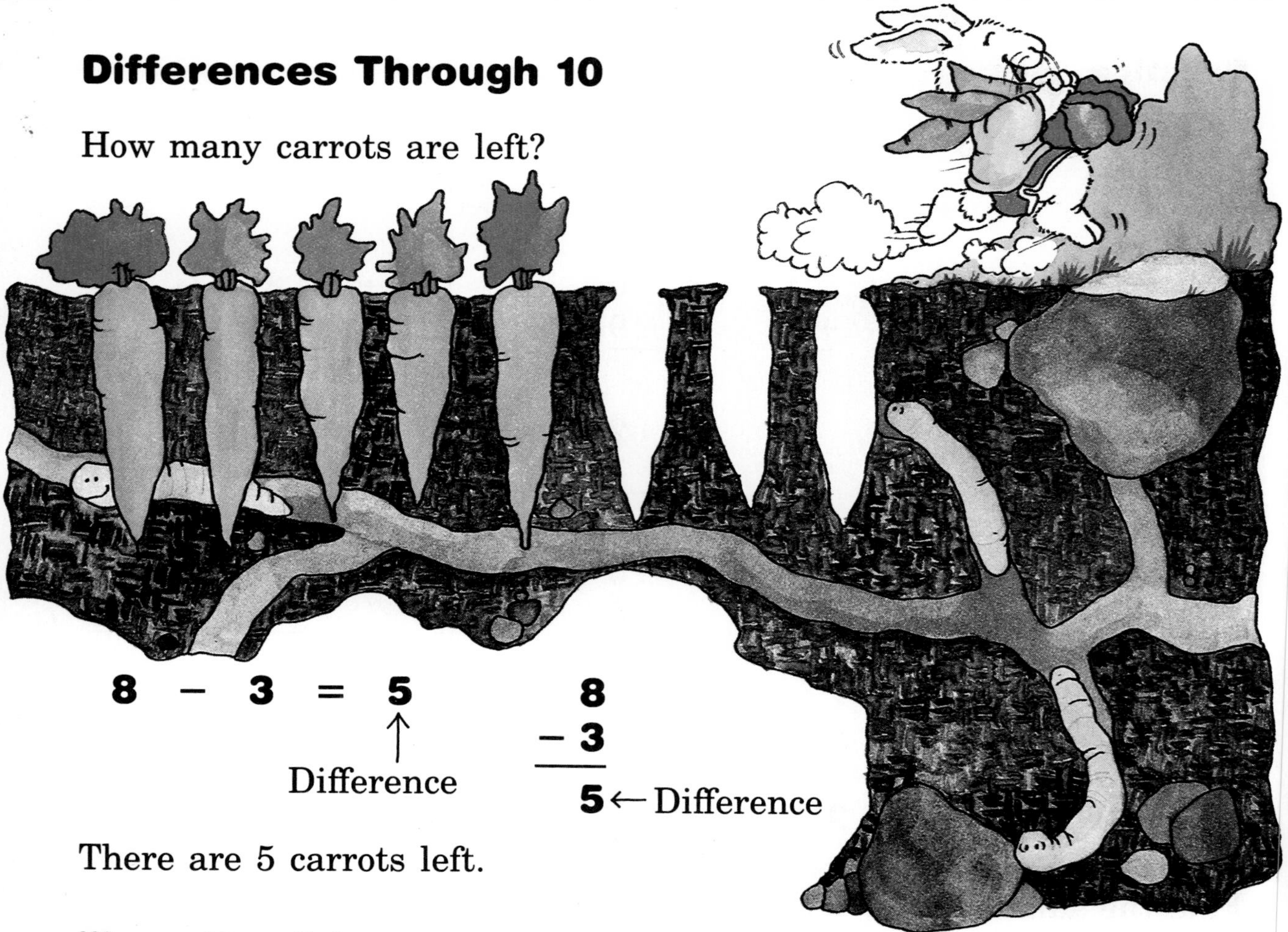

8 − 3 = 5

↑

Difference

$$\begin{array}{r} 8 \\ -\ 3 \\ \hline 5 \end{array}$$ ← Difference

There are 5 carrots left.

Warm Up Subtract.

1. $\begin{array}{r} 5 \\ -\ 2 \\ \hline \end{array}$

2. $\begin{array}{r} 10 \\ -\ 2 \\ \hline \end{array}$

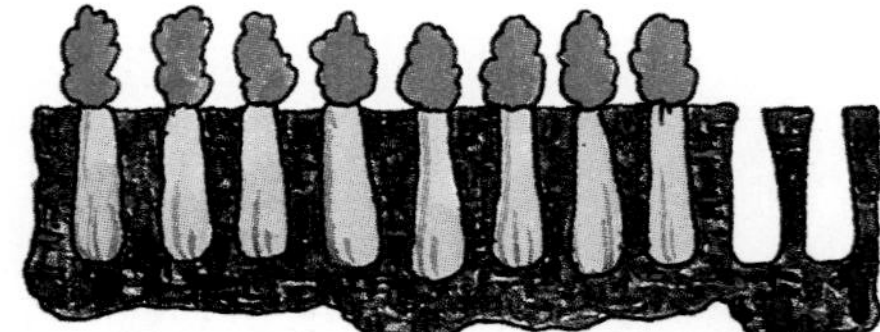

Read each number sentence aloud and give the difference.

Example We read 9 − 4 = 5 as **"Nine minus four equals five."**

3. 9 − 3 = ____ **4.** 3 − 1 = ____ **5.** 8 − 4 = ____ **6.** 10 − 8 = ____

7. 2 − 2 = ____ **8.** 8 − 6 = ____ **9.** 10 − 4 = ____ **10.** 7 − 3 = ____

11. 5 − 5 = ____ **12.** 9 − 7 = ____ **13.** 5 − 1 = ____ **14.** 4 − 2 = ____

15. 4 − 1 = ____ **16.** 7 − 5 = ____ **17.** 10 − 2 = ____ **18.** 9 − 5 = ____

19. 8 − 2 = ____ **20.** 10 − 9 = ____ **21.** 9 − 1 = ____ **22.** 6 − 3 = ____

Practice Subtract.

1. $\begin{array}{r}5\\-\ 3\\\hline\end{array}$	2. $\begin{array}{r}9\\-\ 3\\\hline\end{array}$	3. $\begin{array}{r}10\\-\ 3\\\hline\end{array}$	4. $\begin{array}{r}4\\-\ 2\\\hline\end{array}$	5. $\begin{array}{r}7\\-\ 3\\\hline\end{array}$	6. $\begin{array}{r}10\\-\ 5\\\hline\end{array}$	7. $\begin{array}{r}8\\-\ 6\\\hline\end{array}$
8. $\begin{array}{r}6\\-\ 2\\\hline\end{array}$	9. $\begin{array}{r}9\\-\ 7\\\hline\end{array}$	10. $\begin{array}{r}7\\-\ 4\\\hline\end{array}$	11. $\begin{array}{r}10\\-\ 1\\\hline\end{array}$	12. $\begin{array}{r}8\\-\ 3\\\hline\end{array}$	13. $\begin{array}{r}9\\-\ 6\\\hline\end{array}$	14. $\begin{array}{r}6\\-\ 3\\\hline\end{array}$
15. $\begin{array}{r}8\\-\ 5\\\hline\end{array}$	16. $\begin{array}{r}10\\-\ 7\\\hline\end{array}$	17. $\begin{array}{r}9\\-\ 9\\\hline\end{array}$	18. $\begin{array}{r}7\\-\ 2\\\hline\end{array}$	19. $\begin{array}{r}9\\-\ 4\\\hline\end{array}$	20. $\begin{array}{r}10\\-\ 8\\\hline\end{array}$	21. $\begin{array}{r}8\\-\ 7\\\hline\end{array}$
22. $\begin{array}{r}10\\-\ 2\\\hline\end{array}$	23. $\begin{array}{r}5\\-\ 5\\\hline\end{array}$	24. $\begin{array}{r}9\\-\ 2\\\hline\end{array}$	25. $\begin{array}{r}8\\-\ 4\\\hline\end{array}$	26. $\begin{array}{r}6\\-\ 4\\\hline\end{array}$	27. $\begin{array}{r}10\\-\ 0\\\hline\end{array}$	28. $\begin{array}{r}4\\-\ 3\\\hline\end{array}$

29. $10 - 9$	30. $6 - 1$	31. $8 - 2$	32. $9 - 8$
33. $7 - 5$	34. $8 - 8$	35. $10 - 4$	36. $6 - 0$

Find the difference for each pair of numbers.

37.

38.

39.

40.

THINK

Logical Reasoning

There are 7 rabbits in all.
How many rabbits are inside the house?

MATH

More Practice, page 379, Set B

Sums Through 18

How many toys are there in all?

8 + 5 = 13

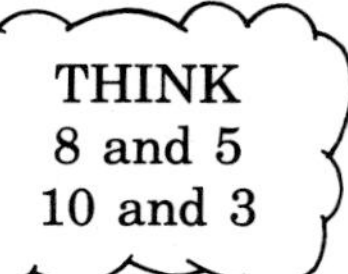

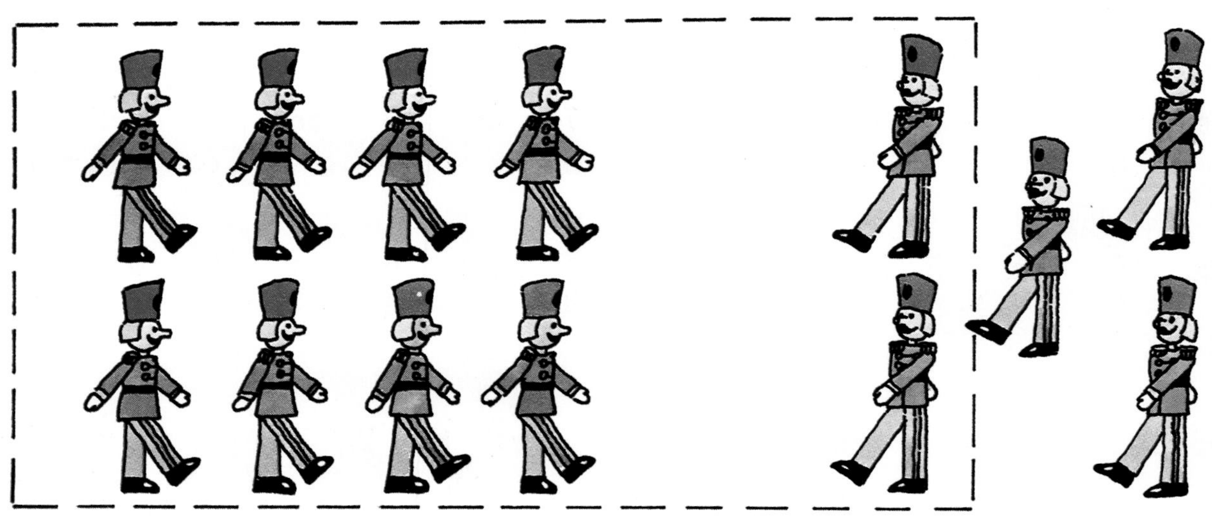

There are 13 toys in all.

Warm Up Give each sum.

1. $\begin{array}{r} 9 \\ +\ 5 \\ \hline \end{array}$

2. $\begin{array}{r} 8 \\ +\ 4 \\ \hline \end{array}$

Give each sum aloud.

3. 8 + 3 = ____	**4.** 9 + 4 = ____	**5.** 9 + 3 = ____	**6.** 6 + 5 = ____
7. 4 + 8 = ____	**8.** 4 + 7 = ____	**9.** 7 + 5 = ____	**10.** 9 + 6 = ____
11. 5 + 8 = ____	**12.** 8 + 8 = ____	**13.** 5 + 9 = ____	**14.** 3 + 8 = ____
15. 9 + 2 = ____	**16.** 4 + 9 = ____	**17.** 7 + 4 = ____	**18.** 7 + 9 = ____
19. 7 + 6 = ____	**20.** 3 + 9 = ____	**21.** 5 + 7 = ____	**22.** 5 + 6 = ____

Practice Add.

1. $\begin{array}{r} 4 \\ +\ 9 \\ \hline \end{array}$ 2. $\begin{array}{r} 7 \\ +\ 9 \\ \hline \end{array}$ 3. $\begin{array}{r} 2 \\ +\ 9 \\ \hline \end{array}$ 4. $\begin{array}{r} 8 \\ +\ 9 \\ \hline \end{array}$ 5. $\begin{array}{r} 7 \\ +\ 7 \\ \hline \end{array}$ 6. $\begin{array}{r} 5 \\ +\ 9 \\ \hline \end{array}$ 7. $\begin{array}{r} 7 \\ +\ 5 \\ \hline \end{array}$

8. $\begin{array}{r} 4 \\ +\ 8 \\ \hline \end{array}$ 9. $\begin{array}{r} 8 \\ +\ 6 \\ \hline \end{array}$ 10. $\begin{array}{r} 6 \\ +\ 7 \\ \hline \end{array}$ 11. $\begin{array}{r} 3 \\ +\ 9 \\ \hline \end{array}$ 12. $\begin{array}{r} 3 \\ +\ 8 \\ \hline \end{array}$ 13. $\begin{array}{r} 9 \\ +\ 6 \\ \hline \end{array}$ 14. $\begin{array}{r} 7 \\ +\ 4 \\ \hline \end{array}$

15. $\begin{array}{r} 6 \\ +\ 6 \\ \hline \end{array}$ 16. $\begin{array}{r} 5 \\ +\ 6 \\ \hline \end{array}$ 17. $\begin{array}{r} 9 \\ +\ 4 \\ \hline \end{array}$ 18. $\begin{array}{r} 7 \\ +\ 8 \\ \hline \end{array}$ 19. $\begin{array}{r} 9 \\ +\ 9 \\ \hline \end{array}$ 20. $\begin{array}{r} 4 \\ +\ 7 \\ \hline \end{array}$ 21. $\begin{array}{r} 8 \\ +\ 5 \\ \hline \end{array}$

22. $\begin{array}{r} 5 \\ +\ 7 \\ \hline \end{array}$ 23. $\begin{array}{r} 9 \\ +\ 8 \\ \hline \end{array}$ 24. $\begin{array}{r} 9 \\ +\ 5 \\ \hline \end{array}$ 25. $\begin{array}{r} 7 \\ +\ 6 \\ \hline \end{array}$ 26. $\begin{array}{r} 9 \\ +\ 2 \\ \hline \end{array}$ 27. $\begin{array}{r} 9 \\ +\ 7 \\ \hline \end{array}$ 28. $\begin{array}{r} 9 \\ +\ 3 \\ \hline \end{array}$

29. $6 + 9$ 30. $8 + 4$ 31. $8 + 8$ 32. $5 + 8$

33. $6 + 8$ 34. $8 + 3$ 35. $3 + 9$ 36. $4 + 7$

SKILLKEEPER

Add or subtract.

1. $\begin{array}{r} 5 \\ -\ 2 \\ \hline \end{array}$ 2. $\begin{array}{r} 8 \\ +\ 1 \\ \hline \end{array}$ 3. $\begin{array}{r} 4 \\ +\ 3 \\ \hline \end{array}$ 4. $\begin{array}{r} 10 \\ -\ 6 \\ \hline \end{array}$ 5. $\begin{array}{r} 7 \\ +\ 2 \\ \hline \end{array}$ 6. $\begin{array}{r} 9 \\ -\ 0 \\ \hline \end{array}$

7. $\begin{array}{r} 8 \\ -\ 5 \\ \hline \end{array}$ 8. $\begin{array}{r} 6 \\ +\ 4 \\ \hline \end{array}$ 9. $\begin{array}{r} 2 \\ +\ 3 \\ \hline \end{array}$ 10. $\begin{array}{r} 1 \\ +\ 0 \\ \hline \end{array}$ 11. $\begin{array}{r} 10 \\ -\ 8 \\ \hline \end{array}$ 12. $\begin{array}{r} 7 \\ -\ 6 \\ \hline \end{array}$

More Practice, page 380, Set A

Differences Through 18

How many grapes are left in the bunch?

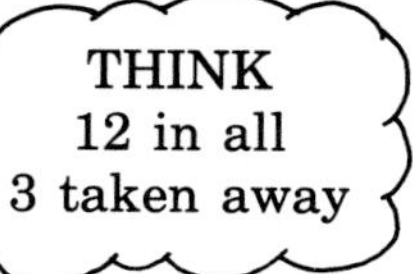

12 − 3 = 9

There are 9 grapes left in the bunch.

Warm Up Give each difference.

1. $\begin{array}{r} 11 \\ -\ 4 \\ \hline \end{array}$ **2.** $\begin{array}{r} 13 \\ -\ 5 \\ \hline \end{array}$ **3.** $\begin{array}{r} 14 \\ -\ 8 \\ \hline \end{array}$

Give each difference aloud.

4. 15 − 7 = ____ **5.** 12 − 8 = ____ **6.** 13 − 9 = ____ **7.** 14 − 8 = ____

8. 10 − 7 = ____ **9.** 16 − 8 = ____ **10.** 11 − 7 = ____ **11.** 13 − 5 = ____

12. 7 − 0 = ____ **13.** 9 − 5 = ____ **14.** 11 − 5 = ____ **15.** 17 − 8 = ____

16. 11 − 3 = ____ **17.** 14 − 6 = ____ **18.** 11 − 9 = ____ **19.** 13 − 7 = ____

20. 8 − 8 = ____ **21.** 12 − 9 = ____ **22.** 14 − 9 = ____ **23.** 16 − 7 = ____

Practice Subtract.

1. $\begin{array}{r} 14 \\ -\ 9 \\ \hline \end{array}$	**2.** $\begin{array}{r} 11 \\ -\ 5 \\ \hline \end{array}$	**3.** $\begin{array}{r} 17 \\ -\ 8 \\ \hline \end{array}$	**4.** $\begin{array}{r} 13 \\ -\ 5 \\ \hline \end{array}$	**5.** $\begin{array}{r} 12 \\ -\ 4 \\ \hline \end{array}$	**6.** $\begin{array}{r} 11 \\ -\ 6 \\ \hline \end{array}$
7. $\begin{array}{r} 15 \\ -\ 9 \\ \hline \end{array}$	**8.** $\begin{array}{r} 12 \\ -\ 5 \\ \hline \end{array}$	**9.** $\begin{array}{r} 18 \\ -\ 9 \\ \hline \end{array}$	**10.** $\begin{array}{r} 14 \\ -\ 5 \\ \hline \end{array}$	**11.** $\begin{array}{r} 11 \\ -\ 3 \\ \hline \end{array}$	**12.** $\begin{array}{r} 15 \\ -\ 6 \\ \hline \end{array}$
13. $\begin{array}{r} 13 \\ -\ 6 \\ \hline \end{array}$	**14.** $\begin{array}{r} 12 \\ -\ 7 \\ \hline \end{array}$	**15.** $\begin{array}{r} 16 \\ -\ 8 \\ \hline \end{array}$	**16.** $\begin{array}{r} 11 \\ -\ 9 \\ \hline \end{array}$	**17.** $\begin{array}{r} 13 \\ -\ 8 \\ \hline \end{array}$	**18.** $\begin{array}{r} 14 \\ -\ 8 \\ \hline \end{array}$
19. $\begin{array}{r} 12 \\ -\ 3 \\ \hline \end{array}$	**20.** $\begin{array}{r} 11 \\ -\ 7 \\ \hline \end{array}$	**21.** $\begin{array}{r} 13 \\ -\ 9 \\ \hline \end{array}$	**22.** $\begin{array}{r} 15 \\ -\ 7 \\ \hline \end{array}$	**23.** $\begin{array}{r} 12 \\ -\ 8 \\ \hline \end{array}$	**24.** $\begin{array}{r} 14 \\ -\ 7 \\ \hline \end{array}$

25. 14 − 6 **26.** 17 − 9 **27.** 11 − 4 **28.** 15 − 8

29. 13 − 4 **30.** 11 − 3 **31.** 12 − 6 **32.** 16 − 8

Find the difference for each pair of numbers.

33.

34.

35.

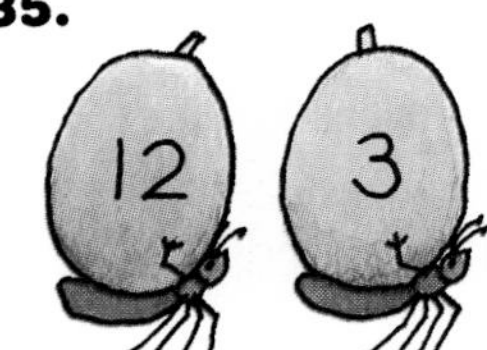

36.

37.

38.

THINK

Estimation

Choose the better estimate.

About how many people are in a

full bus?

A 3 **B** 30 **C** 300

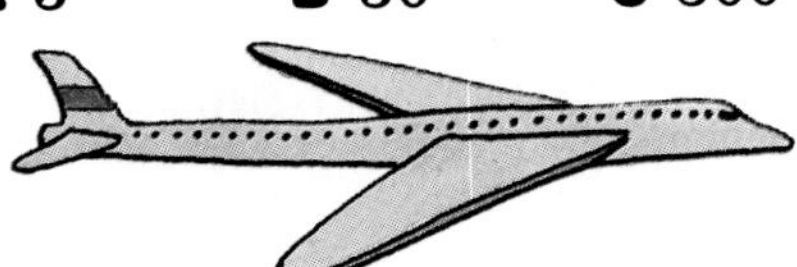

full jet?

A 3 **B** 30 **C** 300

MATH

More Practice, page 380, Set B

Fact Families

7 + 6 = 13

Because
I know this fact,
I know another
addition fact and
two subtraction
facts.

Fact Family

7 + 6 = 13
6 + 7 = 13
13 − 6 = 7
13 − 7 = 6

Warm Up Solve.

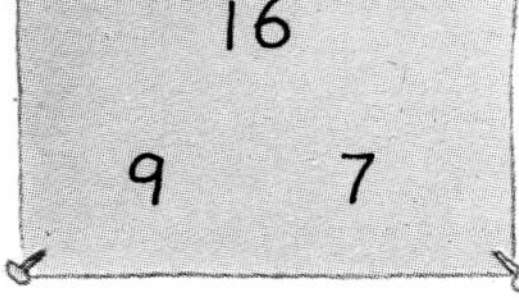

1. 13, 8, 5

Fact-Family Numbers

8 + 5 = ____

5 + 8 = ____

13 − 5 = ____

13 − 8 = ____

2. 16, 9, 7

Fact-Family Numbers

9 + 7 = ____

7 + 9 = ____

16 − 7 = ____

16 − 9 = ____

3. 14, 5, 9

Fact-Family Numbers

5 + 9 = ____

9 + 5 = ____

14 − 9 = ____

14 − 5 = ____

4.

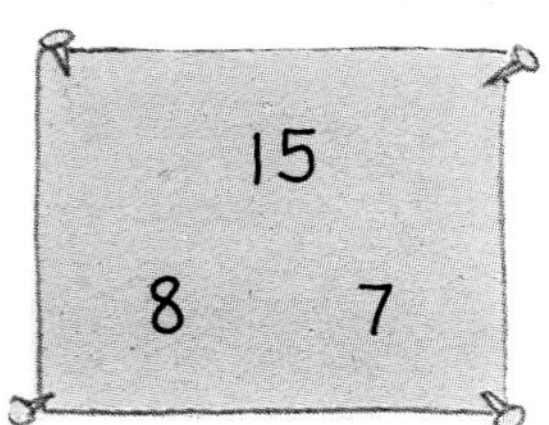
15
8 7

Fact-Family Numbers

$\begin{array}{r} 8 \\ +\ 7 \\ \hline \end{array}$ $\begin{array}{r} 7 \\ +\ 8 \\ \hline \end{array}$

$\begin{array}{r} 15 \\ -\ 7 \\ \hline \end{array}$ $\begin{array}{r} 15 \\ -\ 8 \\ \hline \end{array}$

5.

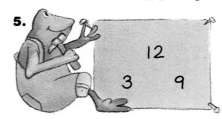

12, 3, 9

Fact-Family Numbers

$\begin{array}{r} 3 \\ +\ 9 \\ \hline \end{array}$ $\begin{array}{r} 9 \\ +\ 3 \\ \hline \end{array}$

$\begin{array}{r} 12 \\ -\ 9 \\ \hline \end{array}$ $\begin{array}{r} 12 \\ -\ 3 \\ \hline \end{array}$

Practice Find the sums and differences.

1.

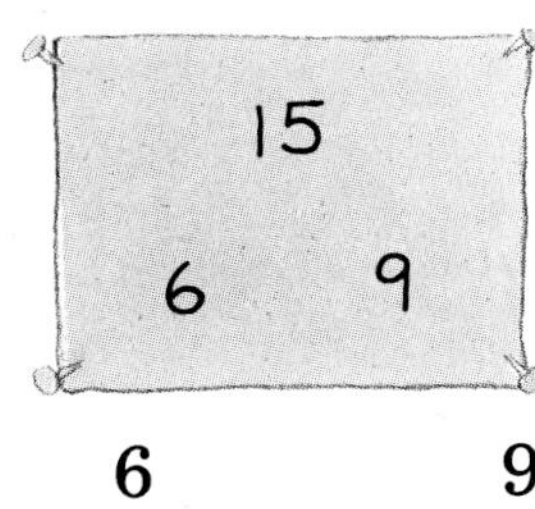

$$\begin{array}{r} 6 \\ +\ 9 \\ \hline \end{array} \qquad \begin{array}{r} 9 \\ +\ 6 \\ \hline \end{array}$$

$$\begin{array}{r} 15 \\ -\ 9 \\ \hline \end{array} \qquad \begin{array}{r} 15 \\ -\ 6 \\ \hline \end{array}$$

2.

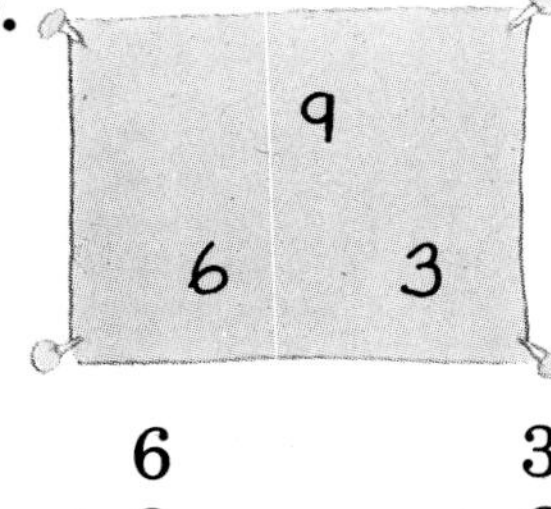

$$\begin{array}{r} 6 \\ +\ 3 \\ \hline \end{array} \qquad \begin{array}{r} 3 \\ +\ 6 \\ \hline \end{array}$$

$$\begin{array}{r} 9 \\ -\ 6 \\ \hline \end{array} \qquad \begin{array}{r} 9 \\ -\ 3 \\ \hline \end{array}$$

3. $\begin{array}{r} 7 \\ +\ 5 \\ \hline \end{array}$ 4. $\begin{array}{r} 4 \\ +\ 6 \\ \hline \end{array}$ 5. $\begin{array}{r} 7 \\ +\ 7 \\ \hline \end{array}$ 6. $\begin{array}{r} 3 \\ +\ 5 \\ \hline \end{array}$ 7. $\begin{array}{r} 4 \\ +\ 9 \\ \hline \end{array}$ 8. $\begin{array}{r} 7 \\ +\ 4 \\ \hline \end{array}$

9. $\begin{array}{r} 12 \\ -\ 5 \\ \hline \end{array}$ 10. $\begin{array}{r} 10 \\ -\ 6 \\ \hline \end{array}$ 11. $\begin{array}{r} 14 \\ -\ 7 \\ \hline \end{array}$ 12. $\begin{array}{r} 8 \\ -\ 5 \\ \hline \end{array}$ 13. $\begin{array}{r} 13 \\ -\ 9 \\ \hline \end{array}$ 14. $\begin{array}{r} 11 \\ -\ 4 \\ \hline \end{array}$

★ Write four number sentences for each set of fact-family numbers.

THINK

Logical Reasoning

I'm the smallest number in my family. The other two numbers are 13 and 9.
WHO AM I?

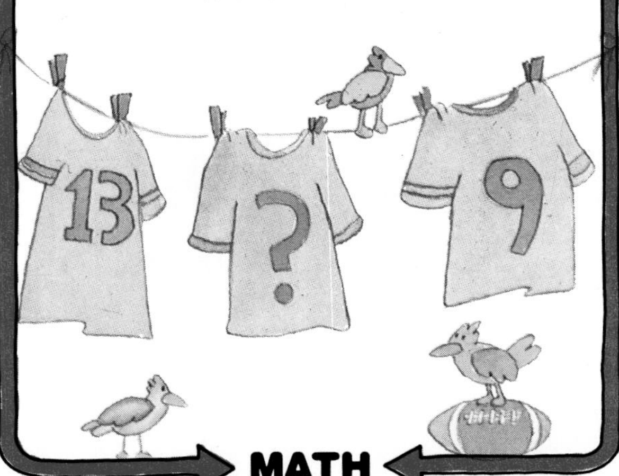

MATH

Practice the Facts

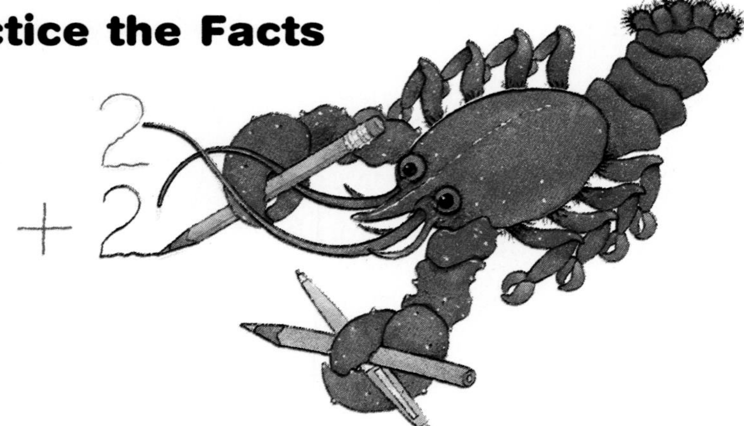

Add.

1. $8 + 7$	2. $4 + 9$	3. $8 + 8$	4. $3 + 9$	5. $9 + 5$	6. $7 + 5$	7. $8 + 9$
8. $6 + 8$	9. $6 + 6$	10. $9 + 6$	11. $9 + 2$	12. $5 + 8$	13. $8 + 4$	14. $7 + 8$
15. $7 + 7$	16. $9 + 9$	17. $6 + 9$	18. $6 + 7$	19. $9 + 8$	20. $8 + 5$	21. $8 + 3$
22. $7 + 4$	23. $7 + 9$	24. $9 + 4$	25. $8 + 6$	26. $6 + 5$	27. $5 + 9$	28. $9 + 3$

Subtract.

29. $11 - 2$	30. $15 - 7$	31. $11 - 5$	32. $18 - 9$	33. $14 - 6$	34. $17 - 8$
35. $12 - 4$	36. $14 - 9$	37. $16 - 7$	38. $11 - 8$	39. $12 - 3$	40. $13 - 8$
41. $15 - 8$	42. $12 - 7$	43. $12 - 5$	44. $16 - 8$	45. $14 - 8$	46. $13 - 5$
47. $15 - 9$	48. $11 - 4$	49. $13 - 4$	50. $13 - 7$	51. $14 - 5$	52. $16 - 9$

Practice Add or subtract.

1. $\begin{array}{r} 4 \\ +\ 7 \\ \hline \end{array}$
2. $\begin{array}{r} 5 \\ +\ 7 \\ \hline \end{array}$
3. $\begin{array}{r} 11 \\ -\ 5 \\ \hline \end{array}$
4. $\begin{array}{r} 15 \\ -\ 7 \\ \hline \end{array}$
5. $\begin{array}{r} 9 \\ +\ 7 \\ \hline \end{array}$
6. $\begin{array}{r} 14 \\ -\ 5 \\ \hline \end{array}$
7. $\begin{array}{r} 12 \\ -\ 4 \\ \hline \end{array}$
8. $\begin{array}{r} 8 \\ +\ 6 \\ \hline \end{array}$
9. $\begin{array}{r} 9 \\ +\ 5 \\ \hline \end{array}$
10. $\begin{array}{r} 16 \\ -\ 7 \\ \hline \end{array}$
11. $\begin{array}{r} 9 \\ +\ 4 \\ \hline \end{array}$
12. $\begin{array}{r} 13 \\ -\ 6 \\ \hline \end{array}$
13. $\begin{array}{r} 6 \\ +\ 5 \\ \hline \end{array}$
14. $\begin{array}{r} 5 \\ +\ 8 \\ \hline \end{array}$
15. $\begin{array}{r} 11 \\ -\ 7 \\ \hline \end{array}$
16. $\begin{array}{r} 14 \\ -\ 7 \\ \hline \end{array}$
17. $\begin{array}{r} 3 \\ +\ 9 \\ \hline \end{array}$
18. $\begin{array}{r} 7 \\ +\ 6 \\ \hline \end{array}$
19. $\begin{array}{r} 13 \\ -\ 4 \\ \hline \end{array}$
20. $\begin{array}{r} 3 \\ +\ 8 \\ \hline \end{array}$
21. $\begin{array}{r} 12 \\ -\ 7 \\ \hline \end{array}$
22. $\begin{array}{r} 11 \\ -\ 8 \\ \hline \end{array}$
23. $\begin{array}{r} 8 \\ +\ 7 \\ \hline \end{array}$
24. $\begin{array}{r} 12 \\ -\ 9 \\ \hline \end{array}$

25. $13 - 5$
26. $9 + 8$
27. $9 + 9$
28. $16 - 8$
29. $9 + 5$
30. $9 + 6$
31. $12 - 3$
32. $13 - 5$
33. $14 - 6$
34. $6 + 6$
35. $16 - 7$
36. $7 + 5$

THINK

Patterns

Guess each rule. Then give the missing numbers.

	Gina said	Mike answered
	4	13
	6	15
	2	11
1.	9	
2.		14

	Mike said	Gina answered
	8	1
	7	0
	10	3
3.	9	
4.		6

	Gina said	Mike answered
	1	2
	2	4
	3	6
	4	8
5.	5	

MATH

PROBLEM SOLVING ★ The 5-Point Checklist

QUESTION
DATA
PLAN
ANSWER
CHECK

To solve a problem

★ **1. Understand the Question**

★ **2. Find the needed Data**

★ **3. Plan what to do**

★ **4. Find the Answer**

★ **5. Check back**

Use the 5-Point Checklist to help you solve the following problem.

Sally took 8 pictures at the park.
She took 7 more pictures at the beach.
How many pictures did Sally take?

1. Understand the QUESTION
What is the total number of pictures?

2. Find the needed DATA
Park: 8 pictures   Beach: 7 pictures

3. PLAN what to do
We want the total number.
We should add.

4. Find the ANSWER
$8 + 7 = 15$ Sally took 15 pictures.

5. CHECK back
Read the problem again.
15 seems about right.

Solve. Use the 5-Point Checklist.

1. Sally put some pictures in a book. She put 6 on one page and 8 on another. How many pictures are on both pages?

2. Only 13 of Sally's pictures were good. She gave 5 of them to friends. How many does she have left?

Solve.

1. Tom took 9 pictures of his friends. He took 8 more of his family. How many pictures did Tom take in all?

2. Betty has 6 pictures of her brother. She has 7 pictures of her sister. How many does she have of both of them?

3. Yuri had 14 animal pictures. He lost 6 of them. How many animal pictures does Yuri have left?

4. Kay had 17 pictures in her picture book. She took 8 of them to school. How many did she leave in the book?

5. Dan took 5 pictures of his dog to school. He left 8 more of them at home. How many pictures of his dog does Dan have?

6. Maria bought a roll of film for 16 pictures. She has taken 8 of them. How many does she have left to take?

7. Dom sent these pictures to his grandmother: 4 of himself and 5 of the whole family. How many did he send?

8. Carla had 12 pictures of a family party. She sent 4 of them to her uncle Joe. How many does she have left?

Three Addends

Maria put 4 small striped fish in the tank. Ben put 5 small goldfish in the tank. Rita put 3 large goldfish in the tank. How many fish are now in the tank?

$(4 + 5) + 3$	$4 + (5 + 3)$
$9 + 3 = 12$	$4 + 8 = 12$
9 ↑ Small fish; 3 ↑ Large fish; 12 ↑ Fish in all	4 ↑ Striped fish; 8 ↑ Goldfish; 12 ↑ Fish in all

12 fish are in the tank.

When you add, you can change the grouping and get the same sum.

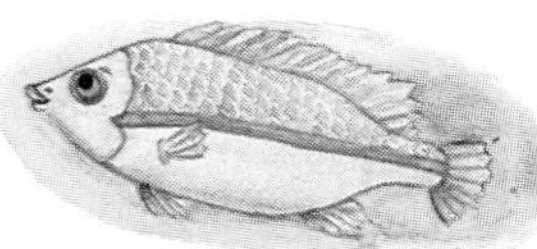

Other Examples

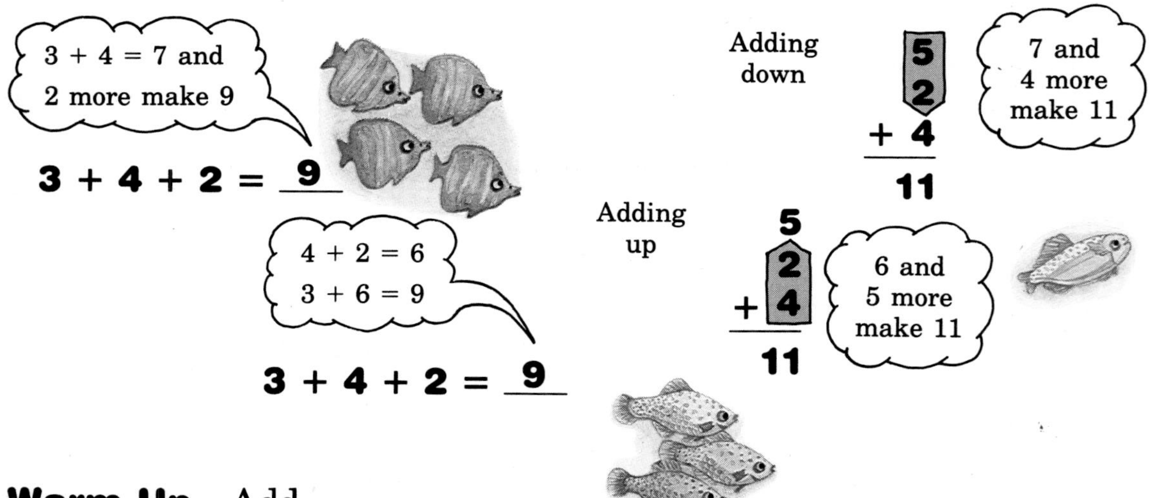

Warm Up Add.

1. $6 + 2 + 4 =$ ____ **2.** $3 + 5 + 2 =$ ____ **3.** $2 + 7 + 3 =$ ____

4.	**5.**	**6.**	**7.**	**8.**	**9.**	**10.**
6	1	5	8	3	5	4
3	7	2	1	7	4	1
+ 2	+ 2	+ 4	+ 1	+ 2	+ 5	+ 3

Practice Add.

1. 2 3 + 1	**2.** 5 1 + 6	**3.** 2 3 + 2	**4.** 4 2 + 3	**5.** 5 3 + 2	**6.** 2 5 + 3
7. 6 2 + 1	**8.** 7 1 + 4	**9.** 6 3 + 5	**10.** 2 8 + 1	**11.** 3 4 + 3	**12.** 4 5 + 3
13. 8 2 + 4	**14.** 7 2 + 3	**15.** 6 3 + 5	**16.** 3 6 + 2	**17.** 4 5 + 4	**18.** 6 1 + 4

Look for the sums of 10.

19. 5 2 (10) + 5	**20.** 8 (10) 2 + 8	**21.** 6 4 + 5	**22.** 3 7 + 2	**23.** 7 6 + 3	**24.** 4 3 + 6

25. 2 + 7 + 3 (10)	**26.** 5 + 4 + 5 (10)	**27.** 3 + 7 + 1
28. 5 + 3 + 4	**29.** 8 + 2 + 7	**30.** 4 + 3 + 6
31. 3 + 7 + 2	**32.** 2 + 3 + 5	**33.** 5 + 3 + 5
34. 4 + 2 + 5	**35.** 6 + 1 + 8	**36.** 7 + 3 + 5

SKILLKEEPER

Add.

1. 8 + 3	**2.** 6 + 9	**3.** 9 + 8	**4.** 7 + 6	**5.** 8 + 7	**6.** 4 + 4
7. 5 + 2	**8.** 1 + 7	**9.** 4 + 9	**10.** 5 + 8	**11.** 6 + 5	**12.** 8 + 4

More Practice, page 381, Set A

PROBLEM SOLVING
Understanding the Question

Short story problems let you think mostly about the **question.**

Solve.

1. Music:
   6 old songs
   4 new songs
   How many songs are there?

2. Spelling:
   10 words
   Missed 2
   How many were right?

3. Reading:
   Red book—8 pages
   Blue book—7 pages
   How many pages are in both?

4. Lunch:
   12 children at a table
   3 left the table
   How many are still there?

5. Recess:
   8 large swings
   4 small swings
   How many swings are there?

6. Math:
   12 problems
   9 right
   How many were missed?

7. Game:
   4 players on Team A
   5 players on Team B
   4 players on Team C
   How many are there in all?

8. Science:
   13 white mice
   4 got away
   How many are left?

PROBLEM SOLVING
Using Data from a Picture

Use the data in the pictures to solve these problems.

1. How many shells did Sally and Sam find together?

Ted

2. Pam gave 5 of her shells to a friend. How many does she have left?

Pam

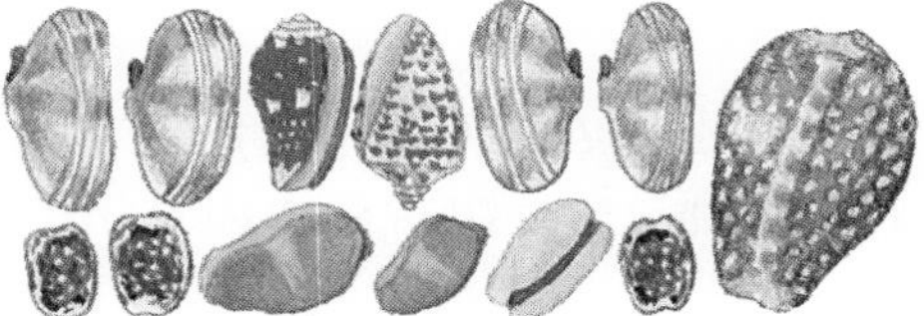

3. Al broke 2 of his shells. How many does he have now?

Sally

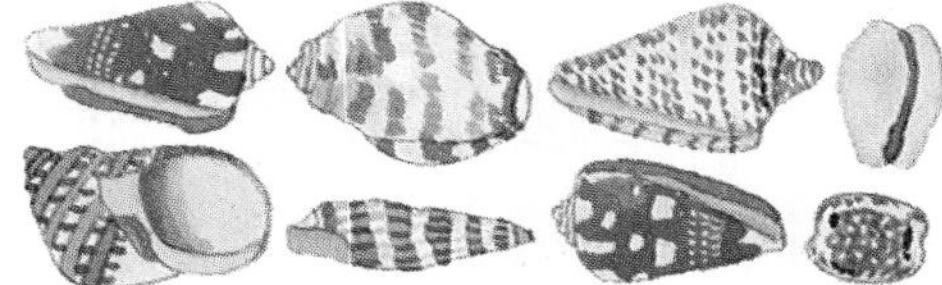

4. Sally and Jane put their shells together. How many did they have then?

Sam

5. Ted lost 4 of his shells. How many does he have now?

Al

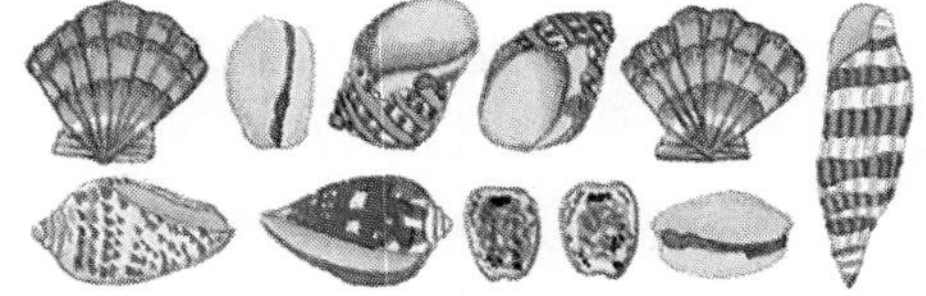

6. Sam found 5 more shells. How many does he have now?

Jane

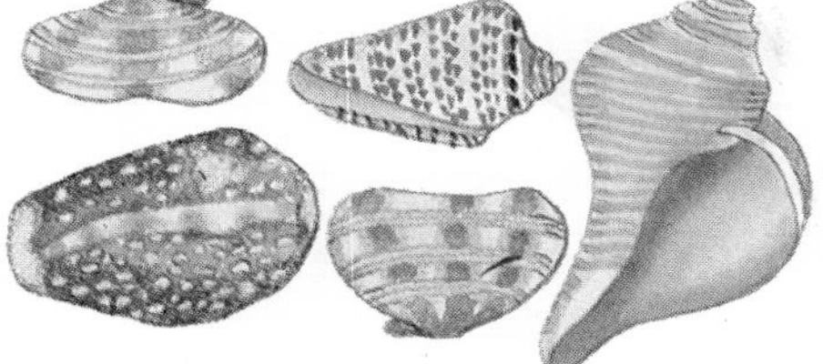

PROBLEM SOLVING
Choose the Operations

There are 4 frogs in a pond.
7 ladybugs are on a limb.

How many animals is this in all?

PUT TOGETHER

7 + 4 = 11

Each frog ate a bug.
How many bugs were left?

How many more bugs are there than frogs?

TAKE AWAY

COMPARE

7 − 4 = 3

7 − 4 = 3

▷ PUT TOGETHER ⟶ Choose addition.
▷ TAKE AWAY ⟶ Choose subtraction.
▷ COMPARE (more or fewer) ⟶ Choose subtraction.

Solve.

1. There were 12 birds in a tree. 9 of the birds flew away. How many of the birds were still in the tree?

2. There are 7 bugs on a leaf. There are 8 more on another leaf. How many bugs are on the two leaves?

3. There are 15 fish in the pond. 6 turtles are in the pond. How many more fish are there than turtles?

4. There are 14 tadpoles in the pond. 5 frogs are on the bank. How many fewer frogs are there than tadpoles?

CHAPTER REVIEW/TEST

Find the sum or difference.

1. $\begin{array}{r} 4 \\ +\ 5 \\ \hline \end{array}$ 2. $\begin{array}{r} 3 \\ +\ 2 \\ \hline \end{array}$ 3. $\begin{array}{r} 6 \\ -\ 3 \\ \hline \end{array}$ 4. $\begin{array}{r} 5 \\ +\ 3 \\ \hline \end{array}$ 5. $\begin{array}{r} 2 \\ -\ 1 \\ \hline \end{array}$ 6. $\begin{array}{r} 8 \\ -\ 4 \\ \hline \end{array}$ 7. $\begin{array}{r} 2 \\ +\ 7 \\ \hline \end{array}$

8. $\begin{array}{r} 2 \\ +\ 8 \\ \hline \end{array}$ 9. $\begin{array}{r} 7 \\ -\ 3 \\ \hline \end{array}$ 10. $\begin{array}{r} 4 \\ -\ 3 \\ \hline \end{array}$ 11. $\begin{array}{r} 3 \\ +\ 4 \\ \hline \end{array}$ 12. $\begin{array}{r} 5 \\ -\ 2 \\ \hline \end{array}$ 13. $\begin{array}{r} 6 \\ +\ 2 \\ \hline \end{array}$ 14. $\begin{array}{r} 7 \\ -\ 5 \\ \hline \end{array}$

Add or subtract.

15. $\begin{array}{r} 7 \\ +\ 5 \\ \hline \end{array}$ 16. $\begin{array}{r} 7 \\ +\ 7 \\ \hline \end{array}$ 17. $\begin{array}{r} 12 \\ -\ 3 \\ \hline \end{array}$ 18. $\begin{array}{r} 11 \\ -\ 7 \\ \hline \end{array}$ 19. $\begin{array}{r} 12 \\ -\ 4 \\ \hline \end{array}$ 20. $\begin{array}{r} 9 \\ +\ 6 \\ \hline \end{array}$ 21. $\begin{array}{r} 8 \\ +\ 5 \\ \hline \end{array}$

22. $\begin{array}{r} 15 \\ -\ 7 \\ \hline \end{array}$ 23. $\begin{array}{r} 7 \\ +\ 6 \\ \hline \end{array}$ 24. $\begin{array}{r} 14 \\ -\ 8 \\ \hline \end{array}$ 25. $\begin{array}{r} 9 \\ +\ 9 \\ \hline \end{array}$ 26. $\begin{array}{r} 13 \\ -\ 9 \\ \hline \end{array}$ 27. $\begin{array}{r} 7 \\ +\ 9 \\ \hline \end{array}$ 28. $\begin{array}{r} 17 \\ -\ 8 \\ \hline \end{array}$

Find the sums.

29. $\begin{array}{r} 4 \\ 2 \\ +\ 4 \\ \hline \end{array}$ 30. $\begin{array}{r} 6 \\ 2 \\ +\ 4 \\ \hline \end{array}$ 31. $\begin{array}{r} 3 \\ 2 \\ +\ 3 \\ \hline \end{array}$ 32. $\begin{array}{r} 5 \\ 2 \\ +\ 3 \\ \hline \end{array}$ 33. $\begin{array}{r} 7 \\ 1 \\ +\ 4 \\ \hline \end{array}$

Solve.

34. Anita took 12 pictures of her kitten. She gave 4 of them away. How many did she keep?

35. Ted has 5 pictures of his dog. He has 9 pictures of his cat. How many pictures does Ted have?

36. Jan found 8 shells. Jo found 7 shells. They put them together. How many did they have then?

37. There were 14 ducks on the pond. 8 frogs were in the pond. How many more ducks were there than frogs?

ANOTHER LOOK

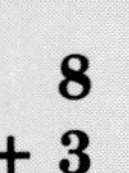

$$\begin{array}{r} 8 \\ +\ 3 \\ \hline 11 \end{array}$$

Start with **8**.

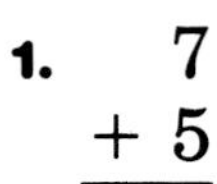

Add **3** more.

Get **11** in all.

Find the sums.

1. $\begin{array}{r} 7 \\ +\ 5 \\ \hline \end{array}$ 2. $\begin{array}{r} 6 \\ +\ 8 \\ \hline \end{array}$ 3. $\begin{array}{r} 5 \\ +\ 3 \\ \hline \end{array}$

4. $\begin{array}{r} 7 \\ +\ 9 \\ \hline \end{array}$ 5. $\begin{array}{r} 4 \\ +\ 3 \\ \hline \end{array}$ 6. $\begin{array}{r} 7 \\ +\ 6 \\ \hline \end{array}$

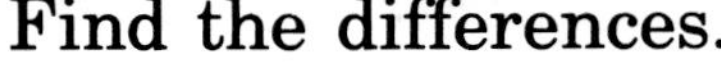

$$\begin{array}{r} 12 \\ -\ 5 \\ \hline 7 \end{array}$$

Start with **12**.

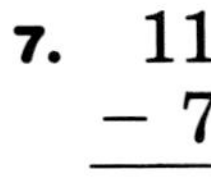

Take away **5**.
7 are left.

Find the differences.

7. $\begin{array}{r} 11 \\ -\ 7 \\ \hline \end{array}$ 8. $\begin{array}{r} 16 \\ -\ 8 \\ \hline \end{array}$ 9. $\begin{array}{r} 7 \\ -\ 5 \\ \hline \end{array}$

10. $\begin{array}{r} 8 \\ -\ 3 \\ \hline \end{array}$ 11. $\begin{array}{r} 13 \\ -\ 8 \\ \hline \end{array}$ 12. $\begin{array}{r} 10 \\ -\ 4 \\ \hline \end{array}$

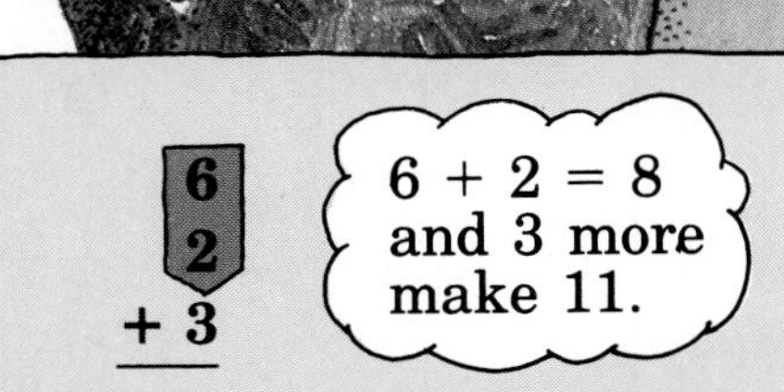

$$\begin{array}{r} 6 \\ 2 \\ +\ 3 \\ \hline 11 \end{array}$$

6 + 2 = 8
and 3 more
make 11.

Find the sums.

13. $\begin{array}{r} 5 \\ 1 \\ +\ 3 \\ \hline \end{array}$ 14. $\begin{array}{r} 6 \\ 4 \\ +\ 2 \\ \hline \end{array}$ 15. $\begin{array}{r} 3 \\ 5 \\ +\ 2 \\ \hline \end{array}$

16. $\begin{array}{r} 5 \\ 3 \\ +\ 6 \\ \hline \end{array}$ 17. $\begin{array}{r} 5 \\ 4 \\ +\ 5 \\ \hline \end{array}$ 18. $\begin{array}{r} 4 \\ 5 \\ +\ 3 \\ \hline \end{array}$

ENRICHMENT

Logical Reasoning

Try a game of Nim with a friend.

1. Start with 11 counters.
2. When it is your turn, you must pick up 1, 2, or 3 counters.
3. To win, make your friend have to pick up the last counter.

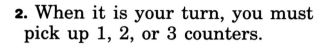

Hints for Reasoning

1. It is your turn. There are 2 counters left. How can you be sure to win?
2. It is your turn. There are 4 counters left. How can you be sure to win?
3. It is your turn. There are 6 counters left. How can you be sure to win?

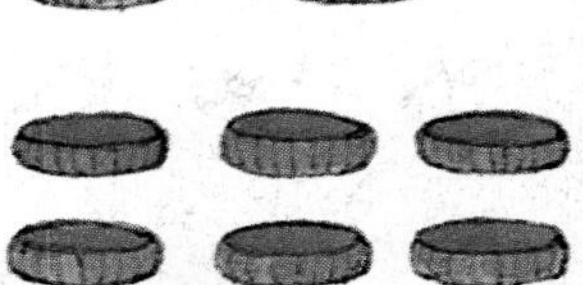

CUMULATIVE REVIEW

Give the letter for the correct answer.

1. $2 + 4 =$ ____
   - A 2 B 8
   - C 6 D not given

2. $5 + 3 =$ ____
   - A 6 B 8
   - C 2 D not given

3. $9 - 4 =$ ____
   - A 6 B 13
   - C 5 D not given

4. $4 + 4 =$ ____
   - A 0 B 9
   - C 8 D not given

5. $6 - 5 =$ ____
   - A 2 B 1
   - C 11 D not given

6. $8 + 1 =$ ____
   - A 6 B 7
   - C 8 D not given

7. $\begin{array}{r} 3 \\ +\ 3 \\ \hline \end{array}$
   - A 0
   - B 3
   - C 6
   - D not given

8. $\begin{array}{r} 10 \\ -\ 5 \\ \hline \end{array}$
   - A 5
   - B 15
   - C 6
   - D not given

9. $\begin{array}{r} 3 \\ +\ 2 \\ \hline \end{array}$
   - A 1
   - B 5
   - C 7
   - D not given

10. $\begin{array}{r} 8 \\ +\ 0 \\ \hline \end{array}$
    - A 0
    - B 16
    - C 8
    - D not given

11. $\begin{array}{r} 2 \\ -\ 1 \\ \hline \end{array}$
    - A 3
    - B 1
    - C 2
    - D not given

12. $\begin{array}{r} 5 \\ -\ 0 \\ \hline \end{array}$
    - A 10
    - B 0
    - C 5
    - D not given

13. Amy had 7 stamps. She used 5. How many were left?
    - A 12 B 7
    - C 2 D not given

14. Jim caught 3 fish. Then he caught 1 more. How many fish did he catch?
    - A 3 B 4
    - C 2 D not given

PLACE VALUE 2

Josh was once in a book-reading contest called a "Read-A-Thon." He asked people to give money for each book he read. In thirty-one days Josh read twenty-three books. Josh's mother gave seventy-five cents for each book he read. His neighbor gave fifteen cents for each book. The money went to help people who have multiple sclerosis.

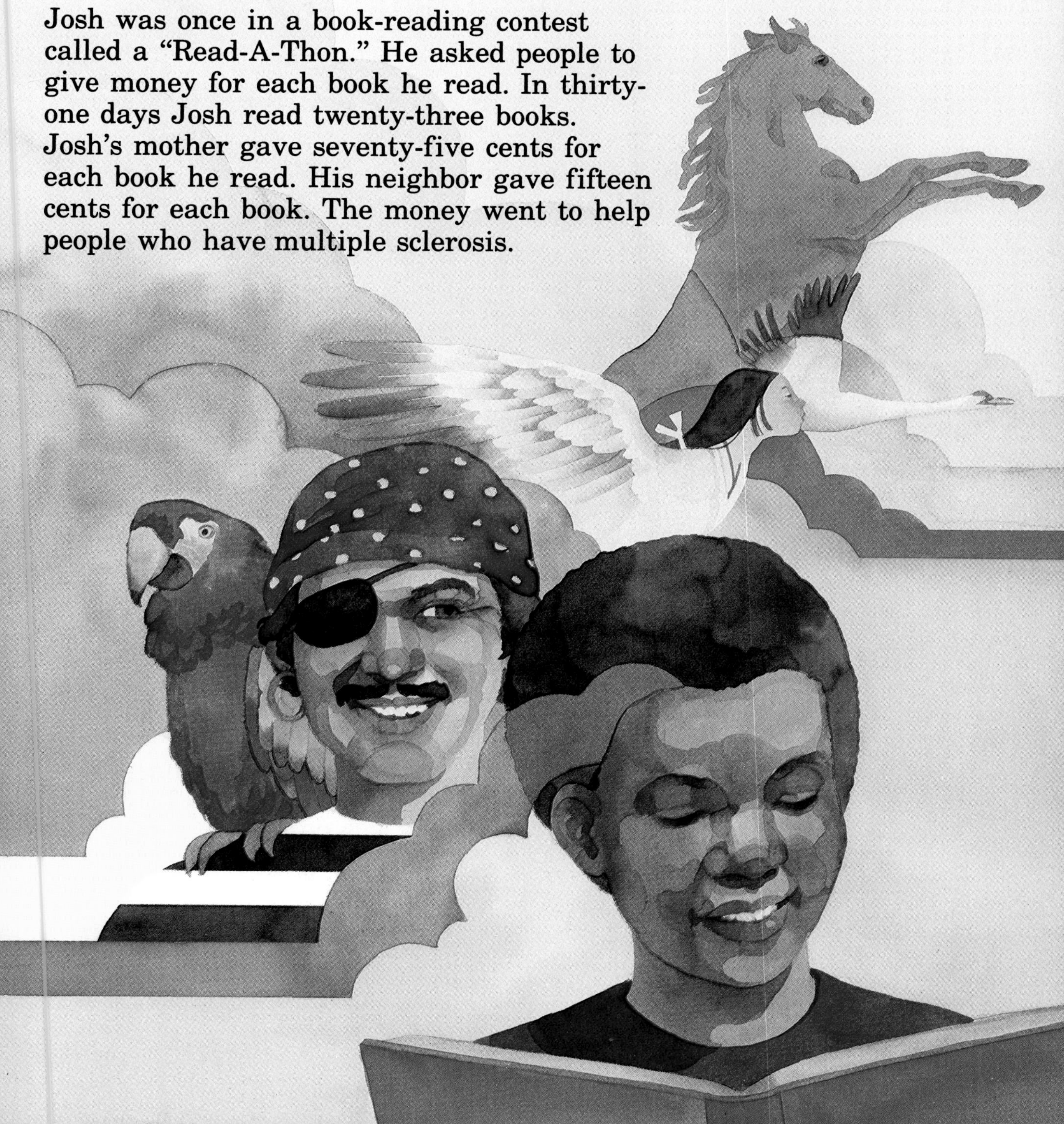

Tens and Ones

Jeff is gluing ten cubes together. He is showing that ten ones equal **one ten.**

ten ones  **one ten (10)**

0, 1, 2, 3, 4, 5, 6, 7, 8, and 9 are called **digits.** We use digits and **place value** to write larger numbers.

Examples

2 tens and **3** ones = **23**
We read, "**twenty-three.**"

3 tens and **5** ones = **35**
We read, "**thirty-five.**"

Warm Up Give the number for each picture.

1. 2 tens and 4 ones = ____

2. 4 tens and 1 one = ____

3.

4.

Practice Write the number for each picture.

1.

2.

Write the number. Be careful!

3. 6 tens and 8 ones

4. 4 tens and 0 ones

5. 3 ones and 1 ten

6. 9 tens and 7 ones

7. 3 ones and 7 tens

8. 1 ten and 0 ones

9. 5 ones and 2 tens

10. 2 ones and 6 tens

Write the number.

11. twenty-three

12. thirty-six

13. seventy-five

14. ninety-two

15. eighty

16. fifty-one

17. seventeen

18. forty-eight

19. thirteen

20. sixty-seven

21. twelve

22. eighty-four

23. forty-one

24. sixty-six

25. nineteen

THINK

Estimation and Place Value

1. Estimate how many cubes are in the picture.
2. Check your estimate *without counting higher than ten.*

   Hint: How many tens could you make?

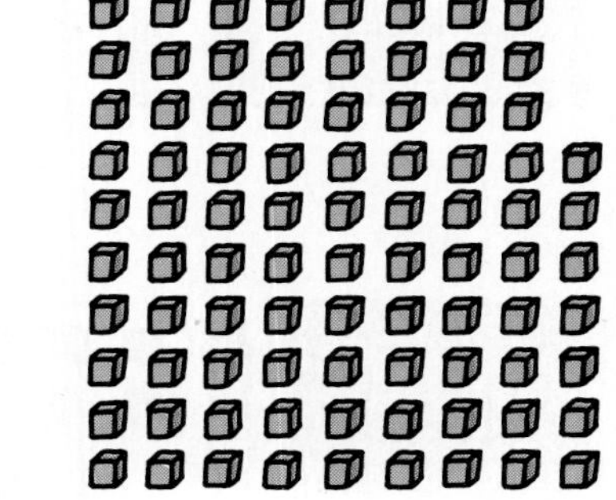

MATH

Hundreds, Tens, and Ones

Jean is gluing blocks together to show that ten tens are equal to **one hundred.**

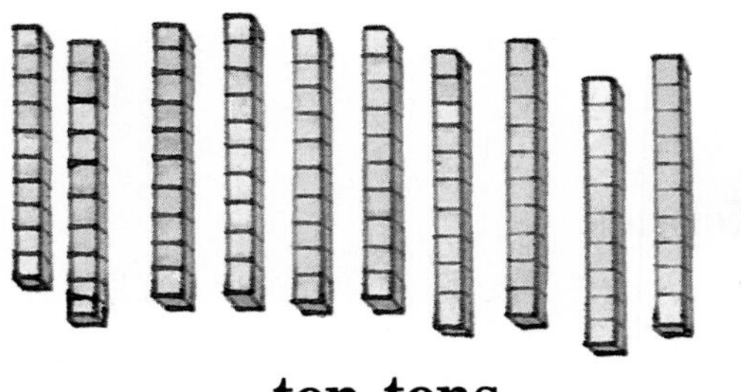

ten tens

one hundred (100)

We use hundreds, tens, and ones to write larger numbers.

Examples

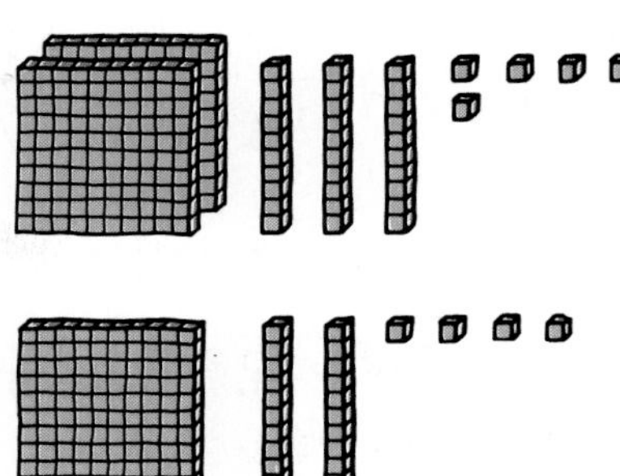

2 hundreds, **3** tens, and **5** ones = **235**
We read, **"two hundred thirty-five."**

1 hundred, **2** tens, and **4** ones = **124**
We read, **"one hundred twenty-four."**

Warm Up Give the number for each picture.

1. 

2.

3. 

4. 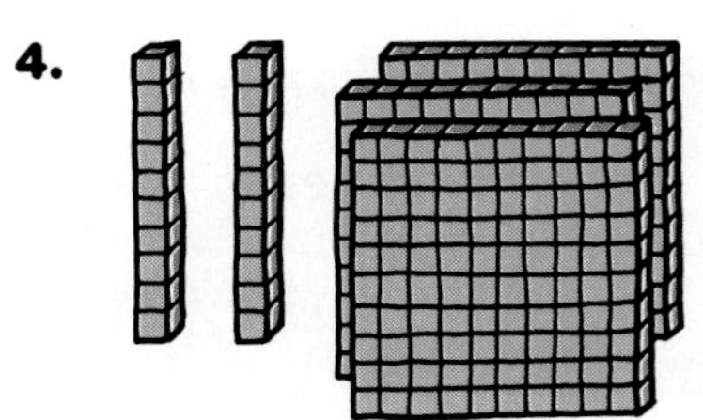

Practice Write the number.

Example

Hundreds	Tens	Ones
3	4	8

Answer 348

1.

Hundreds	Tens	Ones
3	2	4

2.

Hundreds	Tens	Ones
5	9	1

3.

Hundreds	Tens	Ones
2	0	7

4.

Hundreds	Tens	Ones
6	4	7

5.

Hundreds	Tens	Ones
1	2	5

6.

Hundreds	Tens	Ones
4	0	7

7.

Hundreds	Tens	Ones
5	3	0

8.

Hundreds	Tens	Ones
6	0	0

9.

Hundreds	Tens	Ones
7	5	3

10.

Hundreds	Tens	Ones
8	0	4

11.

Hundreds	Tens	Ones
2	6	0

12.

Hundreds	Tens	Ones
9	4	1

13. 6 tens
2 ones
7 hundreds

14. 4 hundreds
0 ones
2 tens

15. 5 ones
3 hundreds
9 tens

16. 7 ones
0 tens
6 hundreds

17. five hundred sixty-seven

18. three hundred twenty-nine

19. nine hundred forty-one

20. six hundred eighty

21. two hundred five

22. four hundred

THINK

Patterns

Make a copy of this figure. Put the numbers 1, 2, 3, 4, 5, and 6 in the circles so that the sum along each line is 14. Use each number only once.

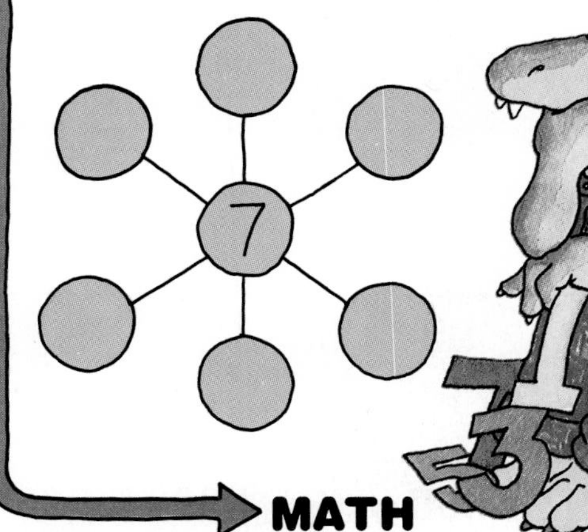

MATH

Counting and Order

Numbers have an order. The pages of a book are numbered. This gives an order to the pages. Page 48 comes **before** page 49. Page 50 comes **after** page 49.

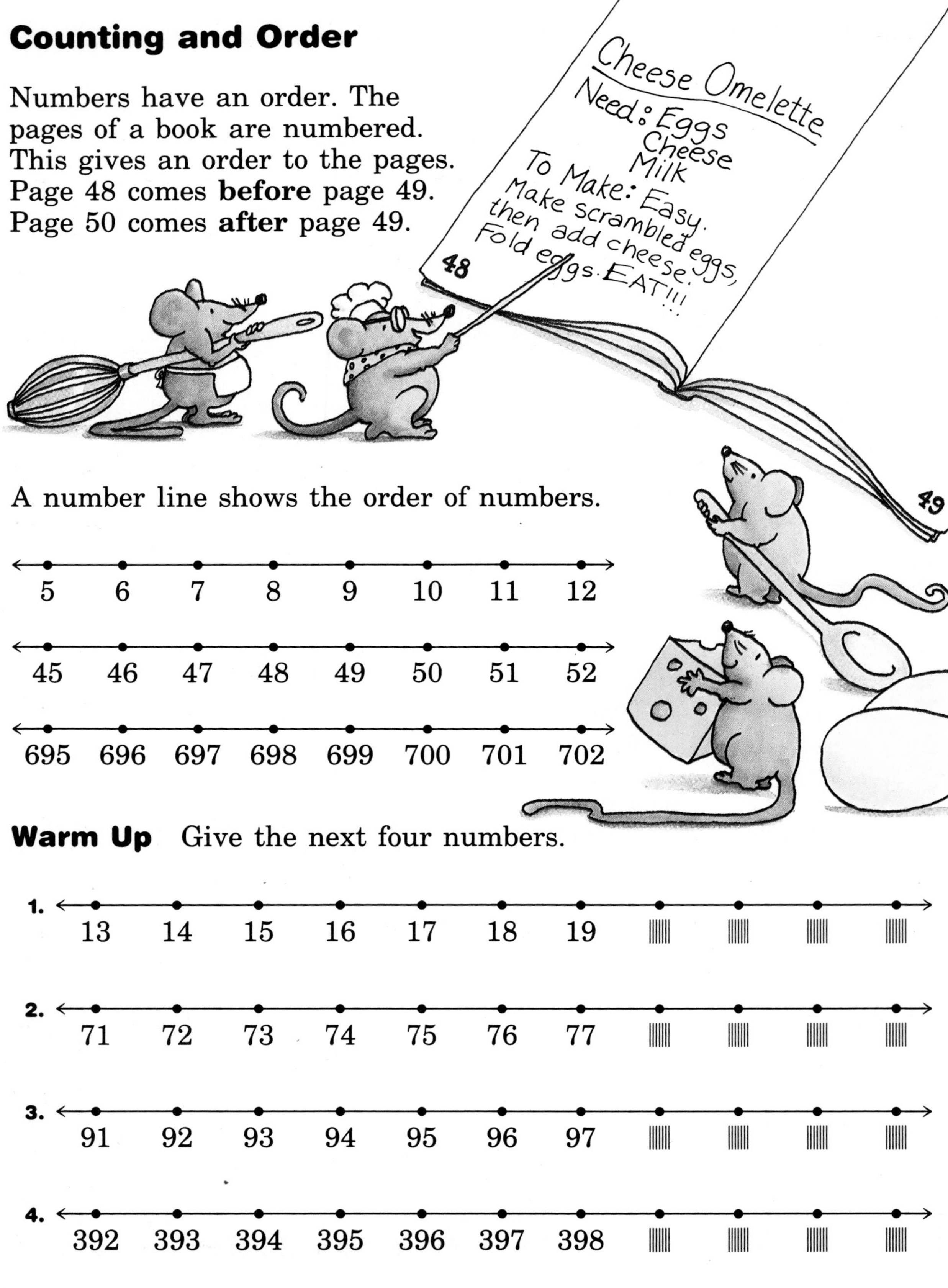

A number line shows the order of numbers.

5 6 7 8 9 10 11 12

45 46 47 48 49 50 51 52

695 696 697 698 699 700 701 702

Warm Up Give the next four numbers.

1. 13 14 15 16 17 18 19 ▯ ▯ ▯ ▯

2. 71 72 73 74 75 76 77 ▯ ▯ ▯ ▯

3. 91 92 93 94 95 96 97 ▯ ▯ ▯ ▯

4. 392 393 394 395 396 397 398 ▯ ▯ ▯ ▯

Practice Write the number of the "next" page.

1. 

2. 

3. 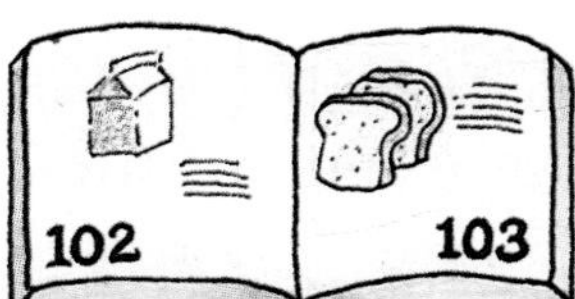

4. 

5. 

6. 

Write the number that comes after.

7. 37 **8.** 58 **9.** 79 **10.** 90 **11.** 19 **12.** 39

13. 126 **14.** 129 **15.** 350 **16.** 499 **17.** 659 **18.** 399

Give the number that comes before.

19. 23 **20.** 41 **21.** 50 **22.** 69 **23.** 70 **24.** 40

25. 134 **26.** 130 **27.** 151 **28.** 670 **29.** 500 **30.** 380

★ Write the number that is between.

31. 329 and 331 **32.** 209 and 211 **33.** 619 and 621

34. 729 and 731 **35.** 846 and 848 **36.** 499 and 501

SKILLKEEPER

Subtract.

1. $17 - 8$ **2.** $15 - 7$ **3.** $13 - 4$ **4.** $11 - 6$ **5.** $14 - 7$ **6.** $12 - 3$

7. $15 - 6$ **8.** $11 - 9$ **9.** $13 - 7$ **10.** $10 - 8$ **11.** $16 - 7$ **12.** $18 - 9$

More Practice, page 381, Set B

Skip Counting

Skip count by 2s beginning with 0. You get the even numbers.

Skip count by 2s beginning with 1. You get the odd numbers.

Skip count by 5s beginning with 0. You get numbers that end in 0 or 5. 0, 5, 10, 15, 20, 25, 30, . . .

Count by twos.

1. Begin at 20. Stop at 30.

2. Begin at 41. Stop at 51.

3. Begin at 85. Stop at 95.

Count by fives.

4. Begin at 30. Stop at 80.

5. Begin at 100. Stop at 150.

6. Begin at 210. Stop at 260.

Is the number even or odd?

7. 68 **8.** 75 **9.** 39 **10.** 124 **11.** 357 **12.** 1,283

Count by tens. Give the next four numbers.

13. 40, 50, 60, ▥, ▥, ▥, ▥

14. 230, 240, 250, 260, ▥, ▥, ▥, ▥

More Practice, page 381, Set C

Counting Money

penny	nickel	dime	quarter	half dollar
1 cent	5 cents	10 cents	25 cents	50 cents
1¢	5¢	10¢	25¢	50¢

Skip counting can help you count money.

Example

Lay out these coins.

Skip Count. **25 35 45 50 55 60**

These coins are worth **60 cents.**

Practice Give the value of each set of coins.

1.

2.

3.

4.

5.

6.

7.

8.

Counting Change

Tina bought a birthday card for 37¢. She gave the clerk 50¢. The clerk counted out her change. He started with the cost of the card and stopped at 50¢. Tina counted with him to make sure the change was correct.

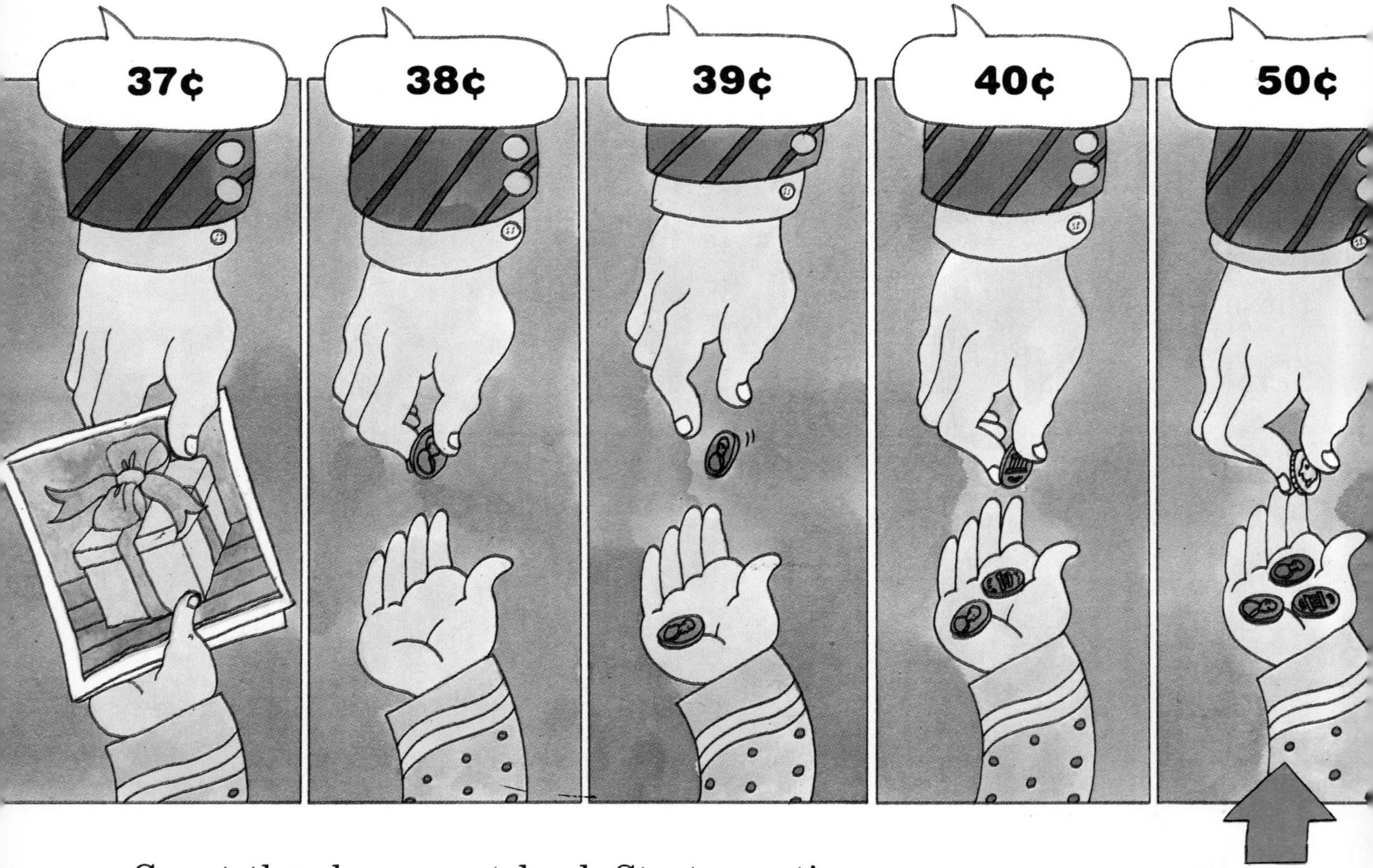

37¢ 38¢ 39¢ 40¢ 50¢

Tina's change is correct.

Count the change out loud. Start counting with the cost of the card. Stop with the amount of money handed to the clerk.

1. Andrea handed the clerk 50¢.

2. Mark handed the clerk $1.00.

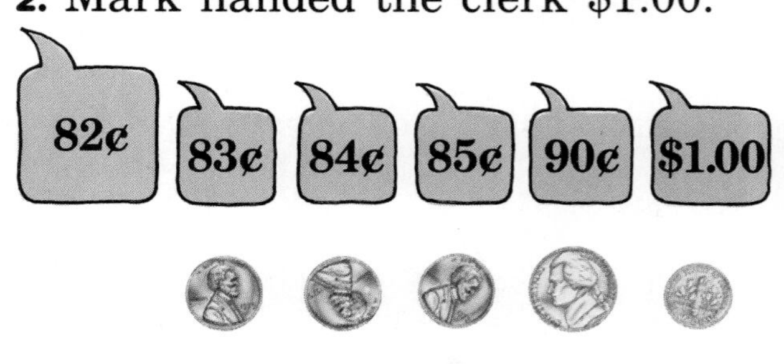

Practice Count the change out loud. Write the numbers the clerk would say.

1. James handed the clerk 50¢.

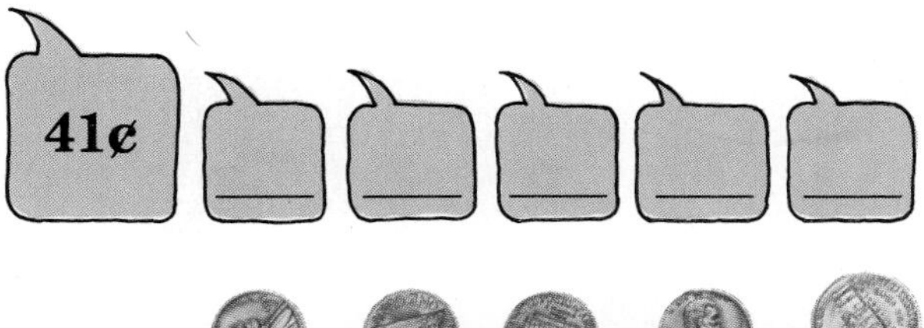

2. Sue handed the clerk 50¢.

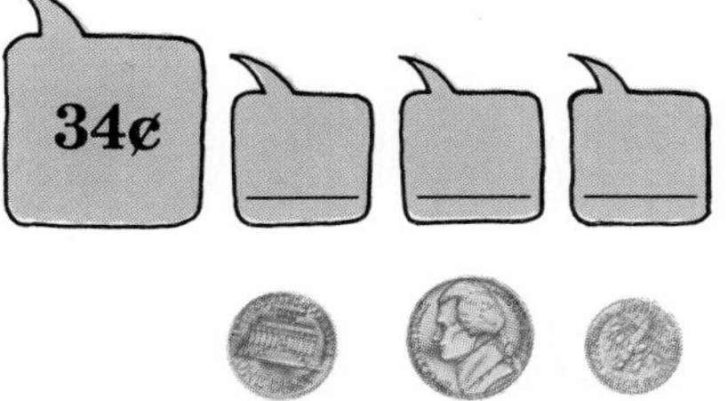

3. Janet handed the clerk 75¢.

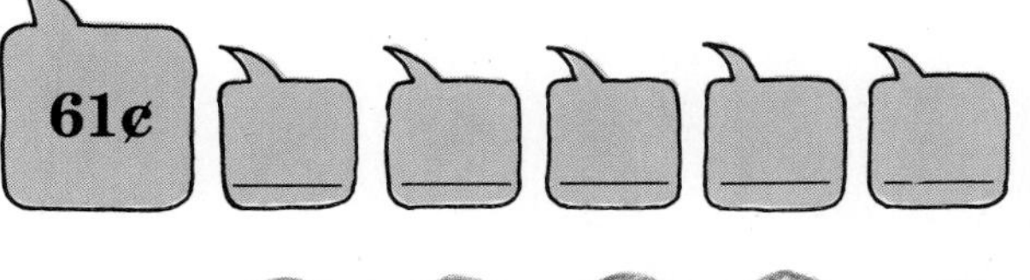

4. Sam handed the clerk 75¢.

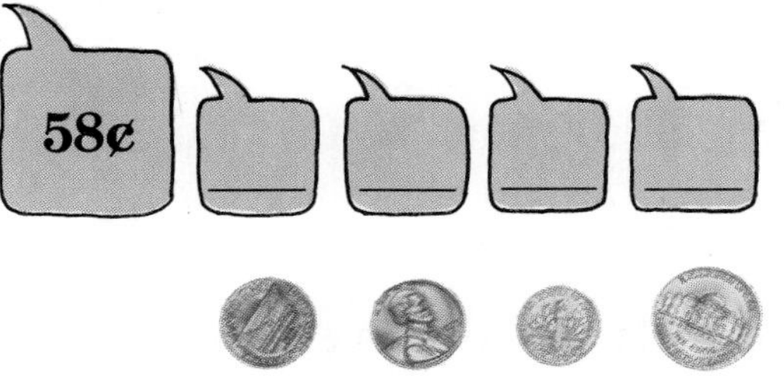

5. Lisa handed the clerk $1.00.

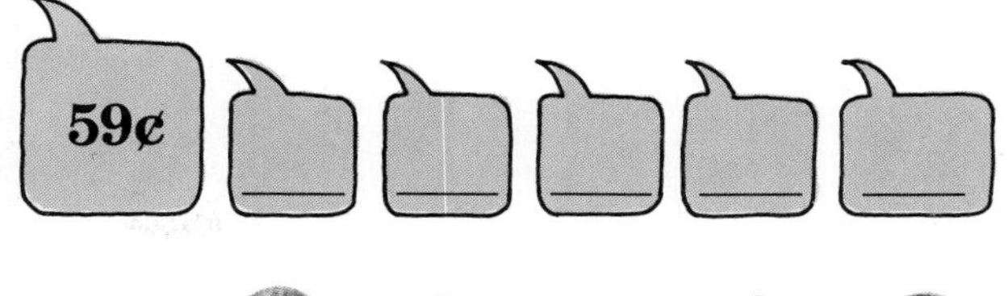

6. Dana handed the clerk $1.00.

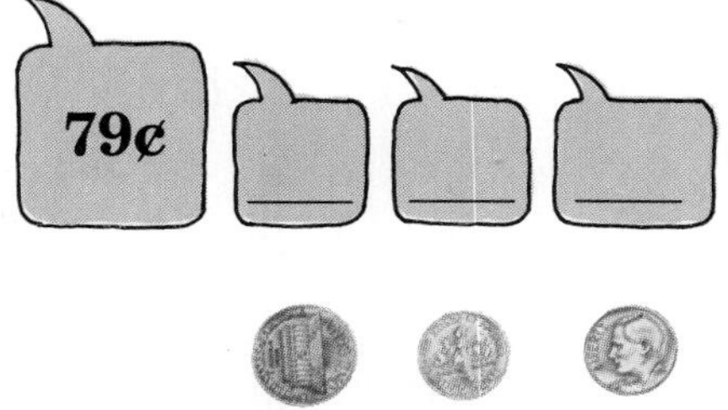

7. Gene handed the clerk $1.00.

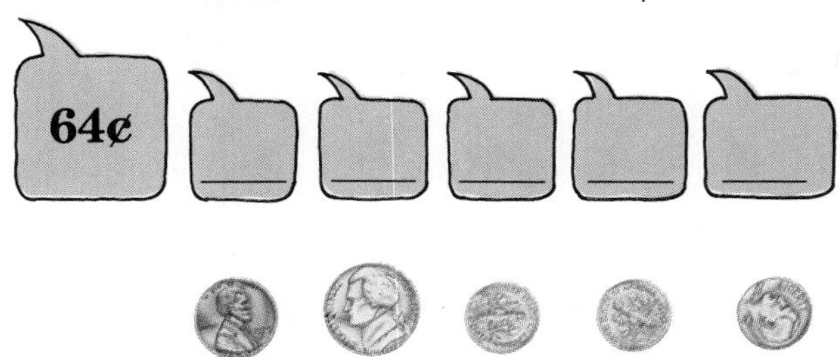

THINK

Logical Reasoning

Marcia handed the clerk $1.00 to buy a card for 74¢. When the clerk counted the change, this is what she said:

What coins did she get back in change?

MATH

Dollars and Cents

dollar
100 cents
100¢

dime
10 cents
10¢

penny
1 cent
1¢

3 dollars
300 cents

2 dimes
20 cents

4 pennies
4 cents

324 cents
We write, **$3.24**
We read, "**three dollars and twenty-four cents.**"

Other Examples

We write, **$0.32**
We read, "**32 cents.**"

We write, **$0.03**
We read, "**3 cents.**"

Warm Up Read each amount aloud.

1. $4.38 **2.** $9.80 **3.** $7.98 **4.** $0.65 **5.** $2.95 **6.** $5.00 **7.** $0.08

8. $3.88 **9.** $0.75 **10.** $2.16 **11.** $7.04 **12.** $1.00 **13.** $8.05 **14.** $2.39

15. $8.01 **16.** $3.90 **17.** $0.98 **18.** $1.69 **19.** $9.85 **20.** $6.75 **21.** $0.01

22. $3.95 **23.** $0.05 **24.** $6.00 **25.** $9.50 **26.** $0.49 **27.** $4.87 **28.** $5.25

The money shows the price of the toy. What amount should be on the price tag?

1.

2.

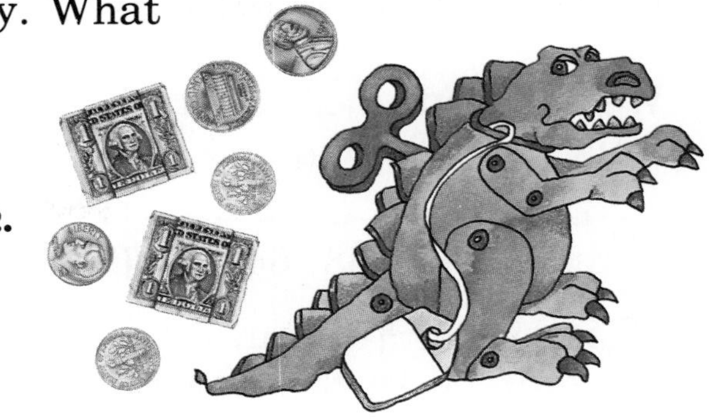

3.

4.

Practice Write each amount.

5. 2 dollars, 4 dimes, 6 pennies
6. 5 dollars, 7 dimes
7. 4 dollars, 3 pennies
8. 6 dollars
9. 3 dollars and 27 cents
10. 57 cents
11. 5 dollars, 6 dimes, 3 pennies
12. 8 dollars, 2 dimes
13. 2 dollars, 5 pennies
14. 7 dollars and 95 cents
15. 75 cents

THINK

Place-Value Game

Make two sets of digit cards.

Each player makes a place-value chart.

Hundreds	Tens	Ones

1. Mix the cards and turn them face down.
2. On your turn, draw the top card. Show the digit.
3. Write that digit in any place on your chart.
4. Take turns until each chart is full.
5. The greatest number wins.

MATH

More Practice, page 382, Set A

Estimation Readiness: Rounding

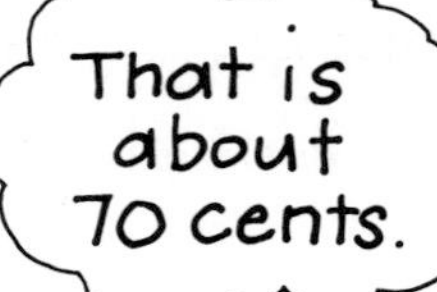

We can **round** numbers to give an estimate that tells about how many. 68 is between 60 and 70.

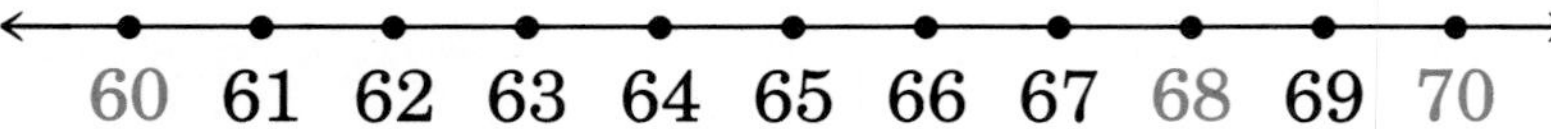

68 is nearer 70 than 60.
68 rounded **to the nearest 10** is 70.

85 is between 80 and 90.

80 81 82 83 84 85 86 87 88 89 90

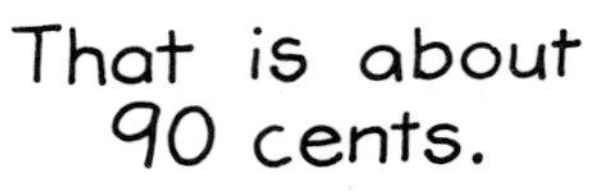

When a number is halfway between, round to the larger number.

85 rounded to the nearest 10 is 90.

Warm Up Where is the number? Use the number line.

Example 53 is between ▥ and ▥.

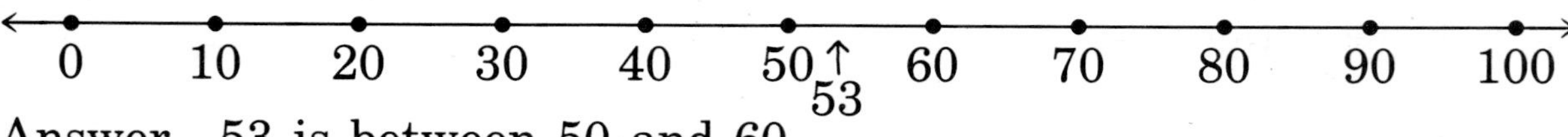

Answer 53 is between 50 and 60.

1. 77 is between ▥ and ▥.
2. 42 is between ▥ and ▥.
3. 63 is between ▥ and ▥.
4. 17 is between ▥ and ▥.
5. 88 is between ▥ and ▥.
6. 49 is between ▥ and ▥.
7. 24 is between ▥ and ▥.
8. 95 is between ▥ and ▥.
9. 31 is between ▥ and ▥.
10. 85 is between ▥ and ▥.

Practice Round to the nearest ten. Which red number is the better choice?

1. 28 → 20 or 30
2. 44 → 40 or 50
3. 75 → 70 or 80
4. 82 → 80 or 90
5. 36 → 30 or 40
6. 61 → 60 or 70
7. 77 → 70 or 80
8. 25 → 20 or 30
9. 54 → 50 or 60
10. 45 → 40 or 50
11. 63 → 60 or 70
12. 89 → 80 or 90

Round to the nearest ten.

Examples 36 ▒ Answer 40 53 ▒ Answer 50

13. 29 ▒
14. 81 ▒
15. 36 ▒
16. 44 ▒
17. 52 ▒
18. 79 ▒
19. 67 ▒
20. 45 ▒
21. 13 ▒
22. 77 ▒
23. 24 ▒
24. 61 ▒

Give the price to the nearest ten cents.

25.

26.

27.

THINK

Rounding

What numbers can you find for the ▒?

▒ rounded to the nearest ten is 60.

Which two numbers have digits that add to the same sum?

MATH

More about Rounding

Sometimes you want to round to the nearest hundred.

230 is between 200 and 300

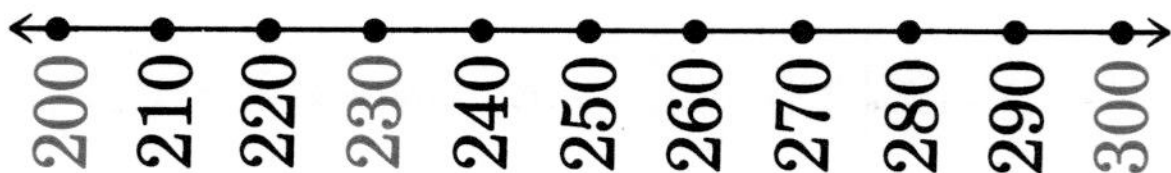

230 rounded to the nearest hundred is 200.

Sometimes you want to round to the nearest dollar.

$2.79 is between $2.00 and $3.00.

$2.79 is nearer to $3.00.

$2.79 rounded to the nearest dollar is $3.00

Warm Up Where is the number? Use the number line.

Example 675 is between ▯ and ▯.

100 200 300 400 500 600 700 800 900 1,000

675

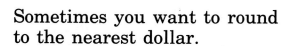

Answer 675 is between 600 and 700.

1. 231 is between ▯ and ▯.

2. 880 is between ▯ and ▯.

3. 524 is between ▯ and ▯.

4. 650 is between ▯ and ▯.

5. 449 is between ▯ and ▯.

6. 362 is between ▯ and ▯.

7. $6.29 is between $▯ and $▯.

8. $4.75 is between $▯ and $▯.

9. $8.98 is between $▯ and $▯.

10. $7.19 is between $▯ and $▯.

11. $6.54 is between $▯ and $▯.

12. $3.48 is between $▯ and $▯.

Practice Round to the nearest hundred or dollar. Which red number is the better choice?

1. 769→700 or 800
2. 427→400 or 500
3. 562→500 or 600
4. 850→800 or 900
5. 539→500 or 600
6. 728→700 or 800
7. \$3.98→\$3.00 or \$4.00
8. \$4.29→\$4.00 or \$5.00
9. \$6.15→\$6.00 or \$7.00
10. \$3.85→\$3.00 or \$4.00

Round to the nearest hundred.

11. 244 ______	12. 685 ______	13. 437 ______	14. 552 ______
15. 579 ______	16. 708 ______	17. 650 ______	18. 376 ______

Round to the nearest dollar.

19. \$4.85 \$______	20. \$9.25 \$______	21. \$2.37 \$______	22. \$6.95 \$______
23. \$6.48 \$______	24. \$1.98 \$______	25. \$4.77 \$______	26. \$3.29 \$______
27. \$5.64 \$______	28. \$8.13 \$______	29. \$3.50 \$______	30. \$7.39 \$______

Give the price to the nearest dollar.

31.

32.

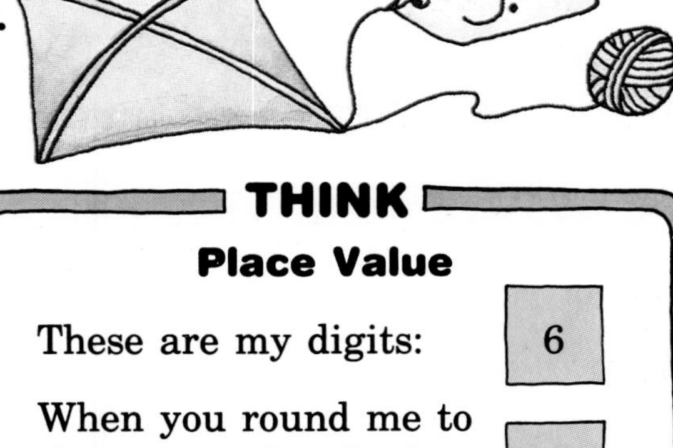

33.

THINK

Place Value

These are my digits: 6 4 3

When you round me to the nearest hundred, you get 500.

WHO AM I?

MATH

More Practice, page 382, Set C

Thousands

10 hundred pieces can be glued together to make **one thousand.**

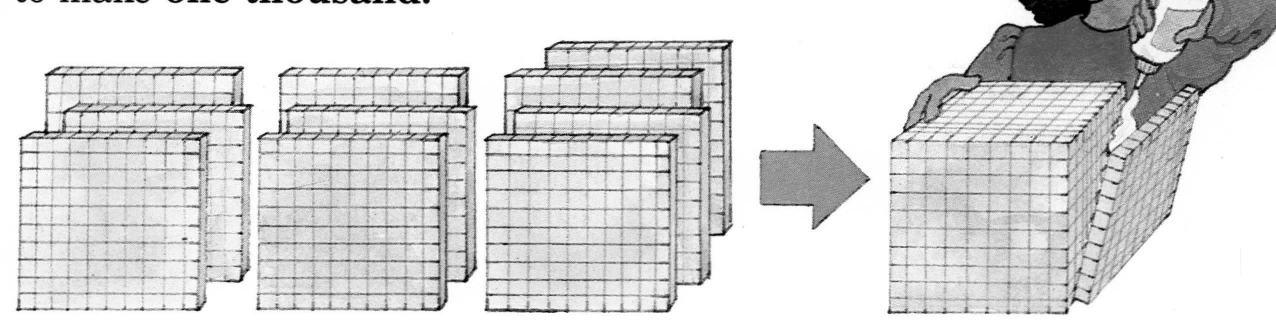

ten hundreds **one thousand (1,000)**

We use thousands, hundreds, tens, and ones to write larger numbers.

Example

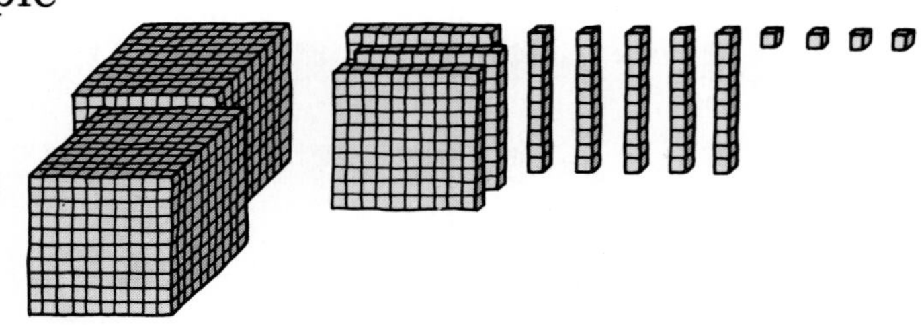

2 thousands, **3** hundreds, **5** tens, and **4** ones = **2,354**
We read, "**two thousand, three hundred fifty-four.**"

Warm Up Read each number aloud.

1. 4,751	**2.** 2,029	**3.** 5,846	**4.** 1,975	**5.** 6,152
6. 8,010	**7.** 1,002	**8.** 3,678	**9.** 6,027	**10.** 7,843
11. 8,942	**12.** 2,000	**13.** 1,391	**14.** 5,300	**15.** 3,012
16. 7,924	**17.** 8,516	**18.** 9,406	**19.** 2,345	**20.** 6,532
21. 1,058	**22.** 7,643	**23.** 9,999	**24.** 4,251	**25.** 4,726
26. 5,301	**27.** 2,640	**28.** 8,765	**29.** 5,206	**30.** 1,001
31. 9,779	**32.** 8,007	**33.** 2,443	**34.** 7,038	**35.** 5,549

Practice Write the number.

1.

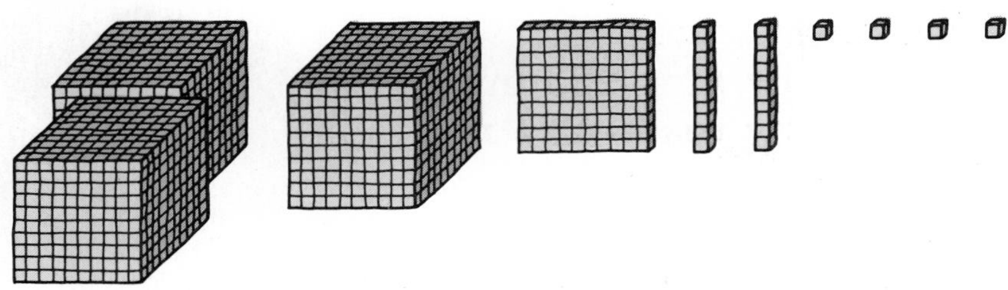

2.

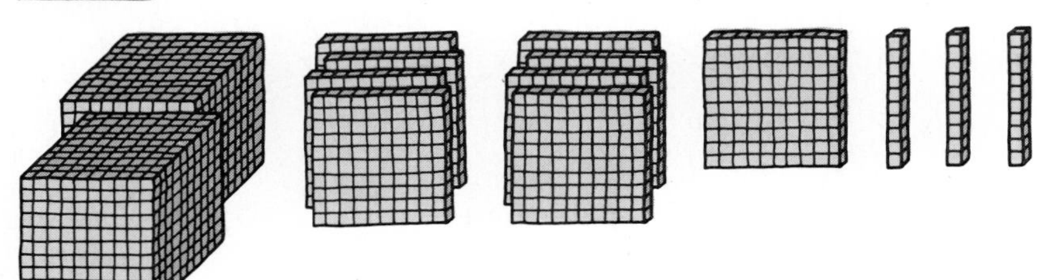

3.

Thousands	Hundreds	Tens	Ones
2	6	8	3

4.

Thousands	Hundreds	Tens	Ones
3	0	9	4

5.

Thousands	Hundreds	Tens	Ones
5	0	7	3

6.

Thousands	Hundreds	Tens	Ones
8	4	0	6

What does the 5 mean in each number? Write **thousands, hundreds, tens,** or **ones.**

7. 3,506 **8.** 2,785 **9.** 5,264 **10.** 3,750

11. 4,605 **12.** 2,582

13. 5,807 **14.** 9,562

Write the number.

15. 2 tens
6 thousands
3 ones
5 hundreds

16. 5 tens
0 ones
0 hundreds
3 thousands

THINK

Place Value

How many 4-digit numbers can you find that have only 0s and 1s?
What are they?

MATH

Comparing Numbers

Which distance is greater?
New York to Washington by air—223 mi.
New York to Washington by road—231 mi.
To find which of two numbers is greater, you compare them.

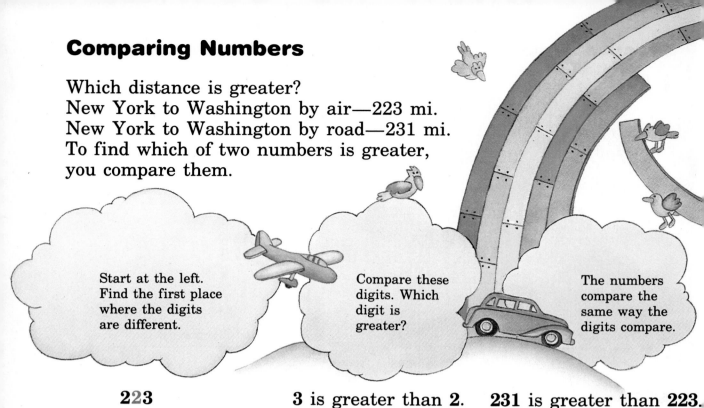

Start at the left. Find the first place where the digits are different.

Compare these digits. Which digit is greater?

The numbers compare the same way the digits compare.

223
231

3 is greater than **2**. **231** is greater than **223**.

The road distance is greater.

231 is greater than **223**.

$\mathbf{231 > 223}$

223 is less than **231**.

$\mathbf{223 < 231}$

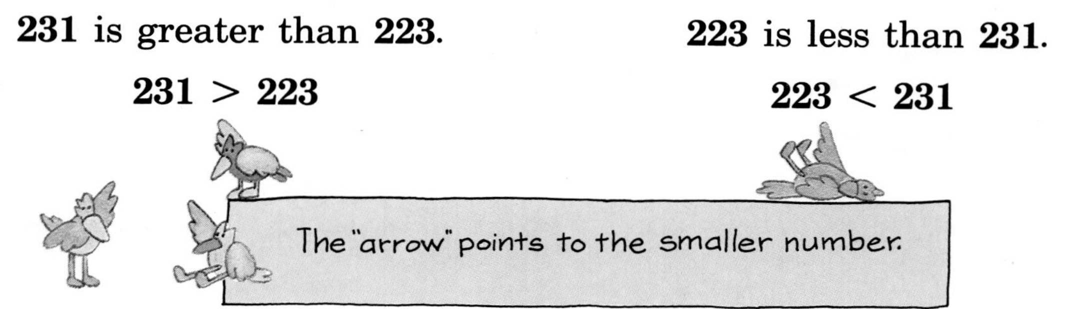

The "arrow" points to the smaller number.

Other Examples **5,236** is less than **5,273**. **43** is greater than **39**.

$\mathbf{5{,}236 < 5{,}273}$ $\mathbf{43 > 39}$

Warm Up Which of the two numbers is greater?

1. 67
63

2. 426
423

3. 692
598

4. 3,629
3,630

5. 5,280
5,340

6. 7,268
7,264

Practice Write $>$ or $<$ for each ●.

1. 8 ● 3	2. 7 ● 9	3. 20 ● 40
4. 60 ● 30	5. 300 ● 500	6. 700 ● 400
7. 900 ● 800	8. 3,000 ● 2,000	9. 4,000 ● 7,000
10. 36 ● 38	11. 47 ● 37	12. 59 ● 62
13. 75 ● 68	14. 234 ● 236	15. 754 ● 750
16. 623 ● 643	17. 874 ● 774	18. 396 ● 412
19. 2,834 ● 2,831	20. 4,675 ● 4,679	21. 3,260 ● 3,250

★ Give the number that is 1,000 more.

22. 3,000 **23.** 4,765 **24.** 2,843 **25.** 6,400 **26.** 5,628

★ Give the number that is 100 more.

27. 200 **28.** 428 **29.** 7,643 **30.** 2,480 **31.** 3,657

★ Give the number that is 1,000 less.

32. 3,000 **33.** 8,432 **34.** 7,651 **35.** 3,281 **36.** 9,467

SKILLKEEPER

Add. Look for sums of 10.

1.	2.	3.	4.	5.	6.
2	4	7	1	2	4
1	3	6	2	5	3
+ 5	+ 5	+ 3	+ 6	+ 5	+ 3

7.	8.	9.	10.	11.	12.
4	3	7	6	8	5
3	5	1	2	2	3
+ 6	+ 3	+ 3	+ 2	+ 7	+ 2

More Practice, page 383, Set A

More About Thousands

The red digits tell the number of thousands.

4,000 four thousand
40,000 forty thousand
400,000 four hundred thousand

Read these numbers aloud.

1. 6,000	**2.** 20,000	**3.** 400,000
4. 50,000	**5.** 800,000	**6.** 2,000
7. 100,000	**8.** 200,000	**9.** 4,000

Read these numbers aloud.

Example We read **654,000** as
"six hundred fifty-four thousand."

10. 23,000	**11.** 423,000	**12.** 68,000	**13.** 168,000
14. 480,000	**15.** 327,000	**16.** 562,000	**17.** 34,000

Read these numbers aloud.

Example We read **465,281** as
"four hundred sixty-five thousand, two hundred eighty-one."

18. 751,324	**19.** 28,600	**20.** 369,070	**21.** 115,280
22. 37,008	**23.** 269,095	**24.** 481,300	**25.** 7,604
26. 692,000	**27.** 840,035	**28.** 31,007	**29.** 111,224
30. 751,217	**31.** 684,500	**32.** 95,090	**33.** 327,006
34. 816,400	**35.** 92,328	**36.** 4,007	**37.** 300,600
38. 802,325	**39.** 26,781	**40.** 384,000	**41.** 975,617

Write the number. Use a comma to separate thousands.

Example Write six hundred twelve thousand as 612,000.

1. forty-two thousand, eight hundred eighty

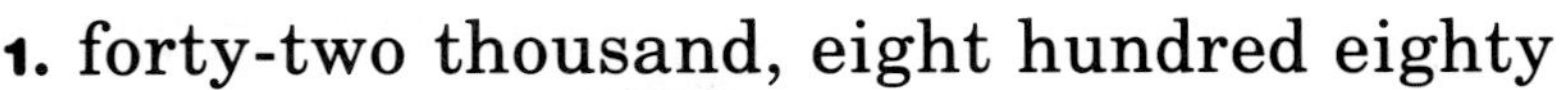

2. forty-two thousand, eight hundred eighty-eight
3. seventy-eight thousand

4. nine thousand, four hundred
5. one hundred twenty thousand
6. fifty-two thousand, ninety
7. fifty-two thousand, nine
8. fifty-two thousand, nineteen
9. seven thousand, sixteen
10. nine hundred ninety thousand

Choose a reasonable estimate.

11. The number of people in a large city:
    A 500 **B** 5,000 **C** 500,000
12. The cost of a pair of shoes:
    A \$4 **B** \$40 **C** \$400
13. The number of miles across the United States:
    A 300 **B** 3,000 **C** 30,000
14. The number of seats in a large football stadium:
    A 750 **B** 7,500 **C** 75,000

THINK MATH

Patterns

Give the next two numbers in each column. Read down.

1.	**2.**
269	4,158
369	4,257
469	4,356
569	4,455
669	4,554
769	4,653
▮▮▮	▮▮▮▮
▮▮▮	▮▮▮▮

More Practice, page 383, Set B

Ordinal Numbers

We can use numbers to tell order.
The Galaxians are in line for tickets.

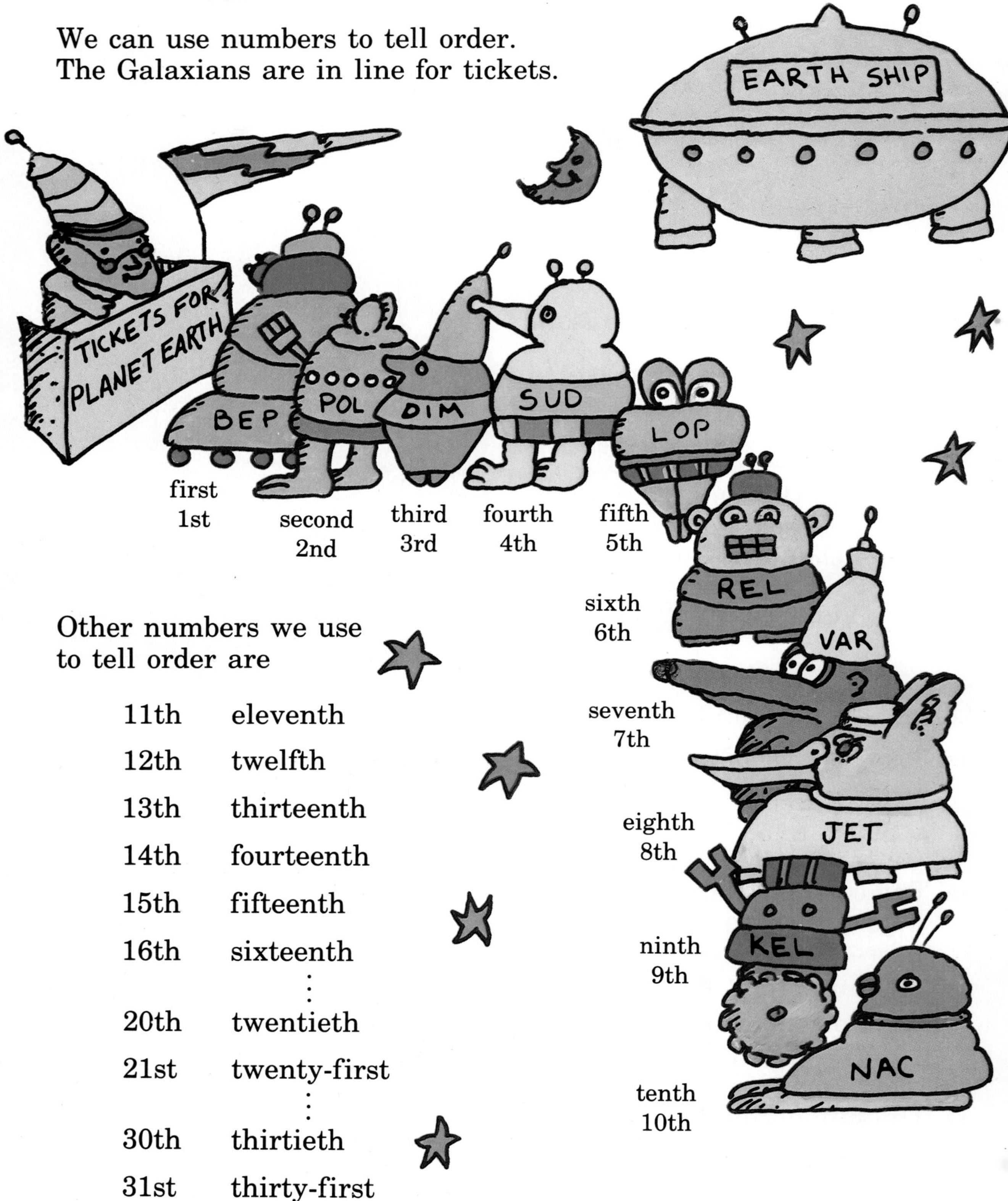

Other numbers we use to tell order are

11th	eleventh
12th	twelfth
13th	thirteenth
14th	fourteenth
15th	fifteenth
16th	sixteenth
⋮	⋮
20th	twentieth
21st	twenty-first
⋮	⋮
30th	thirtieth
31st	thirty-first

Practice Use the pictures on page 48 to answer questions 1–7.

1. Bep is first. Who is last?
2. Where is Dim in line?
3. How many are ahead of Jet?
4. What place is next to last?
5. How many are behind Lop?
6. After Bep and Pol get tickets, who is third in line?
7. If everyone turned around so Nac was first, who would be in fourth place?

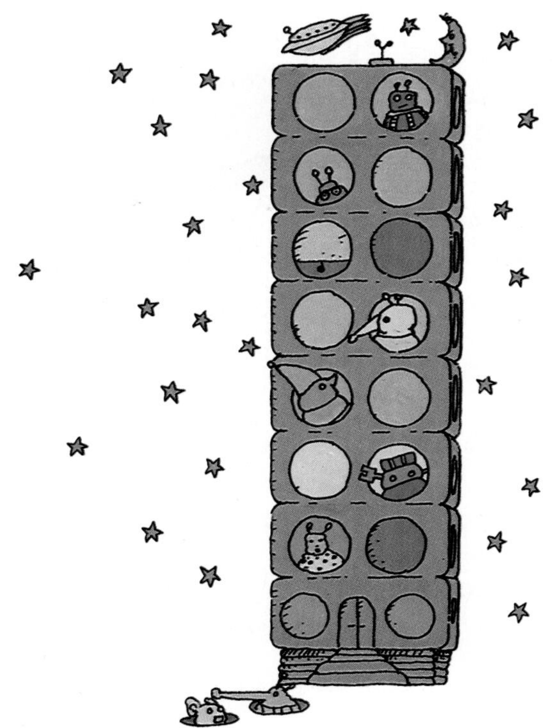

Solve.

8. Chris is 12th in line. How many are ahead of him?
9. Terri is 16th in line. How many are ahead of her?
10. There are 20 people in a race. Sandy is 4th. How many are behind her?
11. There are 14 cars in a race. The red car is 12th. How many cars are in front?
12. There are 20 people in line. Tim is next to last. Name his place in line.

★ 13. How many days are between the 13th day and the 19th day of the month?

★ 14. If Mike is next to last in line and he is also third from first place, how many people are in line?

THINK

Ordinal Numbers

What is one of the tallest buildings in the world?

First Word	*Second Word*
Second letter E	Third letter W
Fifth letter S	Fifth letter R
First letter S	Second letter O
Fourth letter R	First letter T
Third letter A	Fourth letter E

MATH

PROBLEM-SOLVING STRATEGY
Guess and Check

QUESTION
DATA
PLAN
ANSWER
CHECK
To solve a problem like this, you must do more than just quickly add or subtract. A strategy that can help you with this kind of problem is given below.
Try This Two families went on a picnic together. There were 13 people at the picnic. Which families went on the picnic?
Family
Number of People
Clark 9
Ross 5
Hart 6
Hill 8

GUESS AND CHECK

First Guess: Try Clark (9) and Ross (5).
Check 9 + 5 = 14

Too many. Only 13 went on the picnic.

Second Guess: Try Ross (5) and Hart (6).
Check 5 +6 = 11

Too few. There were 13 at the picnic.

Third Guess: Try Ross (5) and Hill (8).
Check 5 + 8 = 13

Just right!

The Ross and Hill families went on the picnic.

Solve.

1. Ann has \$8. Jan has \$5. Fay has \$7. Sue has \$3. Two of the girls put their money together. Then they had \$11. Who were the girls?

2. Bert has 6 cards. Joe has 4 cards. Tom has 7 cards. Fred has 8 cards. Cal has 9 cards. Three boys put their cards together. Then they had 17 cards. Who were the boys?

CHAPTER REVIEW/TEST

Write the number.

1.

2. 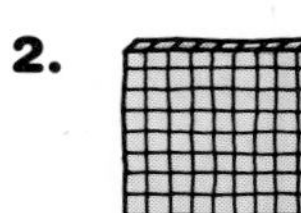 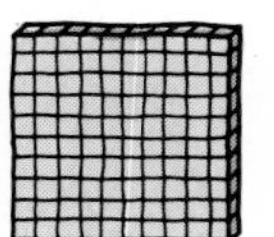 

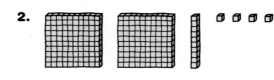

3.

Tens	Ones
5	6

4.

Hundreds	Tens	Ones
8	0	5

Give the next four numbers.

5. 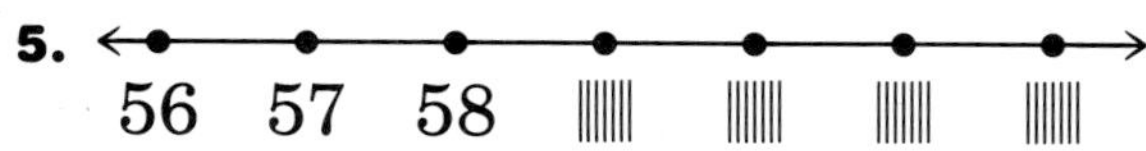

56 57 58 ▒ ▒ ▒ ▒

6. 0, 5, 10, 15, 20, ▒, ▒, ▒, ▒.

How much money?

7. 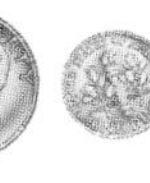   

8.    

Round to the nearest ten.

9. 26 **10.** 75 **11.** 83

Round to the nearest hundred.

12. 139 **13.** 365 **14.** 850

15. Write the number.
six thousand, seven hundred eighty-five

Write > or < for each ▒.

16. 76 ▒ 81 **17.** 324 ▒ 298 **18.** 1,267 ▒ 1,272

19. Write the number.
seven hundred twenty-eight thousand

20. Jesse is eighth in line. How many people are in front of him?

ANOTHER LOOK

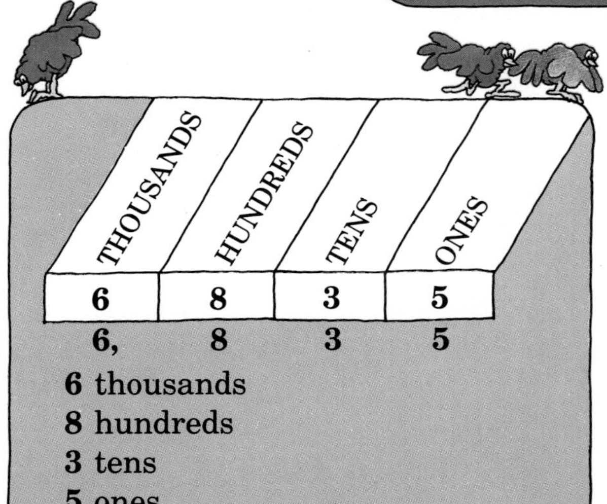

Write the numbers.

1.

Tens	Ones
6	2

2.

Hundreds	Tens	Ones
4	7	5

3.

Thousands	Hundreds	Tens	Ones
3	9	8	4

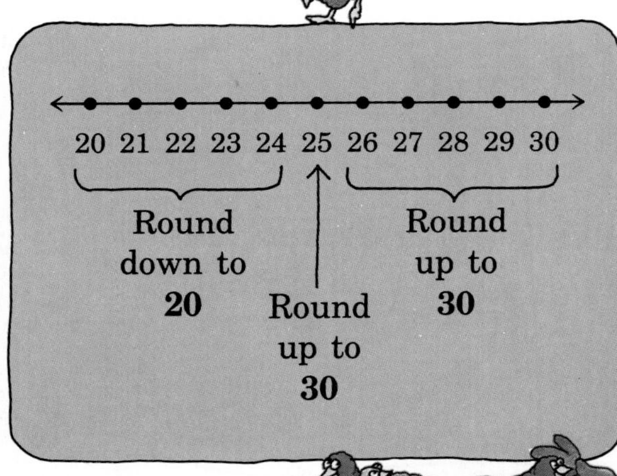

Round to the nearest ten.

4. 23 5. 29 6. 25 7. 83

8. 89 9. 85 10. 46 11. 42

Round to the nearest hundred.

12. 685 13. 624 14. 650

15. 316 16. 392 17. 348

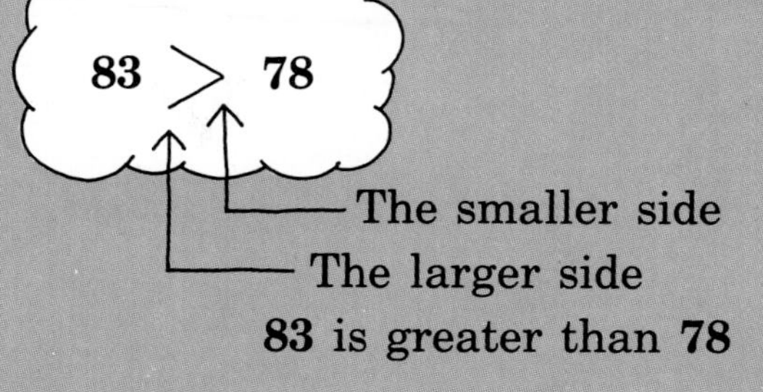

Write > or < for each ●.

18. 32 ● 36 19. 43 ● 33

20. 75 ● 72 21. 68 ● 78

22. 59 ● 62 23. 71 ● 69

24. 235 ● 241 25. 368 ● 361

ENRICHMENT

Roman Numerals

The Romans used letters to write their numbers. Three of the letters were I, V, and X.

I = 1
V = 5
X = 10

The chart shows the first twenty **Roman Numerals.** Give the Roman Numeral for each number.

1. 3 **2.** 6 **3.** 9

4. 14 **5.** 17 **6.** 19

Give the number for each Roman Numeral.

7. II **8.** IV **9.** XI

10. XVI **11.** XVIII **12.** XX

13. Draw a clock face. Put Roman Numerals on it.

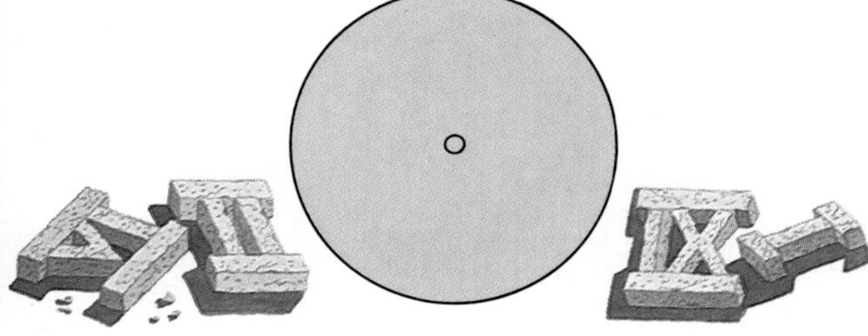

★ **14.** Write the Roman Numerals from 20 to 31. Here is a start. XX, XXI, XXII, . . .

★ **15.** Copy the calendar for this month. Use Roman Numerals.

NUMBER	ROMAN NUMERAL	
1	I	
2	II	1 + 1
3	III	1 + 1 + 1
4	IV	5 - 1
5	V	
6	VI	5 + 1
7	VII	5 + 2
8	VIII	5 + 3
9	IX	10 - 1
10	X	
11	XI	10 + 1
12	XII	10 + 2
13	XIII	10 + 3
14	XIV	10 + 4
15	XV	10 + 5
16	XVI	10 + 6
17	XVII	10 + 7
18	XVIII	10 + 8
19	XIX	10 + 9
20	XX	10 + 10

CALCULATOR

Entering and Erasing Numbers

Press ON to make your calculator work.
Then press the key for your number.
Press CLEAR to erase the number.

Enter **6**  Press ON ⟶  Press 6 ⟶ 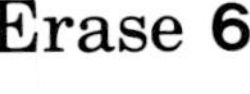 Erase **6**  Press C

Entering Large Numbers

Enter **806**. Press 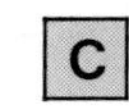 C  8  0 6 ⟶ See 

Adding Numbers

Clear the calculator. Enter each number and the + key. Press the = key for the answer. Add 5 + 2 + 3.

First add the numbers in your head.
Now check your answer.

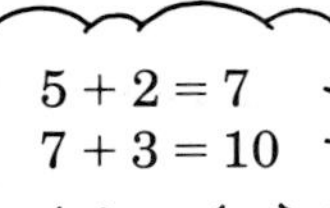

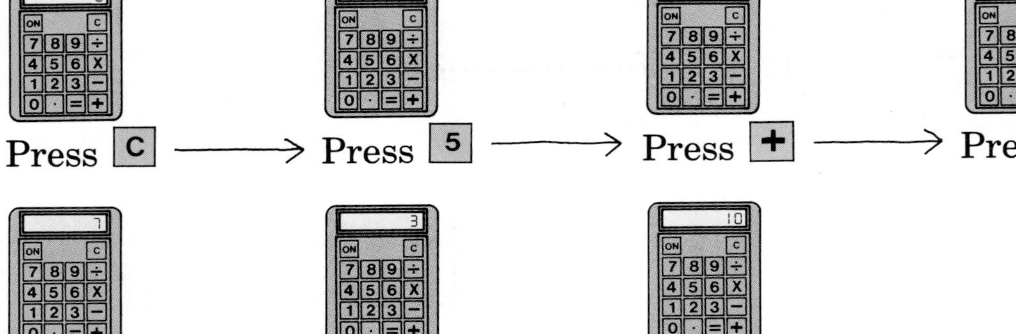

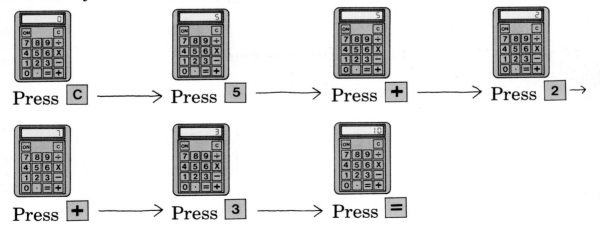

Sue went birdwatching. She counted 8 sparrows, 9 robins, 8 bluejays, and 7 hawks. What is the total number of birds she saw?

When using the calculator, we use estimation to see if the answer on the calculator seems reasonable.

Write the problem.

$$\begin{array}{r} 8 \\ 9 \\ 8 \\ +\ 7 \\ \hline \end{array}$$

Which answer would make sense?

More than 100? No.

Less than 50? Yes.

More than 0? Yes.

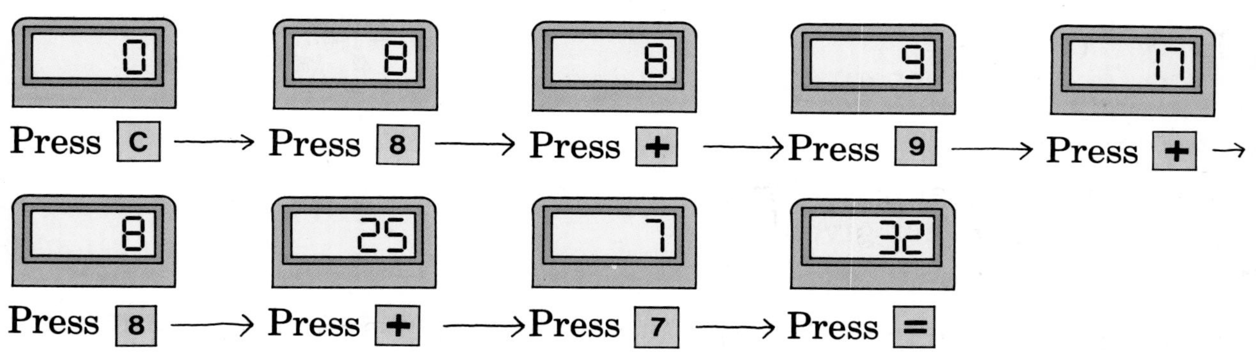

The answer is 32 birds. That answer makes sense. It is less than 50 and more than 0.

Solve. Use the calculator to find the sums. Estimate whether the answer should be more than 50 or less than 50.

1. $\begin{array}{r} 8 \\ 9 \\ 9 \\ +\ 7 \\ \hline \end{array}$

2. $\begin{array}{r} 4 \\ 9 \\ 6 \\ 8 \\ +\ 5 \\ \hline \end{array}$

3. $\begin{array}{r} 7 \\ 8 \\ 6 \\ 6 \\ +\ 8 \\ \hline \end{array}$

4. $\begin{array}{r} 6 \\ 4 \\ 2 \\ 0 \\ +\ 9 \\ \hline \end{array}$

CUMULATIVE REVIEW

Give the letter for the correct answer.

1. $14 - 8 =$ ____
   - A 7 B 9
   - C 12 D not given

2. $9 + 8 =$ ____
   - A 1 B 17
   - C 16 D not given

3. $11 - 9 =$ ____
   - A 10 B 5
   - C 2 D not given

4. $12 - 5 =$ ____
   - A 17 B 6
   - C 7 D not given

5. $8 + 7 =$ ____
   - A 15 B 17
   - C 16 D not given

6. $9 + 5 =$ ____
   - A 4 B 14
   - C 13 D not given

7. $\begin{array}{r} 7 \\ +\ 9 \\ \hline \end{array}$
   - A 15
   - B 16
   - C 17
   - D not given

8. $\begin{array}{r} 16 \\ -\ 8 \\ \hline \end{array}$
   - A 8
   - B 7
   - C 14
   - D not given

9. $\begin{array}{r} 12 \\ -\ 3 \\ \hline \end{array}$
   - A 7
   - B 15
   - C 8
   - D not given

10. $\begin{array}{r} 9 \\ +\ 4 \\ \hline \end{array}$
    - A 13
    - B 5
    - C 12
    - D not given

11. $\begin{array}{r} 8 \\ +\ 3 \\ \hline \end{array}$
    - A 5
    - B 11
    - C 10
    - D not given

12. $\begin{array}{r} 18 \\ -\ 9 \\ \hline \end{array}$
    - A 9
    - B 8
    - C 17
    - D not given

13. Sonja needs 8 clams to make soup. She has 6 clams. How many more clams does Sonja need to make soup?
    - A 3 B 14
    - C 2 D not given

14. Raoul caught 6 fish. Then he caught 5 more fish. How many fish did he catch?
    - A 11 B 10
    - C 1 D not given

ADDITION 3

Billy was making a robot from a kit. He needed to buy flashlight batteries to make it run. Billy wanted to get the best kind of batteries. He tested two kinds to see which one would last longer. He put a silver battery into one flashlight. He put a black battery into another flashlight. Then he left them on until the batteries died. The silver battery lasted 8 hours. The black battery lasted 3 more hours than the silver one.

Trading 10 Ones for 1 Ten

Bev has 2 tens and 15 ones. If she trades 10 ones for 1 ten,

1. how many tens will Bev have?
2. how many ones will she have?

Bev will have 3 tens and 5 ones.

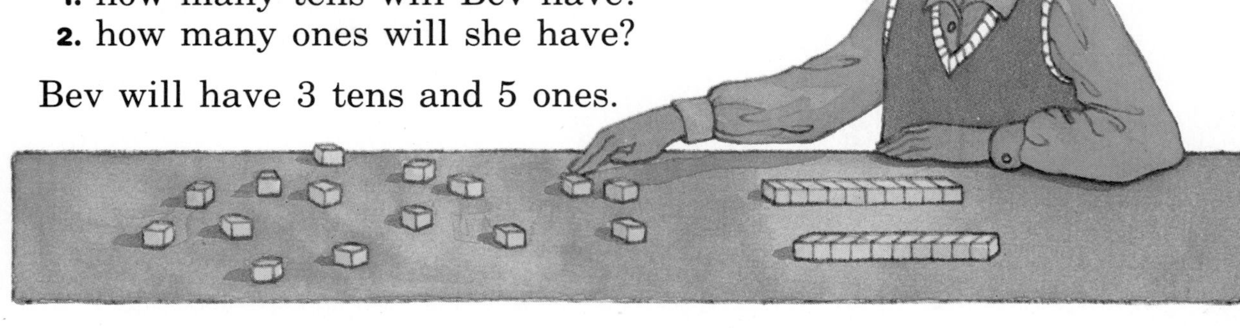

Other Examples

Trade 10 ones for 1 ten.

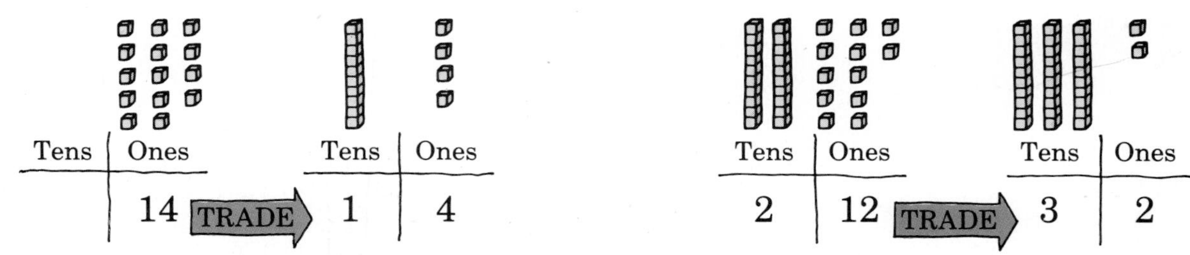

Tens	Ones		Tens	Ones
	14	TRADE	1	4

Tens	Ones		Tens	Ones
2	12	TRADE	3	2

Warm Up Give the numbers of tens and ones after a trade.

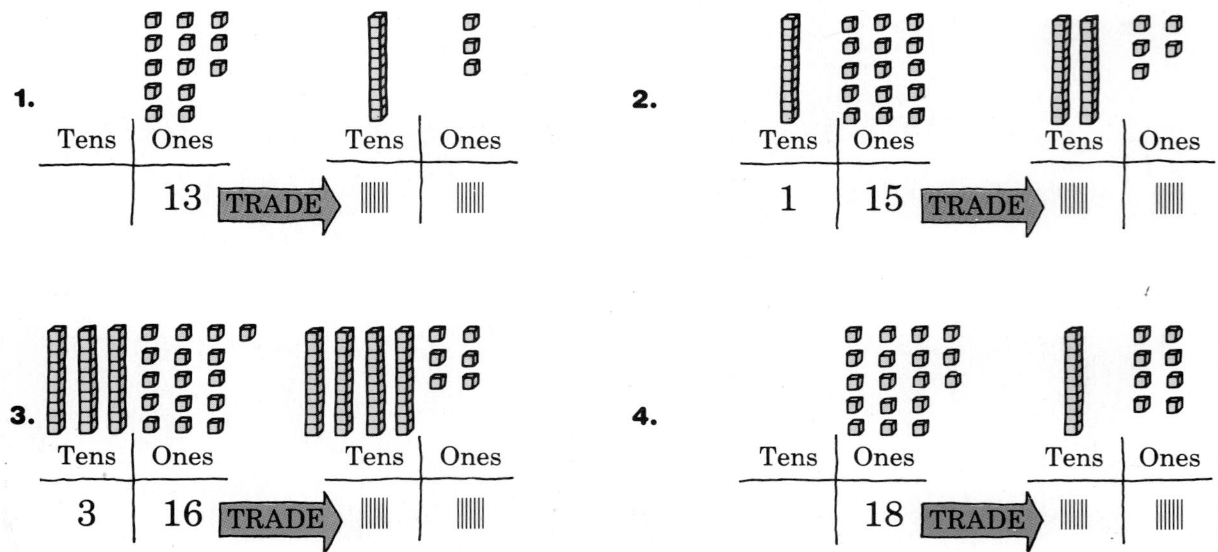

1.

Tens	Ones		Tens	Ones
	13	TRADE		

2.

Tens	Ones		Tens	Ones
1	15	TRADE		

3.

Tens	Ones		Tens	Ones
3	16	TRADE		

4.

Tens	Ones		Tens	Ones
	18	TRADE		

Practice Trade 10 ones for 1 ten.

Example

Tens	Ones
	17

TRADE

Tens	Ones
1	7

1.

Tens	Ones
1	15

TRADE

Tens	Ones

2.

Tens	Ones
3	12

TRADE

Tens	Ones

3.

Tens	Ones
2	16

TRADE

Tens	Ones

4.

Tens	Ones
	11

TRADE

Tens	Ones

5.

Tens	Ones
4	12

TRADE

Tens	Ones

6.

Tens	Ones
5	14

TRADE

Tens	Ones

7.

Tens	Ones
3	10

TRADE

Tens	Ones

8.

Tens	Ones
	16

TRADE

Tens	Ones

9.

Tens	Ones
4	13

TRADE

Tens	Ones

10.

Tens	Ones
5	18

TRADE

Tens	Ones

THINK

Logical Reasoning

Give the missing numbers.

2.
+ 6
15

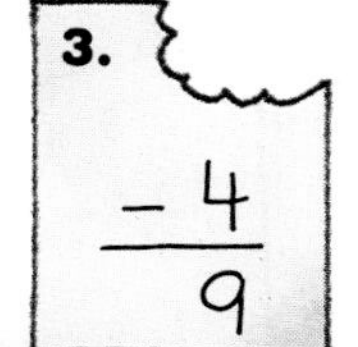

4.
6
+
14

MATH

Adding 2-Digit Numbers: Trading Ones

Jill weighs 35 kg. Jan weighs 29 kg. What is their total weight?

Since we want their total weight, we add.

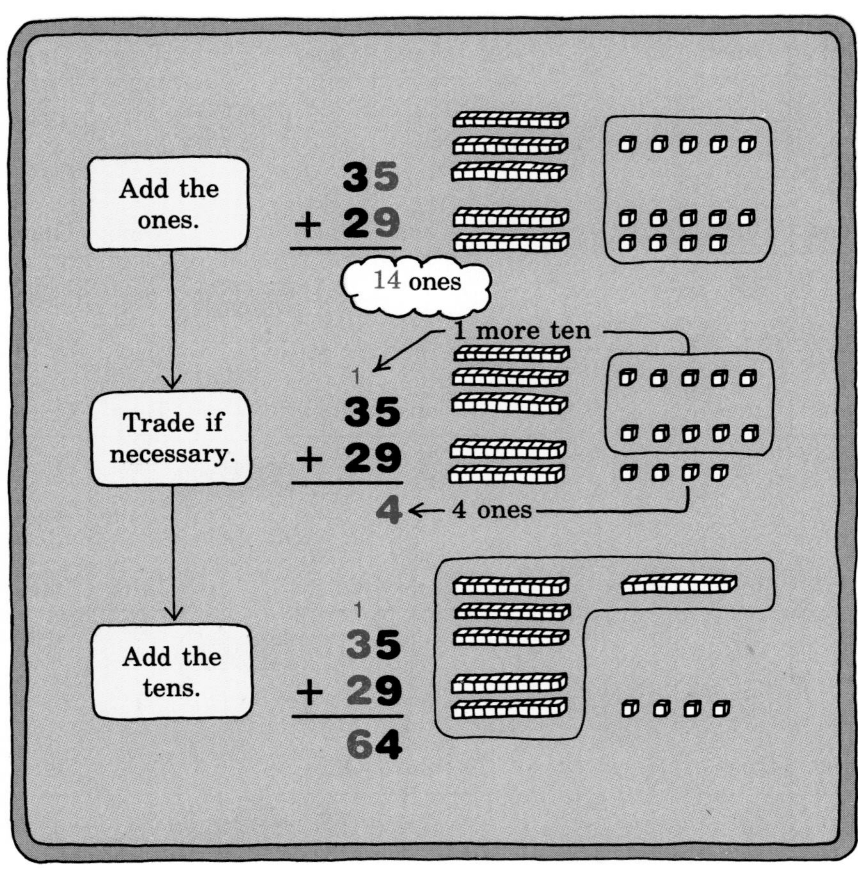

Their total weight is 64 kg.

Other Examples

$$\begin{array}{r} ^{1}27 \\ +\,48 \\ \hline 75 \end{array} \qquad \begin{array}{r} 53 \\ +\,34 \\ \hline 87 \end{array} \qquad \begin{array}{r} ^{1}39 \\ +\;\;4 \\ \hline 43 \end{array} \qquad \begin{array}{r} 30 \\ +\,68 \\ \hline 98 \end{array} \qquad \begin{array}{r} ^{1}7 \\ +\,35 \\ \hline 42 \end{array}$$

NO TRADE NECESSARY (87)

NO TRADE NECESSARY (98)

Warm Up Add.

1. $\begin{array}{r} 24 \\ +\,17 \\ \hline \end{array}$
2. $\begin{array}{r} 36 \\ +\,42 \\ \hline \end{array}$
3. $\begin{array}{r} 54 \\ +\,29 \\ \hline \end{array}$
4. $\begin{array}{r} 68 \\ +\;\;7 \\ \hline \end{array}$
5. $\begin{array}{r} 9 \\ +\,35 \\ \hline \end{array}$
6. $\begin{array}{r} 20 \\ +\,15 \\ \hline \end{array}$

Practice Find the sums.

1. 26 + 37	**2.** 24 + 15	**3.** 47 + 25	**4.** 29 + 55
5. 36 + 51	**6.** 18 + 27	**7.** 7 + 64	**8.** 75 + 3
9. 62 + 28	**10.** 46 + 8	**11.** 16 + 50	**12.** 19 + 54
13. 48 + 20	**14.** 8 + 23	**15.** 67 + 21	**16.** 82 + 11
17. 19 + 24	**18.** 32 + 41	**19.** 45 + 36	**20.** 73 + 18

21. 14 + 85 **22.** 35 + 36 **23.** 20 + 52 **24.** 59 + 7

25. Add 23 to 18 **26.** Add 56 to 27 **27.** Add 39 to 7

Mixed Applications

28. Sandy weighs 28 kg. Pat weighs 34 kg. How much do they weigh together?

29. Ray's dog weighs 13 kg. His cat weighs 4 kg. How much more does the dog weigh than the cat?

30. **DATA HUNT** Find out your weight and the weight of a friend. Altogether how much do the two of you weigh?

THINK

Money Puzzle

Jane has 2 coins in her hand. Give the name of the coins if their value is:

1. 2¢ **2.** 6¢ **3.** 10¢

4. 15¢ **5.** 20¢ **6.** 26¢

7. 30¢ **8.** 35¢ **9.** 50¢

MATH

More Practice, page 383, Set C

Adding 2-Digit Numbers: Trading 10 Tens

Joan checked her pulse rate after riding her bicycle. The first minute it beat 92 times. The second minute her pulse rate slowed to 83 beats. How many times did it beat in the two minutes?

Since we want the total number of beats, we add.

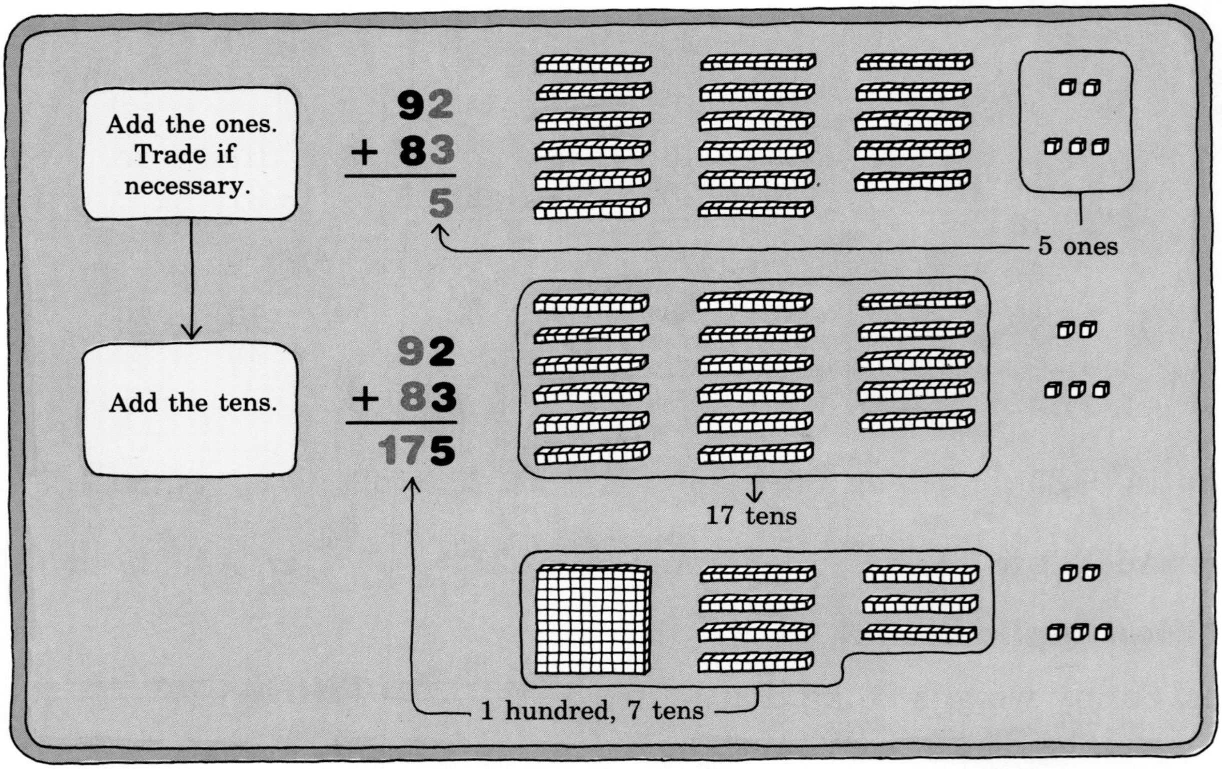

Add the ones. Trade if necessary.

$$\begin{array}{r} 92 \\ +\ 83 \\ \hline 5 \end{array}$$

5 ones

Add the tens.

$$\begin{array}{r} 92 \\ +\ 83 \\ \hline 175 \end{array}$$

17 tens

1 hundred, 7 tens

Joan's pulse beat 175 times in the two minutes.

Other Examples

$$\begin{array}{r} 85 \\ +\ 42 \\ \hline 127 \end{array} \qquad \begin{array}{r} {}^{1} \\ 56 \\ +\ 84 \\ \hline 140 \end{array} \qquad \begin{array}{r} 90 \\ +\ 62 \\ \hline 152 \end{array} \qquad \begin{array}{r} {}^{1} \\ 47 \\ +\ 58 \\ \hline 105 \end{array}$$

Warm Up Add.

1. $\begin{array}{r} 74 \\ +\ 64 \\ \hline \end{array}$ **2.** $\begin{array}{r} 85 \\ +\ 31 \\ \hline \end{array}$ **3.** $\begin{array}{r} 96 \\ +\ 56 \\ \hline \end{array}$ **4.** $\begin{array}{r} 72 \\ +\ 80 \\ \hline \end{array}$ **5.** $\begin{array}{r} 46 \\ +\ 84 \\ \hline \end{array}$ **6.** $\begin{array}{r} 95 \\ +\ 47 \\ \hline \end{array}$

Practice Find the sums.

1. 75 + 86
2. 35 + 94
3. 87 + 83
4. 68 + 73
5. 83 + 54
6. 45 + 26
7. 86 + 30
8. 72 + 98
9. 64 + 68
10. 85 + 64
11. 69 + 53
12. 94 + 96
13. 91 + 23
14. 74 + 36
15. 82 + 18
16. 47 + 21
17. 98 + 83
18. 40 + 72

19. 95 + 68
20. 58 + 67
21. 75 + 13
22. 93 + 40
23. 85 + 49
24. 95 + 85
25. 84 + 21
26. 58 + 96

27. Find the sum of 68 and 72.

28. Find the sum of 96 and 27.

Mixed Applications

29. Tim ran in place for 5 minutes and then took his pulse. Then he rested for 8 minutes and took his pulse. How much longer was he resting than running in place?

30. **DATA HUNT** Check your own pulse rate for each of the first two minutes after running. Find the total number of beats for the two minutes.

SKILLKEEPER

Round to the nearest hundred or dollar.

1. 325 → ▥
2. 550 → ▥
3. 892 → ▥
4. 764 → ▥
5. \$2.59 → ▥
6. \$5.25 → ▥
7. \$8.50 → ▥
8. \$3.49 → ▥

Write > or < for each ●.

9. 28 ● 37
10. 65 ● 55
11. 439 ● 388
12. 638 ● 645

More Practice, page 384, Set A

PROBLEM SOLVING
Using Data from a Graph

The graph shows some of the tickets sold for the school play. The dashed line helps you see that Carla sold 12 tickets.

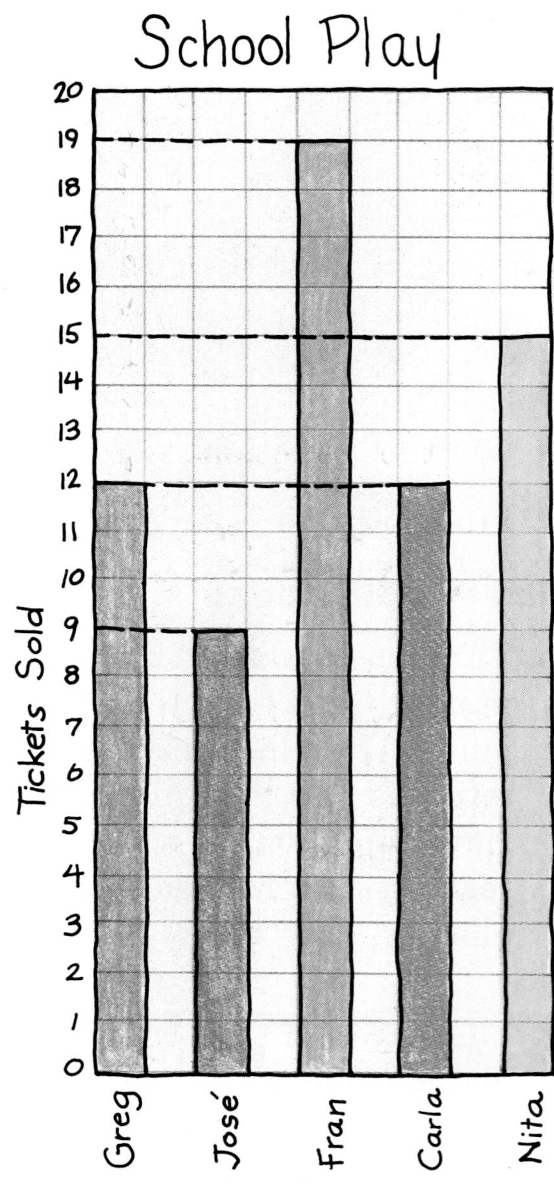

Solve. Use the graph.

1. Who sold the same number of tickets as Carla?
2. Who sold 15 tickets?
3. Who sold the most tickets?
4. How many did Greg sell?
5. How many did José sell?
6. How many tickets did Carla and José sell together?
7. Greg sold 8 more tickets after the graph was made. How many did he sell in all?
8. How many tickets did Fran and Nita sell together?
9. José said, "If I sell 6 more tickets, I will sell the same number as Nita." Check to see if he is right.
10. ***Strategy Practice*** Tickets cost $4, $6, $7, and $9. Amy bought two tickets for $11. What price tickets did she buy? Hint: Guess and check.

PROBLEM SOLVING

Choose the Operations

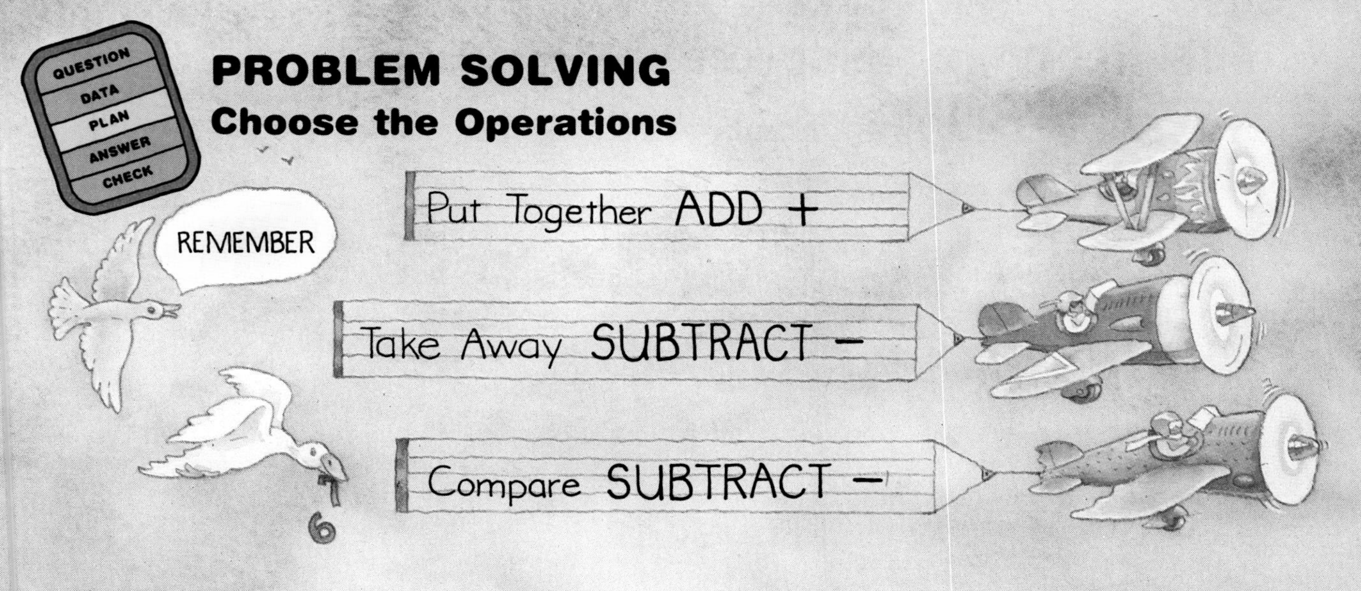

Choose the operations and then solve.

1. There were 17 students from one class and 18 from another class who tried out for the school play. How many students tried out?

2. There were 12 students who got parts in the play. 5 of them were boys. How many were girls?

3. There were 14 students who helped paint. 6 helped clean. How many more students helped paint than clean?

4. There were 17 boys and 8 girls who helped people find seats. How many more boys than girls helped with the seating?

5. The first act was 35 minutes long. The second act lasted for 25 minutes. How long were the two acts?

6. Ann had 15 tickets left to sell. She sold 6 tickets. How many does she have left?

7. On the first night, 96 adults came to the play. On the second night, there were 87. How many adults came altogether?

8. ***Strategy Practice*** The first row had 11 seats. The second had 12. The third row had 13 and the fourth had 14. Which two rows could 26 people just fill?

Adding 3-Digit Numbers: Trading Once

How much do the two animals weigh together?

376 kg
182 kg

Since we want the total weight for both, we add.

Add the ones. Trade if necessary.
Add the tens. Trade if necessary.
Add the hundreds.
182 + 376 = 8
182 + 376 = 58
182 + 376 = 558

The two animals weigh a total of 558 kg.

Other Examples

trading ones	trading tens	trading hundreds
$\begin{array}{r} ^{1} \\ 249 \\ +\ \ 38 \\ \hline 287 \end{array}$	$\begin{array}{r} ^{1} \\ 346 \\ +\ 281 \\ \hline 627 \end{array}$	$\begin{array}{r} 634 \\ +\ 720 \\ \hline 1{,}354 \end{array}$

13 hundreds is 1 thousand and 3 hundreds

Warm Up Add.

1. $\begin{array}{r} 535 \\ +\ 338 \\ \hline \end{array}$ **2.** $\begin{array}{r} 487 \\ +\ 262 \\ \hline \end{array}$ **3.** $\begin{array}{r} 734 \\ +\ 520 \\ \hline \end{array}$ **4.** $\begin{array}{r} 234 \\ +\ 283 \\ \hline \end{array}$ **5.** $\begin{array}{r} 59 \\ +\ 713 \\ \hline \end{array}$

Practice Find the sums.

1. $\begin{array}{r} 575 \\ +\ 802 \\ \hline \end{array}$
2. $\begin{array}{r} 526 \\ +\ 446 \\ \hline \end{array}$
3. $\begin{array}{r} 166 \\ +\ 253 \\ \hline \end{array}$
4. $\begin{array}{r} 817 \\ +\ 46 \\ \hline \end{array}$
5. $\begin{array}{r} 173 \\ +\ 183 \\ \hline \end{array}$
6. $\begin{array}{r} 216 \\ +\ 635 \\ \hline \end{array}$
7. $\begin{array}{r} 543 \\ +\ 76 \\ \hline \end{array}$
8. $\begin{array}{r} 933 \\ +\ 346 \\ \hline \end{array}$
9. $\begin{array}{r} 72 \\ +\ 672 \\ \hline \end{array}$
10. $\begin{array}{r} 284 \\ +\ 800 \\ \hline \end{array}$
11. $\begin{array}{r} 467 \\ +\ 517 \\ \hline \end{array}$
12. $\begin{array}{r} 302 \\ +\ 433 \\ \hline \end{array}$
13. $\begin{array}{r} 678 \\ +\ 51 \\ \hline \end{array}$
14. $\begin{array}{r} 284 \\ +\ 181 \\ \hline \end{array}$
15. $\begin{array}{r} 776 \\ +\ 14 \\ \hline \end{array}$
16. 134 + 718
17. 492 + 497
18. 844 + 93
19. 548 + 327
20. 58 + 327
21. 151 + 681
22. 632 + 293
23. 903 + 755
24. Add 731 and 226.
25. Add 729 and 550.

Mixed Applications

26. A zoo has 6 tigers and 13 bears. How many fewer tigers than bears are there in the zoo?
27. Find the total weight of these two animals.
    Tiger: 182 kg Deer: 125 kg
28. Make up a question you can answer using data in this story. Then find the answer.
    A brown bear weighs 353 kg.
    A black bear weighs 371 kg.
29. **DATA BANK** See page 375. Find the total weight of the buffalo and the camel.

THINK MATH

Logical Reasoning

Find the missing digits.

1. $\begin{array}{r} 7\square \\ +\ \square 3 \\ \hline 159 \end{array}$
2. $\begin{array}{r} \square 8 \\ +\ 7\square \\ \hline 143 \end{array}$
3. $\begin{array}{r} 3\square \\ +\ \square 2 \\ \hline 119 \end{array}$
4. $\begin{array}{r} \square 6 \\ +\ 4\square \\ \hline 101 \end{array}$
5. $\begin{array}{r} 7\square \\ +\ \square 2 \\ \hline 130 \end{array}$

Adding 3-Digit Numbers: Two or More Trades

Emil's collie needs 596 grams of dry dog food each day. His sister's cocker spaniel needs 355 grams each day. How many grams do both dogs need in one day?

Since we want the total number of grams, we add.

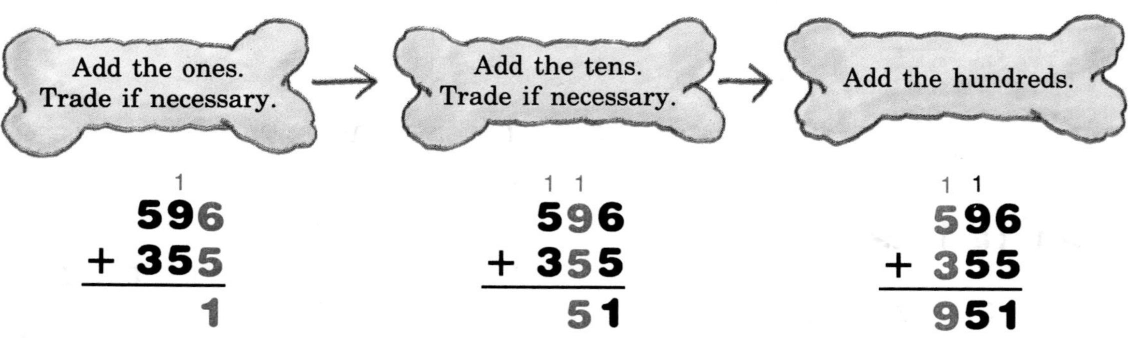

Add the ones. Trade if necessary.
Add the tens. Trade if necessary.
Add the hundreds.
1
596
+ 355
1
1 1
596
+ 355
51
1 1
596
+ 355
951

The two dogs need a total of 951 grams in one day.

Other Examples

$$\begin{array}{r} {}^{1} \\ 472 \\ +\ 856 \\ \hline 1{,}328 \end{array} \qquad \begin{array}{r} {}^{1\,1} \\ 765 \\ +\ 847 \\ \hline 1{,}612 \end{array} \qquad \begin{array}{r} {}^{1\,1} \\ 975 \\ +\ \ 96 \\ \hline 1{,}071 \end{array}$$

Warm Up Add.

1. 784 + 752
2. 256 + 68
3. 247 + 946
4. 765 + 840
5. 324 + 170
6. 649 + 87
7. 764 + 478
8. 615 + 239
9. 559 + 614
10. 279 + 978

Practice Find the sums.

1. $\begin{array}{r} 238 \\ +\ 195 \\ \hline \end{array}$ 2. $\begin{array}{r} 764 \\ +\ 482 \\ \hline \end{array}$ 3. $\begin{array}{r} 953 \\ +\ 649 \\ \hline \end{array}$ 4. $\begin{array}{r} 287 \\ +\ 954 \\ \hline \end{array}$ 5. $\begin{array}{r} 855 \\ +\ 792 \\ \hline \end{array}$

6. $\begin{array}{r} 742 \\ +\ 682 \\ \hline \end{array}$ 7. $\begin{array}{r} 758 \\ +\ 428 \\ \hline \end{array}$ 8. $\begin{array}{r} 327 \\ +\ 610 \\ \hline \end{array}$ 9. $\begin{array}{r} 87 \\ +\ 863 \\ \hline \end{array}$ 10. $\begin{array}{r} 483 \\ +\ 462 \\ \hline \end{array}$

11. $\begin{array}{r} 657 \\ +\ 648 \\ \hline \end{array}$ 12. $\begin{array}{r} 686 \\ +\ 921 \\ \hline \end{array}$ 13. $\begin{array}{r} 493 \\ +\ 976 \\ \hline \end{array}$ 14. $\begin{array}{r} 76 \\ +\ 556 \\ \hline \end{array}$ 15. $\begin{array}{r} 507 \\ +\ 758 \\ \hline \end{array}$

16. 516 + 230 17. 756 + 58 18. 351 + 284 19. 840 + 585

20. 61 + 279 21. 964 + 320 22. 720 + 393 23. 369 + 543

24. Find the sum of 399 and 208.

25. Find the sum of 871 and 371.

26. Find the sum of 285 and 199.

27. Find the sum of 76 and 385.

Mixed Applications

28. Jay's dog needs 156 grams of dog food each day. Tom's dog needs 255 grams. How many grams do both dogs need?

29. Sue's dog eats 16 cans of food a week. Her cat eats 7 cans of food. How many more cans of food does her dog eat?

30. **DATA BANK** See page 376. Find the total number of grams of dry dog food needed by a bulldog and a German shepherd in one day.

THINK

Using a Calculator

Show 806 on your calculator. Now show 876 by **adding one** number.

Now try these the same way.

1. 908 → 928

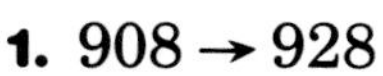

2. 704 → 754
3. 8,064 → 8,364
4. 7,086 → 7,986

MATH

Adding Amounts of Money

GIGANTIC TAPE SALE!!
COUNTRY-WESTERN
EASY LISTENING
CLASSICAL
ROCK
JAZZ
$3.49
$3.88
$4.98
$6.75
$4.75

How much would it cost for a Country-Western tape and an Easy Listening tape?

Since we want the total cost for the tapes, we add the prices.

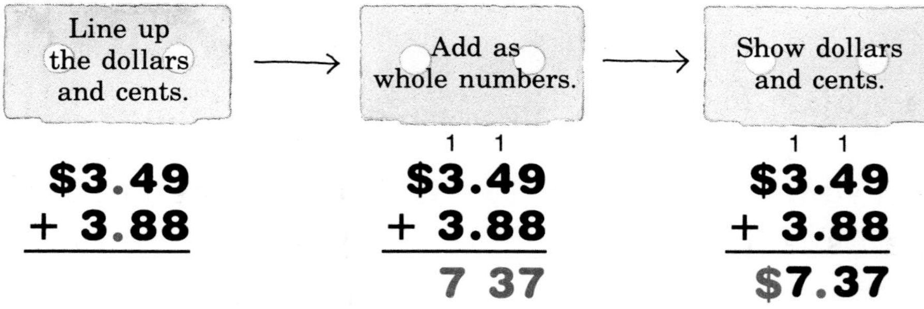

Line up the dollars and cents.
Add as whole numbers.
Show dollars and cents.
$3.49
+ 3.88
1 1
$3.49
+ 3.88
7 37
1 1
$3.49
+ 3.88
$7.37

The total cost for both tapes is $7.37.

Find the total amounts.

1. $6.43 + 5.76	**2.** $3.85 + 4.29	**3.** $7.86 + 9.00	**4.** $0.69 + 1.56	**5.** $8.15 + 7.35
6. $6.59 + 3.98	**7.** $7.50 + 5.50	**8.** $0.78 + 0.57	**9.** $8.75 + 6.98	**10.** $3.75 + 2.98

11. $4.85 + $3.49 **12.** $6.50 + $5.90 **13.** $2.49 + $9.00

14. $1.98 + $0.75 **15.** $8.35 + $6.75 **16.** $0.59 + $0.63

17. $6.75 + $5.95 **18.** $7.50 + $9.95 **19.** $0.08 + $0.69

More Practice, page 385, Set B

PROBLEM SOLVING
Estimating More or Less

Use the advertisement on page 70. Which pairs of tapes could you buy with $10? Answer **yes** or **no.**

1. Country-Western
   Classical
2. Classical
   Rock
3. Country-Western
   Jazz
4. Easy Listening
   Classical
5. Rock
   Jazz
6. Easy Listening
   Jazz
7. Classical
   Jazz
8. Rock
   Easy Listening
9. Rock
   Country-Western

10. Kay bought some tape cleaner for $2.00. She also bought an Easy Listening tape. Can she pay with a $5 bill?

11. Don bought a record for $4.49. He also bought a Classical tape. Can he pay with $10?

12. Mr. Hernandez wants to buy one of each kind of tape. Can he pay with $20?

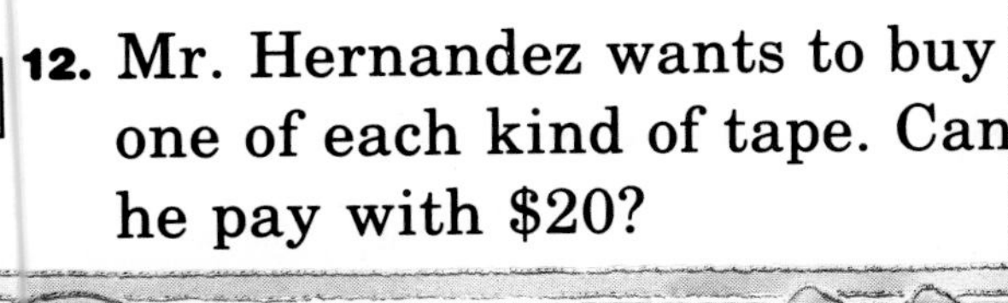

13. Ms. Tanaka bought a record for $5.50 and a Jazz tape. The tax was $0.51. Can she pay with a $10 bill?

14. ***Strategy Practice*** Some special tapes were on sale for $4, $5, $6, and $7. Jeanna bought two of them for $13. What price was on each tape?

Special Sums: Mental Math

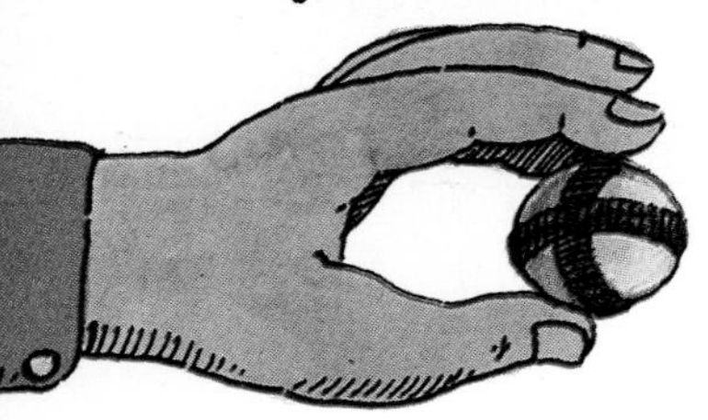

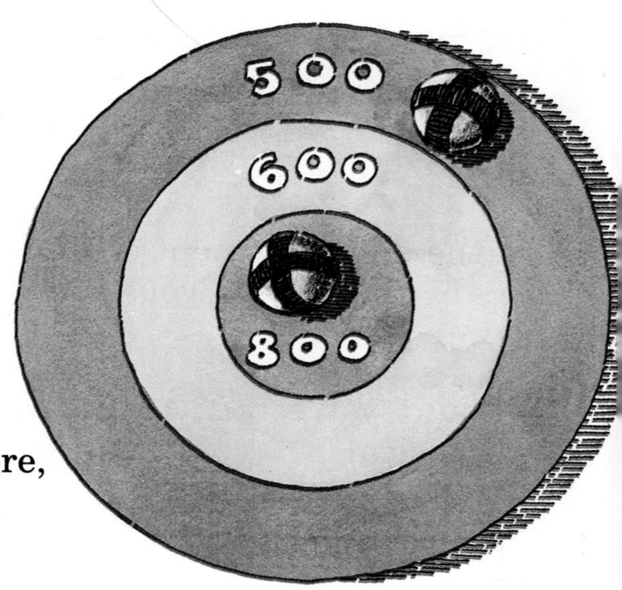

First, Jerry scored 800 points. Then he scored 500 points. What was his total score?

Since we want to know the total score, we need to add.

Think about hundreds.

8 hundreds	+	**5 hundreds**	=	**13 hundreds**
800	+	**500**	=	**1,300**

Other Examples **40 + 30 = 70** **700 + 500 = 1,200**

THINK
4 tens + 3 tens = 7 tens

THINK
7 hundreds + 5 hundreds = 12 hundreds

Practice Find the sums. Write only the answers.

1. 50 + 20	**2.** 80 + 60	**3.** 80 + 30	**4.** 30 + 50
5. 50 + 50	**6.** 70 + 30	**7.** 60 + 10	**8.** 70 + 60
9. 50 + 60	**10.** 60 + 30	**11.** 80 + 40	**12.** 50 + 40
13. 900 + 200	**14.** 800 + 700	**15.** 400 + 400	**16.** 400 + 900
17. 700 + 200	**18.** 200 + 800	**19.** 500 + 800	**20.** 600 + 600
21. 700 + 500	**22.** 800 + 900	**23.** 300 + 600	**24.** 600 + 400

More Practice, page 386, Set A

Using Special Sums: Mental Math

Sometimes you can use special sums to find other sums in your head.

$$46 + 22 = 68$$

(40 + 20) (6 + 2)

Find the sums. Write answers only.

1. 34 + 23 (30 + 20) (4 + 3)
2. 54 + 25 (50 + 20) (4 + 5)
3. 26 + 32
4. 43 + 11
5. 51 + 24
6. 32 + 41
7. 52 + 26
8. 72 + 16
9. 41 + 25
10. 16 + 73
11. 48 + 21
12. 60 + 34
13. 13 + 12
14. 15 + 13
15. 11 + 11
16. 12 + 12
17. 13 + 13
18. 14 + 14
19. 16 + 16
20. 18 + 18

Mixed Applications

21. Cindy scored 24 points. Then she scored 31 points. What was her total score?

22. This problem has missing data. Make up the needed data. Then solve the problem.

    Ted scored 600 points on the first toss. What was his total score for the two tosses?

THINK

Patterns

Give the next number.

1. 200, 400, 600, 800, ▮.
2. 10, 30, 50, 70, ▮.
3. 10, 20, 40, 80, ▮.
4. 100, 200, 400, 700, ▮.

MATH

Estimating Sums Using Rounding

About how much would both cost?
$32.
$19.

Sometimes you want an answer that is only close to the exact answer. One way to estimate how much the sweater and jeans will cost is to **round** and add.

$19	nearest ten	**$20**
+ 32	nearest ten	**+ 30**
		$50

The sweater and jeans cost about $50.

Other Examples

nearest ten

48	→	**50**
+ 53	→	**+ 50**
		100

nearest hundred

296	→	**300**
+ 412	→	**+ 400**
		700

nearest dollar

$3.98	→	**$4.00**
+ 2.25	→	**+ 2.00**
		$6.00

Warm Up Estimate by rounding to the nearest ten.

1. 41 + 18

2. 38 + 29

3. 48 + 33

4. 27 + 52

Estimate by rounding to the nearest hundred.

5. 199 + 289

6. 396 + 402

7. 511 + 295

8. 195 + 604

Estimate by rounding to the nearest dollar.

9. $3.89 + 1.20

10. $5.75 + 4.98

11. $3.88 + 4.25

12. $1.29 + 3.69

Practice Estimate by rounding to the nearest ten.

1. $\begin{array}{r} 68 \\ +\ 24 \\ \hline \end{array}$
2. $\begin{array}{r} 51 \\ +\ 23 \\ \hline \end{array}$
3. $\begin{array}{r} 47 \\ +\ 34 \\ \hline \end{array}$
4. $\begin{array}{r} 65 \\ +\ 23 \\ \hline \end{array}$
5. $\begin{array}{r} 78 \\ +\ 69 \\ \hline \end{array}$
6. $\begin{array}{r} 64 \\ +\ 38 \\ \hline \end{array}$
7. $\begin{array}{r} 55 \\ +\ 25 \\ \hline \end{array}$
8. $\begin{array}{r} 81 \\ +\ 56 \\ \hline \end{array}$
9. $\begin{array}{r} 72 \\ +\ 43 \\ \hline \end{array}$
10. $\begin{array}{r} 59 \\ +\ 34 \\ \hline \end{array}$

Estimate by rounding to the nearest hundred or dollar.

11. $\begin{array}{r} 280 \\ +\ 390 \\ \hline \end{array}$
12. $\begin{array}{r} 412 \\ +\ 167 \\ \hline \end{array}$
13. $\begin{array}{r} 289 \\ +\ 427 \\ \hline \end{array}$
14. $\begin{array}{r} 350 \\ +\ 137 \\ \hline \end{array}$
15. $\begin{array}{r} \$7.89 \\ +\ 1.25 \\ \hline \end{array}$
16. $\begin{array}{r} \$2.75 \\ +\ 3.89 \\ \hline \end{array}$
17. $\begin{array}{r} \$4.15 \\ +1.95 \\ \hline \end{array}$
18. $\begin{array}{r} \$2.78 \\ +\ 3.35 \\ \hline \end{array}$

Use the catalog below.
Estimate the total cost by rounding to the nearest dollar.

19. How much for D and A?
20. How much for C and D?
21. How much for B and A?
22. How much for E and B?

More Practice, page 386, Set B

Adding: Mental Math

Look at the map. How far is it from Hope to Mills?

Since we want the total of the three distances, we add.

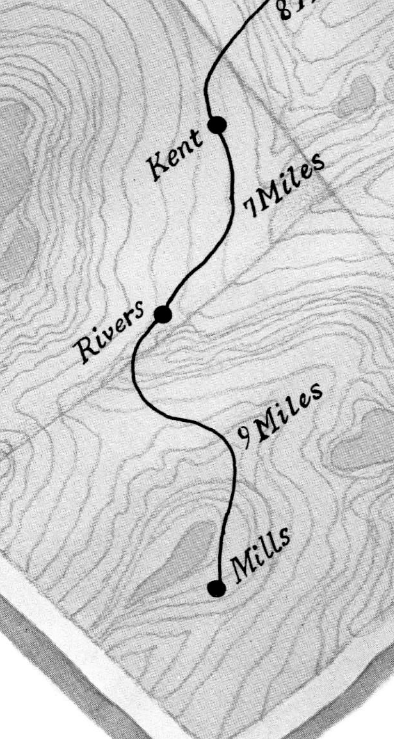

It is 24 miles from Hope to Mills.

Sometimes when you add three or more numbers, you need to find sums such as **15 + 9** "in your head."

Other Examples

13 + 4	**28 + 5**	**17 + 8**
THINK Since 3 + 4 = 7, I know 13 + 4 = 17.	THINK Since 8 + 5 = 13, I know 28 + 5 = 33.	THINK Since 7 + 8 = 15, I know 17 + 8 = 25.

Warm Up Give each sum aloud.

1. 16 + 3	**2.** 14 + 2	**3.** 18 + 3	**4.** 17 + 6
5. 12 + 8	**6.** 22 + 9	**7.** 19 + 5	**8.** 24 + 3
9. 15 + 7	**10.** 18 + 3	**11.** 25 + 2	**12.** 13 + 9
13. 23 + 6	**14.** 11 + 8	**15.** 15 + 6	**16.** 14 + 6
17. 12 + 3	**18.** 12 + 9	**19.** 27 + 7	**20.** 25 + 8

Practice Find the sums. Write answers only.

1. 16 + 5	2. 16 + 4	3. 12 + 6	4. 11 + 7
5. 14 + 9	6. 13 + 2	7. 18 + 5	8. 27 + 8
9. 19 + 2	10. 24 + 3	11. 18 + 4	12. 14 + 5
13. 12 + 6	14. 11 + 9	15. 21 + 8	16. 17 + 7
17. 26 + 6	18. 28 + 5	19. 17 + 4	20. 13 + 3

21. $\begin{array}{r} 8 \\ 6 \\ +\ 7 \\ \hline \end{array}$ (8 + 6 = 14; 14 + 7)

22. $\begin{array}{r} 9 \\ 6 \\ +\ 8 \\ \hline \end{array}$ (9 + 6 = 15; 15 + 8)

23. $\begin{array}{r} 6 \\ 7 \\ +\ 4 \\ \hline \end{array}$ (6 + 7 = 13; 13 + 4)

24. $\begin{array}{r} 8 \\ 9 \\ +\ 7 \\ \hline \end{array}$ (8 + 9 = 17; 17 + 7)

25. $\begin{array}{r} 6 \\ 9 \\ +\ 7 \\ \hline \end{array}$ 26. $\begin{array}{r} 4 \\ 7 \\ +\ 8 \\ \hline \end{array}$ 27. $\begin{array}{r} 7 \\ 7 \\ +\ 7 \\ \hline \end{array}$ 28. $\begin{array}{r} 9 \\ 8 \\ +\ 6 \\ \hline \end{array}$ 29. $\begin{array}{r} 6 \\ 5 \\ +\ 8 \\ \hline \end{array}$ 30. $\begin{array}{r} 8 \\ 8 \\ +\ 8 \\ \hline \end{array}$

Mixed Applications

31. Joe rode his bicycle 17 miles one day. He rode 8 miles the next day. How many more miles did he ride the first day?

32. Sally walked 8 miles one day, 7 miles the second day, and 8 miles the third day. How many miles did Sally walk in the three days?

SKILLKEEPER

Write the number.

1. 3 ones, 4 hundreds, 2 tens
2. 4 hundreds, 9 ones, 5 tens
3. 7 tens, 9 ones, 6 hundreds
4. 6 tens, 2 hundreds, 0 ones
5. eighty-three
6. seven hundred forty-nine
7. two hundred twenty
8. nine hundred five

Column Addition

How many children voted in the "Favorite Wheels" poll?

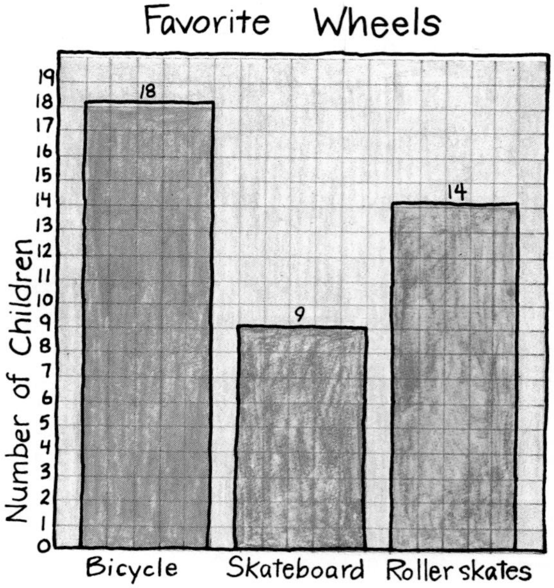

Since we want the total number of children, we add the numbers.

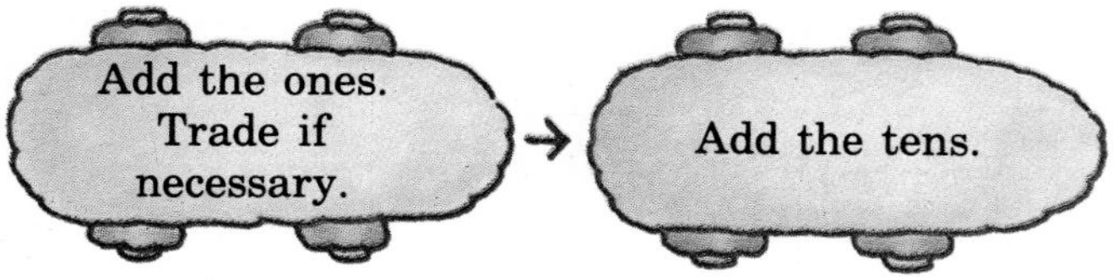


```
 2  ← 2 tens ┐          2
 18          │         18
  9        [21]         9
+14          │       + 14
---          │       ----
  1  ← 1 one ┘         41
```

41 children voted.

Other Examples

```
  1         2         1        2 1
  32        28        46       276
  27         7        37       477
+ 16      + 39        52     +  84
----      ----      + 21     -----
  75        74      ----       837
                     156
```

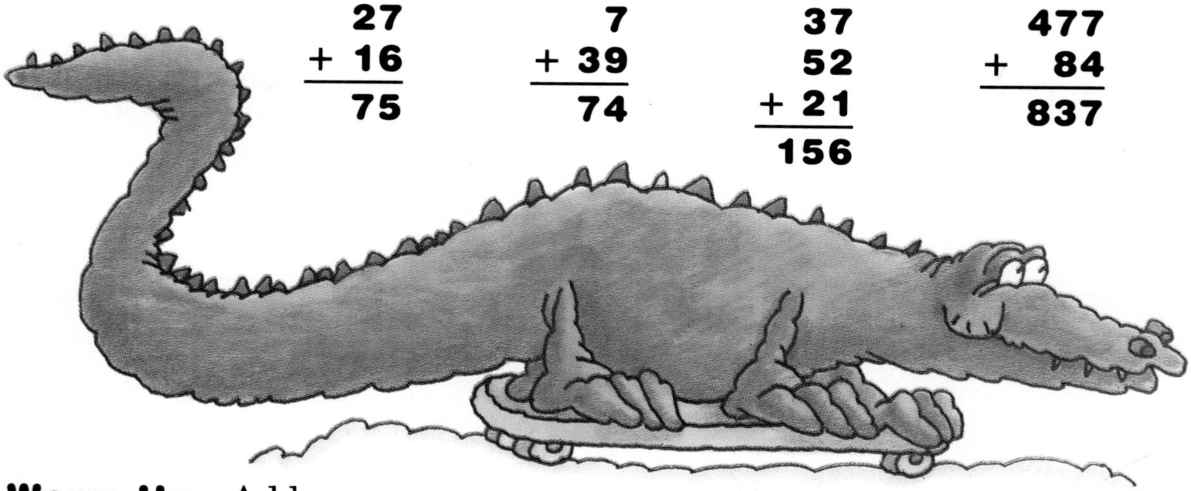

Warm Up Add.

```
1.   34     2.   57     3.   19     4.   48     5.   123     6.   485
     26          34           8          36           48          534
   + 13        + 65        + 17          55        + 307          627
   ----        ----        ----        + 32        -----        + 102
                                       ----                     -----
```

Practice Find the sums.

1. $\begin{array}{r} 26 \\ 15 \\ +\ 34 \\ \hline \end{array}$ **2.** $\begin{array}{r} 48 \\ 7 \\ +\ 14 \\ \hline \end{array}$ **3.** $\begin{array}{r} 32 \\ 41 \\ +\ 10 \\ \hline \end{array}$ **4.** $\begin{array}{r} 57 \\ 24 \\ +\ 35 \\ \hline \end{array}$ **5.** $\begin{array}{r} 8 \\ 42 \\ +\ 68 \\ \hline \end{array}$

6. $\begin{array}{r} 325 \\ 105 \\ +\ 246 \\ \hline \end{array}$ **7.** $\begin{array}{r} 371 \\ 256 \\ +\ 30 \\ \hline \end{array}$ **8.** $\begin{array}{r} 418 \\ 375 \\ +\ 186 \\ \hline \end{array}$ **9.** $\begin{array}{r} 371 \\ 486 \\ +\ 721 \\ \hline \end{array}$ **10.** $\begin{array}{r} 82 \\ 671 \\ +\ 389 \\ \hline \end{array}$

11. $\begin{array}{r} 37 \\ 29 \\ 18 \\ +\ 20 \\ \hline \end{array}$ **12.** $\begin{array}{r} 65 \\ 42 \\ 79 \\ +\ 32 \\ \hline \end{array}$ **13.** $\begin{array}{r} 684 \\ 93 \\ 765 \\ +\ 421 \\ \hline \end{array}$ **14.** $\begin{array}{r} 817 \\ 695 \\ 283 \\ +\ 140 \\ \hline \end{array}$ **15.** $\begin{array}{r} 143 \\ 287 \\ 651 \\ +\ 830 \\ \hline \end{array}$

16. 24 + 37 + 16

17. 327 + 408 + 75

18. 43 + 24 + 55 + 62

19. 327 + 146 + 83 + 276

Mixed Applications

20. There were 28 votes for roller skates, 17 for skateboards, and 15 for bicycles. How many votes were there?

21. In one class 8 children voted for skateboards. 12 voted for bicycles. 2 did not vote. How many more voted for bicycles than skateboards?

22. Estimate by rounding to the nearest hundred. Check your estimate.

287 + 539 + 496

THINK

Mental Math: "Easy" Sums

25 + 75 = 100
60 + 40 = 100
50 + 50 = 100
80 + 20 = 100

Use "easy" sums to help you find these sums mentally.

1. 50 + 37 + 50
2. 25 + 68 + 75
3. 93 + 40 + 60
4. 80 + 43 + 20
5. 75 + 87 + 25

MATH

More Practice, page 387, Set A

Adding 4-Digit Numbers

Look at the table. How many people attended the first two games?

Since we want the total number of people, we add the two numbers.

BASKETBALL ATTENDANCE	
First game	1,928
Second game	2,306
Third game	3,265
Fourth game	1,876

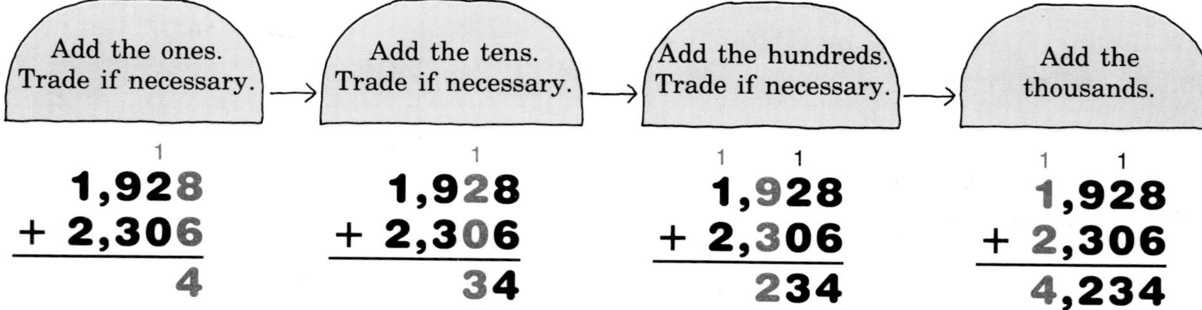

Add the ones. Trade if necessary.
Add the tens. Trade if necessary.
Add the hundreds. Trade if necessary.
Add the thousands.
1,928 + 2,306 = 4
1,928 + 2,306 = 34
1,928 + 2,306 = 234
1,928 + 2,306 = 4,234

4,234 people attended the first two games.

Other Examples

$$\begin{array}{r} 3{,}287 \\ +\ 4{,}165 \\ \hline 7{,}452 \end{array} \qquad \begin{array}{r} 5{,}672 \\ +\ 495 \\ \hline 6{,}167 \end{array} \qquad \begin{array}{r} 5{,}875 \\ +\ 1{,}659 \\ \hline 7{,}534 \end{array}$$

Warm Up Add.

1. 4,236 + 1,357
2. 2,173 + 4,592
3. 6,713 + 2,940
4. 3,627 + 1,809
5. 3,247 + 1,485
6. 2,761 + 3,783
7. 4,653 + 178
8. 6,275 + 980
9. 3,679 + 1,856
10. 2,037 + 1,590

Practice Find the sums.

1. $3{,}729 + 5{,}549$
2. $6{,}751 + 2{,}684$
3. $1{,}254 + 3{,}298$
4. $472 + 6{,}089$
5. $4{,}290 + 4{,}841$
6. $5{,}761 + 4{,}086$
7. $2{,}463 + 562$
8. $5{,}668 + 1{,}246$
9. $4{,}662 + 4{,}791$
10. $1{,}824 + 5{,}567$
11. $3{,}124 + 488$
12. $3{,}750 + 5{,}775$
13. $7{,}772 + 1{,}473$
14. $3{,}393 + 5{,}870$
15. $7{,}858 + 1{,}954$

16. 7,624 + 1,294
17. 3,765 + 3,052
18. 3,908 + 465
19. 2,853 + 5,677
20. 385 + 2,367
21. 5,841 + 3,628

22. Add 3,251 and 4,009.
23. Add 1,265 and 8,308.
24. Add 2,725 and 5,304.
25. Add 6,060 and 3,783.

Mixed Applications

Use the table on page 80 for problems 26 and 27.

26. How many people attended the third and fourth games?
27. How many attended all four games?
28. The basketball team has lost 5 games this year. They have won 13 games. How many more games have they won than lost?

THINK

Estimation

Two of these numbers have a sum of exactly 1,400. Use **estimation** to find them. Check by adding.

816	952
698	286
508	584

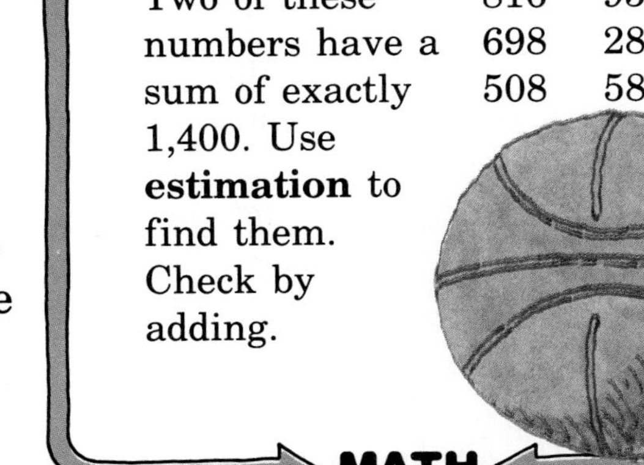

MATH

More Practice, page 387, Set B

PROBLEM SOLVING ★ Using the 5-Point Checklist

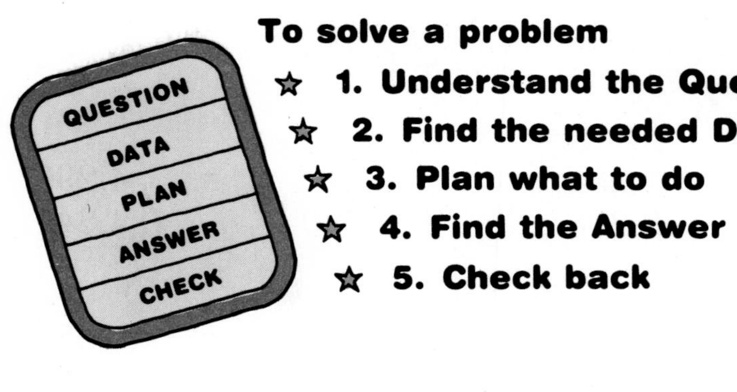

To solve a problem

★ **1. Understand the Question**

★ **2. Find the needed Data**

★ **3. Plan what to do**

★ **4. Find the Answer**

★ **5. Check back**

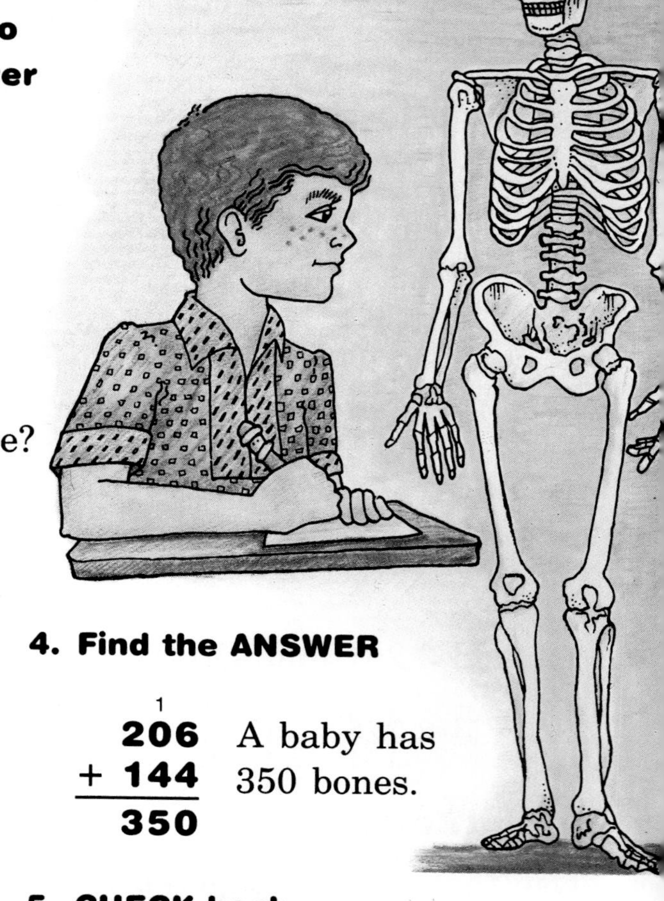

An adult has about 206 bones. A baby may have as many as 144 more bones than an adult. How many bones could a baby have?

Use the 5-Point Checklist to help you solve the problem.

1. Understand the QUESTION
What is the total number of bones a baby could have?

2. Find the needed DATA
An adult has 206 bones.
A baby has 144 more.

3. PLAN what to do
Since we want to increase 206 by 144, we must add.

4. Find the ANSWER

$$\begin{array}{r} \overset{1}{2}06 \\ +\ 144 \\ \hline 350 \end{array}$$

A baby has 350 bones.

5. CHECK back

$$\begin{array}{r} 206 \\ +\ 144 \\ \hline \end{array} \quad \xrightarrow{\text{nearest hundred}} \quad \begin{array}{r} 200 \\ +\ 100 \\ \hline 300 \end{array}$$

350 seems about right.

Solve. Use the 5-Point Checklist.

1. The face has 14 bones. The spinal column has 26 bones. How many bones is this altogether?

2. There are 28 bones in the fingers. There are 28 bones in the toes. How many bones are in both?

Where Your Bones Are Found

Head		Trunk		Limbs	
Cranium	8	Spinal column	26	Arms	60
Face	14	Ribs	24	Legs	60
Ears	6	Breast bone	1		
Throat	1	Collar bones	2		
		Shoulder bones	2		
		Hip bones	2		

Solve.

1. How many bones are in the arms and legs?

2. What is the total number of bones in the spinal column and ribs?

3. How many more bones are in the face than in the cranium?

4. What is the total number of bones in the head?

5. How many more bones are in the face than the ears?

6. How many more bones are in the arms than in the face?

7. There are 8 bones in a wrist, 5 in a palm, and 14 bones in the fingers. How many is this in all?

8. The arm has 3 large bones. How many fewer is this than the 8 bones in the wrist?

9. How many bones are in the trunk?

10. ***Strategy Practice*** The dentist cleaned the teeth of 12 people Monday, 10 people Tuesday, 8 people Thursday, and 11 people Friday. Which two days did he clean the teeth of 21 people?

PROBLEM-SOLVING STRATEGY Use Logical Reasoning

QUESTION
DATA
PLAN
ANSWER
CHECK
To solve this problem, you may need to organize your work in a different way. You cannot just quickly add or subtract. A strategy that can help you is given below.
Try This Melinda was asked how old she is. She said, "I am less than 12 years old. My age is more than 9. I have lived an even number of years." How old is Melinda?

USE LOGICAL REASONING

Listing what you know helps you to reason logically.

Melinda's age is less than 12.

First, list the numbers less than 12.

0 1 2 3 4 5 6 7 8 9 10 11

It is more than 9.

Second, cross out all numbers on the list that are **not** greater than 9.

~~0~~ ~~1~~ ~~2~~ ~~3~~ ~~4~~ ~~5~~ ~~6~~ ~~7~~ ~~8~~ ~~9~~ 10 11

It is even.

Third, cross out all **odd** numbers still on the list.

~~0~~ ~~1~~ ~~2~~ ~~3~~ ~~4~~ ~~5~~ ~~6~~ ~~7~~ ~~8~~ ~~9~~ 10 ~~11~~

Melinda must be 10 years old because 10 is the only number left on the list.

Solve.

1. Doug said, "The number of goldfish I have is between 25 and 35. It is more than 32. I have an odd number of goldfish." How many goldfish does Doug have?

2. Candy said, "The number of people in my family is more than 3 and less than 4 and 4. It is an odd number and it is not 7." How many are in Candy's family?

CHAPTER REVIEW/TEST

Add.

1. 16 + 25
2. 42 + 13
3. 84 + 65
4. 36 + 47
5. 28 + 59
6. 370 + 985
7. 567 + 242
8. 475 + 68
9. 933 + 474
10. 165 + 237
11. $5.26 + 3.15
12. $1.02 + 3.98
13. $3.87 + 1.64
14. $2.79 + 8.56
15. $7.95 + 4.69

Estimate by rounding to the nearest ten or dollar.

16. 17 + 23
17. 34 + 65
18. $7.09 + 2.98
19. $6.81 + 3.22

Add.

20. 23 + 18 + 31
21. 2,476 + 1,282
22. 6,417 + 1,958
23. 42 + 65 + 28 + 19
24. 276 + 128 + 315

Use the table to solve problems 25–26.

25. How much more did Sue grow than Jo?

26. What was Jo's height at the end of the year?

Name	Height	Growth in 1 year
Ben	118 cm	13 cm
Jo	124 cm	9 cm
Sue	119 cm	12 cm

Solve.

27. How much do both A and B cost?

A.

B.

$1.49

ANOTHER LOOK

Find the sums.

1. 26 + 48
2. 58 + 15
3. 67 + 24
4. 79 + 46
5. 37 + 99
6. 89 + 64
7. 274 + 372
8. 640 + 185
9. 394 + 350
10. 193 + 179
11. 246 + 465
12. 348 + 57
13. 367 + 249
14. 158 + 472
15. 647 + 275
16. 25 + 17 + 46
17. 24 + 28 + 23
18. 16 + 35 + 28
19. 57 + 8 + 76
20. 29 + 87 + 46
21. 36 + 69 + 56

Front-end Estimation

You have learned to estimate by rounding. Another way to estimate is to use the front-end numbers.

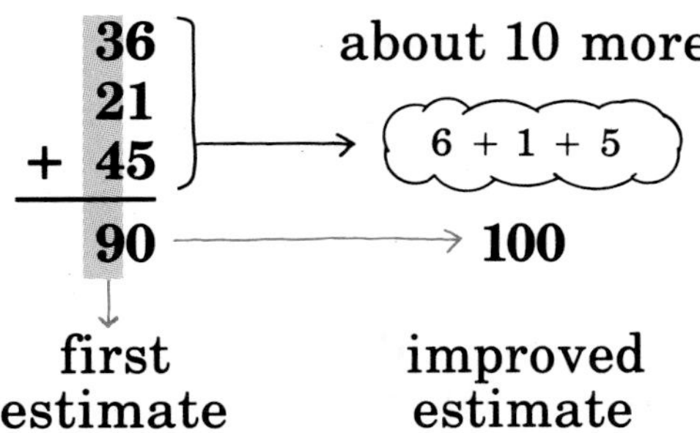

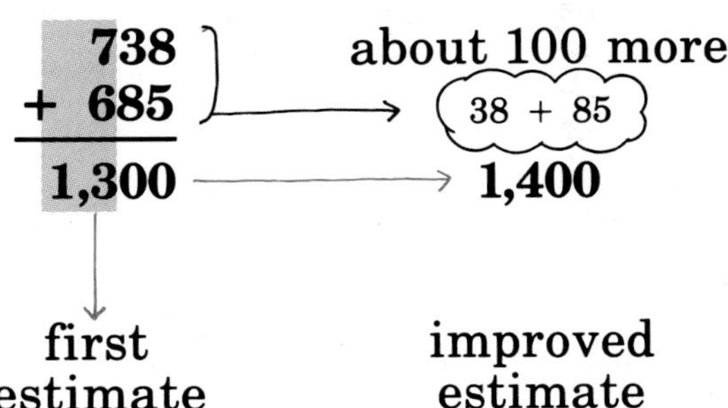

Estimate the sums. Use front-end estimation.

1. 26 + 32 + 24
2. 43 + 11 + 34
3. 51 + 40 + 31
4. 65 + 21 + 76
5. 44 + 34 + 64
6. 63 + 41 + 20
7. 46 + 32 + 45
8. 57 + 16 + 38
9. 65 + 22 + 74
10. 49 + 36 + 54
11. 23 + 90 + 66
12. 88 + 35 + 45
13. 618 + 283
14. 546 + 750
15. 310 + 425
16. \$8.63 + 6.51
17. \$7.04 + 9.13
18. \$5.76 + 8.20

19. Jack bought an apple for 32¢, an orange for 35¢, and a pear for 23¢. About how much did he spend?

20. Betty bought a pair of gloves for \$8.75 and a scarf for \$6.50. About how much did she spend?

CUMULATIVE REVIEW

Give the letter for the correct answer.

1. $3 + 4 + 6 =$ ____
   A 14   B 12
   C 13   D not given

2. $5 + 1 + 9 =$ ____
   A 14   B 16
   C 15   D not given

3. $3 + 2 + 6 =$ ____
   A 9   B 11
   C 10   D not given

4. $\begin{array}{r} 3 \\ 4 \\ +\ 5 \\ \hline \end{array}$
   A 7
   B 8
   C 9
   D not given

5. $\begin{array}{r} 3 \\ 3 \\ +\ 7 \\ \hline \end{array}$
   A 7
   B 8
   C 9
   D not given

6. $\begin{array}{r} 8 \\ 2 \\ +\ 5 \\ \hline \end{array}$
   A 14
   B 15
   C 16
   D not given

7. 6 tens and 7 ones
   A 76   B 77
   C 67   D not given

8. 7 hundreds, 3 tens, 2 ones
   A 372   B 732
   C 273   D not given

9. What is the next number?
   26, 27, 28, 29, ▯
   A 20   B 40
   C 30   D not given

10. What is the next number?
    96, 97, 98, 99, ▯
    A 100   B 80
    C 90   D not given

11. What is the next number?
    127, 128, 129, ▯
    A 148   B 120
    C 130   D not given

12. What is the next number?
    396, 397, 398, 399, ▯
    A 200   B 400
    C 300   D not given

13. Mariko has 2 guppies and 1 angel fish. She bought 2 zebra fish. How many fish does she have?
    A 2   B 5
    C 3   D not given

14. Allen bought 6 bananas, 4 oranges, and 3 apples. How many pieces of fruit did he buy?
    A 13   B 11
    C 12   D not given

SUBTRACTION 4

Dan lives in Alaska. He is 15 years old. Dan carves totem poles like the Alaskan Indians once did. The Indians carved poles when a chief died. They carved poles after winning a battle. Poles were even used to make fun of people. Dan knows many legends about the animals he carves. A legend is an old story. The eagle on the top is 55 cm high. The beaver on the bottom is 42 cm high.

Trading 1 Ten for 10 Ones

Mark has 4 tens and 3 ones. If he trades 1 ten for 10 ones,

1. how many tens will Mark have?
2. how many ones will Mark have?

Mark will have 3 tens and 13 ones.

Other Examples

Trade 1 ten for 10 ones.

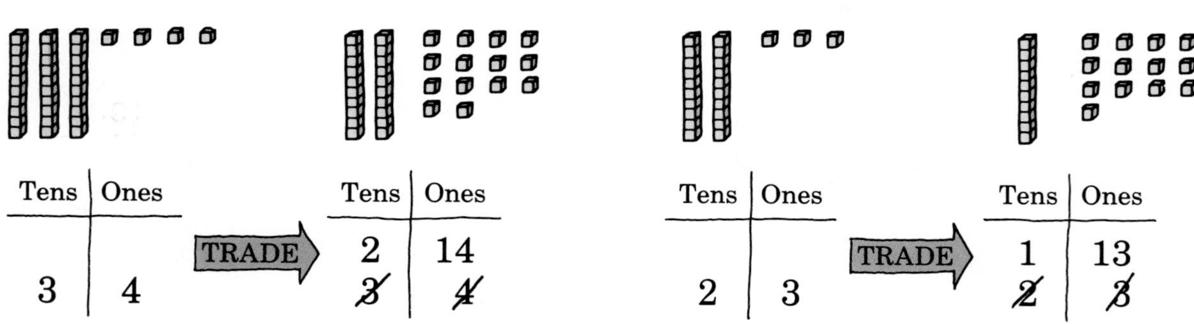

Tens	Ones
3	4

TRADE

Tens	Ones
2	14
~~3~~	~~4~~

Tens	Ones
2	3

TRADE

Tens	Ones
1	13
~~2~~	~~3~~

Warm Up Give the numbers of tens and ones after a trade.

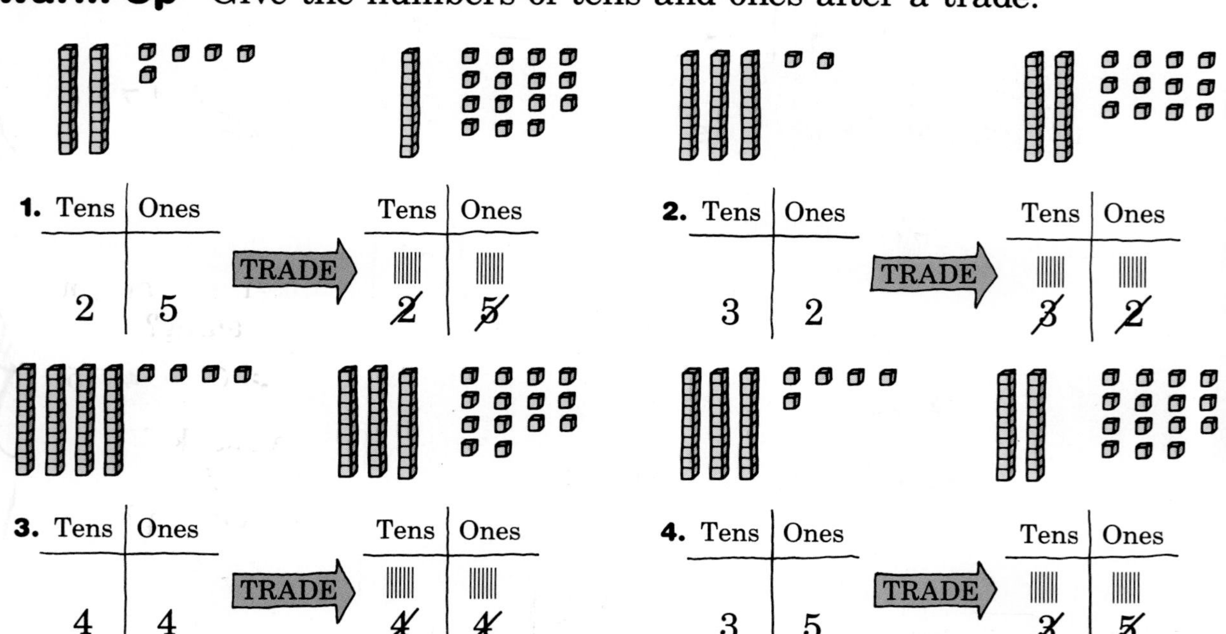

1.

Tens	Ones
2	5

TRADE

Tens	Ones
~~2~~	~~5~~

2.

Tens	Ones
3	2

TRADE

Tens	Ones
~~3~~	~~2~~

3.

Tens	Ones
4	4

TRADE

Tens	Ones
~~4~~	~~4~~

4.

Tens	Ones
3	5

TRADE

Tens	Ones
~~3~~	~~5~~

Practice Trade 1 ten for 10 ones.

Example

Tens	Ones
6	7

TRADE →

Tens	Ones
5	17
~~6~~	~~7~~

1.

Tens	Ones
4	7

TRADE →

Tens	Ones
▯▯▯	▯▯▯
~~4~~	~~7~~

2.

Tens	Ones
5	5

TRADE →

Tens	Ones
▯▯▯	▯▯▯
~~5~~	~~5~~

3.

Tens	Ones
7	2

TRADE →

Tens	Ones
▯▯▯	▯▯▯
~~7~~	~~2~~

4.

Tens	Ones
3	6

TRADE →

Tens	Ones
▯▯▯	▯▯▯
~~3~~	~~6~~

5.

Tens	Ones
2	1

TRADE →

Tens	Ones
▯▯▯	▯▯▯
~~2~~	~~1~~

6.

Tens	Ones
5	0

TRADE →

Tens	Ones
▯▯▯	▯▯▯
~~5~~	~~0~~

7.

Tens	Ones
8	3

TRADE →

Tens	Ones
▯▯▯	▯▯▯
~~8~~	~~3~~

Copy the number. Trade 1 ten for 10 ones.

Example 56→~~5~~~~6~~ (4 16)

8. 76 **9.** 36 **10.** 47

11. 60 **12.** 15 **13.** 92

14. 24 **15.** 67 **16.** 80

17. 86 **18.** 73 **19.** 66

20. 29 **21.** 82 **22.** 55

THINK

Place Value

Each stick is made up of ten cubes. Which numbers can you pick up without trading?

1. 23 **2.** 31 **3.** 6 **4.** 15

If you trade a ten-stick for ten single cubes, which numbers can you pick up?

5. 9 **6.** 29 **7.** 5 **8.** 18

MATH

Subtracting 2-Digit Numbers: Trading Tens

Carla and Paul were trying to estimate one minute (60 seconds). Carla estimated 48 seconds. By how much did she miss 60 seconds?

Since we want the difference between 48 and 60, we subtract.

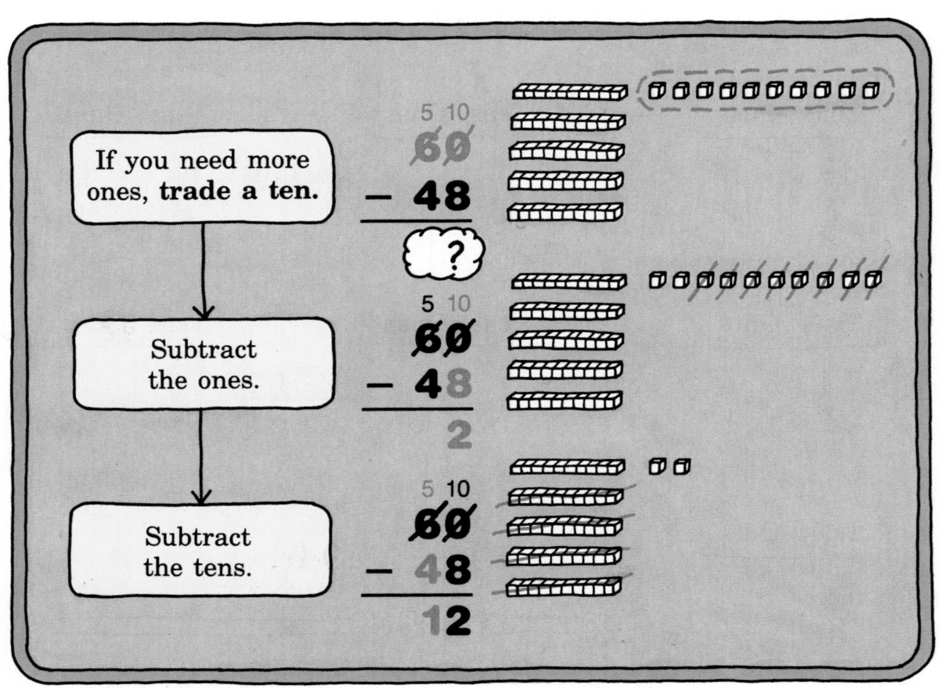

Carla missed by 12 seconds.

Other Examples

5 15	6 15		7 15	
~~65~~	~~75~~	68	~~85~~	54
− 28	− 69	− 27	− 7	− 3
37	6	41	78	51
		NO TRADE NECESSARY		NO TRADE NECESSARY

Warm Up Subtract.

1.	2.	3.	4.	5.
74	80	72	76	57
− 18	− 26	− 8	− 34	− 49

Practice Find the differences.

1. 72 − 18	**2.** 62 − 34	**3.** 58 − 22	**4.** 64 − 58	**5.** 52 − 7	**6.** 70 − 22
7. 48 − 3	**8.** 95 − 56	**9.** 43 − 15	**10.** 72 − 63	**11.** 71 − 9	**12.** 44 − 19
13. 50 − 35	**14.** 79 − 36	**15.** 71 − 14	**16.** 46 − 28	**17.** 76 − 67	**18.** 37 − 29
19. 80 − 42	**20.** 64 − 29	**21.** 97 − 49	**22.** 95 − 70	**23.** 56 − 37	**24.** 55 − 28

25. 83 − 56 **26.** 64 − 8 **27.** 51 − 34 **28.** 43 − 12

29. 63 − 27 **30.** 90 − 78 **31.** 75 − 7 **32.** 85 − 65

33. 42 − 17 **34.** 98 − 39 **35.** 77 − 29 **36.** 36 − 7

37. Subtract 25 from 33.

38. Subtract 19 from 32.

Mixed Applications

39. Salvador tried to estimate one minute. His estimate was 75 seconds. By how much did Salvador miss 60 seconds?

40. Sammy's first 5 estimates were less than one minute. His next 7 tries were greater than one minute. How many times did Sammy try to estimate one minute?

41. Jose's first estimate was 5 seconds over 1 minute. His second estimate was 8 seconds less than 1 minute. How many seconds apart were Jose's two estimates?

42. **DATA HUNT** Have a friend time you with a stopwatch. Close your eyes and try to estimate one minute. Find the difference between your estimate and one minute.

More Practice, page 388, Set A

PROBLEM SOLVING

Understanding the Question

The data in the following problems is given in "short form" to help you think about the **question.**

1. Running once around the track:
Jan: 59 seconds
Tom: 72 seconds
How many more seconds did Tom take than Jan?

2. Sit-ups:
Rob: 41
Ben: 27
How many fewer sit-ups did Ben do than Rob?

3. Push-ups:
Pam on first try: 17
Pam on second try: 15
How many push-ups did Pam do in two tries?

4. Baseball throw:
First try: 28 yards
Second try: 46 yards
How much longer was the second try than the first?

5. Four-person relay race:
1st: 17 seconds
2nd: 18 seconds
3rd: 18 seconds
4th: 16 seconds
What was the total time for the relay?

6. ***Strategy Practice*** School record baseball throw: 47 yards
Sally's own record baseball throw: 36 yards
Sally broke her own record but not the school record. Her throw ends in 0. How far was her throw? Hint: Use logical reasoning.

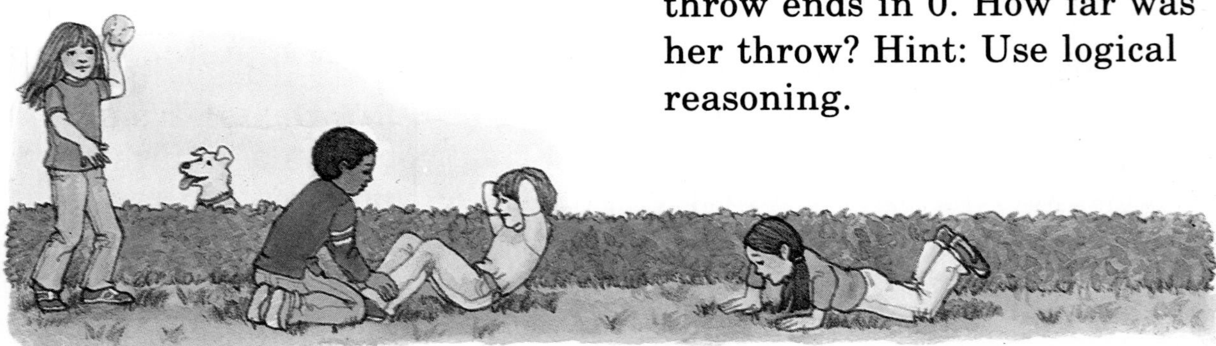

Subtraction Practice

Find the differences.

1. 63 − 15	**2.** 84 − 16	**3.** 52 − 34	**4.** 81 − 16	**5.** 38 − 9	**6.** 26 − 18
7. 79 − 46	**8.** 95 − 7	**9.** 80 − 29	**10.** 76 − 21	**11.** 55 − 47	**12.** 49 − 39
13. 64 − 37	**14.** 70 − 55	**15.** 48 − 3	**16.** 91 − 68	**17.** 52 − 37	**18.** 71 − 36
19. 46 − 22	**20.** 63 − 49	**21.** 47 − 18			

22. 52 − 17 **23.** 63 − 24

24. 75 − 18 **25.** 37 − 29

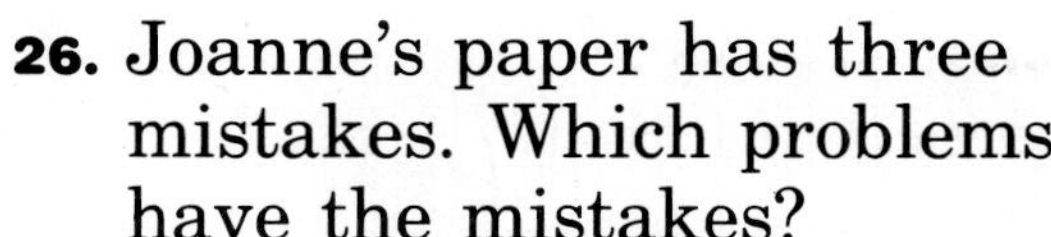

26. Joanne's paper has three mistakes. Which problems have the mistakes?

SKILLKEEPER

Add.

1. 25 + 74	**2.** 63 + 28	**3.** 56 + 95	**4.** 321 + 69	**5.** 684 + 352
6. 366 + 642	**7.** 193 + 408	**8.** 579 + 847	**9.** 908 + 214	**10.** 788 + 556

Subtracting 3-Digit Numbers: Trading Hundreds

Brian works in a bicycle store. In March, the store sold 132 bicycles. In April, the store sold 315 bicycles. How many fewer bicycles did the store sell in March?

To find out how many fewer bicycles, we subtract.

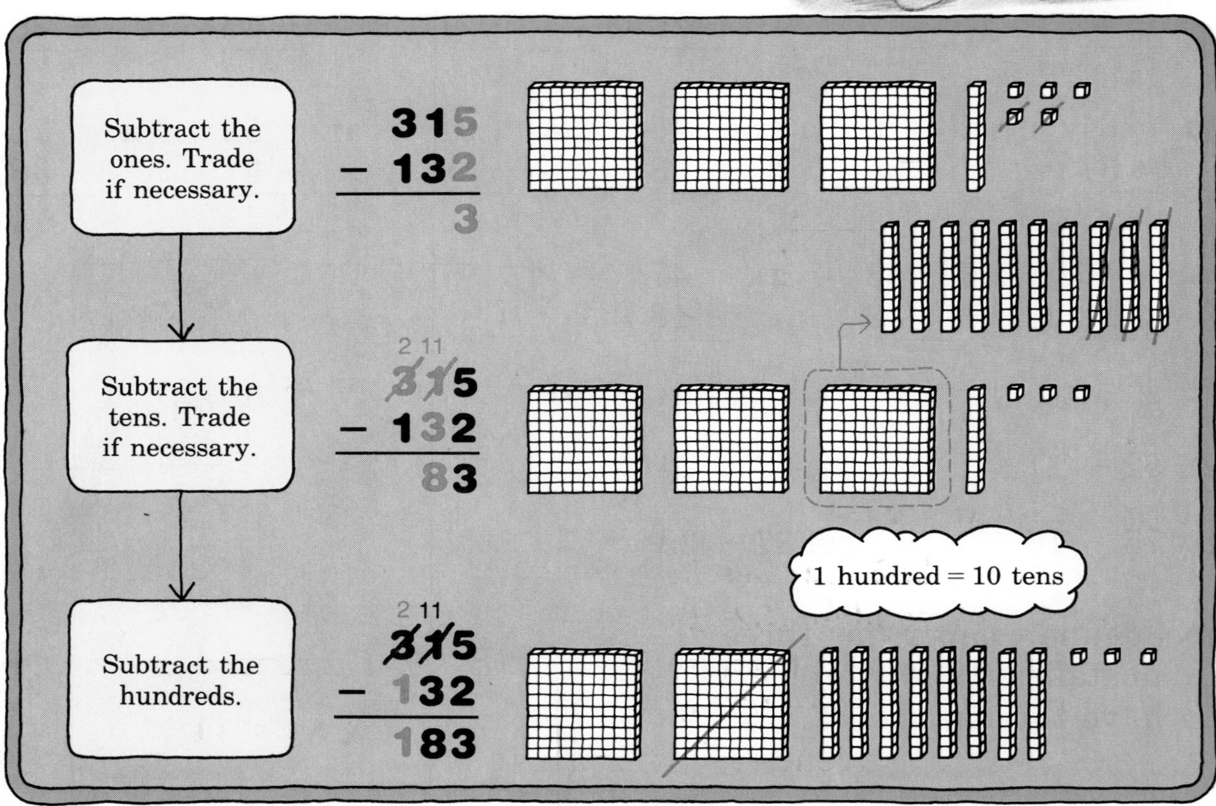

The store sold 183 fewer bicycles in March.

Other Examples

6 12 ~~72~~6	5 10 ~~60~~5	3 12 ~~42~~8	2 15 ~~35~~6	138
− 251	− 183	− 375	− 92	− 53
475	422	53	264	85

Warm Up Subtract.

1.	**2.**	**3.**	**4.**	**5.**
837	708	643	725	127
− 372	− 156	− 560	− 81	− 82

Practice Find the differences.

1. 716 − 231
2. 417 − 83
3. 603 − 420
4. 154 − 70
5. 516 − 432
6. 168 − 95
7. 819 − 168
8. 127 − 92
9. 435 − 240
10. 524 − 71
11. 904 − 312
12. 418 − 24
13. 156 − 72
14. 768 − 692
15. 544 − 281
16. 854 − 648
17. 708 − 49
18. 135 − 127
19. 624 − 65
20. 312 − 187
21. 307 − 172
22. 424 − 70
23. 738 − 474
24. How much greater is 823 than 170?
25. How much less is 271 than 348?

Mixed Applications

26. In October 355 bicycles were sold. In November 132 more bicycles were sold than in October. How many bicycles were sold in November?
27. In May the store sold 414 bicycles. In June the store sold 280. How many fewer bicycles were sold in June?

★ 28. Use the following data to write your own question. Then solve it. The bicycle store had 183 girl's bicycles and 327 boy's bicycles.

THINK

Using a Calculator

Show 582 on your calculator. Now show 502 by **subtracting one** number.

Now try these the same way.

1. 573 → 503
2. 924 → 904
3. 8,267 → 8,067
4. 9,146 → 9,046

MATH

Subtracting 3-Digit Numbers: Two Trades

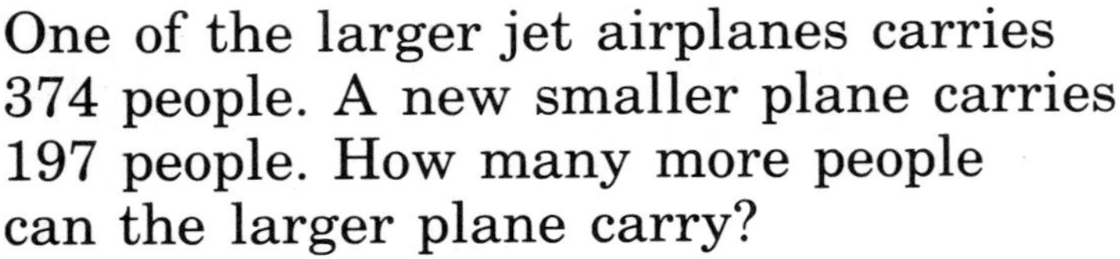

One of the larger jet airplanes carries 374 people. A new smaller plane carries 197 people. How many more people can the larger plane carry?

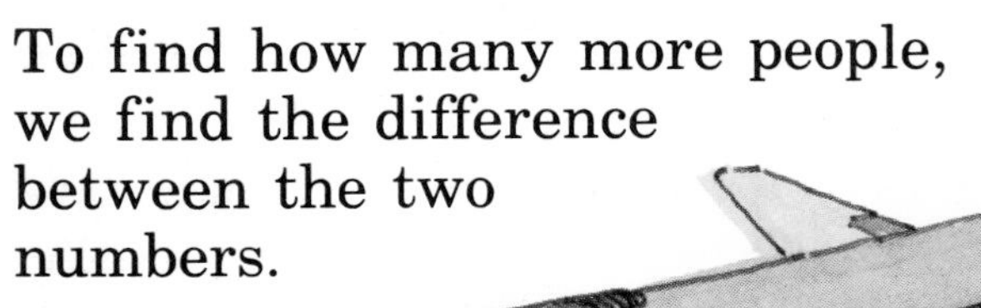

To find how many more people, we find the difference between the two numbers.

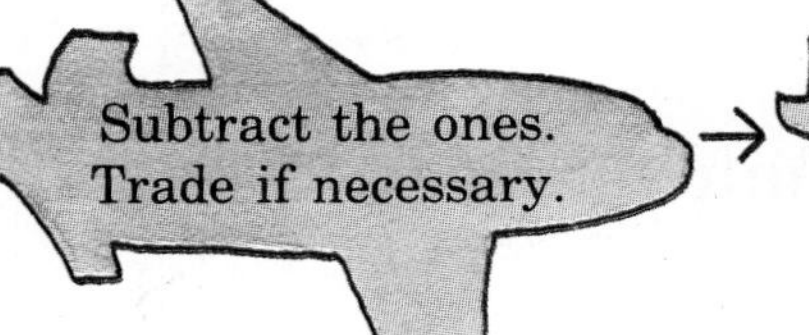
Subtract the ones.
Trade if necessary.

→ Subtract the tens. Trade if necessary. → Subtract the hundreds.

6 14	2 16 14	2 16 14
374	374	374
− 197	− 197	− 197
7	77	177

The larger plane carries 177 more people.

Other Examples

6 10 14	8 13 13	5 12 14	3 12
714	943	634	142
− 189	− 878	− 89	− 68
525	65	545	74

Warm Up Subtract.

1. 324 − 167	**2.** 854 − 175	**3.** 712 − 638	**4.** 126 − 88	**5.** 927 − 258
6. 228 − 79	**7.** 437 − 359	**8.** 516 − 97	**9.** 135 − 77	**10.** 643 − 578

Practice Find the differences.

1. $743 - 555$
2. $154 - 86$
3. $654 - 590$
4. $123 - 87$
5. $324 - 68$
6. $815 - 337$
7. $483 - 45$
8. $530 - 364$
9. $327 - 213$
10. $122 - 24$
11. $435 - 267$
12. $311 - 172$
13. $462 - 325$
14. $146 - 73$
15. $654 - 88$

16. 627 − 463 17. 153 − 78 18. 412 − 385 19. 567 − 234

20. How much less is 69 than 835? 21. How much less is 57 than 124?

Mixed Applications

22. One section of a plane seats 125 people. The other seats 188. How many people does this plane seat?

23. A jet plane has 214 seats. 167 people get on. How many seats are empty?

24. **DATA BANK** See page 377. Find how many people the largest jet can carry. Find how many people another jet can carry. What is the difference between your choice and the largest jet?

THINK

Using a Calculator

Start with a 3-digit number. 287

Reverse the digits and subtract the smaller number from the larger number.

$$\begin{array}{r} 782 \\ -\ 287 \\ \hline 495 \end{array}$$

Reverse the digits and add.

$$\begin{array}{r} 495 \\ +\ 594 \\ \hline 1{,}089 \end{array}$$

Try this with other 3-digit numbers. What do you notice?

MATH

Checking Subtraction

You can check subtraction by adding.

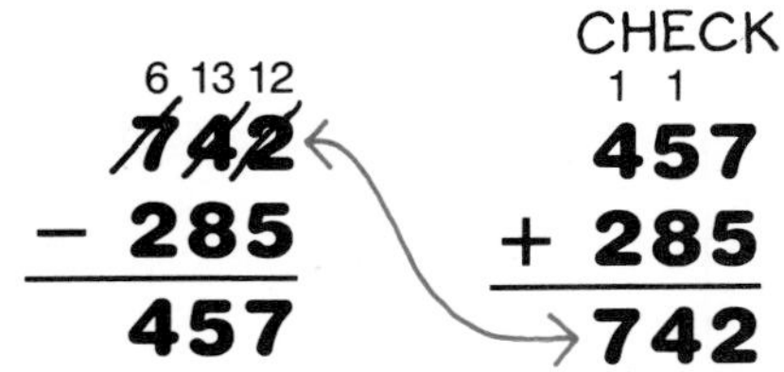

Janet missed two subtraction problems. **Check** her problems for her. Which ones did she miss? What are the correct answers?

Janet

1. 62 − 27 = 35 CHECK 35 + 27
2. 56 − 32 = 24 CHECK 24 + 32
3. 123 − 56 = 67 CHECK 67 + 56
4. 150 − 73 = 77 CHECK 77 + 73
5. 418 − 172 = 246 CHECK 246 + 172
6. 753 − 128 = 625 CHECK 625 + 128
7. 922 − 437 = 485 CHECK 485 + 437
8. 835 − 379 = 556 CHECK 556 + 379

Warm Up Subtract. Check each answer.

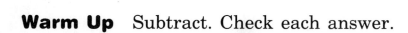

1. 85 − 28

2. 62 − 57

3. 78 − 24

4. 120 − 36

5. 141 − 75

6. 382 − 158

7. 436 − 285

8. 724 − 76

9. 840 − 175

10. 927 − 869

Practice Find the differences. Check your answers.

1. $\begin{array}{r} 72 \\ -\ 25 \\ \hline \end{array}$	2. $\begin{array}{r} 64 \\ -\ 56 \\ \hline \end{array}$	3. $\begin{array}{r} 92 \\ -\ 7 \\ \hline \end{array}$	4. $\begin{array}{r} 76 \\ -\ 34 \\ \hline \end{array}$	5. $\begin{array}{r} 40 \\ -\ 25 \\ \hline \end{array}$
6. $\begin{array}{r} 136 \\ -\ 63 \\ \hline \end{array}$	7. $\begin{array}{r} 152 \\ -\ 76 \\ \hline \end{array}$	8. $\begin{array}{r} 124 \\ -\ 80 \\ \hline \end{array}$	9. $\begin{array}{r} 116 \\ -\ 39 \\ \hline \end{array}$	10. $\begin{array}{r} 130 \\ -\ 52 \\ \hline \end{array}$
11. $\begin{array}{r} 827 \\ -\ 153 \\ \hline \end{array}$	12. $\begin{array}{r} 706 \\ -\ 284 \\ \hline \end{array}$	13. $\begin{array}{r} 657 \\ -\ 583 \\ \hline \end{array}$	14. $\begin{array}{r} 948 \\ -\ 83 \\ \hline \end{array}$	15. $\begin{array}{r} 765 \\ -\ 290 \\ \hline \end{array}$
16. $\begin{array}{r} 824 \\ -\ 175 \\ \hline \end{array}$	17. $\begin{array}{r} 623 \\ -\ 564 \\ \hline \end{array}$	18. $\begin{array}{r} 726 \\ -\ 87 \\ \hline \end{array}$	19. $\begin{array}{r} 650 \\ -\ 188 \\ \hline \end{array}$	20. $\begin{array}{r} 514 \\ -\ 257 \\ \hline \end{array}$

21. 83 − 47 **22.** 60 − 8 **23.** 67 − 21 **24.** 124 − 76

25. 832 − 280 **26.** 643 − 129 **27.** 644 − 389

28. Find the difference between 68 and 136.

29. Subtract 79 from 624.

30. How much more is 726 than 581?

31. How much less is 295 than 632?

SKILLKEEPER

Subtract.

1. $\begin{array}{r} 15 \\ -\ 9 \\ \hline \end{array}$	2. $\begin{array}{r} 16 \\ -\ 8 \\ \hline \end{array}$	3. $\begin{array}{r} 14 \\ -\ 6 \\ \hline \end{array}$	4. $\begin{array}{r} 13 \\ -\ 4 \\ \hline \end{array}$	5. $\begin{array}{r} 11 \\ -\ 8 \\ \hline \end{array}$
6. $\begin{array}{r} 16 \\ -\ 7 \\ \hline \end{array}$	7. $\begin{array}{r} 17 \\ -\ 9 \\ \hline \end{array}$	8. $\begin{array}{r} 10 \\ -\ 3 \\ \hline \end{array}$	9. $\begin{array}{r} 15 \\ -\ 7 \\ \hline \end{array}$	10. $\begin{array}{r} 12 \\ -\ 4 \\ \hline \end{array}$

PROBLEM SOLVING
Using Data from a Map

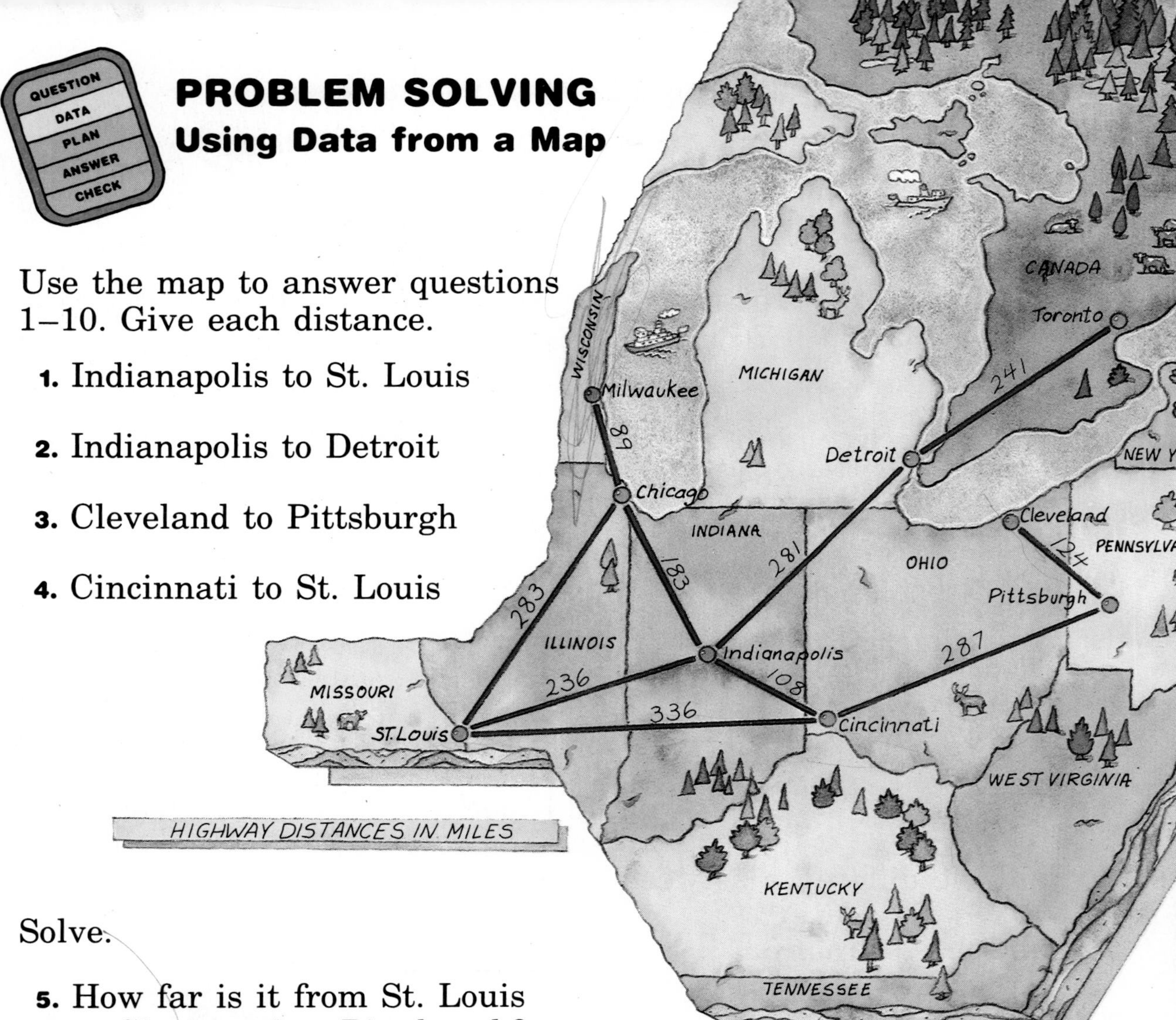

Use the map to answer questions 1–10. Give each distance.

1. Indianapolis to St. Louis
2. Indianapolis to Detroit
3. Cleveland to Pittsburgh
4. Cincinnati to St. Louis

Solve.

5. How far is it from St. Louis to Cincinnati to Pittsburgh?
6. How much farther is it from St. Louis to Chicago than from St. Louis to Indianapolis?
7. How far is it from Indianapolis to Detroit to Toronto?
8. How much shorter is the trip from Chicago to Milwaukee than from Chicago to Indianapolis?
9. **DATA BANK** See page 378. How far is it from Tampa to Atlanta to Birmingham?
10. ***Strategy Practice*** Pretend you take one of the trips on the map above. Your trip is more than 200 miles and less than 300 miles. You go an even number of miles. What two cities do you visit?

PROBLEM SOLVING
Using Data from a Table

The yellow shading shows you how to read the table. The distance from New York to Pittsburgh is 384 miles.

	Boston	Buffalo	New York	Philadelphia	Pittsburgh	Washington
Boston	–	454	212	302	593	437
Buffalo	454	–	434	381	217	384
New York	212	434	–	93	384	227
Philadelphia	302	381	93	–	302	139
Pittsburgh	593	217	384	302	–	240
Washington	437	384	227	139	240	–

Mileage Table

Other Examples

Philadelphia to Buffalo: 381 miles

Boston to Washington: 437 miles

Use the table to answer questions 1–8.

Give each distance.

1. Pittsburgh to Buffalo
2. New York to Washington
3. Buffalo to New York
4. Philadelphia to Boston

Solve.

5. What is the distance from Boston to Buffalo and then to Pittsburgh?
6. How much farther is the distance from Buffalo to Philadelphia than the distance from Pittsburgh to Philadelphia?
7. How far is it from Boston to Washington to Buffalo to Pittsburgh to Philadelphia to Boston?
8. ***Strategy Practice*** Joe lives less than 500 miles from Boston. It is an odd number of miles. Where does Joe live?

Subtracting Across a Middle Zero

How many more cars passed Main Street between 7:00 a.m. and 8:00 a.m. than between 9:00 a.m. and 10:00 a.m.?

To find how many more cars, we subtract.

Monday Car Count- Main Street	
Time	Number of cars
7:00-8:00 a.m.	405
8:00-9:00 a.m.	302
9:00-10:00 a.m.	128
10:00-11:00 a.m.	137

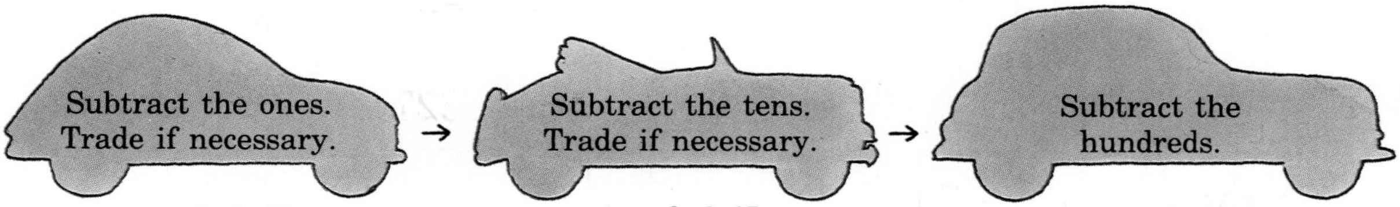

Subtract the ones		Subtract the tens	Subtract the hundreds
3 9 15		3 9 15	3 9 15
~~405~~	THINK "40 tens"	~~405~~	~~405~~
− 128		− 128	− 128
7		77	277

277 more cars passed Main Street between 7:00 a.m. and 8:00 a.m. than between 9:00 a.m. and 10:00 a.m.

Other Examples

6 9 10	7 9 16	5 9 15	9 13	6 10
~~700~~	~~806~~	~~605~~	~~103~~	~~70~~5
− 367	− 759	− 88	− 76	− 382
333	47	517	27	323

Warm Up Subtract.

1. 602 − 273	**2.** 906 − 528	**3.** 401 − 89	**4.** 504 − 392	**5.** 703 − 634
6. 104 − 36	**7.** 502 − 287	**8.** 703 − 59	**9.** 800 − 342	**10.** 605 − 416

Practice Find the differences.

1. $\begin{array}{r} 702 \\ -\ 237 \\ \hline \end{array}$
2. $\begin{array}{r} 504 \\ -\ 146 \\ \hline \end{array}$
3. $\begin{array}{r} 400 \\ -\ 164 \\ \hline \end{array}$
4. $\begin{array}{r} 623 \\ -\ 508 \\ \hline \end{array}$
5. $\begin{array}{r} 904 \\ -\ 627 \\ \hline \end{array}$
6. $\begin{array}{r} 506 \\ -\ 458 \\ \hline \end{array}$
7. $\begin{array}{r} 712 \\ -\ 285 \\ \hline \end{array}$
8. $\begin{array}{r} 309 \\ -\ 142 \\ \hline \end{array}$
9. $\begin{array}{r} 600 \\ -\ 536 \\ \hline \end{array}$
10. $\begin{array}{r} 805 \\ -\ 723 \\ \hline \end{array}$
11. $\begin{array}{r} 803 \\ -\ 439 \\ \hline \end{array}$
12. $\begin{array}{r} 107 \\ -\ 29 \\ \hline \end{array}$
13. $\begin{array}{r} 435 \\ -\ 67 \\ \hline \end{array}$
14. $\begin{array}{r} 205 \\ -\ 76 \\ \hline \end{array}$
15. $\begin{array}{r} 900 \\ -\ 285 \\ \hline \end{array}$

16. 204 − 154
17. 600 − 316
18. 906 − 78
19. 746 − 359
20. 304 − 168
21. 503 − 188
22. 705 − 627
23. 108 − 59
24. Subtract 275 from 704.
25. Subtract 364 from 907.

Mixed Applications

Use the table on page 104.

26. How many more cars passed between 8:00 a.m. and 9:00 a.m. than between 10:00 a.m. and 11:00 a.m.?
27. What was the total number of cars that passed from 9:00 a.m. to 11:00 a.m.?

★ 28. Make up the missing data and solve this problem. How many more cars passed Elm Street between 6:00 a.m. and 7:00 a.m. than between 1:00 p.m. and 2:00 p.m.?

THINK

Smallest Difference Game

1. Make this set of cards.

0	1	2	3	4	5	6	7	8	9
0	1	2	3	4	5	6	7	8	9

2. Mix the cards face down.
3. Give each player four cards.
4. Each player makes a subtraction problem.

Example

$\begin{array}{r} 80 \\ -\ 73 \\ \hline 7 \end{array}$ $\quad$ $\begin{array}{r} 42 \\ -\ 39 \\ \hline 3 \end{array}$ ←Winner

5. Smallest difference wins.

MATH

Subtracting Amounts of Money

How much more money does the book about robots cost than the book about dinosaurs?

To find out how much more money, we subtract the smaller amount from the larger amount.

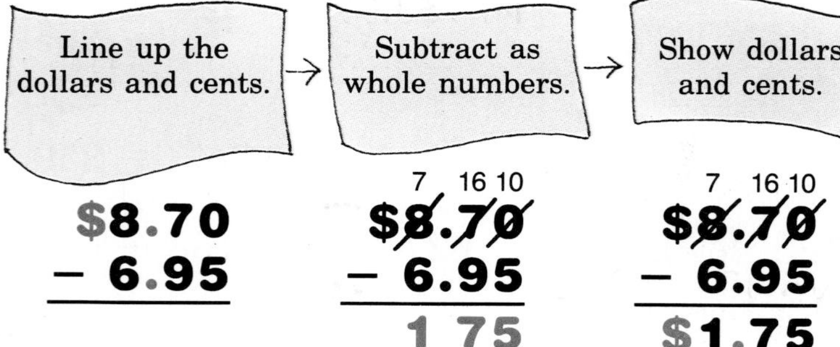

Line up the dollars and cents.
Subtract as whole numbers.
Show dollars and cents.
$8.70
− 6.95
7 16 10
$8.70
− 6.95
1 75
7 16 10
$8.70
− 6.95
$1.75

The book about robots costs $1.75 more than the book about dinosaurs.

Other Examples

7 11 15 $8.25 − 2.49 $5.76	4 9 10 $5.00 − 0.98 $4.02	9 10 $1.00 − 0.69 $0.31

Warm Up Subtract.

1. $6.15 − 1.30	**2.** $7.25 − 2.50	**3.** $5.00 − 2.47	**4.** $7.50 − 0.75	**5.** $8.00 − 6.25
6. $1.00 − 0.49	**7.** $5.00 − 1.75	**8.** $3.69 − 1.25	**9.** $5.00 − 2.75	**10.** $8.50 − 1.75

Practice Find the differences in the amounts.

1. \$6.25 − 1.50	**2.** \$5.50 − 1.70	**3.** \$7.42 − 0.98	**4.** \$5.00 − 2.25	**5.** \$1.00 − 0.75
6. \$4.25 − 0.75	**7.** \$8.00 − 3.50	**8.** \$1.00 − 0.45	**9.** \$7.50 − 0.98	**10.** \$5.00 − 2.89
11. \$8.25 − 6.75	**12.** \$4.00 − 0.95	**13.** \$6.32 − 4.44	**14.** \$3.09 − 1.99	**15.** \$1.36 − 1.27

16. \$4.35 − \$2.50 **17.** \$6.50 − \$3.75 **18.** \$7.25 − \$0.79

19. \$4.00 − \$1.25 **20.** \$5.00 − \$2.65 **21.** \$6.00 − \$1.98

Mixed Applications

22. How much for A and B?

23. How much more is B than C?

24. How much for B and C?

25. How much less is C than A?

26. How much more is A than B?

27. How much for A and C?

28. How much for A, B, and C?

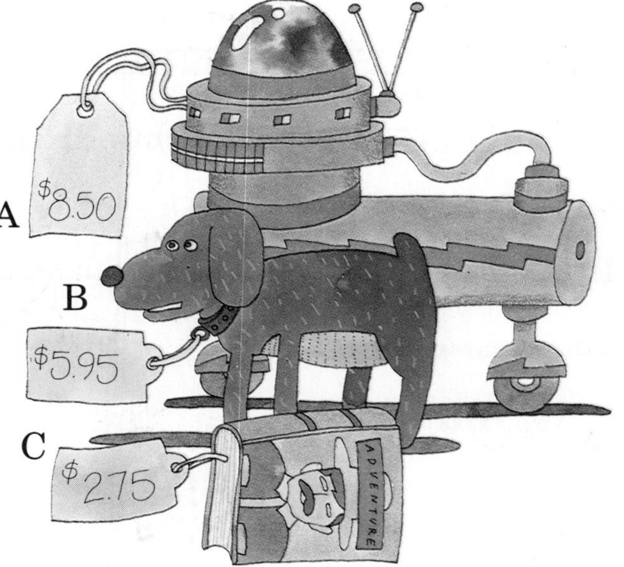

THINK

Estimation

Two of these numbers have a difference of 187. Use **estimation** to find them.

Check by subtracting.

413	587
600	313
487	513

MATH

Special Differences: Mental Math

It is 1,100 yards from the Tree to the Treasure if you go past Big Rock. It is only 800 yards if you cross the Dangerous Bridge. How much farther is it to go past Big Rock?

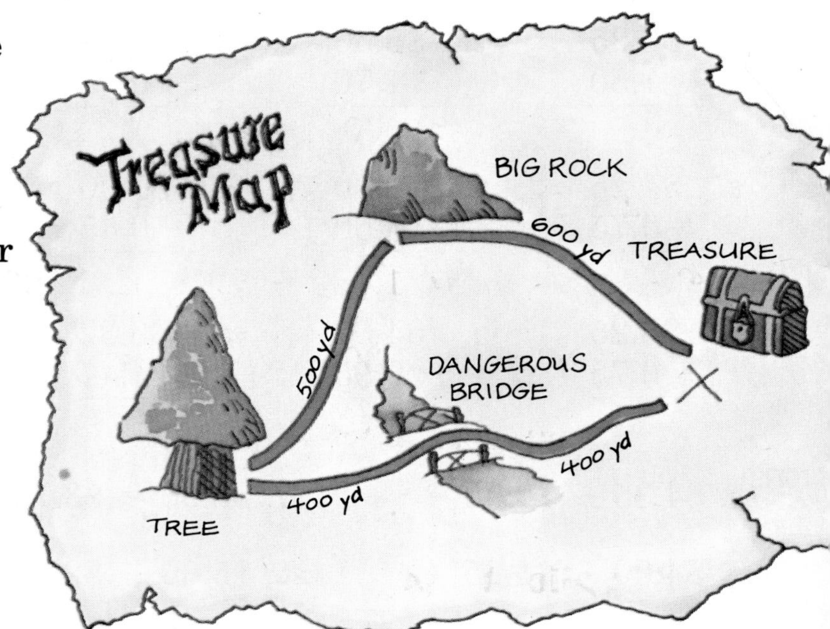

Since we are comparing, we subtract.

Think about hundreds.
11 hundreds − 8 hundreds = 3 hundreds

11 hundreds

8 hundreds

1,100 − 800 = 300

It is 300 yards farther to go past Big Rock.

Other Examples

1,300 − 600 = 700

THINK
13 hundreds − 6 hundreds = 7 hundreds

150 − 80 = 70

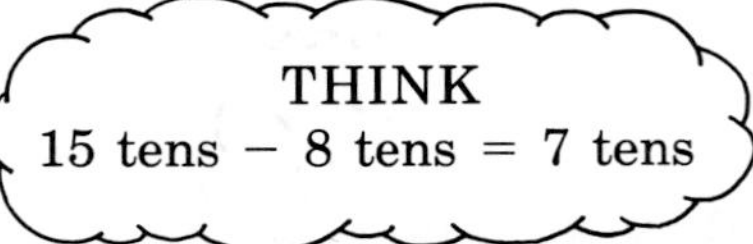

Warm Up Give the differences aloud.

1. 110 − 50	**2.** 80 − 30	**3.** 1,200 − 600	**4.** 100 − 20
5. 130 − 40	**6.** 1,700 − 900	**7.** 900 − 500	**8.** 1,400 − 800
9. 120 − 70	**10.** 1,000 − 400	**11.** 140 − 60	**12.** 1,100 − 200

Practice Find the differences. Write only the answers.

1. 90 − 10	**2.** 1,400 − 800	**3.** 120 − 60	**4.** 60 − 50
5. 160 − 80	**6.** 800 − 600	**7.** 1,500 − 600	**8.** 1,000 − 700
9. 1,200 − 900	**10.** 50 − 20	**11.** 150 − 90	**12.** 100 − 40
13. 80 − 30	**14.** 1,100 − 600	**15.** 1,400 − 700	**16.** 700 − 100
17. 900 − 700	**18.** 130 − 90	**19.** 70 − 20	**20.** 1,300 − 800
21. 1,400 − 600	**22.** 70 − 40	**23.** 1,600 − 900	**24.** 120 − 50
25. 130 − 60	**26.** 150 − 80	**27.** 1,700 − 800	**28.** 90 − 30

Mixed Applications

Use the map on page 108 as needed.

29. Kevin walked from the tree to the big rock and then back to the tree. How far did he walk?

30. How much farther is it from the big rock to the treasure than it is from the dangerous bridge to the treasure?

THINK MATH

Mental Math

Sometimes you can find differences in your head.

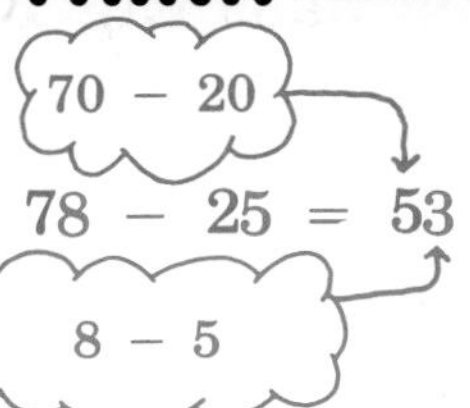

Find the differences. Write only the answers.

1. 89 − 32 (9 − 2)

70 − 40

2. 76 − 45 (6 − 5)

3. 97 − 54 (7 − 4)

4. 76 − 24	**5.** 85 − 33	**6.** 98 − 72	**7.** 67 − 41
8. 59 − 36	**9.** 68 − 43	**10.** 94 − 22	**11.** 46 − 34

Estimating Differences Using Rounding

Sometimes you want an answer that is only close to the exact answer.

About how much less is the blue car?
$7.98
$5.19

To estimate how much less the blue car is than the yellow car, we round and subtract.

$7.98	nearest dollar →	**$8.00**
− 5.19	nearest dollar →	**− 5.00**
		$3.00

The blue car is about $3.00 less than the yellow car.

Other Examples

nearest ten		nearest hundred		nearest dollar	
72 →	**70**	**518 →**	**500**	**$6.95 →**	**$7.00**
− 29 →	**− 30**	**− 195 →**	**− 200**	**− 4.29 →**	**− 4.00**
	40		**300**		**$3.00**

Warm Up Estimate by rounding to the nearest ten.

1. 92 − 48

2. 59 − 13

3. 67 − 39

4. 81 − 33

Estimate by rounding to the nearest hundred.

5. 789 − 207

6. 617 − 321

7. 575 − 187

8. 921 − 498

Estimate by rounding to the nearest dollar.

9. $7.95 − 1.29

10. $5.08 − 1.95

11. $6.98 − 1.99

12. $8.19 − 3.25

Practice Estimate by rounding to the nearest ten.

1. $\begin{array}{r} 87 \\ -\ 19 \\ \hline \end{array}$ **2.** $\begin{array}{r} 63 \\ -\ 39 \\ \hline \end{array}$ **3.** $\begin{array}{r} 79 \\ -\ 42 \\ \hline \end{array}$ **4.** $\begin{array}{r} 67 \\ -\ 38 \\ \hline \end{array}$ **5.** $\begin{array}{r} 92 \\ -\ 43 \\ \hline \end{array}$

6. $\begin{array}{r} 56 \\ -\ 17 \\ \hline \end{array}$ **7.** $\begin{array}{r} 73 \\ -\ 27 \\ \hline \end{array}$ **8.** $\begin{array}{r} 45 \\ -\ 21 \\ \hline \end{array}$ **9.** $\begin{array}{r} 89 \\ -\ 19 \\ \hline \end{array}$ **10.** $\begin{array}{r} 58 \\ -\ 27 \\ \hline \end{array}$

Estimate by rounding to the nearest hundred or dollar.

11. $\begin{array}{r} 921 \\ -\ 196 \\ \hline \end{array}$ **12.** $\begin{array}{r} 804 \\ -\ 295 \\ \hline \end{array}$ **13.** $\begin{array}{r} 795 \\ -\ 319 \\ \hline \end{array}$ **14.** $\begin{array}{r} 817 \\ -\ 595 \\ \hline \end{array}$

15. $\begin{array}{r} \$7.25 \\ -\ 3.19 \\ \hline \end{array}$ **16.** $\begin{array}{r} \$5.98 \\ -\ 2.79 \\ \hline \end{array}$ **17.** $\begin{array}{r} \$9.20 \\ -\ 4.39 \\ \hline \end{array}$ **18.** $\begin{array}{r} \$4.79 \\ -\ 0.95 \\ \hline \end{array}$

Estimate by rounding to the nearest dollar.

19. A costs \$3.95.
A costs \$2.15.
How much for both?

20. A costs \$2.98. How much change should you get from \$5?

21. A costs \$6.95.
A costs \$1.98.
How much less is the ?

22. A costs \$4.98.
A costs \$7.95.
How much for both?

THINK

Mental Math

Use counting to find these differences. Write only the answers.

397, 398, 399, 400

Example: 400 − 397 = 3

1. 500 − 498 **2.** 700 − 697
3. 600 − 596 **4.** 900 − 895
5. 501 − 498 **6.** 402 − 398

MATH

More Practice, page 391, Set A

Subtracting 4-Digit Numbers

Estimate the number of beads.

Student	Estimate
Ken	4,800
Lynn	8,307
Janet	5,675
Juan	6,992

The actual number was 6,354.

Whose estimate was closest?

Since we are comparing numbers, we subtract.

The smallest difference wins.

Ken	Lynn	Janet	Juan
5 13	7 12 10	5 12 14 14	8 12
6,354	**8,307**	**6,354**	**6,992**
− 4,800	**− 6,354**	**− 5,675**	**− 6,354**
1,554	**1,953**	**679**	**638**

Juan's estimate was closest to 6,354.

Warm Up Subtract.

1. 7,287 − 1,532	**2.** 5,759 − 4,287	**3.** 8,746 − 578	**4.** 9,314 − 8,487
5. 9,538 − 5,675	**6.** 7,620 − 6,341	**7.** 6,504 − 3,257	**8.** 4,313 − 2,765

CHAPTER REVIEW/TEST

Subtract.

1. 76 − 15	**2.** 83 − 56	**3.** 95 − 58	**4.** 90 − 53	**5.** 68 − 46
6. 138 − 95	**7.** 924 − 657	**8.** 124 − 78	**9.** 657 − 589	**10.** 135 − 86
11. 304 − 127	**12.** 608 − 239	**13.** \$8.32 − 2.70	**14.** \$6.23 − 2.57	**15.** \$7.50 − 3.90

Estimate by rounding to the nearest hundred or dollar.

16. 795 − 213	**17.** 604 − 379	**18.** \$4.28 − 1.96	**19.** \$5.80 − 3.87

Find the differences.

20. 6,594 − 3,276	**21.** 5,042 − 1,864	**22.** 2,710 − 2,654	**23.** 4,100 − 2,973

Solve.

24. How much less is B than A?

A

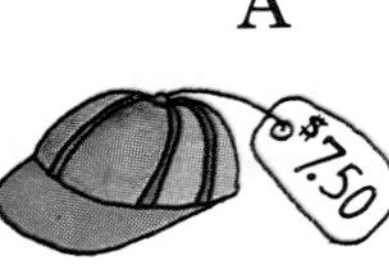

26. How much farther is it from Hilltop to Lake than from Home to Lake?

25. How much for both A and B?

B

27. The IDS Center is 57 stories. The Sears Tower is 110. How many stories are in both?

18. 95 − 8 **19.** 52 − 9 **20.** 43 − 8

21. 75 − 8 **22.** 64 − 9 **23.** 91 − 8 **24.** 82 − 9

ANOTHER LOOK

DO YOU NEED MORE ONES?

Do you need more ones?
Answer YES or NO.

CUMULATIVE REVIEW

Give the letter for the correct answer.

1. $35 + 24$ **A** 58 **B** 69 **C** 59 **D** not given

2. $68 + 26$ **A** 94 **B** 22 **C** 84 **D** not given

3. $78 + 57$ **A** 135 **B** 125 **C** 145 **D** not given

4. $355 + 426$ **A** 771 **B** 781 **C** 761 **D** not given

5. $\$7.49 + 6.25$ **A** \$14.74 **B** \$13.64 **C** \$13.74 **D** not given

6. $367 + 554$ **A** 921 **B** 811 **C** 911 **D** not given

Give the number.

7. 8 tens, 3 ones **A** 88 **B** 38 **C** 83 **D** not given

8. 2 hundreds, 4 tens, 6 ones **A** 624 **B** 426 **C** 264 **D** not given

9. 7 hundreds, 0 tens, 2 ones **A** 207 **B** 720 **C** 702 **D** not given

Which number sentence is correct?

10. **A** $52 < 41$ **B** $52 > 32$ **C** $52 > 108$ **D** not given

11. **A** $325 > 400$ **B** $325 < 250$ **C** $325 < 500$ **D** not given

12. **A** $6{,}508 > 6{,}500$ **B** $6{,}508 > 7{,}296$ **C** $6{,}508 < 3{,}454$ **D** not given

13. Tondi had \$2.75. She earned \$1.50. How much did she have then?
A \$3.25 **B** \$3.17 **C** \$4.25 **D** not given

14. Erin paid \$9.98 for a puppet. He paid \$4.75 for a stage. How much did he pay for both?
A \$5.23 **B** \$14.63 **C** \$14.73 **D** not given

JANUARY

S	M	T	W	T	F	S
		1	2	3	4	5
6	7	8	9	10	11	12
13	14	15	16	17	18	19
20	21	22	23	24	25	26
27	28	29	30	31		

FEBRUARY

S	M	T	W	T	F	S
					1	2
3	4	5	6	7	8	9
10	11	12	13	14	15	16
17	18	19	20	21	22	23
24	25	26	27	28		

MARCH

S	M	T	W	T	F	S
					1	2
3	4	5	6	7	8	9
10	11	12	13	14	15	16
17	18	19	20	21	22	23
24	25	26	27	28	29	30
31						

APRIL

S	M	T	W	T	F	S
	1	2	3	4	5	6
7	8	9	10	11	12	13
14	15	16	17	18	19	20
21	22	23	24	25	26	27
28	29	30				

MAY

S	M	T	W	T	F	S
			1	2	3	4
5	6	7	8	9	10	11
12	13	14	15	16	17	18
19	20	21	22	23	24	25
26	27	28	29	30	31	

JUNE

S	M	T	W	T	F	S
						1
2	3	4	5	6	7	8
9	10	11	12	13	14	15
16	17	18	19	20	21	22
23	24	25	26	27	28	29
30						

JULY

S	M	T	W	T	F	S
	1	2	3	4	5	6
7	8	9	10	11	12	13
14	15	16	17	18	19	20
21	22	23	24	25	26	27
28	29	30	31			

AUGUST

S	M	T	W	T	F	S
				1	2	3
4	5	6	7	8	9	10
11	12	13	14	15	16	17
18	19	20	21	22	23	24
25	26	27	28	29	30	31

SEPTEMBER

S	M	T	W	T	F	S
1	2	3	4	5	6	7
8	9	10	11	12	13	14
15	16	17	18	19	20	21
22	23	24	25	26	27	28
29	30					

OCTOBER

S	M	T	W	T	F	S
		1	2	3	4	5
6	7	8	9	10	11	12
13	14	15	16	17	18	19
20	21	22	23	24	25	26
27	28	29	30	31		

NOVEMBER

S	M	T	W	T	F	S
					1	2
3	4	5	6	7	8	9
10	11	12	13	14	15	16
17	18	19	20	21	22	23
24	25	26	27	28	29	30

DECEMBER

S	M	T	W	T	F	S
1	2	3	4	5	6	7
8	9	10	11	12	13	14
15	16	17	18	19	20	21
22	23	24	25	26	27	28
29	30	31				

January is the first month.
The seventh month is July.

1. Give the months in order from first to twelfth.

Give the name of the day of the week.

2. July 4

3. February 14

4. October 31

5. January 1

6. February 22

7. December 31

Give the date.

Example first Sunday of the third month → March 3

8. second Tuesday of the seventh month

9. third Friday of the tenth month

10. first Monday of the ninth month

11. last Monday of the fifth month

Units for Measuring

Laura is making a ruler. She is using a paper clip as her unit for measuring. Each unit is one paper clip. About how many paper clips long is the brush?

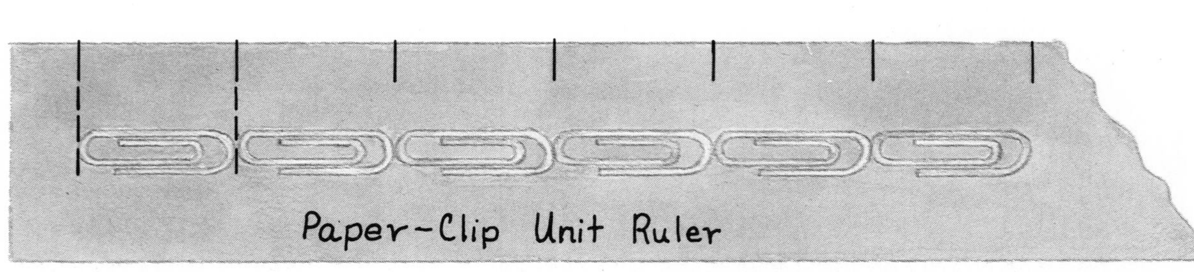

The length of the brush is about 6 paper-clip units.

Give the length of each pencil. Use the paper-clip unit ruler below.

1. 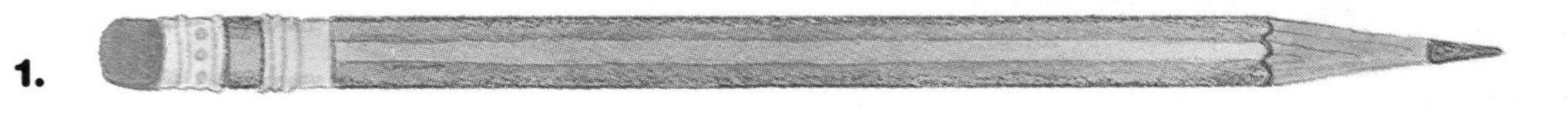

2. 

3. 

4. 

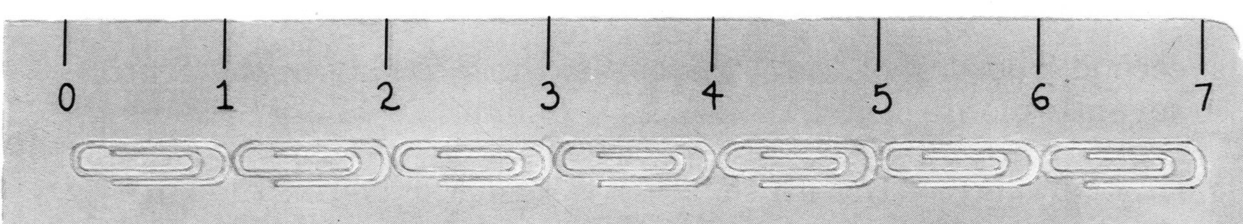

Using the Centimeter Unit

This is a **centimeter** (cm) unit. → ▬
Give the length of each object.
Use the centimeter ruler below.

1. 

2. 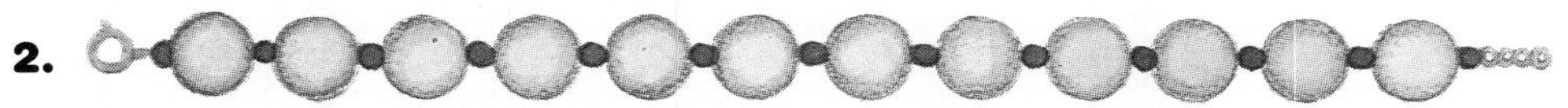

3. 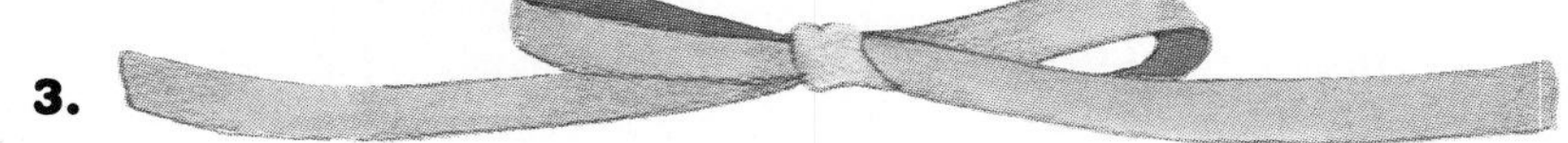

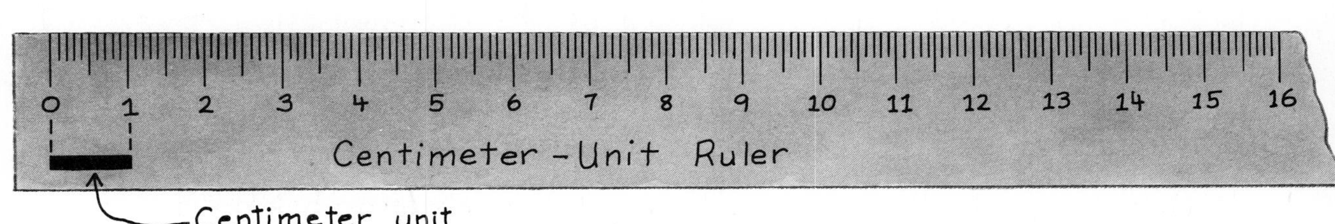

Use your centimeter ruler. Give the length of each object.

4. 

5. 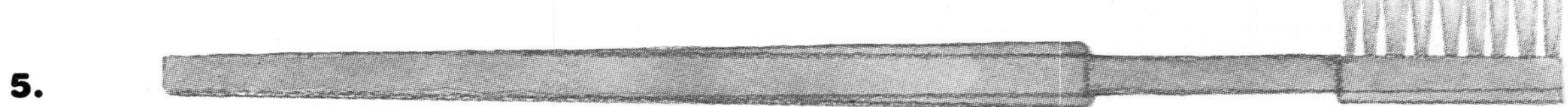

6. 

7. 

Use your centimeter ruler. Draw some lines that have these lengths.

8. 10 cm **9.** 7 cm **10.** 15 cm

Measuring to the Nearest Centimeter

Sometimes measures are not exact. Then you give the measure to the **nearest unit.**

The width of Maria's wrist is closer to 5 cm than to 6 cm. The width to the nearest centimeter is 5 cm.

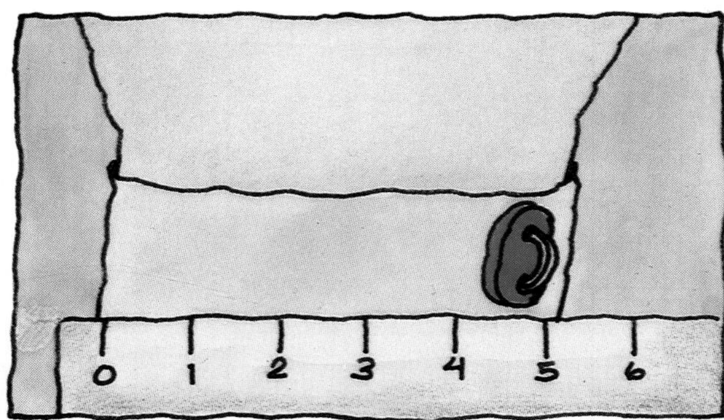

The length of Ted's finger is closer to 6 cm than to 5 cm. The length to the nearest centimeter is 6 cm.

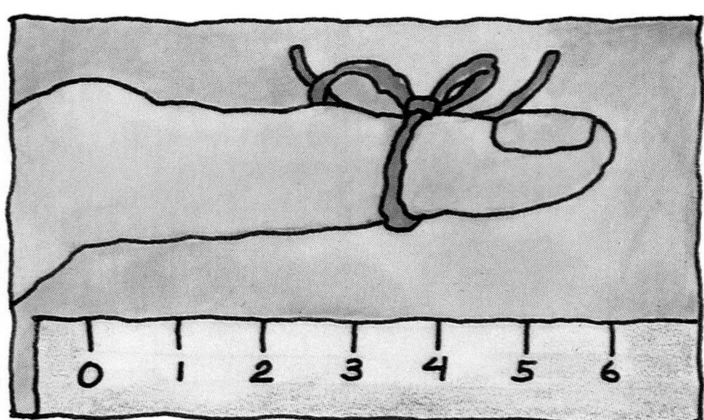

Give each measure to the nearest centimeter.

1. Sue's hand width

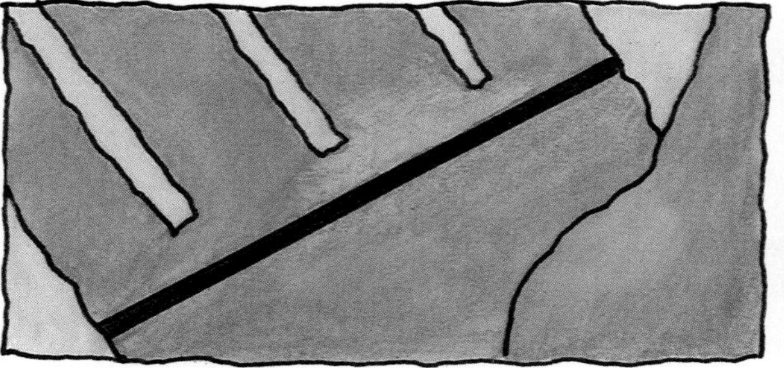

2. Larry's thumb length

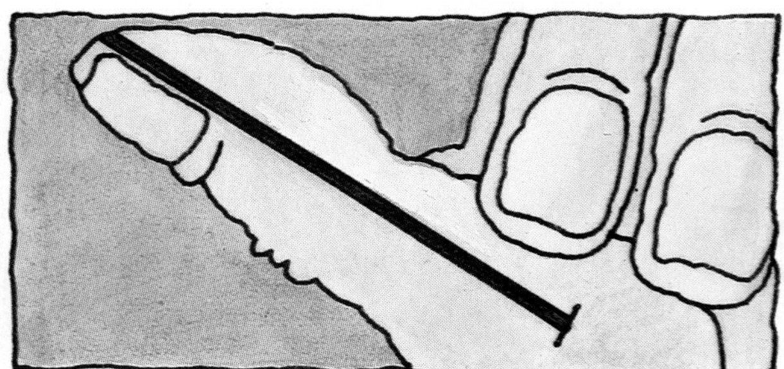

3. Ben's little finger length

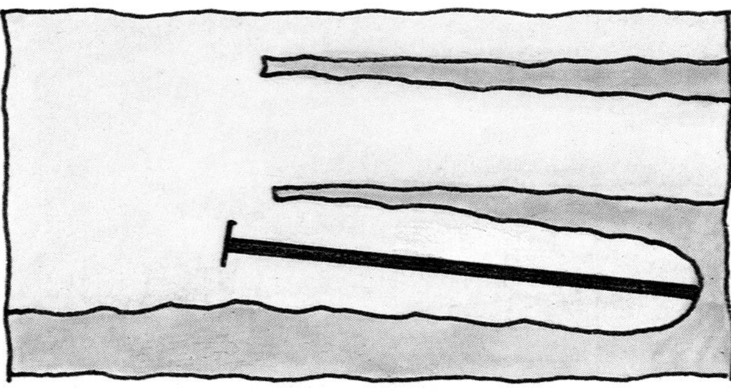

4. Patty's wrist width

This is a picture of Jo's hand.

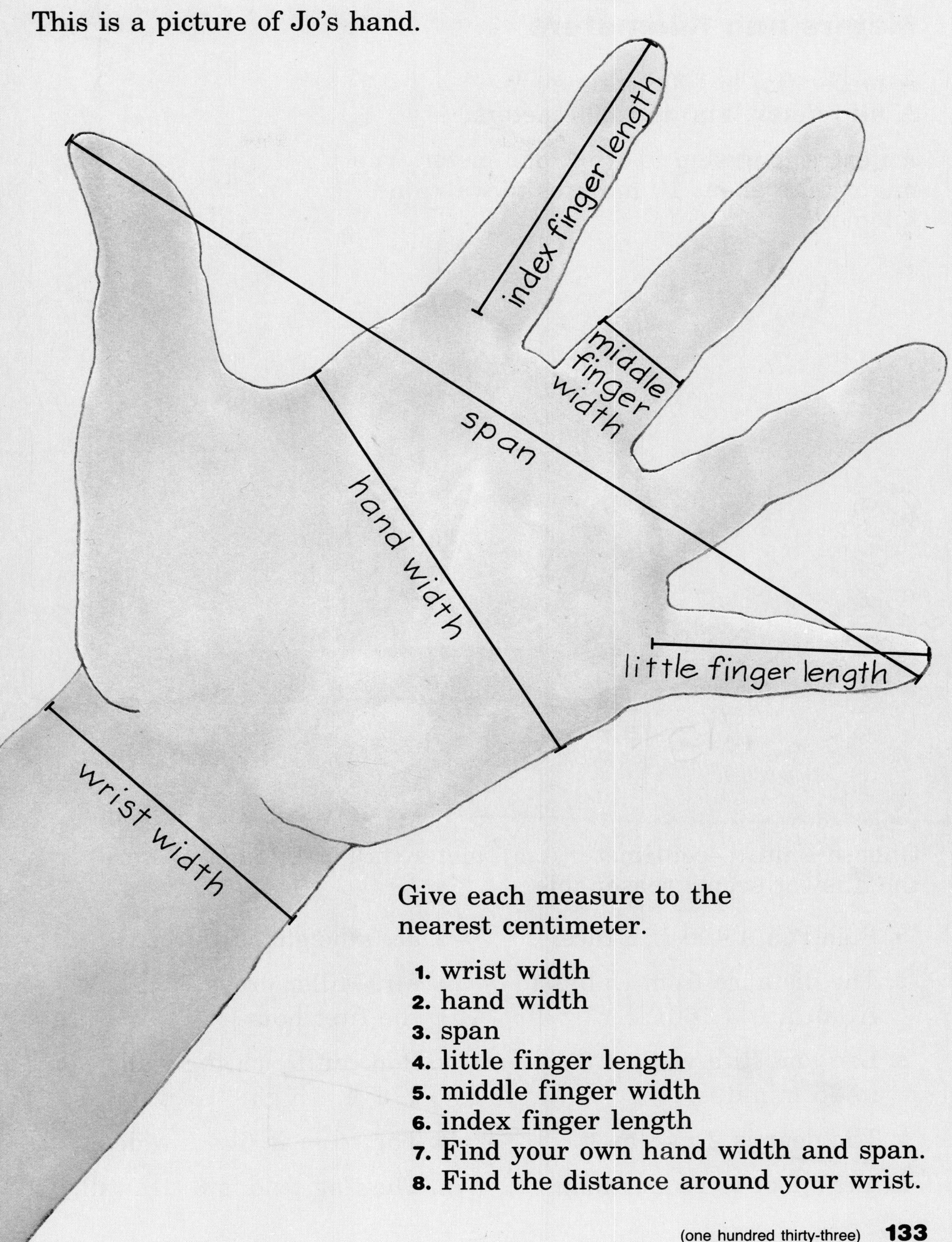

Give each measure to the nearest centimeter.

1. wrist width
2. hand width
3. span
4. little finger length
5. middle finger width
6. index finger length
7. Find your own hand width and span.
8. Find the distance around your wrist.

Meters and Kilometers

A **meter** (m) is 100 centimeters.
A **kilometer** (km) is 1,000 meters.

An extra long step is about one meter. You might take about 10 minutes to walk one kilometer.

Choose a unit—centimeter (cm), meter (m), or kilometer (km)—so the answer seems reasonable.

1. Pam ran a 400 ___ race.
2. Joe's height is 150 ___.
3. The distance from Dallas to Atlanta is 1,160 ___.
4. Mr. Miller drove 75 ___ the first hour.
5. Len and Rita walked 3 ___ in 35 minutes.
6. Ron can touch the wall 176 ___ high.
7. The door is 2 ___ high.
8. The room is 6 ___ wide.
9. Mia's foot is 17 ___ long.
10. The flag pole is 6 ___ tall.

PROBLEM SOLVING
Using Data from a Picture

1. How far is it from Dale to Brook to Troy?

2. How much taller is the building than it is wide?

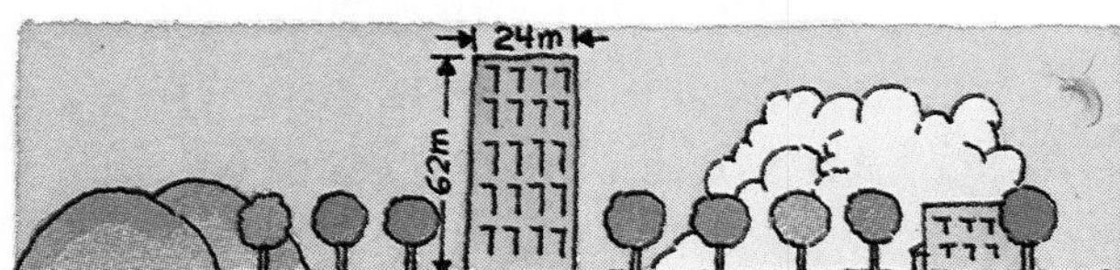

3. How much wider is the brick wall than it is tall?

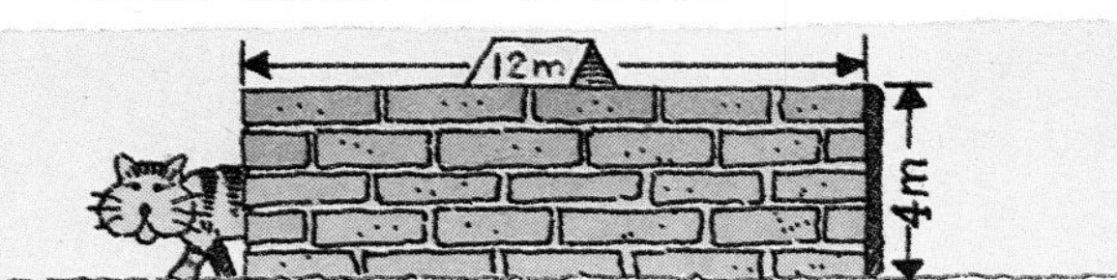

4. How far is it from the ground to the top of the flagpole?

5. How long is the wire holding the birdhouse?

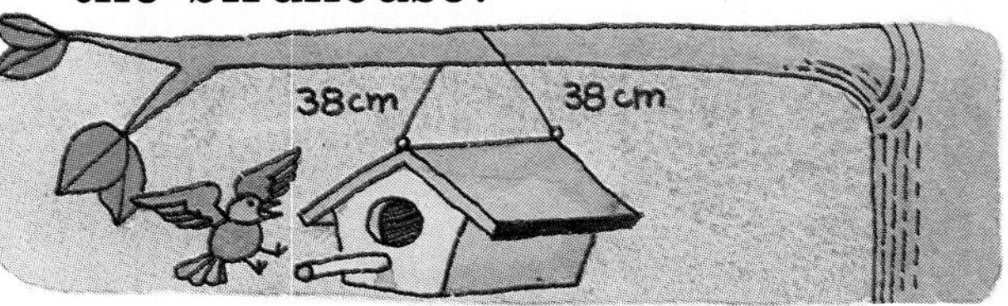

6. How much farther is it to go around the lake than to take the straight road?

7. ***Strategy Practice*** The lake is farther from home than the school, but not as far as the park. The school is farther from home than the store. Which is farthest from home? Hint: Draw a picture.

SKILLKEEPER

Add.

1.	2.	3.	4.	5.	6.
5	12	4	7	3	5
9	4	4	9	3	26
+ 13	+ 6	+ 4	14	3	37
			+ 2	+ 3	+ 14

Perimeter

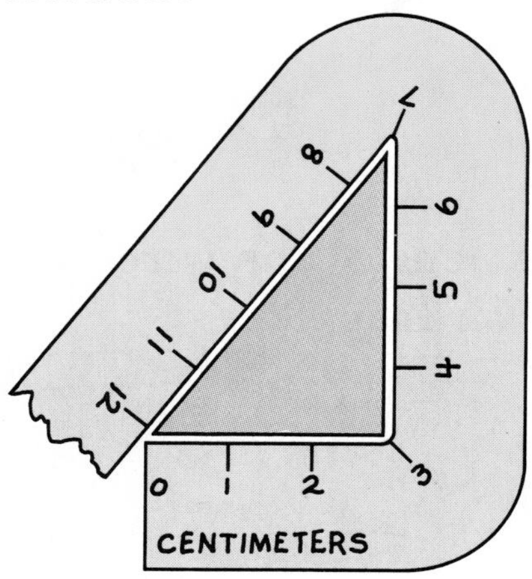

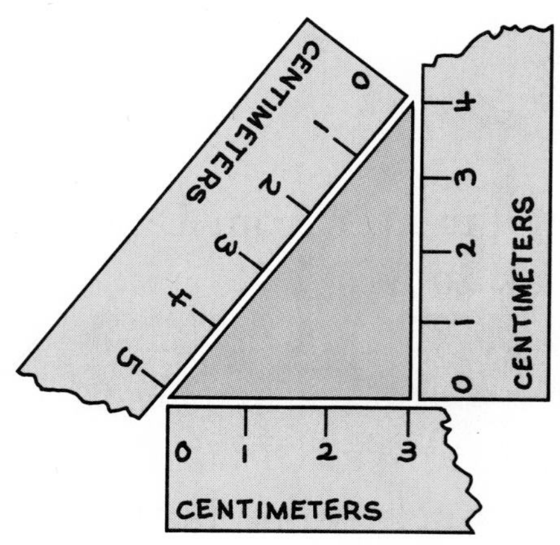

The distance around a figure is its **perimeter**. Look at the **triangle** within the bent ruler. Count the number of centimeters around the triangle. The perimeter is 12 cm.

Most rulers do not bend like the one above. So you may need to add to find the perimeter.

3 + 4 + 5 = 12

The perimeter is 12 cm.

Warm Up Find the perimeter for each figure.

1.

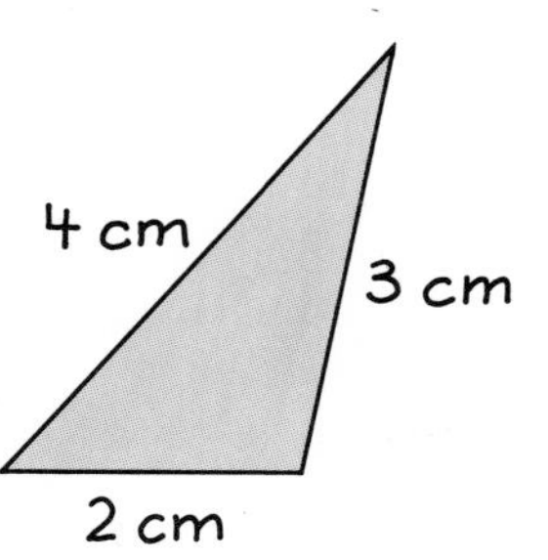

2.

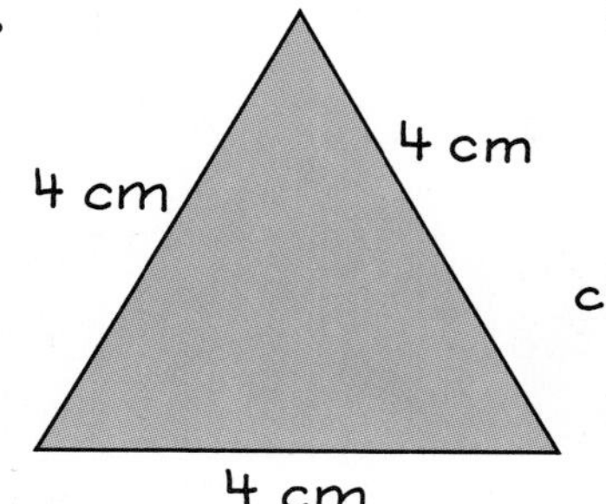

3.

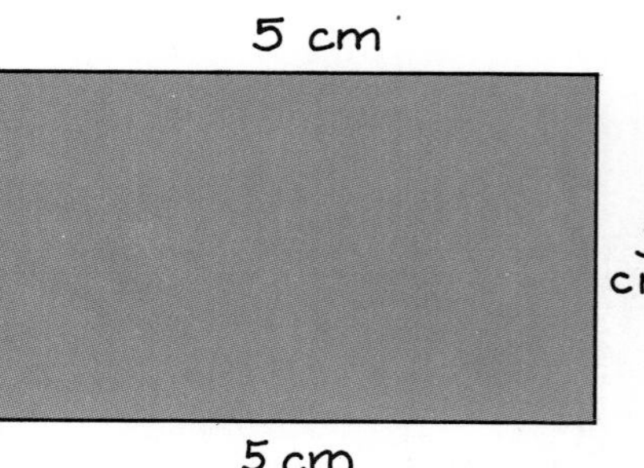

Practice Use your centimeter ruler to measure the sides. Then find the perimeter of each figure.

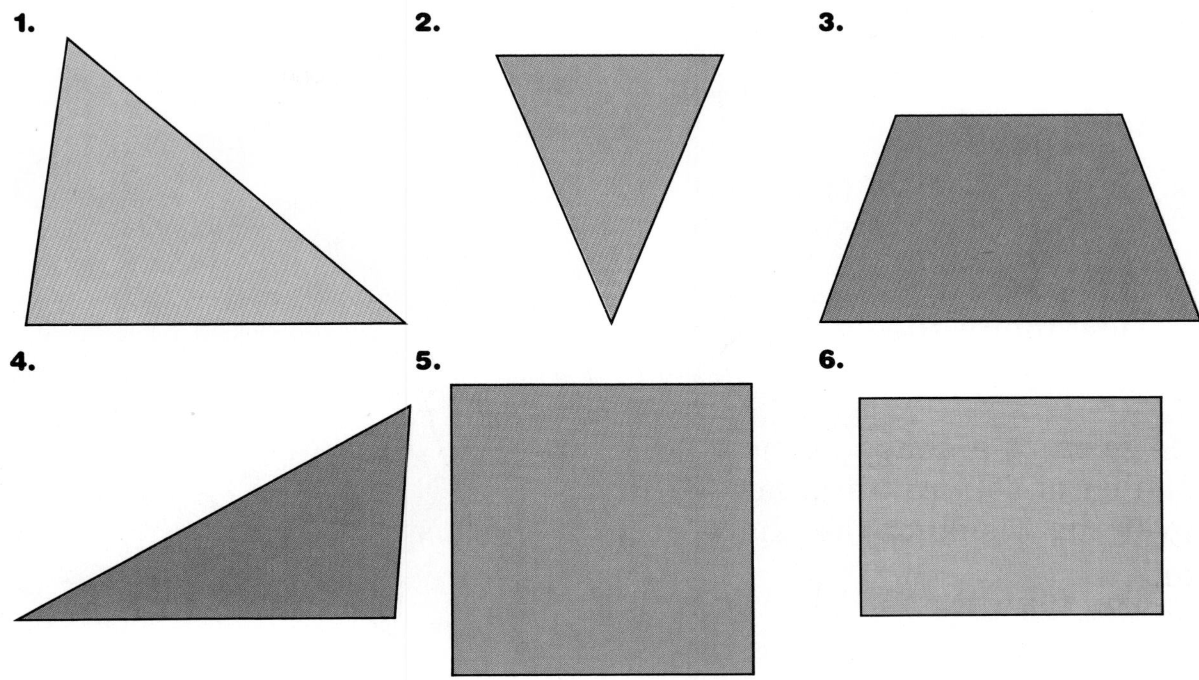

7. How many meters of fence are needed for the yard?

8. How far is it around the picture frame?

9. Find the perimeter of the cover of your math book.

10. Find the perimeter of the top of your desk.

11. A triangle has sides which measure 5,876 m, 7,398 m, and 8,597 m. Find the perimeter of the triangle.

★ 12. The perimeter of a triangle is 24 cm. One side is 7 cm and another side is 9 cm. What is the length of the third side?

Area

Don is covering the top of his table with square tiles.

1. How many tiles are on the table now?
2. How many tiles does Don need to finish covering the table?
3. How many tiles will be on the table when Don finishes?

The **area** of a shape is the number of square units needed to cover the inside of the shape.

4. The blue tile is the unit of measurement. What is the area of Don's table top?

Warm Up This is a **square centimeter** unit. ⟶ Give the area of each shape in square centimeters.

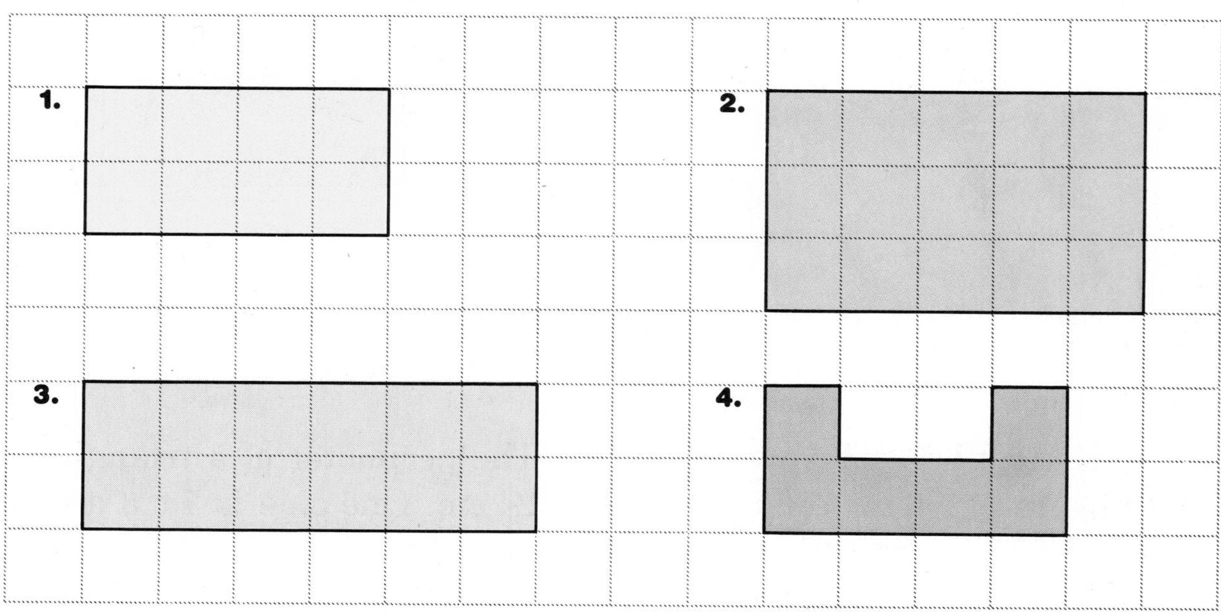

Practice Find the area of each shape in square centimeters.

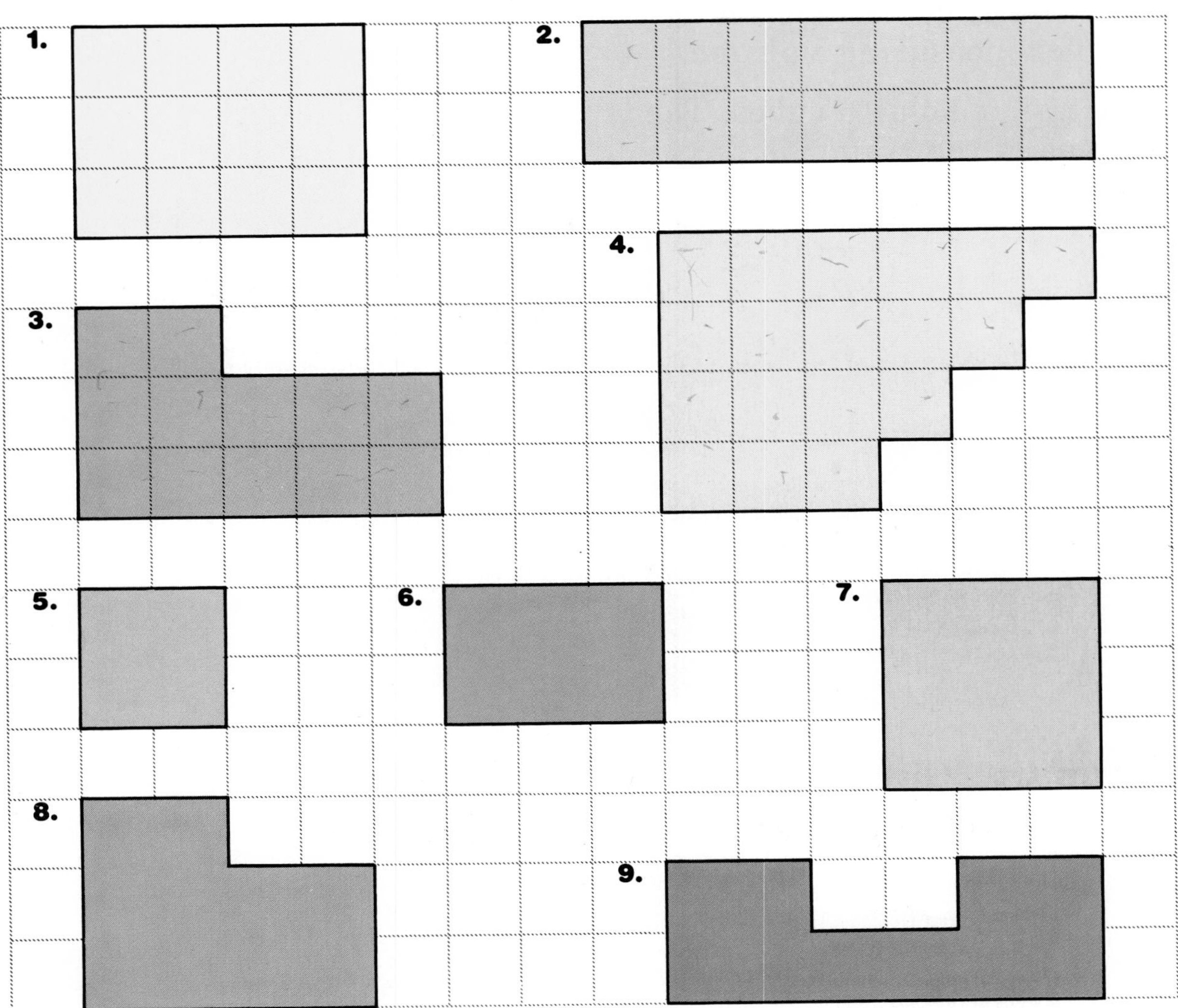

Use graph paper. Draw shapes with these areas.

10. 14 square units
11. 16 square units
12. 24 square units

THINK

Patterns

The shapes in 1, 2, 5, 6, and 7 above are **rectangles**.

Use graph paper. Draw as many different rectangles as you can that have an area of 24 square units.

MATH

Volume

A cube can be used as the unit for measuring **volume**.

The trailer holds 6 cubes. The volume of the trailer is 6 cubic units.

Warm Up Give the volume of each box in cubic units.

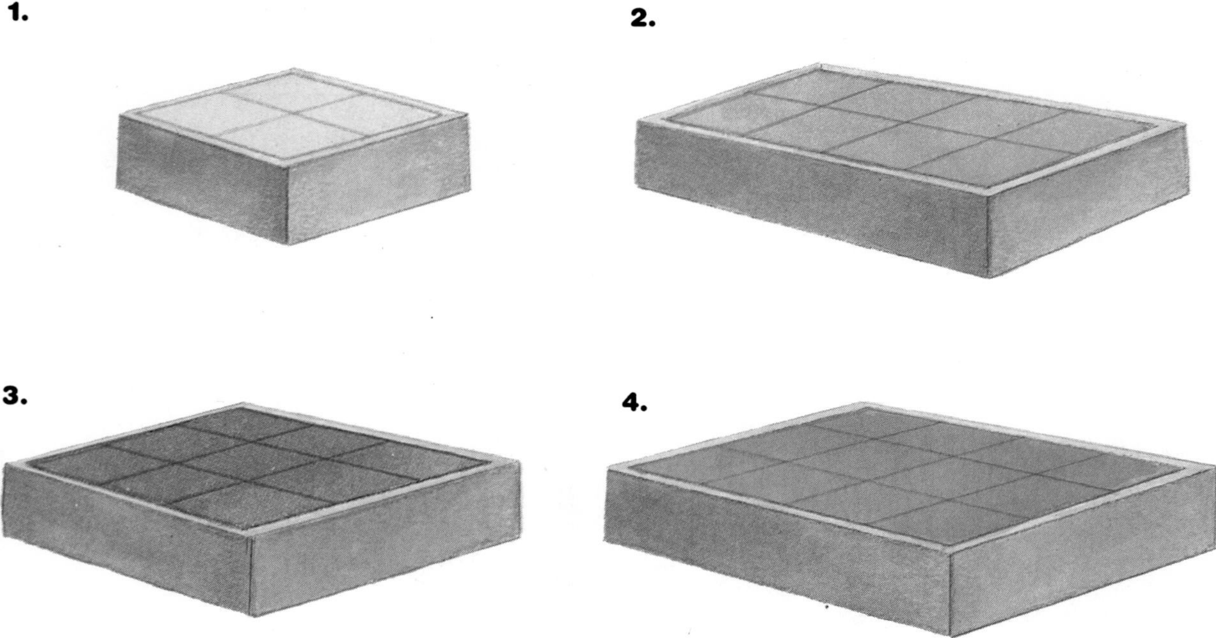

1.

2.

3.

4.

This cubic centimeter is the unit of measurement for the figures below.

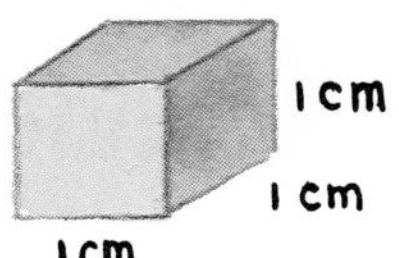

Practice Find the volume of each figure in cubic centimeters.

1.

2.

3.

4.

5.

6.

★7.

THINK

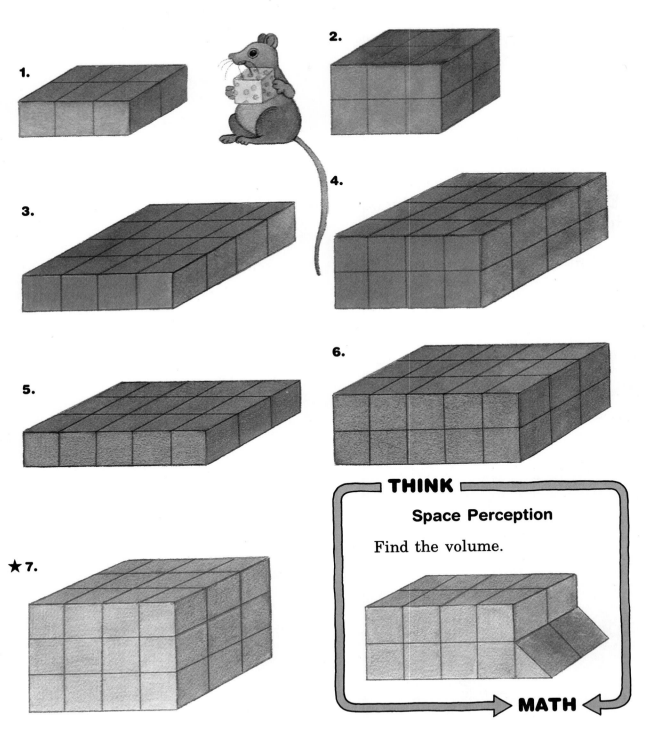

Space Perception

Find the volume.

MATH

Estimating Liquid Measure

This box holds 1,000 cubic centimeters.
It also holds 1 **liter** (L).

1 liter = 1,000 cubic centimeters

1 liter will fill 4 large glasses.

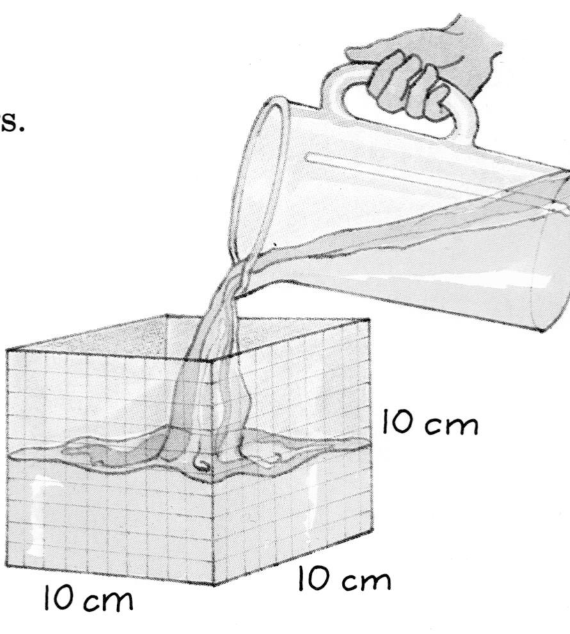

Estimate whether the objects below hold more or less than a liter.

1. Water pail

2. Drinking glass

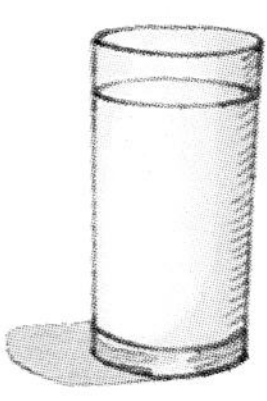

3. Paper cup

4. Aquarium

5. Roasting pan

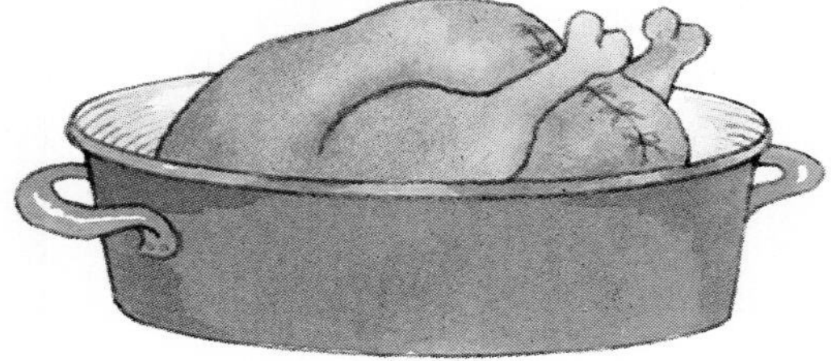

6. Cereal bowl

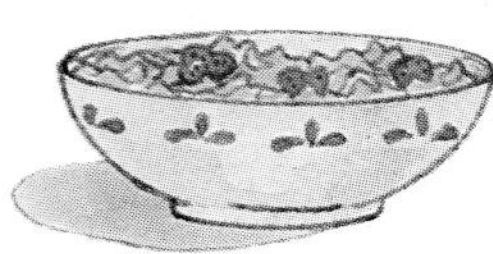

Estimating Weight

The **gram** (g) and **kilogram** (kg) are units for measuring weight. A liter of water has a weight of one kilogram.

1 kilogram = 1,000 grams

A paper clip:
about 1 gram

A large book:
about 1 kilogram

Choose the better estimate for the weight.

1.

Baseball bat
A 1 g **B** 1 kg

2.

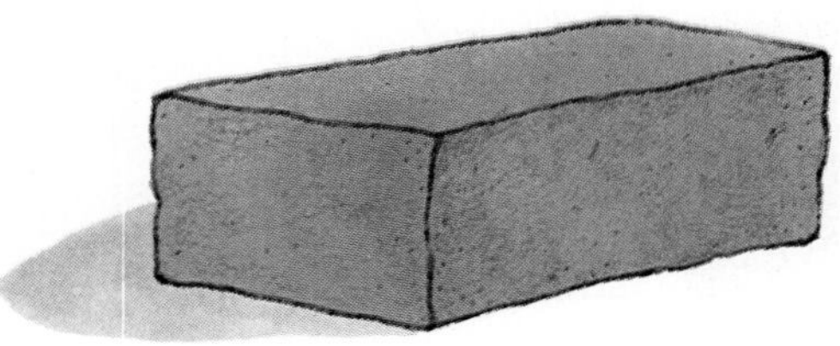

Brick
A 1 g **B** 1 kg

3.

Apple
A 250 g **B** 250 kg

4.

Small dog
A 10 g **B** 10 kg

THINK

Guess and Check

The large block weighs 2 kg more than the small block. Together they weigh 8 kg. How much does the large block weigh?

MATH

Temperature

A unit for measuring temperature is the **degree Celsius** (°C).

The thermometer at the right reads about 20°C (room temperature).

Give the reading for each thermometer below.

1. Boiling point of water

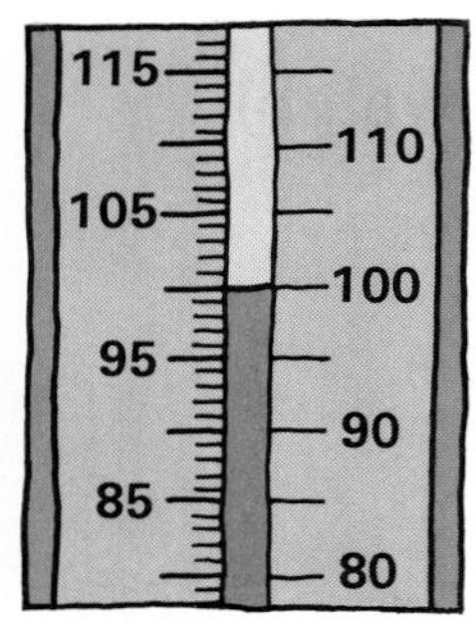

2. Drinking water

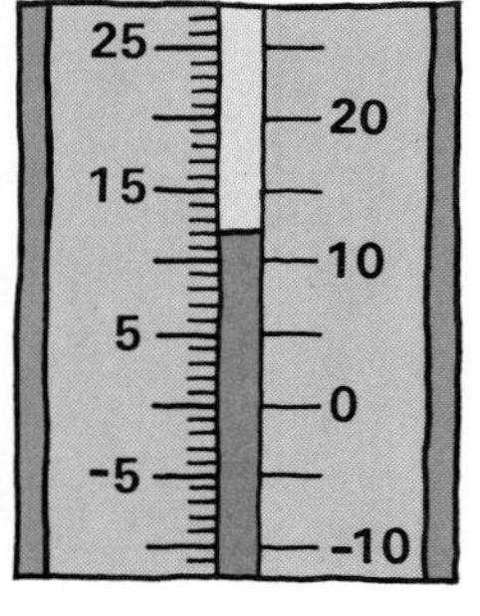

3. Freezing point of water

4. DATA HUNT Get a Celsius thermometer. Record the outside temperature. Record the room temperature. Find the difference between them.

PROBLEM SOLVING
Using Data from a Graph

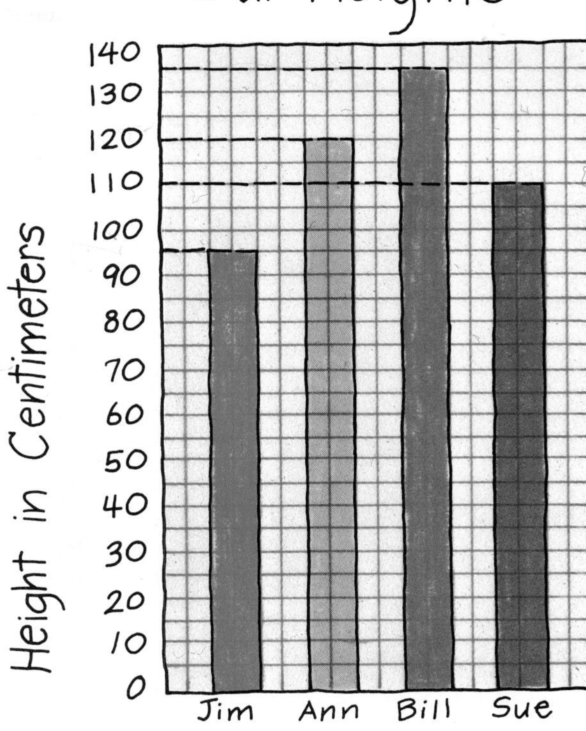

1. The graph shows that Bill is 135 cm tall and Jim is 95 cm tall. How much taller is Bill than Jim?

2. How much taller is Ann than Jim?

3. Jim grew 7 cm a year after the graph was made. How tall was he then?

4. How much taller is Bill than Sue?

5. How much more does Kay weigh than Pam?

6. Joe and Tom both got on the scales. What do they weigh together?

7. How much do Pam and Kay weigh together?

8. ***Strategy Practice*** Peter weighs an odd number of kilograms. His weight is between Tom's and Kay's on the Our Weights graph. It is closer to Tom's. How much does Peter weigh?

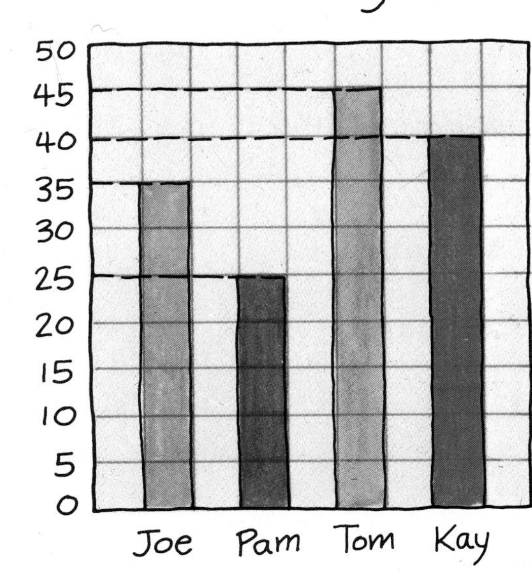

Mixed Skills Practice

Computation

Find the answers.

1. $\begin{array}{r} 7 \\ +\ 5 \\ \hline \end{array}$	**2.** $\begin{array}{r} 13 \\ -\ 6 \\ \hline \end{array}$	**3.** $\begin{array}{r} 11 \\ -\ 7 \\ \hline \end{array}$	**4.** $\begin{array}{r} 9 \\ +\ 8 \\ \hline \end{array}$	**5.** $\begin{array}{r} 10 \\ -\ 4 \\ \hline \end{array}$	**6.** $\begin{array}{r} 6 \\ +\ 7 \\ \hline \end{array}$
7. $\begin{array}{r} 14 \\ -\ 9 \\ \hline \end{array}$	**8.** $\begin{array}{r} 9 \\ +\ 9 \\ \hline \end{array}$	**9.** $\begin{array}{r} 15 \\ -\ 6 \\ \hline \end{array}$	**10.** $\begin{array}{r} 8 \\ +\ 3 \\ \hline \end{array}$	**11.** $\begin{array}{r} 7 \\ +\ 9 \\ \hline \end{array}$	**12.** $\begin{array}{r} 16 \\ -\ 8 \\ \hline \end{array}$
13. $\begin{array}{r} 23 \\ +\ 14 \\ \hline \end{array}$	**14.** $\begin{array}{r} 58 \\ +\ 17 \\ \hline \end{array}$	**15.** $\begin{array}{r} 74 \\ -\ 32 \\ \hline \end{array}$	**16.** $\begin{array}{r} 51 \\ -\ 24 \\ \hline \end{array}$	**17.** $\begin{array}{r} 68 \\ +\ 19 \\ \hline \end{array}$	**18.** $\begin{array}{r} 84 \\ -\ 77 \\ \hline \end{array}$
19. $\begin{array}{r} 36 \\ -\ 20 \\ \hline \end{array}$	**20.** $\begin{array}{r} 57 \\ +\ 88 \\ \hline \end{array}$	**21.** $\begin{array}{r} 135 \\ +\ 267 \\ \hline \end{array}$	**22.** $\begin{array}{r} 412 \\ -\ 130 \\ \hline \end{array}$	**23.** $\begin{array}{r} 506 \\ -\ 148 \\ \hline \end{array}$	**24.** $\begin{array}{r} 367 \\ +\ 955 \\ \hline \end{array}$

Mental Math

Write only the answers.

25. 17 + 2	**26.** 18 + 7	**27.** 34 + 3	**28.** 16 + 9
29. 70 + 30	**30.** 50 − 20	**31.** 80 + 60	**32.** 90 − 40
33. 800 − 300	**34.** 500 + 200	**35.** 600 + 100	**36.** 900 − 700

Estimation

Estimate.

37. 29 + 28	**38.** 51 − 39	**39.** 18 + 41	**40.** 69 − 29
41. 92 − 59	**42.** 38 + 49	**43.** 71 − 37	**44.** 54 + 27
45. 57 + 12	**46.** 68 + 14	**47.** 82 − 39	**48.** 73 − 18

APPLIED PROBLEM SOLVING

QUESTION
DATA
PLAN
ANSWER
CHECK

You are going to spend the afternoon at the zoo. A bus will get you there at 12:00 noon and pick you up at 3:00 p.m. You need to decide which animal areas you will visit.

Some Things to Consider

- The zoo has three animal areas. They are the Water Animals area, the Land Animals area, and the Bird area.
- Suggested amount of time it takes to see each area.
  - Water area—1:00
  - Land area— 1:15
  - Bird area— 0:45
- It takes about 5 minutes to walk between areas and to the bus.
- You want to take about 30 minutes to eat lunch.
- You may want to rest awhile between visits.

Some Questions to Answer

1. About how long will it take to visit both the Land and Bird areas?
2. About how long will it take to visit both the Land and Water areas?
3. Is there time to visit all three areas?
4. Which areas interest you most?

What Is Your Decision?

Plan your afternoon.
Which animal areas will you visit?

PROBLEM-SOLVING STRATEGY

Make a List

To solve a problem like this, you may need to do more than just add or subtract. A strategy that can help you is given below.

Try This You can have one piece of fruit and one cracker. How many choices can you make?

MAKE A LIST

If I choose the apple, then I can choose the square cracker or the round cracker.

Apple-square cracker
Apple-round cracker

If I choose the orange, then I can choose the square cracker or the round cracker.

Orange-square cracker
Orange-round cracker

There are 4 different choices.

1. Apple-square cracker
2. Apple-round cracker
3. Orange-square cracker
4. Orange-round cracker

Solve.

1. Charles has a white shirt and a blue shirt. He has a pair of blue jeans and a pair of white jeans. How many outfits can he wear?

2. Amy makes sandwiches with either cheese, jam, or meat. She uses white bread or rye bread. How many different sandwiches can she make?

CHAPTER REVIEW/TEST

Write each time.

1. **2.** **3.**

4. Use your centimeter ruler. Give the length to the nearest centimeter.

Give the missing unit—cm, m, or km.

5. Tom lives 45 ____ from Reno.

6. The tree is 5 ____ tall.

7. Find the perimeter.

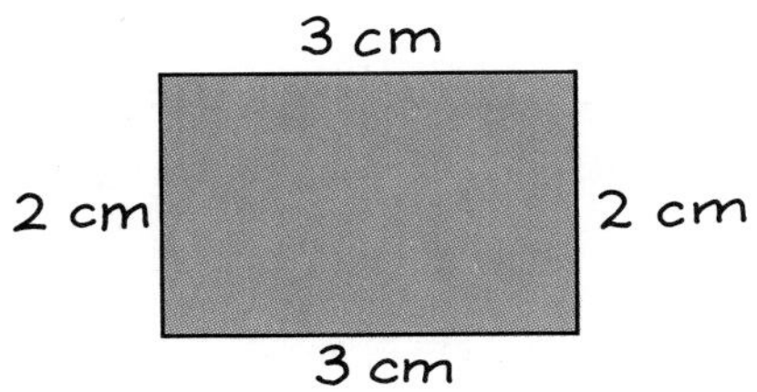

8. Find the area.

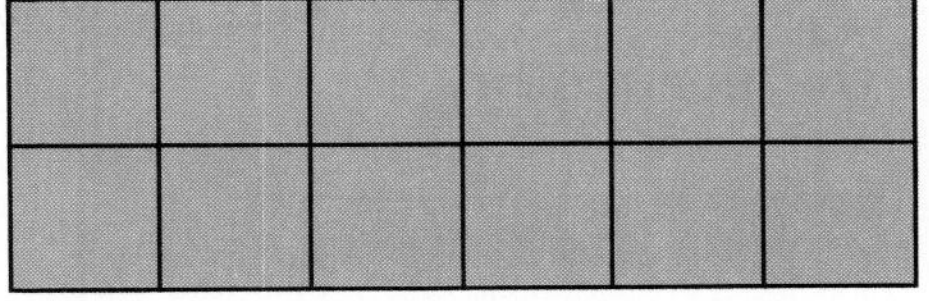

9. Find the volume.

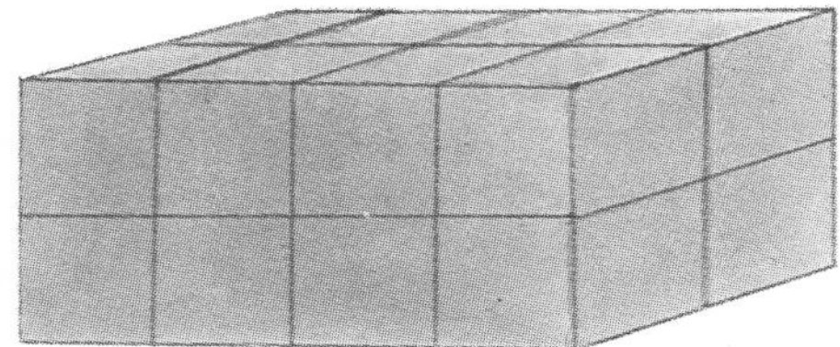

10. Does the bathtub hold more than or less than a liter?

11. Choose the better estimate.

A 12 g **B** 12 kg

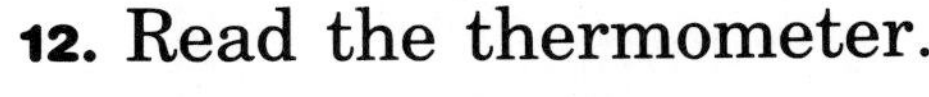

12. Read the thermometer.

Solve.

13. Gym class starts at 2:30. It lasts 45 minutes. What time is gym class over?

ANOTHER LOOK

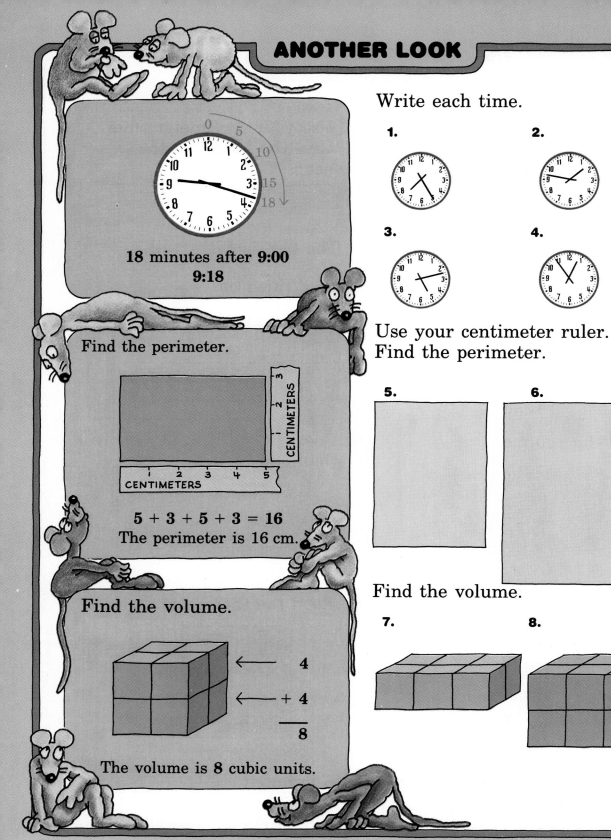

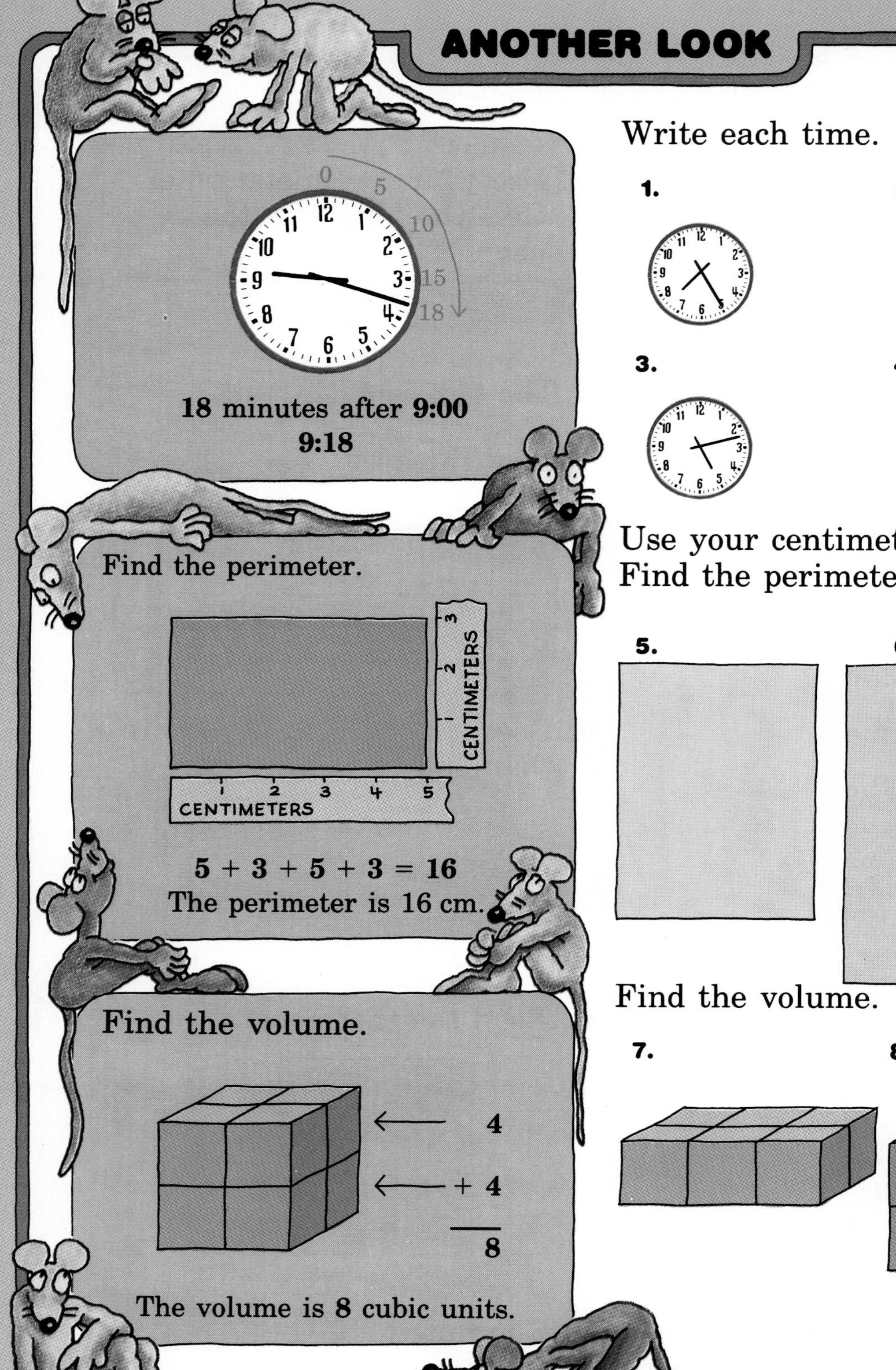

Write each time.

1.

2.

3.

4.

Use your centimeter ruler.
Find the perimeter.

5.

6.

Find the volume.

7.

8.

ENRICHMENT

Estimation in Measurement

1. If this length is 8 units, estimate this length.

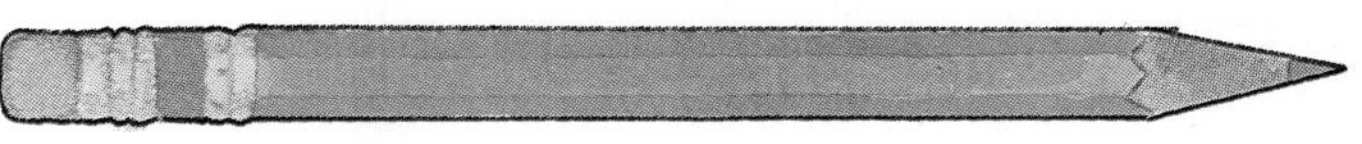

8 units

2. If this area is 6 square units, estimate this area.

6 square units

? square units

3. If this volume is 2 cubic units, estimate this volume.

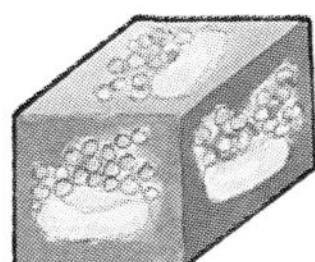

2 cubic units

? cubic units

4. If this perimeter is 20 units, estimate this perimeter.

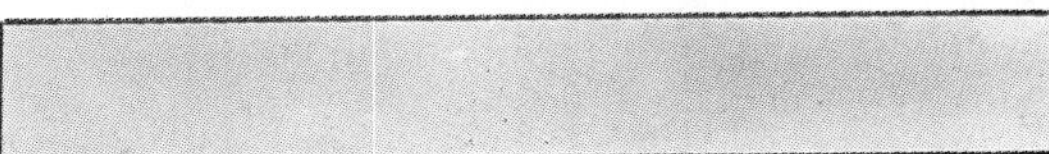

20 units

? units

CUMULATIVE REVIEW

Give the letter for the correct answer.

1. $9 + 9$
   - A 0
   - B 18
   - C 10
   - D not given

2. $6 + 7$
   - A 1
   - B 15
   - C 13
   - D not given

3. $8 + 5$
   - A 3
   - B 13
   - C 12
   - D not given

4. $10 + 0$
   - A 0
   - B 1
   - C 10
   - D not given

5. $3 + 8$
   - A 12
   - B 10
   - C 5
   - D not given

6. $6 + 8$
   - A 16
   - B 2
   - C 14
   - D not given

7. $42 + 86$
   - A 128
   - B 148
   - C 138
   - D not given

8. $276 + 54$
   - A 220
   - B 320
   - C 330
   - D not given

9. $529 + 683$
   - A 1,212
   - B 1,202
   - C 1,102
   - D not given

10. 356 + 825
    - A 1,171
    - B 1,181
    - C 1,281
    - D not given

11. \$9.86 + \$6.02
    - A \$16.88
    - B \$15.16
    - C \$15.88
    - D not given

12. \$9.53 + \$6.78
    - A \$16.31
    - B \$15.23
    - C \$15.21
    - D not given

13. Marisa read 16 pages of a book. Then she read 19 more pages. How many pages did she read altogether?
    - A 25
    - B 36
    - C 35
    - D not given

14. Alex spent \$7.98 for a gift. He spent \$0.75 for a card. How much did he spend?
    - A \$8.63
    - B \$8.73
    - C \$7.73
    - D not given

MULTIPLICATION FACTS

6

Tom's dentist is Dr. Verne. He let Tom ride up and down in the dental chair. Then he cleaned Tom's teeth. He checked Tom's teeth for cavities. Dr. Verne even took X-rays of Tom's mouth. The X-rays looked like a picture of his teeth. Tom learned that his front teeth are called incisors. They are used to cut food. Tom has 4 incisors on top and 4 incisors on the bottom. His pointed teeth are called canines. The canines are good for tearing. The back teeth are called molars. They grind the food.

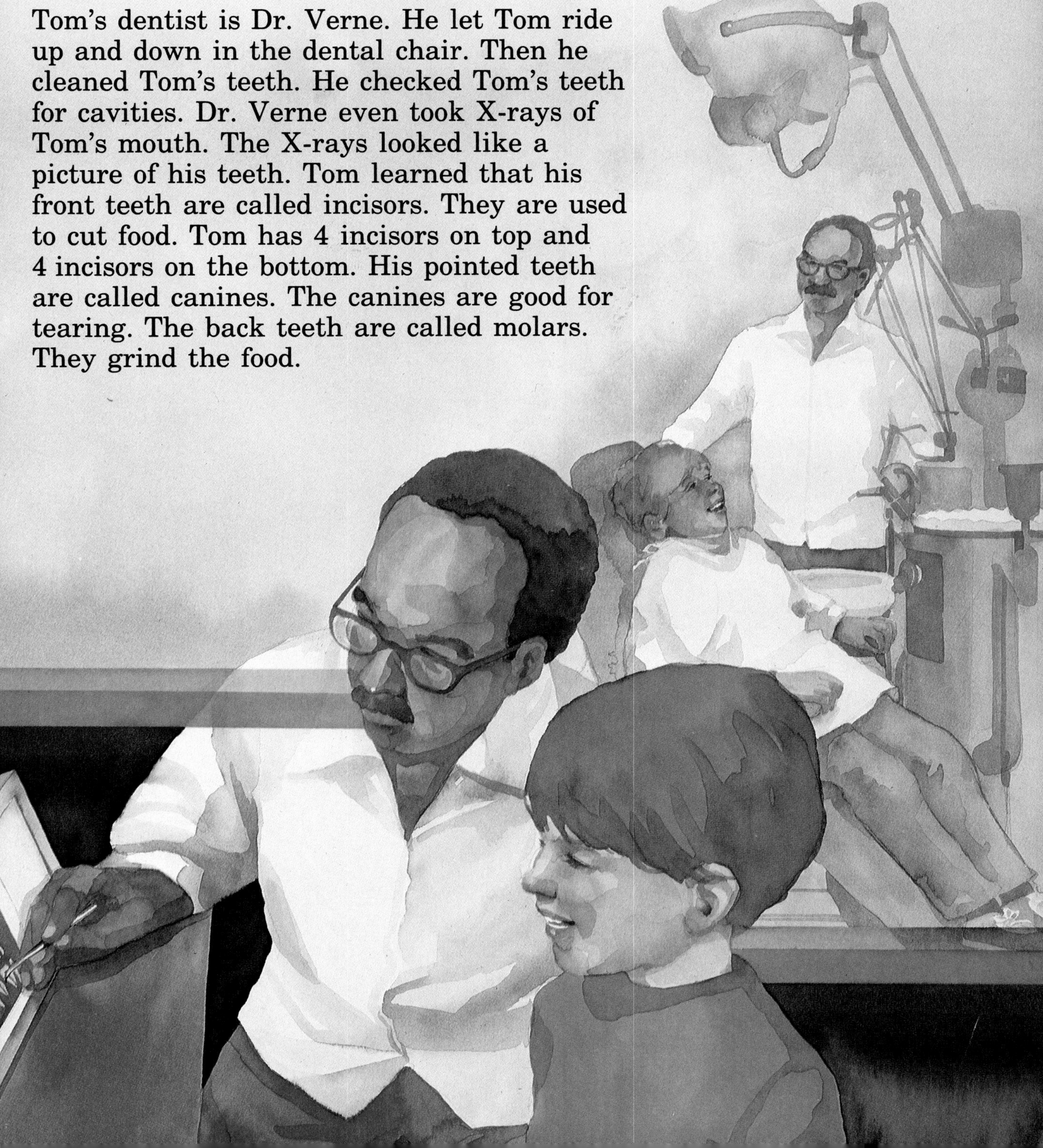

Addition and Multiplication

How many tents are there?

You can find out by adding.

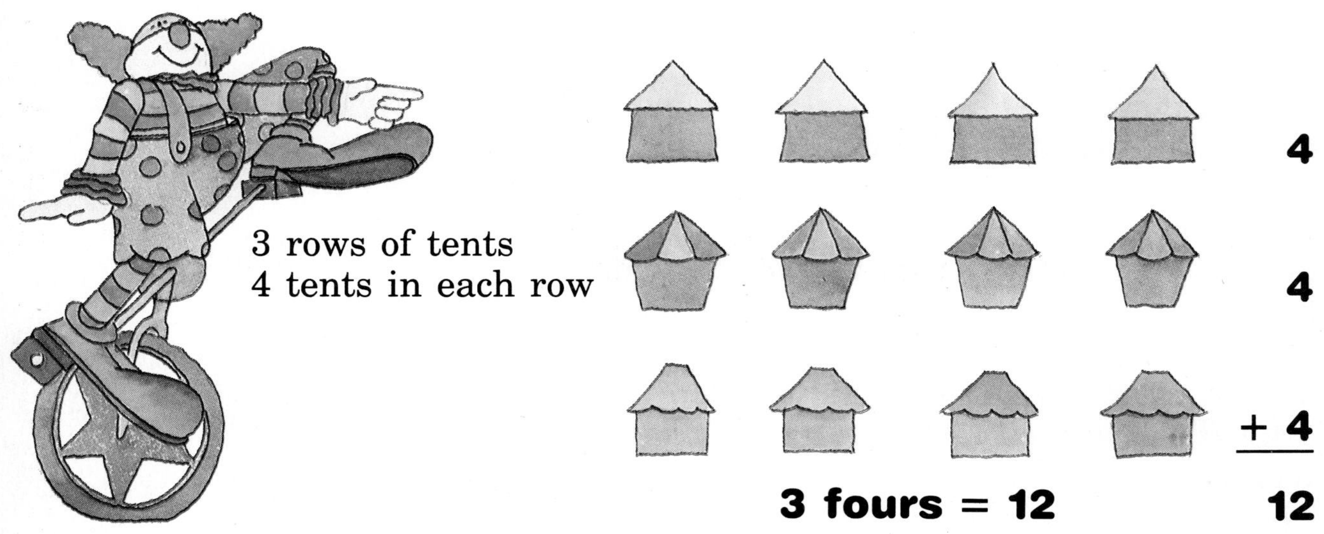

3 rows of tents
4 tents in each row

$$\begin{array}{r} 4 \\ 4 \\ +\ 4 \\ \hline 12 \end{array}$$

3 fours = 12

Warm Up How many are there?

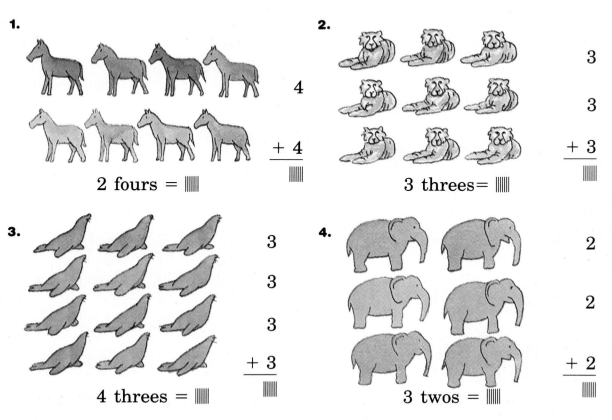

1.

$$\begin{array}{r} 4 \\ +\ 4 \\ \hline \text{\_\_\_\_} \end{array}$$

2 fours = ____

2.

$$\begin{array}{r} 3 \\ 3 \\ +\ 3 \\ \hline \text{\_\_\_\_} \end{array}$$

3 threes = ____

3.

$$\begin{array}{r} 3 \\ 3 \\ 3 \\ +\ 3 \\ \hline \text{\_\_\_\_} \end{array}$$

4 threes = ____

4.

$$\begin{array}{r} 2 \\ 2 \\ +\ 2 \\ \hline \text{\_\_\_\_} \end{array}$$

3 twos = ____

Practice How many are there?

1. 

$$\begin{array}{r} 2 \\ +\ 2 \\ \hline ▥ \end{array}$$

2 twos = ▥

2.

$$\begin{array}{r} 5 \\ 5 \\ +\ 5 \\ \hline ▥ \end{array}$$

3 fives = ▥

3. 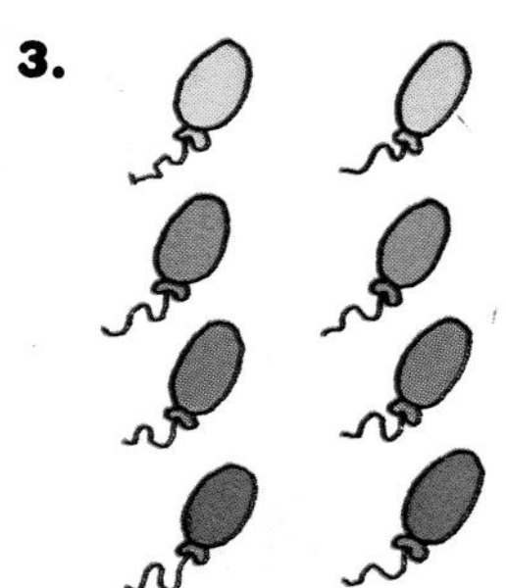

$$\begin{array}{r} 2 \\ 2 \\ 2 \\ +\ 2 \\ \hline ▥ \end{array}$$

4 twos = ▥

4.

$$\begin{array}{r} 3 \\ +\ 3 \\ \hline ▥ \end{array}$$

2 threes = ▥

5.

$$\begin{array}{r} 5 \\ +\ 5 \\ \hline ▥ \end{array}$$

2 fives = ▥

6.

$$\begin{array}{r} 4 \\ 4 \\ 4 \\ +\ 4 \\ \hline ▥ \end{array}$$

4 fours = ▥

How many cents are there?

7.  

2 nickels equal ▥¢

8.  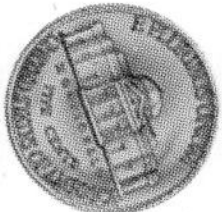 

3 nickels equal ▥¢

9.  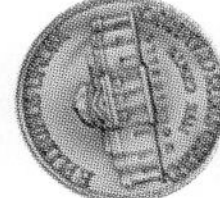  

4 nickels equal ▥¢

THINK

Patterns

Give the next 3 numbers.

1. 2, 4, 6, 8, ▥, ▥, ▥
2. 3, 6, 9, 12, ▥, ▥, ▥
3. 8, 12, 16, 20, ▥, ▥, ▥
4. 15, 20, 25, 30, ▥, ▥, ▥

Understanding Multiplication

Heather has 3 pots of flowers. There are 2 flowers in each pot. How many flowers does Heather have?

Dru has 2 pots of flowers. There are 3 flowers in each pot. How many flowers does Dru have?

The pots have the same number of flowers. You can **multiply** to find how many.

3 twos = 6
3 × 2 = 6

$$\begin{array}{r} 2 \\ \times\ 3 \\ \hline 6 \end{array}$$

Read:
"Three times two equals six."

Heather has 6 flowers.

2 threes = 6
2 × 3 = 6

$$\begin{array}{r} 3 \\ \times\ 2 \\ \hline 6 \end{array}$$

Read:
"Two times three equals six."

Dru has 6 flowers.

Warm Up Multiply.

1. 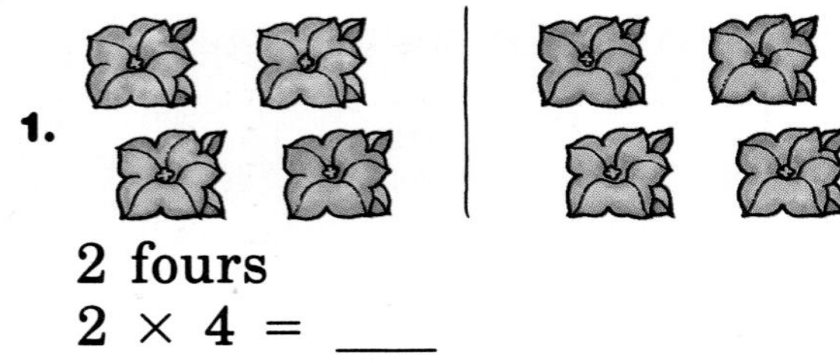

2 fours
2 × 4 = ____

2. 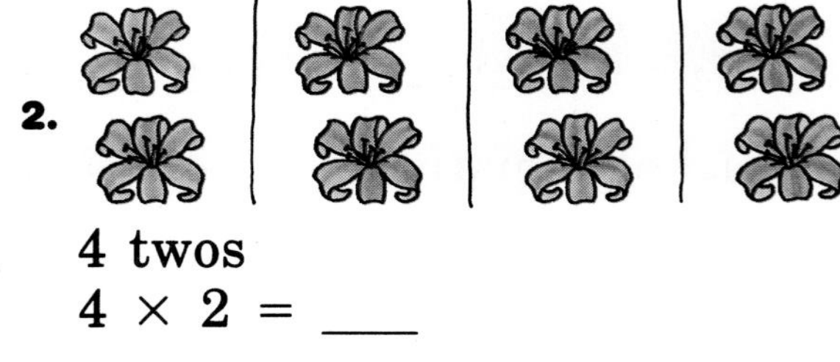

4 twos
4 × 2 = ____

3. 

3 fours

$$\begin{array}{r} 4 \\ \times\ 3 \\ \hline \end{array}$$

4. 

4 threes

$$\begin{array}{r} 3 \\ \times\ 4 \\ \hline \end{array}$$

Practice Multiply.

1. $2 \times 5 =$ ____

2. $5 \times 2 =$ ____

3. $2 \times 3 =$ ____

4. $3 \times 2 =$ ____

5. $\begin{array}{r} 2 \\ \times 4 \\ \hline \end{array}$

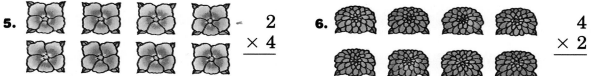

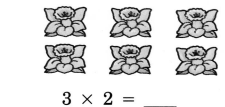

6. $\begin{array}{r} 4 \\ \times 2 \\ \hline \end{array}$

7. $\begin{array}{r} 3 \\ \times 3 \\ \hline \end{array}$

8. $\begin{array}{r} 2 \\ \times 2 \\ \hline \end{array}$

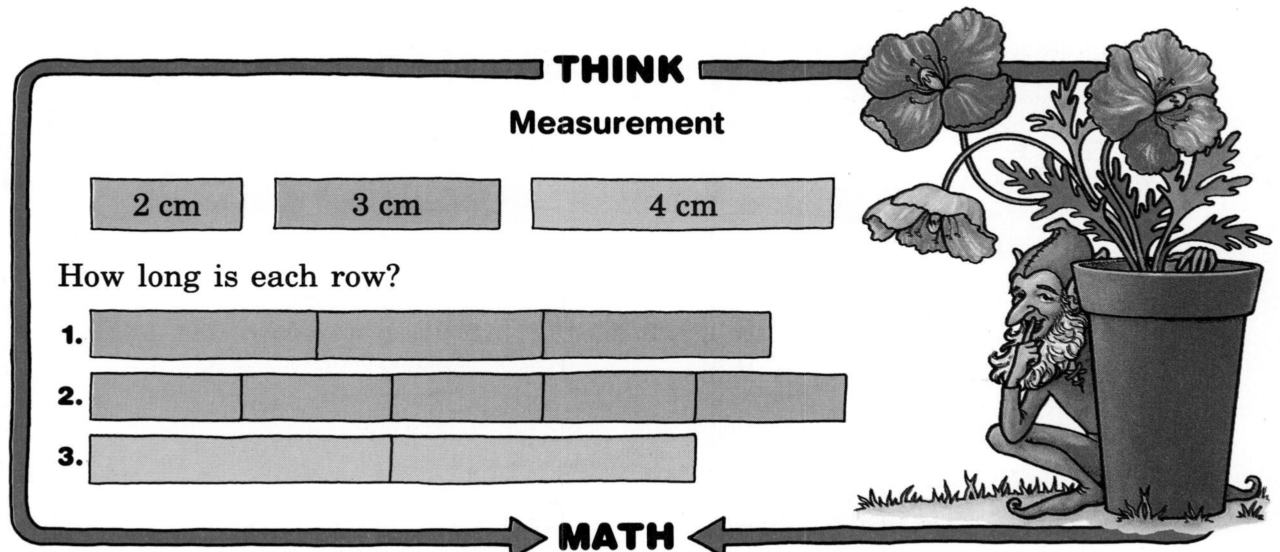

THINK
Measurement
2 cm
3 cm
4 cm
How long is each row?
1.
2.
3.
MATH

2 as a Factor

How many cans of juice are there?

$$\begin{array}{r} 3 \leftarrow \text{Factor} \\ \times\ 2 \leftarrow \text{Factor} \\ \hline 6 \leftarrow \text{Product} \end{array}$$

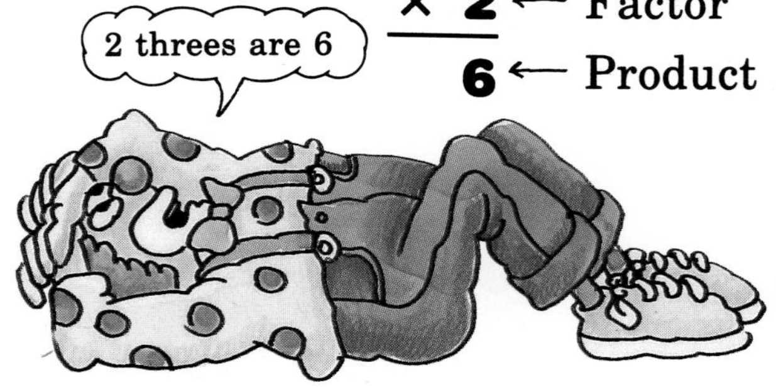

$2 \times 3 = 6$

Factor, Factor, Product

There are 6 cans of juice.

Thinking about the addition doubles may help you find products when 2 is a factor.

Find the products.

1. $2 \times 2 =$ ____
   2 twos
2. $2 \times 3 =$ ____
   2 threes
3. $2 \times 4 =$ ____
   2 fours
4. $2 \times 5 =$ ____
   2 fives

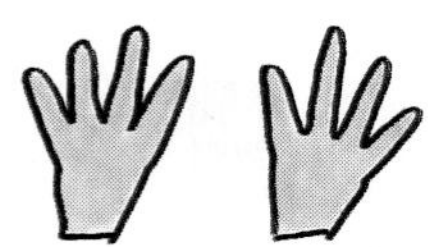

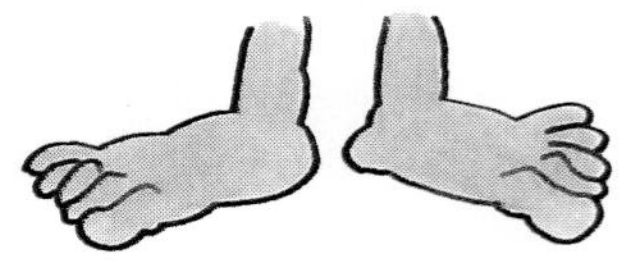

5. $2 \times 6 =$ ____
   2 sixes
6. $2 \times 7 =$ ____
   2 sevens
7. $2 \times 8 =$ ____
   2 eights
8. $2 \times 9 =$ ____
   2 nines

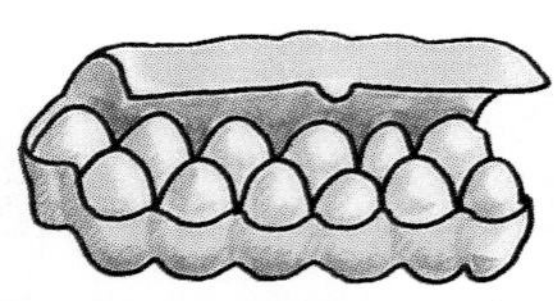

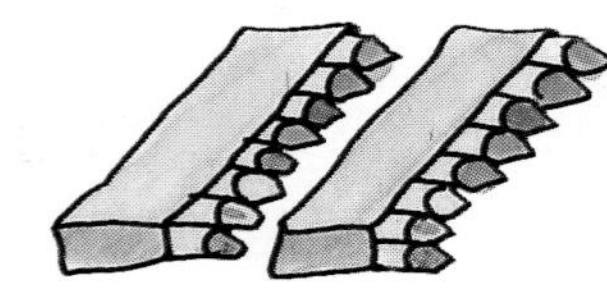

Warm Up Give each product aloud.

9. 8×2
10. 4×2
11. 6×2
12. 9×2
13. 3×2
14. 5×2
15. 7×2
16. 1×2
17. 6×2
18. 2×2
19. 3×2
20. 9×2
21. 8×2
22. 5×2

Practice Multiply.

THINK
2×7

1. 2×7 2. 7×2 3. 2×5 4. 5×2

5. 2×9 6. 9×2 7. 2×4 8. 4×2

9. 4×2 10. 2×7 11. 2×2 12. 8×2 13. 3×2 14. 2×5 15. 9×2

16. 2×8 17. 6×2 18. 7×2 19. 2×5 20. 2×2 21. 2×9 22. 7×2

23. 2×2 24. 2×6 25. 4×2 26. 5×2 27. 2×7 28. 8×2 29. 2×3

Mixed Applications

Each box has 2 shoes. How many shoes are there?

30. 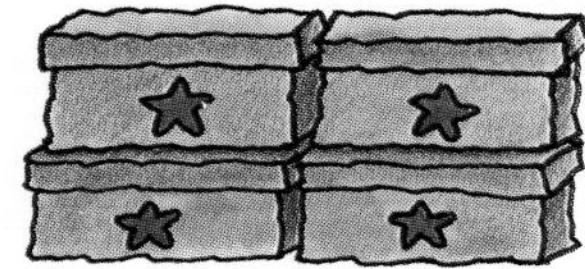

32. 

31. 

33. Make up a story problem that could be solved with this number sentence.

$5 \times 2 = 10$

SKILLKEEPER

Add or subtract.

1. $56 - 35$ 2. $26 + 73$ 3. $38 + 59$ 4. $354 - 108$

5. $349 + 685$ 6. $806 - 687$ 7. $413 + 377$ 8. $361 - 220$

3 as a Factor

How many tennis balls are there?

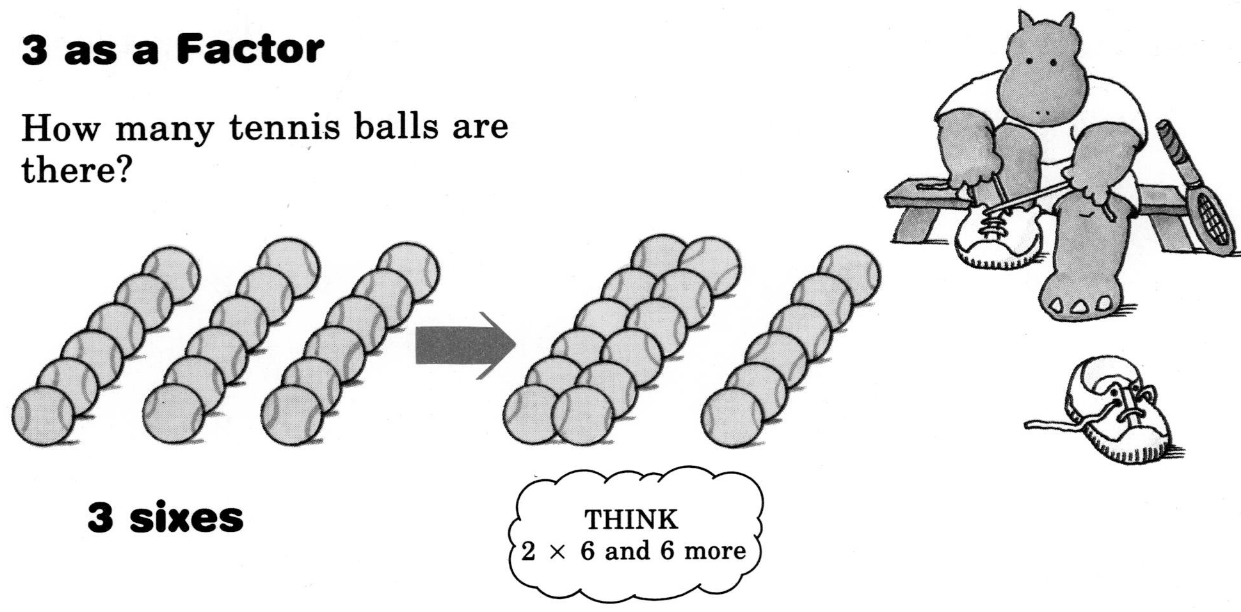

3 × 6 = 18

There are 18 tennis balls in all.

Find the products.

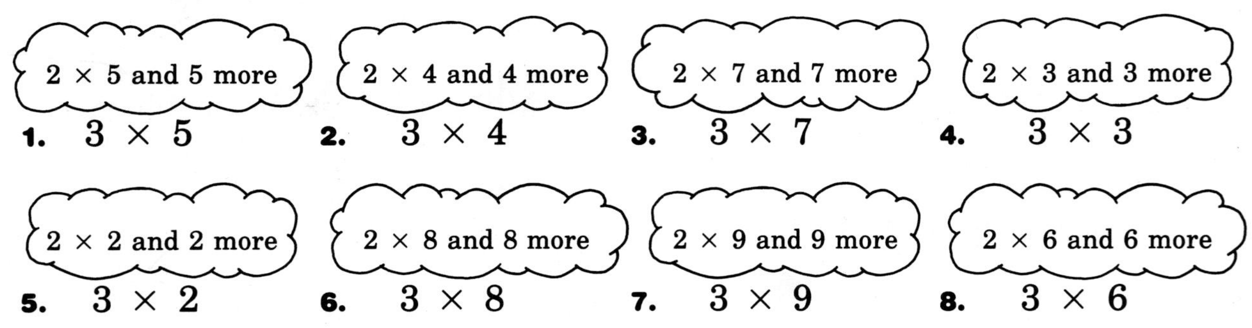

2 × 5 and 5 more
1. 3 × 5
2 × 4 and 4 more
2. 3 × 4
2 × 7 and 7 more
3. 3 × 7
2 × 3 and 3 more
4. 3 × 3
2 × 2 and 2 more
5. 3 × 2
2 × 8 and 8 more
6. 3 × 8
2 × 9 and 9 more
7. 3 × 9
2 × 6 and 6 more
8. 3 × 6

Warm Up Give each product aloud.

9. 5×3
10. 6×3
11. 8×3
12. 3×3
13. 9×3
14. 4×3
15. 7×3
16. 2×3
17. 1×3
18. 4×3
19. 9×3
20. 6×3
21. 8×3
22. 5×3

Practice Multiply.

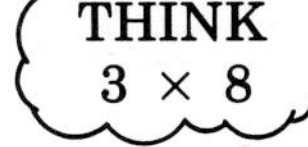

1. 3×5
2. 5×3
3. 3×8
4. 8×3
5. 3×7
6. 7×3
7. 3×6
8. 6×3

9. 4×3
10. 3×9
11. 2×3
12. 8×3
13. 3×6
14. 3×7
15. 5×3

16. 3×3
17. 6×3
18. 9×3
19. 4×3
20. 3×2
21. 5×3
22. 3×9

23. 8×3
24. 3×4
25. 2×3
26. 3×2
27. 3×4
28. 8×3
29. 3×6

Each can has 3 tennis balls.
How many tennis balls are there?

30.

31.

32.

THINK

Shape Perception

Draw a figure like the one below. Color your map using just four colors. You must have different colors on each side of a line.

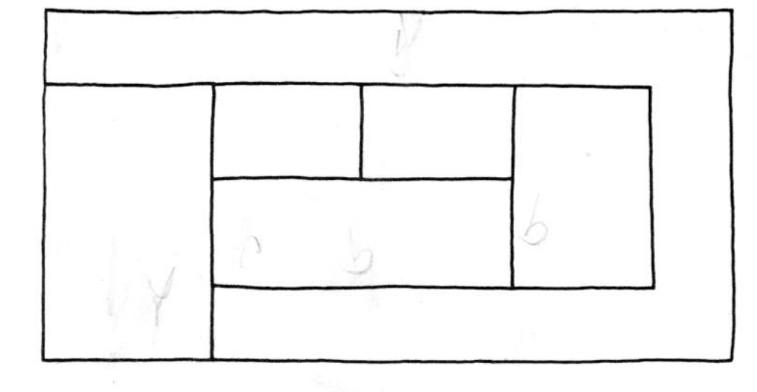

MATH

More Practice, page 392, Set B

PROBLEM SOLVING
Choose the Operations

Now you have a new operation to think about when you make your **plan**.

Choose the operation and solve.

1. Mandy bought 4 boxes of golf balls. Each box had 3 golf balls. How many golf balls did Mandy buy?

2. There were 27 children who played softball in the morning. 35 played in the afternoon. How many children played that day?

3. Justin scored 23 points. Tod scored 16 points. How many more points did Justin score than Tod?

4. There were 45 children who played soccer. 18 of them left the game early. How many were still playing?

5. Becky scored 7 field goals in basketball. Each one was 2 points. How many points did Becky score?

6. Jim's team scored 39 points the first half and 27 points the second half. How many points did they score in all?

7. A field goal in football is 3 points. Gretchen scored 8 field goals. How many points did she score?

8. ***Strategy Practice*** Yolanda and Phil are pitchers. Barb and Luis are catchers. How many different pitcher-catcher pairs can they make? Hint: Make a list.

Practice the Facts

Give each product aloud.

1. 2 × 4 **2.** 7 × 3 **3.** 3 × 5 **4.** 6 × 2

5. 4 × 3 **6.** 2 × 8 **7.** 2 × 2 **8.** 2 × 3

9. 2 × 7 **10.** 3 × 9 **11.** 3 × 8 **12.** 2 × 5

13. 3 × 3 **14.** 3 × 2 **15.** 2 × 9 **16.** 6 × 3

Write each product.

17. 2 × 4 **18.** 8 × 3 **19.** 3 × 4 **20.** 9 × 2 **21.** 3 × 6 **22.** 9 × 3 **23.** 2 × 5

24. 6 × 2 **25.** 3 × 2 **26.** 8 × 3 **27.** 2 × 2 **28.** 6 × 3 **29.** 3 × 7 **30.** 7 × 2

Give the missing numbers.

	× 2	
	8	16
	6	12
31.	4	▥
32.	9	▥
33.	3	▥
34.	5	▥
35.	7	▥

	× 3	
	5	15
	9	27
36.	3	▥
37.	6	▥
38.	7	▥
39.	4	▥
40.	8	▥

THINK MATH

Predictions

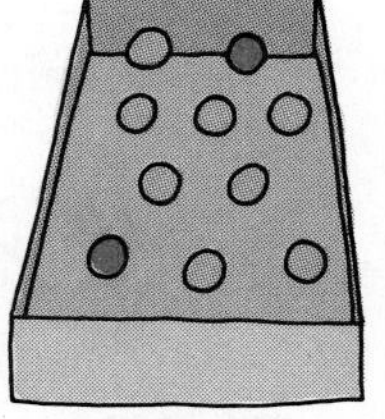

Pretend you closed your eyes and took a marble. Would it be red or blue? Now pretend you put it back. If you did this 50 times, would you get more red or blue marbles? How many blue marbles do you think you might get?

4 as a Factor

How many days are there in 4 weeks?

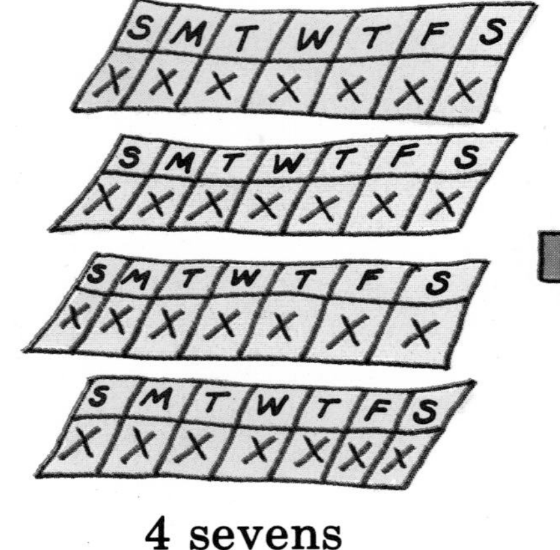

4 sevens

2 × 7 plus 2 × 7

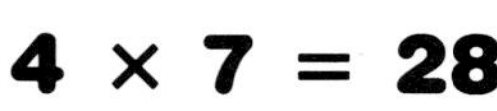

There are 28 days in 4 weeks.

Find the products.

2 × 3 plus 2 × 3

2 × 8 plus 2 × 8

1. 4 × 6 **2.** 4 × 3 **3.** 4 × 8

2 × 4 plus 2 × 4

4. 4 × 5 **5.** 4 × 9 **6.** 4 × 4

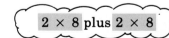

Warm Up Give each product aloud.

7. $\begin{array}{r} 6 \\ \times 4 \\ \hline \end{array}$ **8.** $\begin{array}{r} 8 \\ \times 4 \\ \hline \end{array}$ **9.** $\begin{array}{r} 4 \\ \times 4 \\ \hline \end{array}$ **10.** $\begin{array}{r} 7 \\ \times 4 \\ \hline \end{array}$ **11.** $\begin{array}{r} 3 \\ \times 4 \\ \hline \end{array}$ **12.** $\begin{array}{r} 9 \\ \times 4 \\ \hline \end{array}$ **13.** $\begin{array}{r} 5 \\ \times 4 \\ \hline \end{array}$

14. $\begin{array}{r} 2 \\ \times 4 \\ \hline \end{array}$ **15.** $\begin{array}{r} 7 \\ \times 4 \\ \hline \end{array}$ **16.** $\begin{array}{r} 5 \\ \times 4 \\ \hline \end{array}$ **17.** $\begin{array}{r} 6 \\ \times 4 \\ \hline \end{array}$ **18.** $\begin{array}{r} 8 \\ \times 4 \\ \hline \end{array}$ **19.** $\begin{array}{r} 4 \\ \times 4 \\ \hline \end{array}$ **20.** $\begin{array}{r} 9 \\ \times 4 \\ \hline \end{array}$

Practice Multiply.

THINK
4 × 8

1. 4×6
2. 6×4
3. 4×8
4. 8×4
5. 4×7
6. 7×4
7. 4×5
8. 5×4
9. $\begin{array}{r} 4 \\ \times 5 \\ \hline \end{array}$
10. $\begin{array}{r} 8 \\ \times 4 \\ \hline \end{array}$
11. $\begin{array}{r} 7 \\ \times 3 \\ \hline \end{array}$
12. $\begin{array}{r} 4 \\ \times 4 \\ \hline \end{array}$
13. $\begin{array}{r} 2 \\ \times 9 \\ \hline \end{array}$
14. $\begin{array}{r} 4 \\ \times 3 \\ \hline \end{array}$
15. $\begin{array}{r} 9 \\ \times 4 \\ \hline \end{array}$
16. $\begin{array}{r} 7 \\ \times 4 \\ \hline \end{array}$
17. $\begin{array}{r} 4 \\ \times 2 \\ \hline \end{array}$
18. $\begin{array}{r} 3 \\ \times 6 \\ \hline \end{array}$
19. $\begin{array}{r} 4 \\ \times 9 \\ \hline \end{array}$
20. $\begin{array}{r} 6 \\ \times 4 \\ \hline \end{array}$
21. $\begin{array}{r} 8 \\ \times 2 \\ \hline \end{array}$
22. $\begin{array}{r} 4 \\ \times 3 \\ \hline \end{array}$
23. $\begin{array}{r} 4 \\ \times 2 \\ \hline \end{array}$
24. $\begin{array}{r} 5 \\ \times 4 \\ \hline \end{array}$
25. $\begin{array}{r} 8 \\ \times 3 \\ \hline \end{array}$
26. $\begin{array}{r} 7 \\ \times 4 \\ \hline \end{array}$
27. $\begin{array}{r} 5 \\ \times 2 \\ \hline \end{array}$
28. $\begin{array}{r} 5 \\ \times 3 \\ \hline \end{array}$
29. $\begin{array}{r} 3 \\ \times 2 \\ \hline \end{array}$

Mixed Applications

30. Each plate needs 4 meatballs. How many meatballs are needed?

31. There were 7 small tables and 4 large tables in a restaurant. How many tables were there altogether?

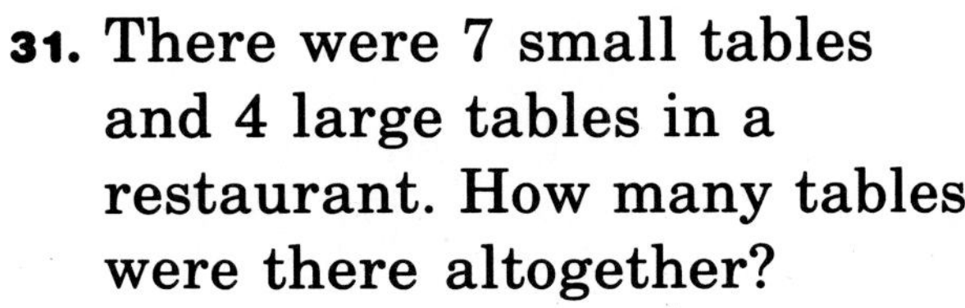

32. This problem has missing data. Make up the needed data. Then solve the problem.

    Only 3 alligators can sit at the round tables in a particular restaurant. How many alligators can sit at all of the round tables in this restaurant?

THINK

Logical Reasoning

Solve these puzzle problems.

1. My digits are 7, 2, and 5. I'm between 500 and 550. Who am I?
2. My digits are 6, 0, and 3. I'm smaller than 350. Who am I?

MATH

More Practice, page 392, Set C

5 as a Factor—Counting by Fives

How many letters are in these
6 words?

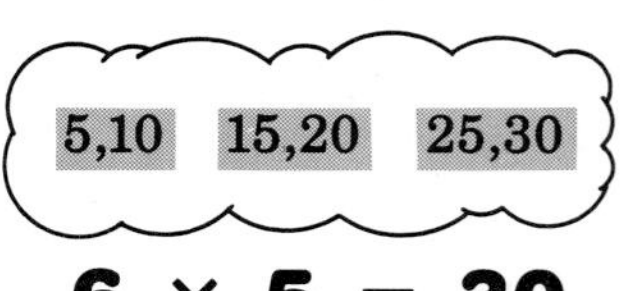

6 × 5 = 30

6 fives

There are 30 letters in the 6 words.

Find the products.

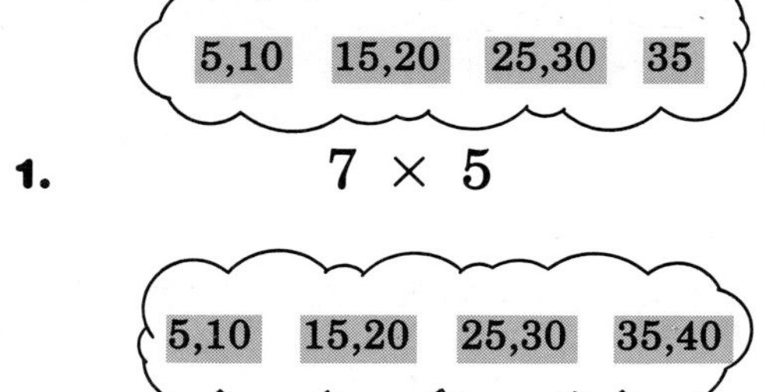

5,10 15,20 25,30 35
5,10 15,20 25,30 35,40

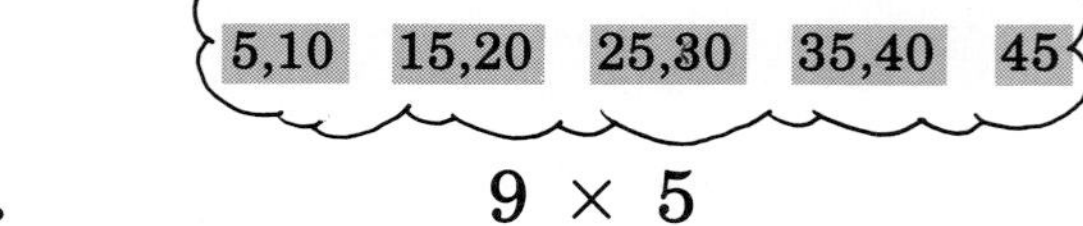

1. 7 × 5

2. 9 × 5

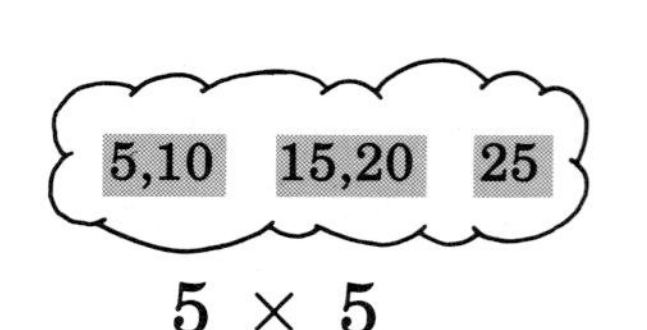

3. 8 × 5

4. 5 × 5

Warm Up Give each product aloud.

5. 5 × 8 **6.** 5 × 4 **7.** 5 × 7 **8.** 5 × 6 **9.** 5 × 5 **10.** 5 × 9 **11.** 5 × 3

12. 5 × 5 **13.** 5 × 9 **14.** 5 × 8 **15.** 5 × 3 **16.** 5 × 2 **17.** 5 × 6 **18.** 5 × 4

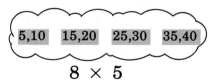

Practice Multiply.

1. 7×5
2. 5×7
3. 8×5
4. 5×8
5. 6×5
6. 5×6
7. 9×5
8. 5×9

9. 5×4
10. 3×6
11. 9×5
12. 5×5
13. 3×9
14. 5×6
15. 2×8
16. 7×4
17. 8×5
18. 9×4
19. 5×2
20. 7×5
21. 6×2
22. 5×3
23. 3×5
24. 3×8
25. 5×7
26. 9×2
27. 4×4
28. 5×9
29. 6×5

Mixed Applications

Here are some number names that have five letters.

30. How many letters are there altogether in the number names first, fifth, and ninth?

31. Count the letters in your last name. Now count the letters in the word "five." Are there more or less letters in your name? How many?

SKILLKEEPER

Give the value of each set of coins.

1. 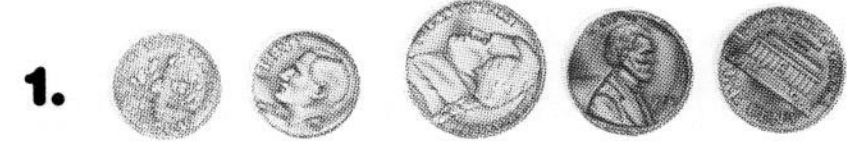
2. 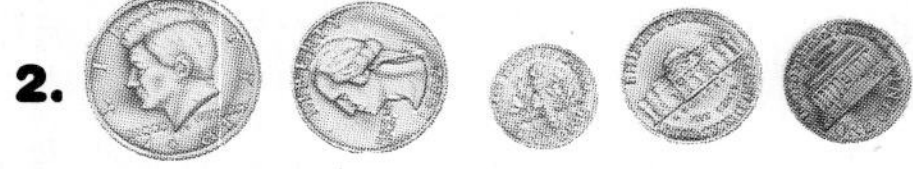
3. 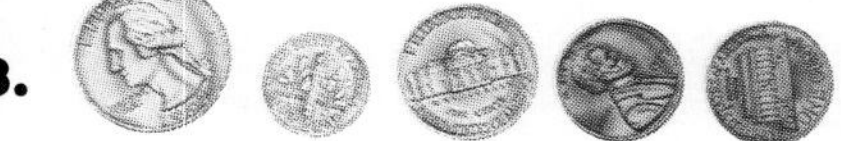
4. 

More Practice, page 393, Set A

PROBLEM SOLVING
Using Data from an Advertisement

Use the advertisement to solve the following problems.

1. How much are E and D?
2. How much are 4 F?
3. How much more is D than B?
4. How much are 6 E?
5. How much are C, D, and E?
6. How much are 6 A?
7. How much more is A than E?
8. How much are 7 F?

★ 9. How much is one of each?

★ 10. How much are 3 E and 4 F?

11. **DATA HUNT** Look at some advertisements. Find something that costs 2, 3, 4, or 5 dollars. How much would it cost to get one for each member of your family?

12. ***Strategy Practice*** Lucia had $10. She spent more than $5. She spent an odd number of dollars. The number is closer to 5 than to 10. How much did Lucia spend?

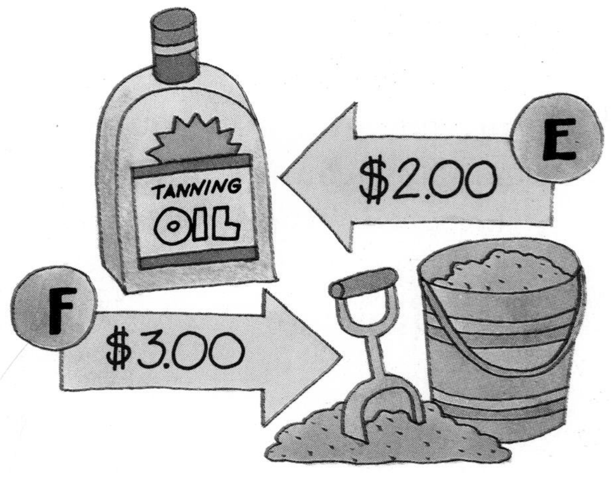

Practice the Facts

Multiply.

1. 3×5
2. 8×2
3. 4×4
4. 3×5
5. 2×6
6. 3×3
7. 9×4
8. 5×2
9. 4×7
10. 2×2
11. 5×5
12. 7×2
13. 5×8
14. 8×3
15. 7×5
16. 2×9
17. 7×3
18. 2×5
19. 4×6
20. 5×6
21. 5×7

22. 4×5
23. 3×8
24. 4×3
25. 4×8
26. 2×7
27. 4×2
28. 9×5
29. 6×3

Give the missing numbers.

	× 3	
	6	18
	2	6
	4	12
30.	3	

	× 2	
	7	14
	5	10
31.	8	
32.	4	

	× 4	
	5	20
33.	7	
34.	9	
35.	8	

	× 3	
	6	18
36.	8	
37.	5	
38.	9	

	× 5	
39.	6	
40.	3	
41.	5	
42.	4	

★ 43.	×	
	4	12
	7	21
★ 44.	6	
★ 45.		6

0 and 1 as Factors

How many birds are there?

4 cages
1 bird in each cage
4 × 1 = 4

When 1 is a factor, the product is the other factor.

How many birds are there?

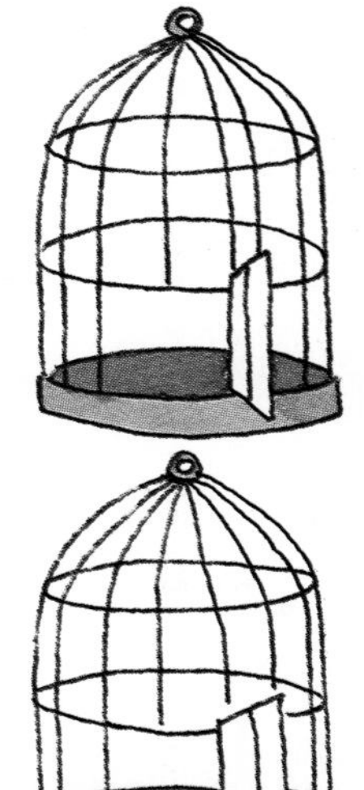

4 cages
0 birds in each cage
4 × 0 = 0

When 0 is a factor, the product is 0.

Warm Up Give each product aloud.

1. $3 \times 0 =$ ____ **2.** $8 \times 1 =$ ____ **3.** $6 \times 1 =$ ____ **4.** $9 \times 0 =$ ____

5. $6 \times 1 =$ ____ **6.** $7 \times 0 =$ ____ **7.** $1 \times 1 =$ ____ **8.** $4 \times 0 =$ ____

9. $5 \times 0 =$ ____ **10.** $9 \times 1 =$ ____ **11.** $0 \times 0 =$ ____ **12.** $4 \times 1 =$ ____

13. 0×3 **14.** 1×7 **15.** 0×6 **16.** 0×4 **17.** 1×9 **18.** 1×2 **19.** 0×8

20. 1×3 **21.** 0×1 **22.** 1×0 **23.** 1×4 **24.** 0×2 **25.** 0×5 **26.** 1×5

More Practice, page 393, Set B

Practice the Facts

Multiply.

1. 4×3	**2.** 2×7	**3.** 5×7	**4.** 0×5	**5.** 3×5	**6.** 4×6	**7.** 1×5
8. 5×8	**9.** 0×6	**10.** 2×2	**11.** 4×4	**12.** 1×3	**13.** 3×8	**14.** 2×8
15. 3×6	**16.** 1×6	**17.** 2×4	**18.** 0×2	**19.** 3×3	**20.** 3×9	**21.** 4×8

22. 9×5 **23.** 4×3 **24.** 9×4 **25.** 6×5

26. 4×0 **27.** 7×3 **28.** 4×1 **29.** 5×5

Give the missing numbers.

	× 5	
	5	25
	9	45
30.	7	|||||
31.	8	|||||
32.	6	|||||
33.	4	|||||
34.	3	|||||

	× 4	
	6	24
	3	12
35.	8	|||||
36.	9	|||||
37.	4	|||||
38.	5	|||||
39.	7	|||||

THINK

Number Puzzle

Make a copy of this figure. Put the numbers 4, 5, 6, 7, 8, 9, and 10 in the circles so that the sum along each line is 21. Use each number only once.

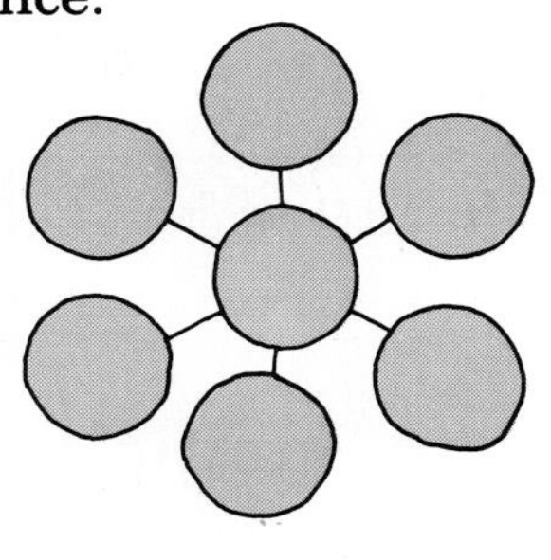

MATH

Multiples

A **multiple** of a number is the product of that number and another factor.
Copy and complete each set of multiples.

1. Multiples of 2

x	0	1	2	3	4	5	6	7	8	9	...
2	0	2	4	6	8	10					

2. Multiples of 3

x	0	1	2	3	4	5	6	7	8	9	...
3	0	3	6	9	12						

3. Multiples of 4

x	0	1	2	3	4	5	6	7	8	9	...
4	0	4	8	12							

4. Multiples of 5

x	0	1	2	3	4	5	6	7	8	9	...
5	0	5	10	15							

5. What set of multiples is the even numbers?

6. What set of multiples always ends in 0 or 5?

Practice Multiply.

1. $\begin{array}{r} 8 \\ \times 3 \\ \hline \end{array}$ 2. $\begin{array}{r} 2 \\ \times 9 \\ \hline \end{array}$ 3. $\begin{array}{r} 1 \\ \times 6 \\ \hline \end{array}$ 4. $\begin{array}{r} 4 \\ \times 8 \\ \hline \end{array}$ 5. $\begin{array}{r} 4 \\ \times 5 \\ \hline \end{array}$

6. $\begin{array}{r} 5 \\ \times 7 \\ \hline \end{array}$ 7. $\begin{array}{r} 5 \\ \times 5 \\ \hline \end{array}$ 8. $\begin{array}{r} 6 \\ \times 3 \\ \hline \end{array}$ 9. $\begin{array}{r} 5 \\ \times 2 \\ \hline \end{array}$ 10. $\begin{array}{r} 7 \\ \times 0 \\ \hline \end{array}$ 11. $\begin{array}{r} 3 \\ \times 4 \\ \hline \end{array}$ 12. $\begin{array}{r} 2 \\ \times 7 \\ \hline \end{array}$

13. $\begin{array}{r} 5 \\ \times 7 \\ \hline \end{array}$ 14. $\begin{array}{r} 3 \\ \times 3 \\ \hline \end{array}$ 15. $\begin{array}{r} 2 \\ \times 6 \\ \hline \end{array}$ 16. $\begin{array}{r} 5 \\ \times 9 \\ \hline \end{array}$ 17. $\begin{array}{r} 4 \\ \times 4 \\ \hline \end{array}$ 18. $\begin{array}{r} 5 \\ \times 8 \\ \hline \end{array}$ 19. $\begin{array}{r} 4 \\ \times 7 \\ \hline \end{array}$

20. 3×9 21. 1×9 22. 4×6 23. 5×6

24. 8×0 25. 8×2 26. 2×4 27. 7×3

28. Find the product of 6 and 3.
29. Find the product of 4 and 9.
30. Find the product of 5 and 6.
31. Find the product of 8 and 2.
32. Find the product of 2 and 4.
33. Find the product of 7 and 5.

Four children tossed number cubes. Multiply to get each child's score.

Eva Lee Paco Tara

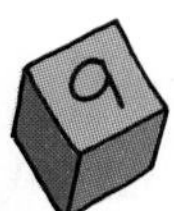

34. Who had the lowest score?
35. Who had the highest score?
36. Who scored 35?

THINK

Logical Reasoning

Find the product of the two numbers that are

1. in the red ring but not the blue ring.
2. not in the red ring.
3. in both the red and the blue rings.

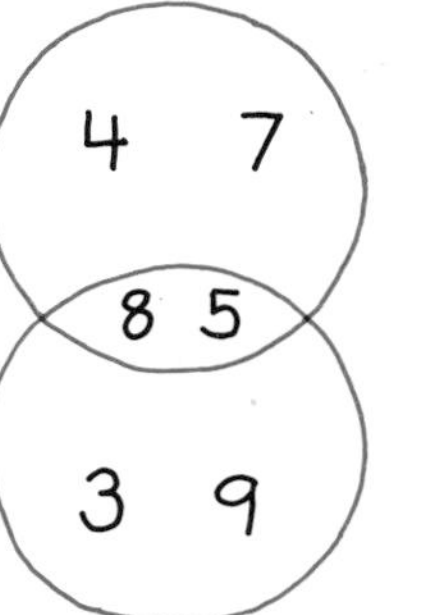

MATH

PROBLEM SOLVING ☆ Using the 5-Point Checklist

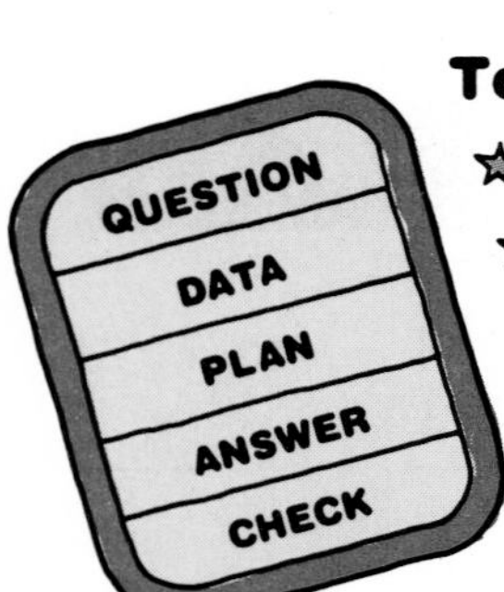

To solve a problem

☆ **1. Understand the Question**

☆ **2. Find the needed Data**

☆ **3. Plan what to do**

☆ **4. Find the Answer**

☆ **5. Check back**

Use the 5-Point Checklist to help you solve the following problem.

There are 6 rows of plants in a box. Each row has 5 plants. How many plants are in the box?

1. Understand the QUESTION
What is the total number of plants?

2. Find the needed DATA
6 rows, 5 plants each

3. PLAN what to do
The sets of plants are equal.
We can multiply.

4. Find the ANSWER
6 fives $6 \times 5 = 30$

5. CHECK back
Read the problem again. 30 plants seems about right.

Solve. Use the 5-Point Checklist.

1. There are 18 plants in a box and 24 in another. How many plants are in the two boxes?

2. There are 42 plants in the garden. 15 of them are cherry tomato plants. How many are not cherry tomatoes?

1. Donna picked 26 apples. She gave 9 to a friend. How many apples does she have left?

2. Ryan puts 5 drops of food on his plant 4 times each year. How many drops is this in one year?

3. Lisa's plant grew 27 cm in one year. It grew 19 cm during the next year. How much did her plant grow in the two years?

4. Casey planted 4 seeds of popcorn in each of 8 holes. How many seeds of popcorn did he plant?

5. Vida picked 42 lemons. Joyce picked 27. How many more lemons did Vida pick?

6. Dale's plants get 4 hours of sunlight each day. How many hours of sunlight do they get in 7 days?

7. Judi uses 8 liters of water to water her plants each week. How many liters of water does she use in 4 weeks?

8. James picked 27 plums and 36 peaches. How many pieces of fruit did he pick?

9. There are 27 rows of trees. Each row has 9 trees. How many trees are there?

10. ***Strategy Practice*** Jamie's plant is taller than Dale's. Nina's plant is shorter than Dale's. Jamie's plant is shorter than Brad's. Whose plant is tallest?

PROBLEM-SOLVING STRATEGY
Make a Table

A problem like this can sometimes be solved by using a table. A strategy that can help you is given below.

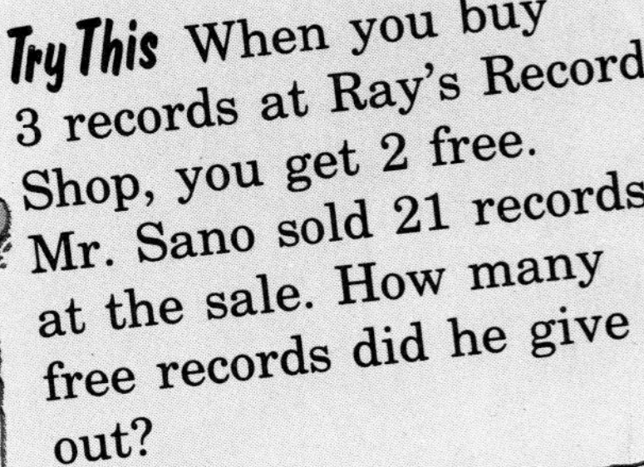

Try This When you buy 3 records at Ray's Record Shop, you get 2 free. Mr. Sano sold 21 records at the sale. How many free records did he give out?

Sell 3 more—3 + 3 = 6
Get 2 more—2 + 2 = 4

MAKE A TABLE

Number sold	3	6	9	12	15	18	21
Free records	2	4	6	8	10	12	14

When the number sold reaches 21, you will have the number of free records in your table.

Mr. Sano gave away 14 free records.

Copy and complete the tables to solve these problems.

1. Tod has the same number of pennies as nickels. He has 30 cents worth of nickels. How many pennies does he have?

Nickel value	5¢	10¢	15¢	
Penny value	1¢	2¢	3¢	

2. Lita sews 4 large buttons and 3 small buttons on each coat. When she has used 28 large buttons, how many small ones has she used?

Large buttons	4	8	12	
Small buttons	3	6	9	

CHAPTER REVIEW/TEST

Solve.

1. $5 \times 4 =$ ____ **2.** $7 \times 2 =$ ____

3. $6 \times 2 =$ ____ **4.** $6 \times 4 =$ ____ **5.** $4 \times 4 =$ ____ **6.** $4 \times 3 =$ ____

7. $3 \times 5 =$ ____ **8.** $7 \times 4 =$ ____ **9.** $3 \times 2 =$ ____ **10.** $5 \times 2 =$ ____

11. $9 \times 4 =$ ____ **12.** $9 \times 3 =$ ____ **13.** $5 \times 5 =$ ____ **14.** $8 \times 4 =$ ____

15. 4×7 **16.** 0×8 **17.** 5×2 **18.** 3×6 **19.** 1×9 **20.** 2×2 **21.** 3×8

22. 5×8 **23.** 3×3 **24.** 4×2 **25.** 0×6 **26.** 5×6 **27.** 2×0 **28.** 1×6

29. 7×1 **30.** 6×4 **31.** 0×5 **32.** 8×5 **33.** 5×4 **34.** 3×5 **35.** 9×4

36. Curtis put 5 drops of plant food on each of his plants. He has 6 plants. How many drops of food did he use?

37. Sara scored 42 points. Bill scored 27 points. How many more points did Sara score than Bill?

ANOTHER LOOK

0 and 1 as factors

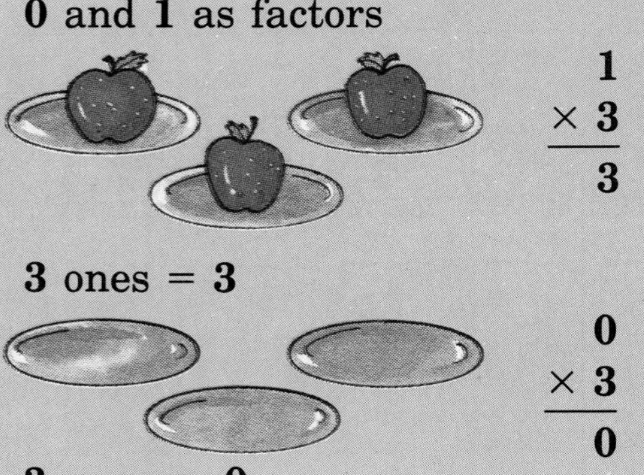

$$\begin{array}{r} 1 \\ \times\ 3 \\ \hline 3 \end{array}$$

3 ones = 3

$$\begin{array}{r} 0 \\ \times\ 3 \\ \hline 0 \end{array}$$

3 zeros = 0

2 and 3 as factors

$$\begin{array}{r} 2 \\ \times\ 4 \\ \hline 8 \end{array}$$

$$\begin{array}{r} 3 \\ \times\ 4 \\ \hline 12 \end{array}$$

4 and 5 as factors

$$\begin{array}{r} 4 \\ \times\ 4 \\ \hline 16 \end{array}$$

$$\begin{array}{r} 5 \\ \times\ 2 \\ \hline 10 \end{array}$$

Multiply.

1. 0×4
2. 1×6
3. 0×2
4. 1×8
5. 1×3
6. 0×7
7. 0×5
8. 1×9
9. 3×8
10. 2×6
11. 2×4
12. 3×6
13. 2×7
14. 3×2
15. 2×9
16. 3×5
17. 4×8
18. 5×9
19. 4×7
20. 5×5
21. 5×6
22. 4×4
23. 4×6
24. 5×2

ENRICHMENT

Finding Patterns

The examples below show the patterns in some number sequences.

1 , 7 , 13 , 19 , ? , ? , ? , . . .

Rule: Add 6 each time.

2 , 4 , 8 , 16 , ? , ? , ? , . . .

Rule: Double the last number.

1 + 2 2 + 3 3 + 5 5 + 8 . . .

1 , 2 , 3 , 5 , 8 , ? , ? , ? , . . .

Rule: Add the last two numbers.

Give the next three numbers in each sequence.

1. 5, 10, 15, 20, . . .

2. 12, 23, 34, 45, . . .

3. 3, 6, 12, 24, . . .

4. 50, 42, 34, 26, . . .

5. 3, 0, 6, 0, 9, 0, . . .

6. 1, 3, 2, 4, 3, 5, 4, 6, . . .

7. 3, 2, 1, 6, 5, 4, 9, 8, 7, . . .

8. 2, 10, 8, 16, 14, 22, . . .

9. 1, 3, 6, 10, 15, 21, . . .

10. 4, 3, 2, 8, 7, 6, 12, 11, 10, . . .

CUMULATIVE REVIEW

Give the letter for the correct answer.

1. 35 rounded to the nearest ten

A 30 **B** 50
C 40 **D** not given

2. 21 rounded to the nearest ten

A 30 **B** 20
C 25 **D** not given

3. 429 rounded to the nearest hundred

A 430 **B** 500
C 400 **D** not given

4. 575 rounded to the nearest hundred

A 600 **B** 500
C 1,000 **D** not given

5. 9 tens and 5 ones

A 95 **B** 905
C 59 **D** not given

6. 2 hundreds, 6 tens, 3 ones

A 623 **B** 263
C 236 **D** not given

7. $\begin{array}{r} 91 \\ -\ 75 \\ \hline \end{array}$

A 16 **B** 24
C 26 **D** not given

8. $\begin{array}{r} 843 \\ -\ 22 \\ \hline \end{array}$

A 21 **B** 811
C 821 **D** not given

9. $\begin{array}{r} \$7.25 \\ -\ 3.19 \\ \hline \end{array}$

A $4.14
B $4.06
C $3.96
D not given

10. $\begin{array}{r} \$6.00 \\ -\ 3.75 \\ \hline \end{array}$

A $2.25
B $3.75
C $3.25
D not given

11. 623 − 27

A 556
B 646
C 546
D not given

12. 702 − 344

A 358
B 442
C 368
D not given

13. Jordan's mother gave him $5.00 to spend at the fair. He spent $3.50. How much money did Jordan have left?

A $8.50 **B** $1.50
C $2.50 **D** not given

14. Melissa bought a plant for $3.20. She bought a pot for $6.65. How much did she spend for both?

A $3.45 **B** $9.45
C $9.85 **D** not given

MORE MULTIPLICATION FACTS 7

Juanita and her grandfather are going to the hot-air balloon festival. It is in Albuquerque, New Mexico. Juanita's grandfather owns a hot-air balloon that will hold 3 people in its basket. At the festival hundreds of many-colored balloons will float up in the air together. Someday Juanita wants to get a private balloon pilot's license. Juanita is 8 years old now. When she is 2 times this age she can be the pilot of her grandfather's balloon.

9 as a Factor

There were 10 carrots in each bunch. The rabbit took 1 carrot from each bunch. How many carrots are in the 6 bunches of nine?

60 − 6

6 × 10 = 60   **6 × 9 = 54**

6 tens   6 tens − 6

There are 54 carrots left.

Multiply.

THINK 4 tens − 4
1. 4 × 9 = ____

THINK 5 tens − 5
2. 5 × 9 = ____

THINK 7 tens − 7
3. 7 × 9 = ____

THINK 8 tens − 8
4. 8 × 9 = ____

THINK 9 tens − 9
5. 9 × 9 = ____

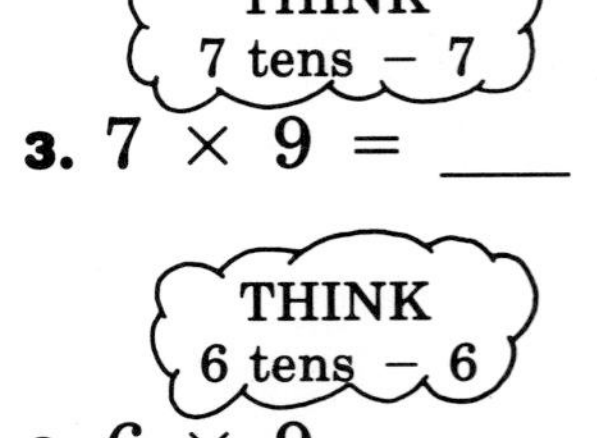

6. 6 × 9 = ____

Warm Up Read each number sentence aloud and give the product.

7. 4 × 9 = ____ **8.** 2 × 9 = ____ **9.** 3 × 9 = ____ **10.** 5 × 9 = ____

11. 8 × 9 = ____ **12.** 6 × 9 = ____ **13.** 9 × 9 = ____ **14.** 7 × 9 = ____

Give each product aloud.

15. 9 × 3 **16.** 9 × 5 **17.** 9 × 2 **18.** 9 × 9 **19.** 9 × 8 **20.** 9 × 6 **21.** 9 × 4

Practice Multiply.

1. 4×9 (THINK 4×9)
2. 9×4
3. 7×9 (THINK 7×9)
4. 9×7
5. 5×9
6. 9×5
7. 8×9
8. 9×8

9. 5×9
10. 9×6
11. 3×9
12. 7×4
13. 8×9
14. 3×6
15. 9×7

16. 4×9
17. 5×8
18. 9×1
19. 9×5
20. 7×5
21. 9×9
22. 9×2

23. 6×9
24. 4×8
25. 9×4
26. 3×7
27. 7×9
28. 9×3
29. 9×0

Mixed Applications

30. Each bunch has 9 carrots. How many carrots are there?

31. One box has 75 bunches of carrots. Another has 68 bunches. How many bunches are in the two boxes?

32. In Exercise 31, how many more bunches did one box have than the other?

THINK → MATH

A Strategy Game

1. Each player writes the numbers 2 through 12.
2. In turn, each player tosses two cubes numbered 1 through 6.
3. Add the top numbers.
4. Cross out your sum or any numbers that add up to your sum.
5. Continue until you cannot cross out a number.
6. The player with the most crossed out numbers wins.

The Squares

How many tiles are on each table top?
Give the product to find out.

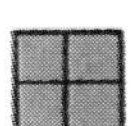
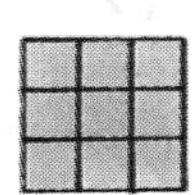
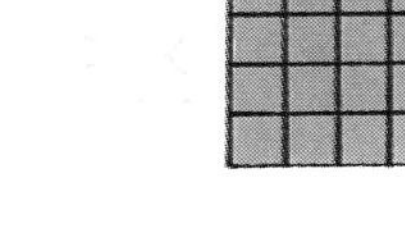
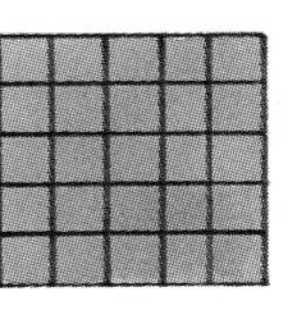
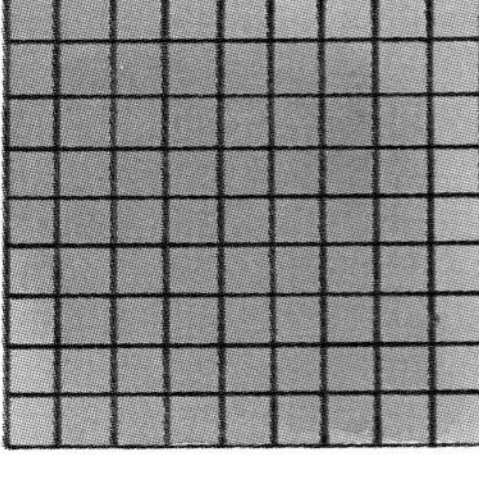

2	3	4	5	9
× 2	× 3	× 4	× 5	× 9

These products are called **squares.**
Do you see why?

Here are other squares. Find each one.
Try to remember them.

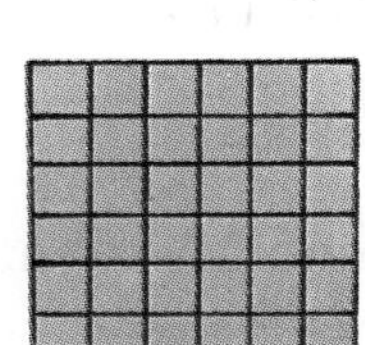

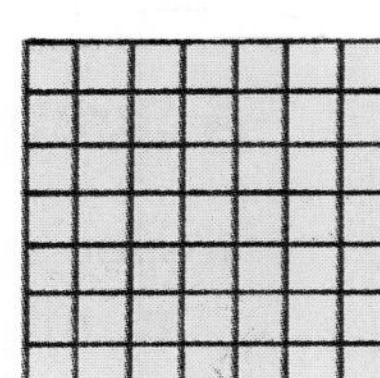
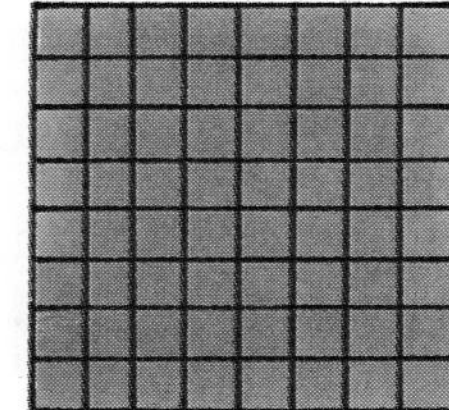

6	7	8
× 6	× 7	× 8

Find the products.

1.	**2.**	**3.**	**4.**	**5.**	**6.**	**7.**
7	5	4	8	2	9	6
× 3	× 5	× 6	× 8	× 2	× 5	× 6

8.	**9.**	**10.**	**11.**	**12.**	**13.**	**14.**
7	8	3	5	9	4	6
× 7	× 4	× 3	× 6	× 9	× 4	× 4

Practice Multiply.

1. 4 × 4
2. 6 × 6
3. 2 × 2
4. 3 × 3
5. 7 × 7
6. 9 × 9
7. 5 × 5
8. 8 × 8

9. 5×5
10. 9×9
11. 4×4
12. 2×2
13. 7×4
14. 6×6
15. 8×8
16. 7×7
17. 5×8
18. 2×2
19. 8×8
20. 6×5
21. 3×3
22. 9×9
23. 4×4
24. 6×6
25. 9×4
26. 3×3
27. 5×5
28. 9×8
29. 7×7

Mixed Applications

30. The table top has a cloth on it. How many tiles does the table top have?

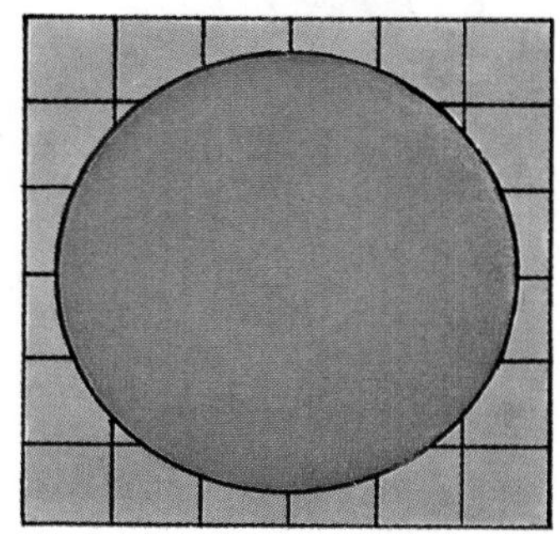

31. Make up a question about this data.

Tan table: 169 tiles
Blue table: 225 tiles

THINK

Patterns

Look at the calendar. Find the sum along each arrow. What do you notice? Try this with another "square" of numbers on the calendar.

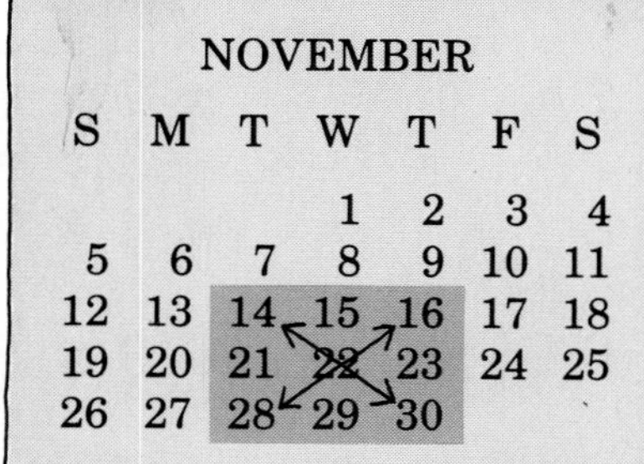

NOVEMBER						
S	M	T	W	T	F	S
			1	2	3	4
5	6	7	8	9	10	11
12	13	14	15	16	17	18
19	20	21	22	23	24	25
26	27	28	29	30		

MATH

The Last Three Facts: 6 × 7, 6 × 8, 7 × 8

The table shows all of the multiplication facts you have had so far. The pink squares are the "new" facts.

See if you can figure out the new facts. Some ways to think are given below.

×	0	1	2	3	4	5	6	7	8	9
0	0	0	0	0	0	0	0	0	0	0
1	0	1	2	3	4	5	6	7	8	9
2	0	2	4	6	8	10	12	14	16	18
3	0	3	6	9	12	15	18	21	24	27
4	0	4	8	12	16	20	24	28	32	36
5	0	5	10	15	20	25	30	35	40	45
6	0	6	12	18	24	30	36	6×7	6 × 8	54
7	0	7	14	21	28	35	7×6	49	7 × 8	63
8	0	8	16	24	32	40	8×6	8×7	64	72
9	0	9	18	27	36	45	54	63	72	81

6 × 7
That is the same as 3 sevens and 3 sevens.
6 × 7 = ___
6 × 8
That is the same as 3 eights and 3 eights.
6 × 8 = ___
7 × 8
That is the same as 6 eights and 8 more.
7 × 8 = ___

Warm Up Give the products.

THINK 6 × 8

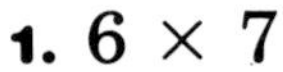

1. 6 × 7 **2.** 7 × 6 **3.** 6 × 8 **4.** 8 × 6

5. 7 × 8 **6.** 8 × 7 **7.** 6 × 5 **8.** 9 × 6

9. 6 × 6 **10.** 9 × 8 **11.** 8 × 8 **12.** 4 × 8

13. $\begin{array}{r} 7 \\ \times 6 \\ \hline \end{array}$ **14.** $\begin{array}{r} 6 \\ \times 7 \\ \hline \end{array}$ **15.** $\begin{array}{r} 8 \\ \times 6 \\ \hline \end{array}$ **16.** $\begin{array}{r} 6 \\ \times 8 \\ \hline \end{array}$ **17.** $\begin{array}{r} 7 \\ \times 8 \\ \hline \end{array}$ **18.** $\begin{array}{r} 8 \\ \times 7 \\ \hline \end{array}$ **19.** $\begin{array}{r} 9 \\ \times 9 \\ \hline \end{array}$

Practice Multiply.

1. 9×8 2. 8×4 3. 6×9 4. 9×9 5. 7×7 6. 7×5 7. 8×9

8. 5×7 9. 9×9 10. 6×6 11. 8×8 12. 5×8 13. 9×5 14. 2×9

15. 8×6 16. 7×9 17. 7×6 18. 5×5 19. 8×3 20. 9×7 21. 3×9

22. 8×2 23. 4×9 24. 7×4 25. 6×5 26. 9×1 27. 8×0 28. 7×3

29. 9×8 30. 6×7 31. 7×8 32. 8×9

33. 7×4 34. 3×9 35. 9×9 36. 9×4

Copy and complete each table.

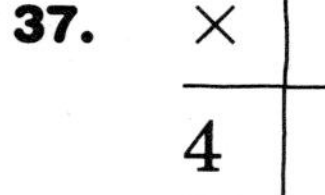

37.

×	5	9	8
4			
6			
3			

38.

×	7	6	8
9			
5			
6			

SKILLKEEPER

Write each time.

1. 

2. 

3. 4. 

PROBLEM SOLVING
Mixed Practice

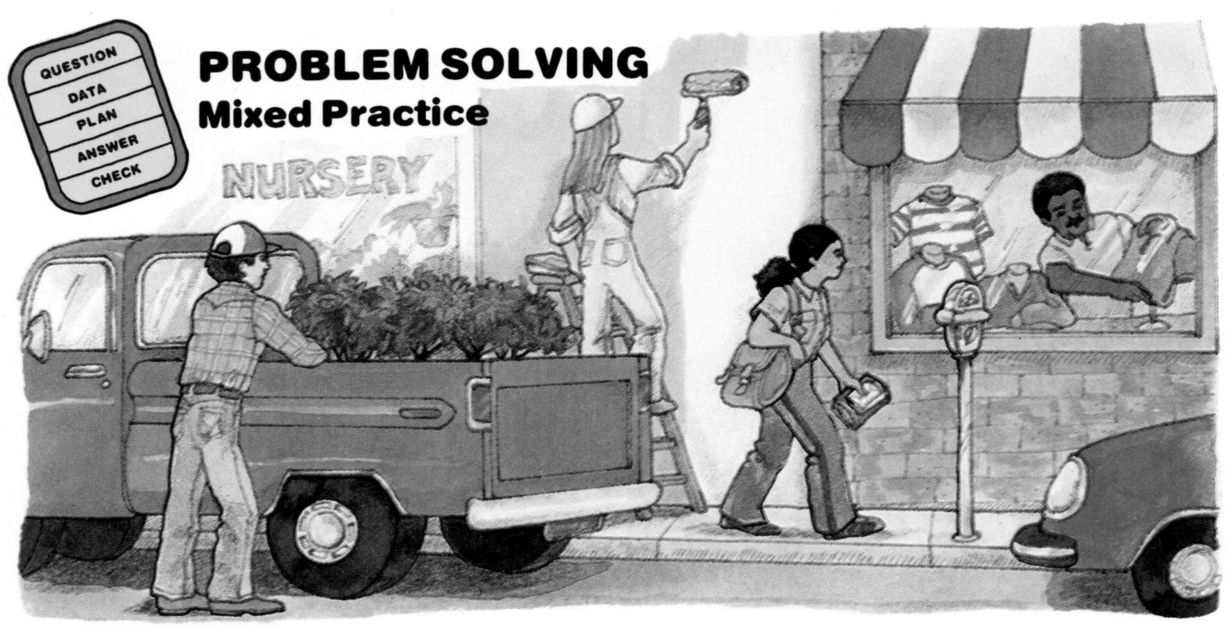

1. Sales Clerk:
T-shirts are \$6 each.
Sold 9 shirts.
How much money did the clerk receive?

2. Mail Carrier:
Delivered 376 letters. Then delivered 295. How many letters were delivered in all?

3. Office Worker:
Had 500 papers to file.
Filed 283 before lunch.
How many are left to file?

4. Waiter:
Served 2 rooms with 3 tables in each room. How many tables were served in all?
Each table had 4 people. How many people were served?

5. Farmer:
Planted 9 rows of trees.
8 trees were in each row.
How many trees did the farmer plant?

6. Painter:
Estimate for job was \$185.
Actual cost was \$208.
How much less was the estimate?

7. ***Strategy Practice*** A worker uses 3 nails for every 2 tacks. When she has used 18 nails, how many tacks has she used? Hint: Make a table.

Nails	3	6	9
Tacks	2	4	6

Practice the Facts

Find the products.

Products: less than 35

1. 3×6	**2.** 3×5	**3.** 4×7	**4.** 2×2	**5.** 5×5	**6.** 4×4	**7.** 5×4
8. 3×8	**9.** 3×4	**10.** 5×1	**11.** 3×7	**12.** 4×2	**13.** 6×5	**14.** 8×3
15. 0×4	**16.** 5×2	**17.** 3×2	**18.** 4×1	**19.** 0×5	**20.** 2×1	**21.** 4×3
22. 3×5	**23.** 4×6	**24.** 4×5	**25.** 3×9	**26.** 8×4	**27.** 5×6	**28.** 7×3

Products: 35 and greater

29. 7×5	**30.** 8×6	**31.** 7×7	**32.** 7×8	**33.** 6×6	**34.** 8×9	**35.** 9×7
36. 7×6	**37.** 8×8	**38.** 9×5	**39.** 5×7	**40.** 6×7	**41.** 8×5	**42.** 9×6
43. 8×7	**44.** 9×8	**45.** 6×8	**46.** 7×9	**47.** 9×9	**48.** 6×9	**49.** 5×9
50. 6×7	**51.** 4×9	**52.** 5×8	**53.** 7×8	**54.** 5×9	**55.** 7×7	**56.** 9×4

Multiplying Three Numbers

There are 3 tennis balls in each can. There are 2 cans in each box. There are 4 boxes. How many tennis balls are in all?

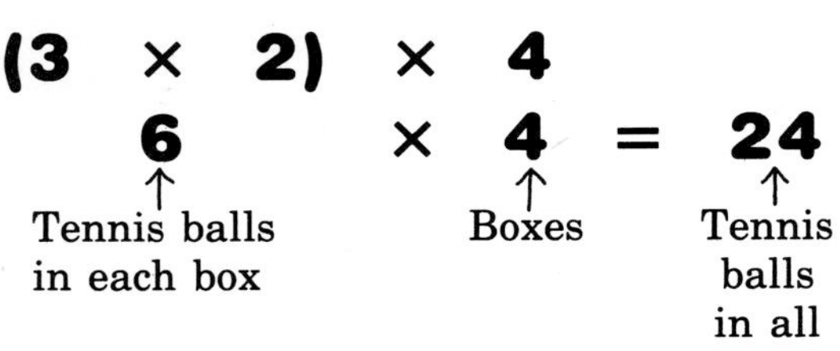

(3 × 2) × 4

6 × 4 = 24

6 — Tennis balls in each box; 4 — Boxes; 24 — Tennis balls in all

3 × (2 × 4)

3 × 8 = 24

3 — Tennis balls in each can; 8 — Cans; 24 — Tennis balls in all

These symbols ( ) tell which multiplication to do first.

Find these products.

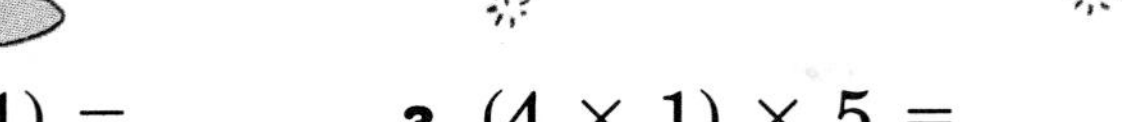

1. $(2 \times 4) \times 1 =$ ____
2. $2 \times (4 \times 1) =$ ____
3. $(4 \times 1) \times 5 =$ ____
4. $4 \times (1 \times 5) =$ ____
5. $(4 \times 2) \times 4 =$ ____
6. $4 \times (2 \times 4) =$ ____

> When you multiply, you can change the grouping and get the same product.

Use the grouping shown. Find the product.

7. $(3 \times 2) \times 5 =$ ____
8. $8 \times (4 \times 2) =$ ____
9. $9 \times (2 \times 2) =$ ____
10. $(3 \times 3) \times 6 =$ ____
11. $7 \times (2 \times 3) =$ ____
12. $(2 \times 4) \times 6 =$ ____

Use any grouping you want. Find the product.

13. $4 \times 2 \times 1 =$ ____
14. $4 \times 2 \times 3 =$ ____
15. $6 \times 1 \times 3 =$ ____
16. $3 \times 2 \times 2 =$ ____
17. $2 \times 4 \times 2 =$ ____
18. $8 \times 9 \times 0 =$ ____
19. $4 \times 1 \times 5 =$ ____
20. $6 \times 0 \times 7 =$ ____
21. $3 \times 3 \times 2 =$ ____
22. $4 \times 2 \times 4 =$ ____
23. $3 \times 1 \times 3 =$ ____
24. $9 \times 1 \times 4 =$ ____

More Practice, page 394, Set C

Missing Factors

Can you tell what 1-digit factors Cathy's mittens are hiding? You cannot tell because

 ×  = 18

2 × 9 = 18 and 3 × 6 = 18

Suppose only one factor is hidden. Can you tell now? The answer is 6.

3 × ___ = 18

Find these factors.

1. 2 × ___ = 6
2. ___ × 3 = 9
3. 4 × ___ = 12
4. ___ × 5 = 15
5. 7 × ___ = 21
6. ___ × 5 = 30
7. 3 × ___ = 15
8. ___ × 2 = 14
9. 4 × ___ = 32
10. ___ × 8 = 40
11. 5 × ___ = 20
12. ___ × 7 = 28
13. 2 × ___ = 18
14. ___ × 4 = 24
15. 3 × ___ = 21
16. ___ × 6 = 36
17. 5 × ___ = 30
18. ___ × 9 = 27
19. 7 × ___ = 35
20. ___ × 3 = 24
21. 5 × ___ = 25
22. ___ × 3 = 12

SKILLKEEPER

Add or subtract.

1. 8 + 7
2. 13 − 4
3. 10 − 8
4. 5 + 9
5. 8 + 3
6. 17 − 9
7. 8 + 8
8. 12 − 5
9. 14 − 7
10. 16 − 9
11. 9 + 9
12. 7 + 6

PROBLEM SOLVING
Using Data from a Table

A dietitian plans meals for people. A dietitian needs to know how many **calories** are in different foods. Calories are the measure of energy supplied by our foods.

Calorie Table

Breakfast	Calories	Lunch	Calories	Dinner	Calories
juice	85	sandwich	395	chicken	283
cereal	95	salad	48	potatoes	197
banana	81	soup	147	peas	60
milk	166	apple	75	orange	64
		milk	166	milk	166

Use the table to solve the following problems.

1. How many calories are in the banana and cereal?

2. How many more calories are in the sandwich than the soup?

3. How many more calories are in the potatoes than the milk?

4. One piece of celery has 7 calories. How many calories are in 6 pieces?

★ 5. Find the total amount of calories for breakfast.

6. **DATA HUNT** Find the number of calories in a poached egg and a fried egg. What is the difference?

7. ***Strategy Practice*** Jack can have a pear, a banana, or an apple for a snack. He can have milk or juice with his snack. How many different ways can Jack choose his snack?

PROBLEM SOLVING
Identifying Needed Data

These problems need more data. Find the data on the Data Sheet. Then solve the problems.

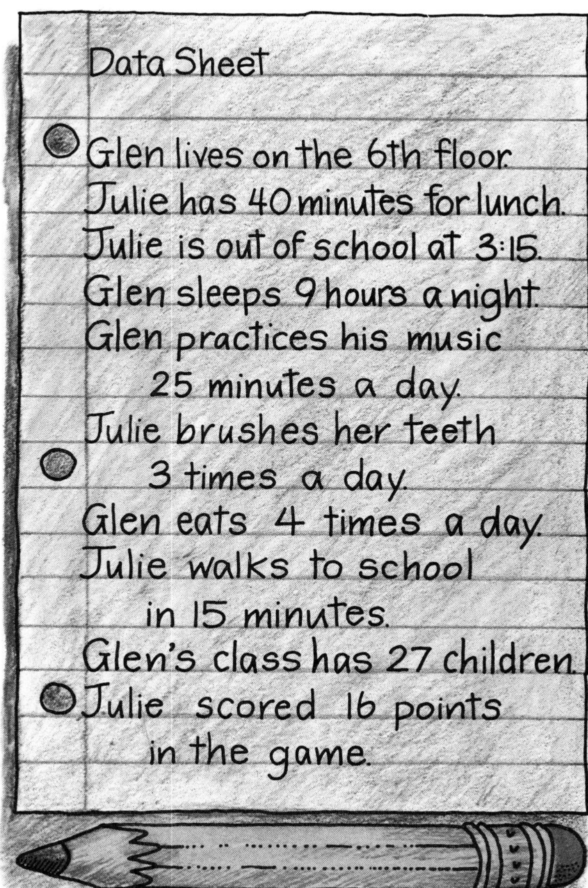

Data Sheet
Glen lives on the 6th floor.
Julie has 40 minutes for lunch.
Julie is out of school at 3:15.
Glen sleeps 9 hours a night.
Glen practices his music
25 minutes a day.
Julie brushes her teeth
3 times a day.
Glen eats 4 times a day.
Julie walks to school
in 15 minutes.
Glen's class has 27 children.
Julie scored 16 points
in the game.

1. Julie practices the piano 40 minutes a day. How much longer does she practice than Glen?

2. Glen has 5 minutes less for lunch than Julie. How long does Glen have for lunch?

3. Julie tries to keep her teeth clean and healthy. How many times does she brush a week (7 days)?

4. Julie's class has 29 children. How many children are in Julie's class and Glen's class?

5. Julie takes 15 minutes to walk home from school. What time does she get home?

6. It takes Glen 22 minutes to walk to school. How much longer does it take Glen than Julie?

7. Glen scored 14 points in the game. How many points did Julie and Glen score in all?

8. ***Strategy Practice*** Glen and Julie live in the same building. Julie lives on the 14th floor. How many floors of apartments are between them? Hint: Draw a picture.

PROBLEM SOLVING
Mixed Practice

People have given many names to the flag of the United States.

THE STARS AND STRIPES
THE STAR-SPANGLED BANNER
OLD GLORY

The flag stands for the land, the people, the government, and the ideals of the United States.

The U.S. Flag Today
50 stars
13 stripes

Solve.

1. The first flag of 1777 had 13 stars. How many fewer stars did the first flag have than today's flag?

2. There were 34 stars on the flag of 1861. How many more stars does today's flag have?

3. The flag of 1912 had 6 rows of stars. There were 8 stars in each row. How many stars did the flag have?

4. The flag of 1912 lasted for 47 years. The flag of 1777 lasted for 18 years. How many more years did the flag of 1912 last than that of 1777?

5. The flag of 1818 had 4 rows of stars with 5 in each row. How many stars did it have?

★ 6. One U.S. flag had 4 rows of stars with 7 in each row and 1 row with only 6 stars. How many stars did it have?

7. **DATA BANK** See page 378. How many more stars does today's flag have than the flag of 1795?

8. ***Strategy Practice*** Mary's flag is between 30 cm and 40 cm long. It is longer than 6×6. It is an even number of centimeters. How long is Mary's flag?

Practice the Facts

Multiply.

1. 6×8 2. 9×9 3. 8×8 4. 3×8 5. 5×9 6. 7×6 7. 9×4

8. 8×9 9. 7×9 10. 8×7 11. 9×8 12. 9×6 13. 7×3 14. 5×6

15. 4×7 16. 7×7 17. 8×6 18. 7×2 19. 6×3 20. 4×8 21. 2×9

22. 6×2 23. 7×4 24. 9×5 25. 8×2 26. 9×1 27. 8×0 28. 5×3

29. 8×4 30. 5×7 31. 8×5 32. 7×0 33. 9×7 34. 8×3 35. 8×1

36. 7×5 37. 5×8 38. 9×3 39. 7×1 40. 4×5

41. 6×7 42. 9×9 43. 6×6 44. 9×6 45. 5×5

Write the products.

	Multiply by 6	
46.	7	▥
47.	9	▥
48.	8	▥
49.	6	▥

	Multiply by 7	
50.	5	▥
51.	8	▥
52.	7	▥
53.	9	▥

	Multiply by 8	
54.	4	▥
55.	8	▥
56.	6	▥
57.	9	▥

	Multiply by 9	
58.	7	▥
59.	6	▥
60.	9	▥
61.	5	▥

PROBLEM-SOLVING STRATEGY
Choose the Operations

To solve this problem you need to use more than one operation. A strategy that can help you is given below.

Try This There were 7 cars and 1 bus to take people to the picnic. Each car took 4 children. The bus took 37. How many children went to the picnic?

CHOOSE THE OPERATIONS

I can **multiply** to find how many children rode in cars.
I can **add** to find how many children rode in both the bus and the cars.

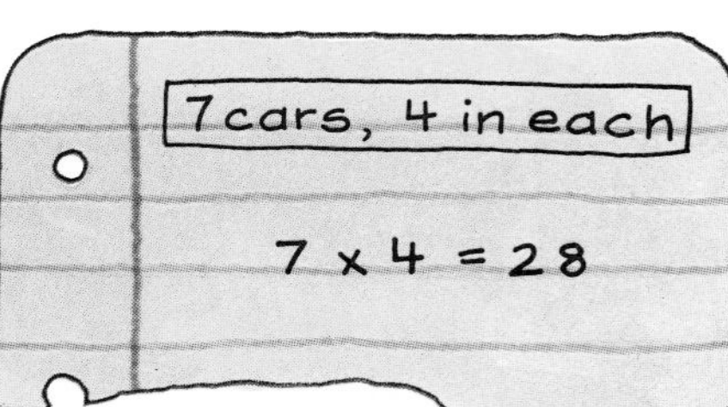

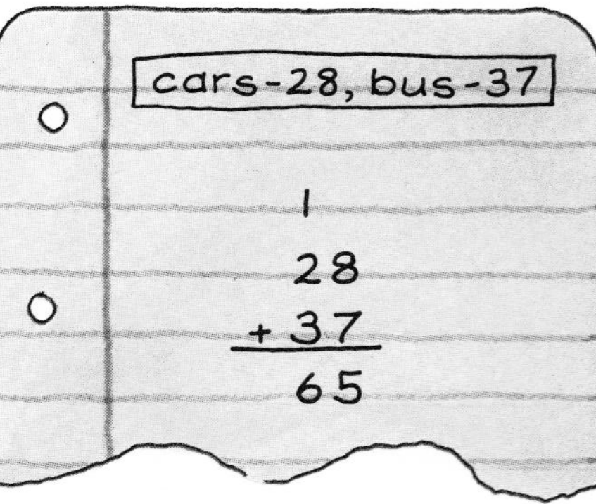

65 children went to the picnic.

Solve.

1. Diane has one book with 72 pictures in it. Another book has 8 pages with 6 pictures on each page. How many pictures are in both books?

2. At the book sale all \$12-books were \$5 off the regular price. Don bought 4 \$12-books at the sale. How much did he pay for the books?

CHAPTER REVIEW/TEST

Multiply.

1. $\begin{array}{r} 8 \\ \times\ 4 \\ \hline \end{array}$	**2.** $\begin{array}{r} 7 \\ \times\ 2 \\ \hline \end{array}$	**3.** $\begin{array}{r} 8 \\ \times\ 3 \\ \hline \end{array}$	**4.** $\begin{array}{r} 8 \\ \times\ 5 \\ \hline \end{array}$	**5.** $\begin{array}{r} 9 \\ \times\ 4 \\ \hline \end{array}$	**6.** $\begin{array}{r} 6 \\ \times\ 5 \\ \hline \end{array}$	**7.** $\begin{array}{r} 7 \\ \times\ 3 \\ \hline \end{array}$
8. $\begin{array}{r} 6 \\ \times\ 8 \\ \hline \end{array}$	**9.** $\begin{array}{r} 6 \\ \times\ 7 \\ \hline \end{array}$	**10.** $\begin{array}{r} 9 \\ \times\ 6 \\ \hline \end{array}$	**11.** $\begin{array}{r} 6 \\ \times\ 6 \\ \hline \end{array}$	**12.** $\begin{array}{r} 6 \\ \times\ 9 \\ \hline \end{array}$	**13.** $\begin{array}{r} 7 \\ \times\ 6 \\ \hline \end{array}$	**14.** $\begin{array}{r} 8 \\ \times\ 6 \\ \hline \end{array}$
15. $\begin{array}{r} 8 \\ \times\ 7 \\ \hline \end{array}$	**16.** $\begin{array}{r} 4 \\ \times\ 7 \\ \hline \end{array}$	**17.** $\begin{array}{r} 7 \\ \times\ 7 \\ \hline \end{array}$	**18.** $\begin{array}{r} 7 \\ \times\ 9 \\ \hline \end{array}$	**19.** $\begin{array}{r} 7 \\ \times\ 8 \\ \hline \end{array}$	**20.** $\begin{array}{r} 7 \\ \times\ 6 \\ \hline \end{array}$	**21.** $\begin{array}{r} 9 \\ \times\ 7 \\ \hline \end{array}$

22. 8×8 **23.** 7×9 **24.** 8×7 **25.** 8×9 **26.** 9×9

27. 6×8 **28.** 5×9 **29.** 7×6 **30.** 9×4 **31.** 3×8

Solve.

32. $2 \times 2 \times 2 =$ ____ **33.** $2 \times 4 \times 2 =$ ____ **34.** $3 \times 2 \times 3 =$ ____

Find the missing factor.

35. $6 \times$ ____ $= 18$ **36.** $5 \times$ ____ $= 25$ **37.** $7 \times$ ____ $= 21$

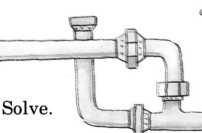

Solve.

38. Cook:
Baked 6 rows of biscuits.
8 biscuits are in each row.
How many are in all?

39. Plumber:
Had a 126-cm pipe.
Cut off 39-cm piece.
How long is the other piece?

ANOTHER LOOK

Multiply.

1. 6×6
2. 6×4
3. 6×9
4. 6×3
5. 6×5
6. 6×8
7. 6×2
8. 6×7
9. 6×1

8 sevens

7 sevens and 1 seven

49 + 7

8 × 7 = 56

10. 7×5
11. 7×9
12. 7×2
13. 7×4
14. 7×6
15. 7×7
16. 7×8
17. 7×3
18. 7×1

9 eights

5 eights and 4 eights

40 + 32

9 × 8 = 72

19. 8×6
20. 9×7
21. 9×9
22. 8×8
23. 9×6
24. 8×9
25. 9×5
26. 8×7
27. 8×5

ENRICHMENT

Making Predictions

To get your score, spin both spinners and add the two numbers. The score shown is 9.

1. What is the greatest sum you can spin?
2. What is the least?
3. How many ways can you spin a sum of 7?

Make a table like this one. Finish it.

Sum	Different ways to spin the sum
6	5 + 1,
7	5 + 2, 6 + 1
8	5 + 3, 6 + 2, 7 +
9	5 + 4,
10	

4. When you spin the spinners, what sum do you think you would get most often?
5. What sums do you think you would get least often?
6. Use two spinners like these. Take 50 turns. Keep a record of your sums. Were your predictions right?

CUMULATIVE REVIEW

Give the letter for the correct answer.

1. $\begin{array}{r} 36 \\ +\ 54 \\ \hline \end{array}$ **A** 90 **B** 80 **C** 70 **D** not given

2. $\begin{array}{r} 185 \\ +\ \ 32 \\ \hline \end{array}$ **A** 117 **B** 227 **C** 217 **D** not given

3. $\begin{array}{r} 589 \\ +\ 176 \\ \hline \end{array}$ **A** 765 **B** 655 **C** 755 **D** not given

4. $\begin{array}{r} \$3.50 \\ +\ 2.82 \\ \hline \end{array}$ **A** $6.22 **B** $5.22 **C** $5.32 **D** not given

5. $\begin{array}{r} 75 \\ +\ 76 \\ \hline \end{array}$ **A** 151 **B** 141 **C** 142 **D** not given

6. $\begin{array}{r} 76 \\ +\ 94 \\ \hline \end{array}$ **A** 180 **B** 170 **C** 160 **D** not given

What time does the clock show?

7. 
A 9:00
B 9:15
C 9:30
D not given

8. 
A 11:50
B 10:50
C 10:55
D not given

9. Use your centimeter ruler. What is the length?
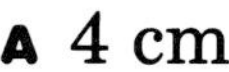
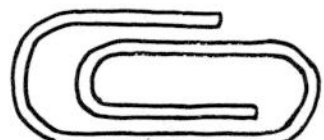
A 4 cm
B 3 cm
C 2 cm
D not given

10. What is the perimeter?
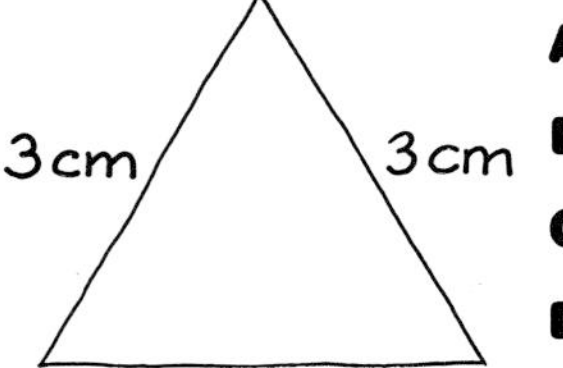

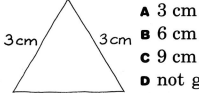

A 3 cm
B 6 cm
C 9 cm
D not given

11. What is the area?
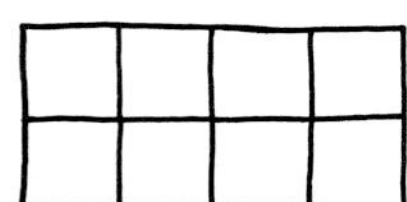
A 6 square units
B 8 square units
C 12 square units
D not given

12. What is the volume?

A 3 cubic units
B 6 cubic units
C 4 cubic units
D not given

13. Rita rode her bike 12 km before lunch. After lunch she rode 9 km. How far did she ride?
A 21 km **B** 11 km
C 3 km **D** not given

14. Dean started hiking at 12:30 p.m. He stopped one hour later. What time did he stop?
A 1:30 a.m. **B** 1:30 p.m.
C 1:00 a.m. **D** not given

GEOMETRY AND GRAPHING 8

Tim was very happy when his baby sister was born. He helped design a card about the baby. The card was to be sent to friends of his family. Tim and his father took the design to a printer. At the printer's shop they picked the shape of the card. They also picked the size and color. The printer showed Tim many ways his sister's name could look on the front of the card. The finished card looked very nice.

Space Figures

Look at the objects below. Think of sorting them into the boxes so the shapes match. Give the name of the box for each object.

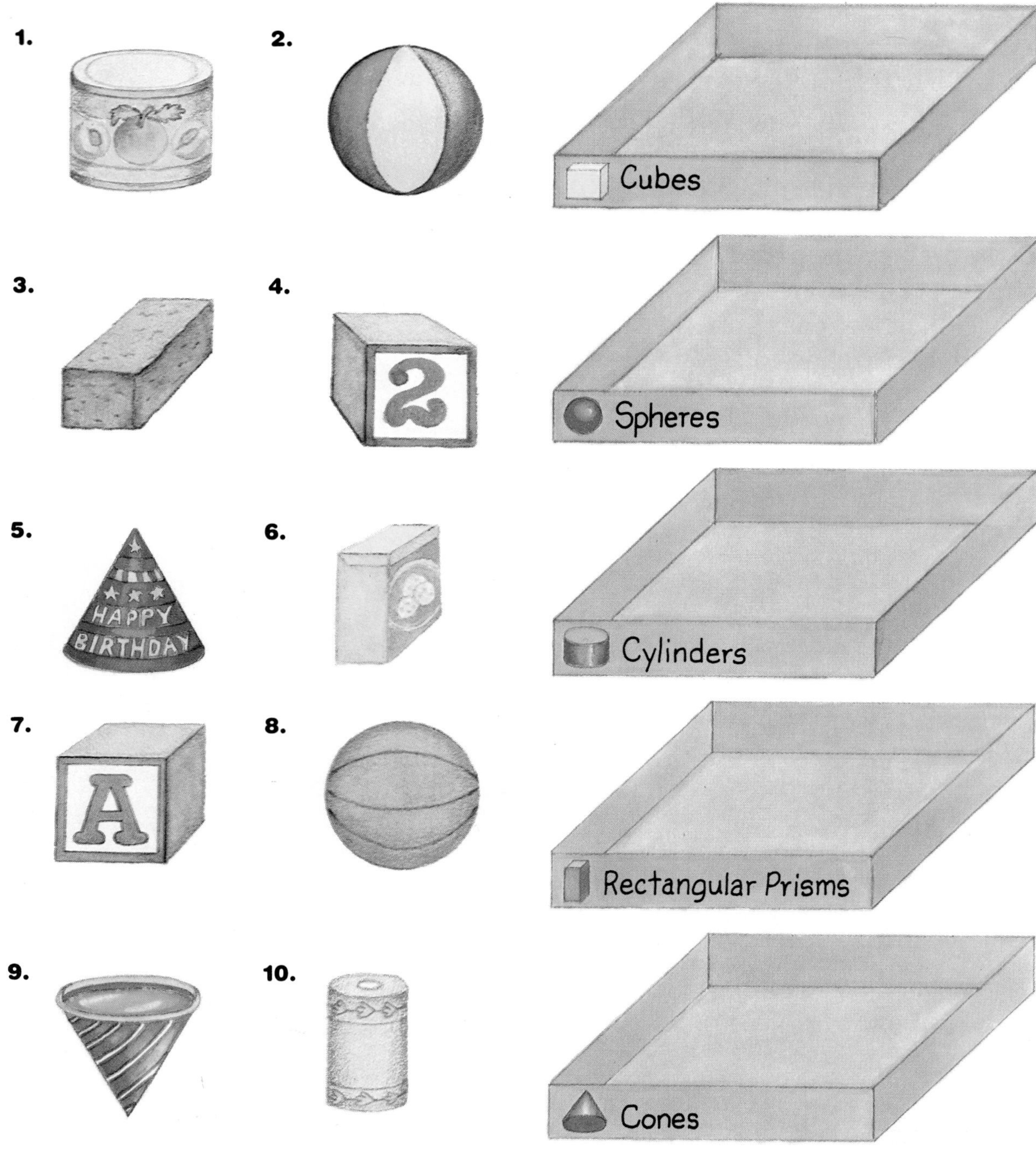

Write **cube, sphere, cone, cylinder,** or **rectangular prism** for each object.

1.

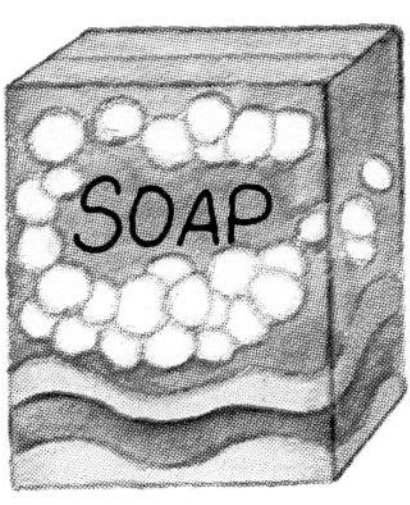

2.

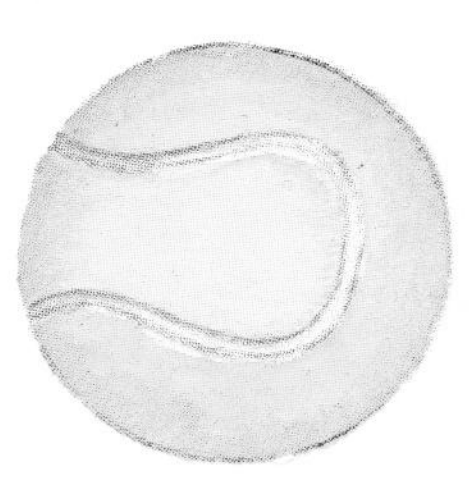

3.

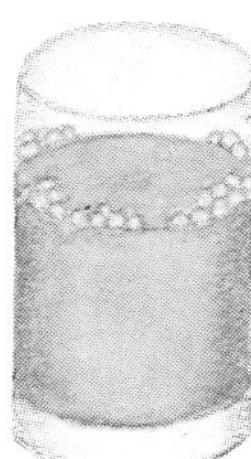

4.

5.

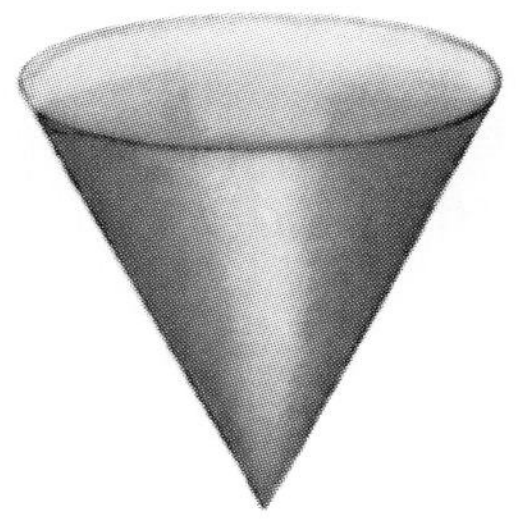

6.

7.

8.

9.

THINK

Space Perception

A cube has 4 dots on each of its faces. You can hold the cube any way you want.

1. What is the greatest number of dots you can see at one time?
2. What is the least number of dots you can see at one time?

MATH

Plane Figures

Plane figures lie on a "flat" surface.

A face of a cube has a **square** shape.

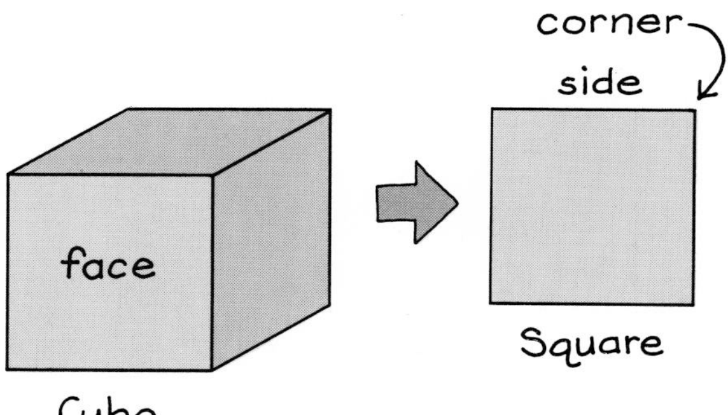

A face of a rectangular prism has a **rectangle** shape.

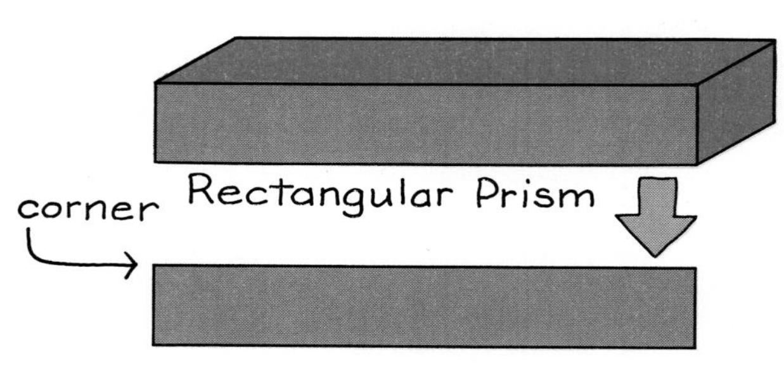

A face of a cylinder has a **circle** shape.

Cut off a corner of a cube to get a **triangle** shape.

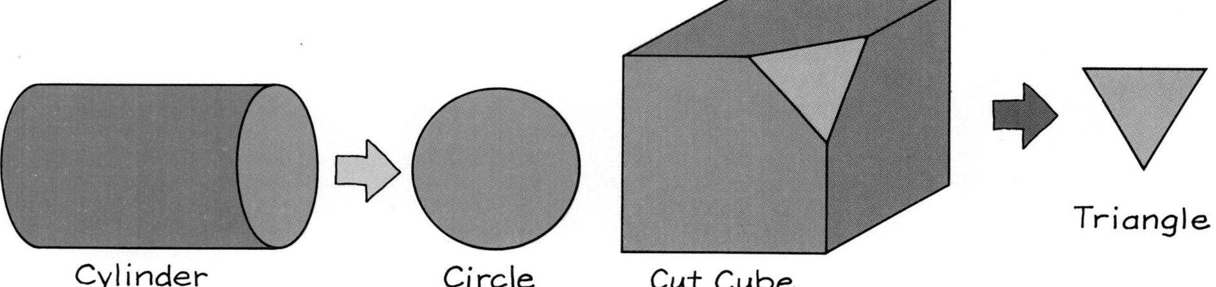

Warm Up Give the name of each figure— **square**, **rectangle**, **circle**, or **triangle**. Then give the number of sides and corners.

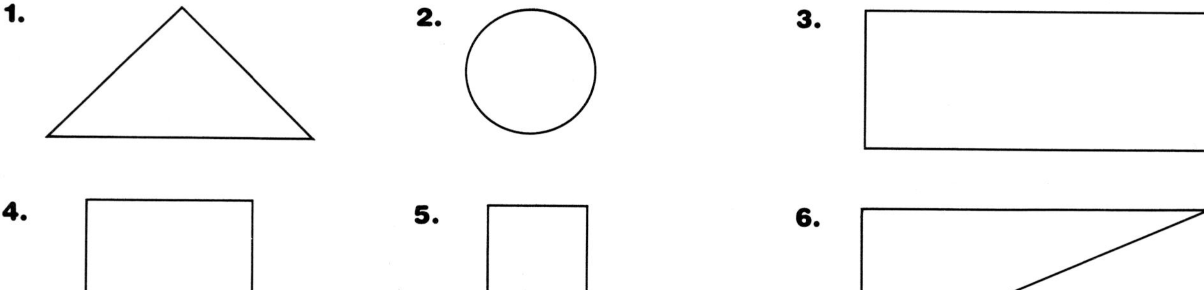

Practice Tell whether the picture reminds you of a square, a rectangle, a circle, or a triangle.

1.

2.

3.

4.

5.

6.

Write **square**, **circle**, **rectangle**, or **triangle** for each figure.

7. 3 sides and 3 corners

8. 4 sides all the same length

9. No straight sides and no corners

10. 4 sides with two longer than the others

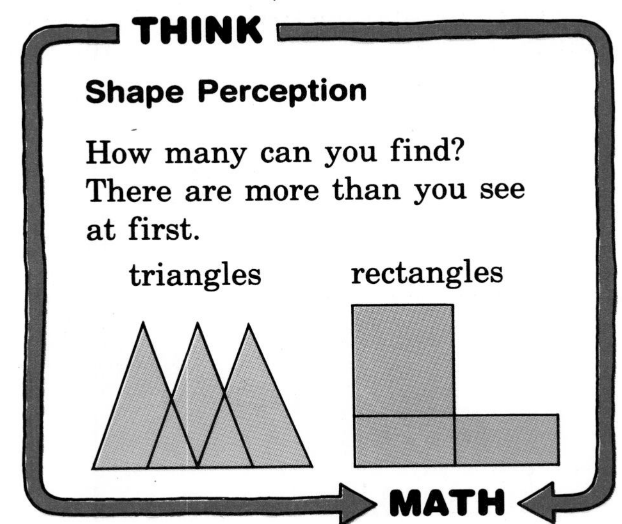
THINK
Shape Perception
How many can you find?
There are more than you see at first.
triangles
rectangles
MATH

Segments

Look at the cardboard strips. You can put them together to make different shapes.

The sides of rectangles, squares, and triangles are **segments**.

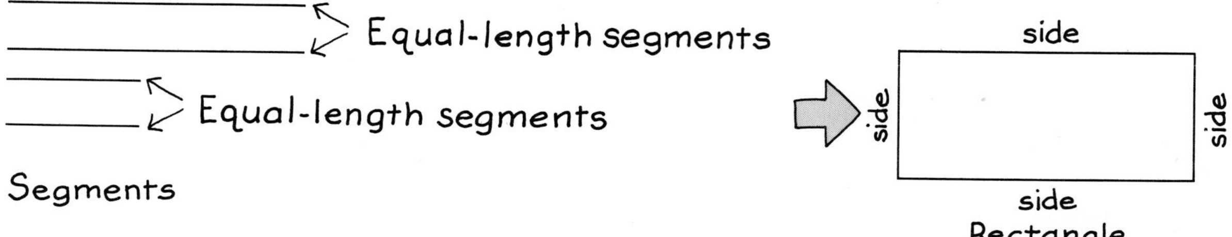

Warm Up Think of the strips as segments.

1. What shape has been made with these strips?

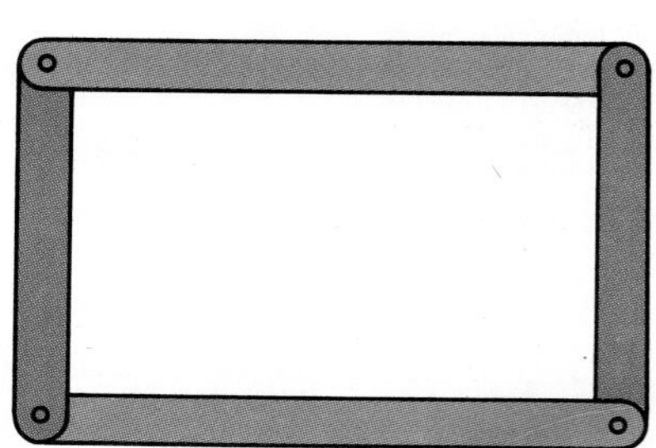

2. What shape could you make with all these strips?

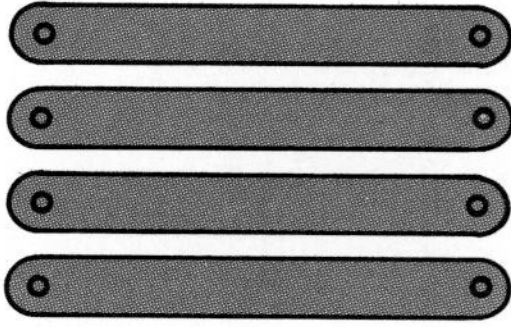

Practice Tell who made each shape.

1. A triangle with all sides that are equal in length
2. A small square
3. A triangle with no sides that are equal in length
4. A rectangle
5. A triangle with just two sides that are equal in length
6. A large square

Ted's strips

Patty's strips

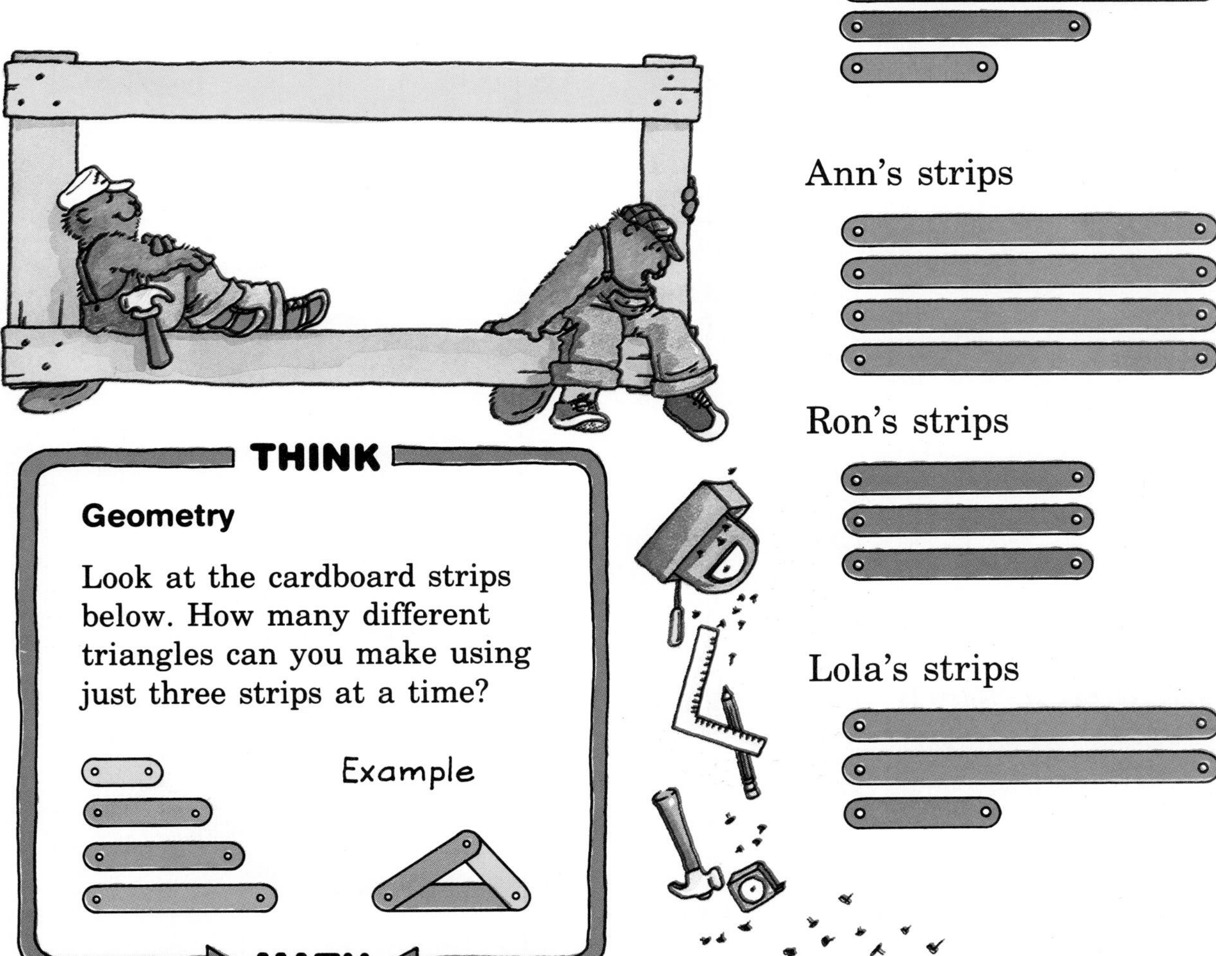

Lola's strips

THINK

Geometry

Look at the cardboard strips below. How many different triangles can you make using just three strips at a time?

Example

MATH

Angles

Many things can remind you of an **angle**.

The corner of a triangle or rectangle can remind you of an angle.

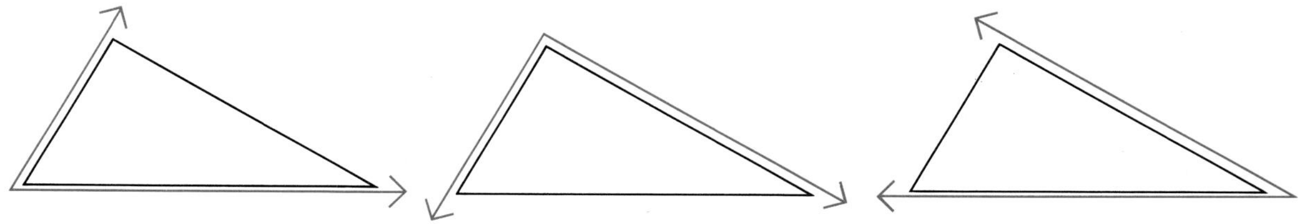

Each triangle has 3 angles.

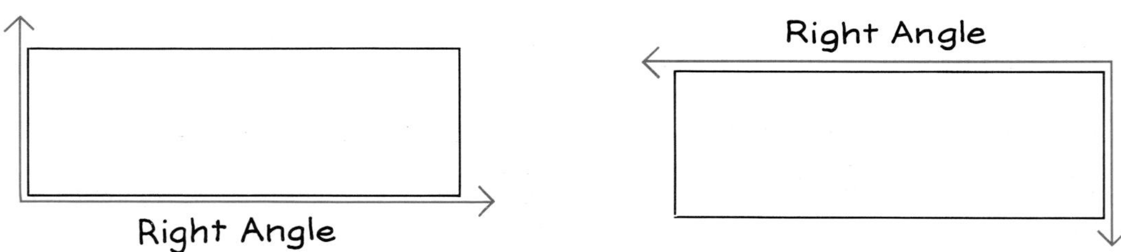

Each rectangle has 4 **right** angles.

Warm Up Which of the angles below are right angles?

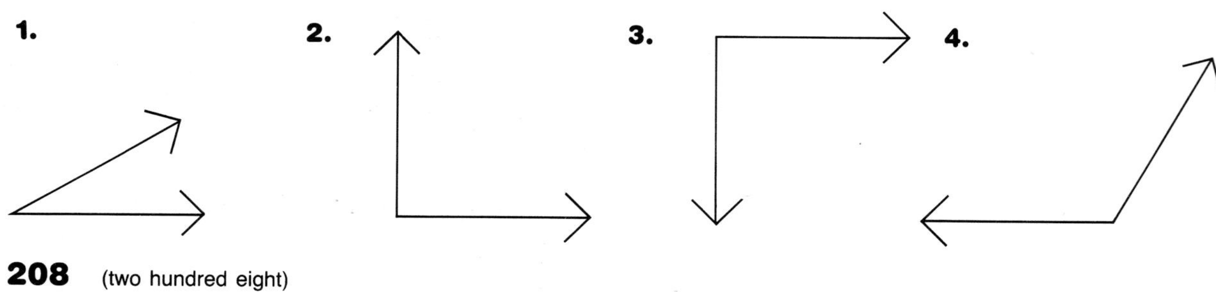

Practice Which of the angles below are right angles?

1.

2.

3.

How many right angles does each figure have?

4.

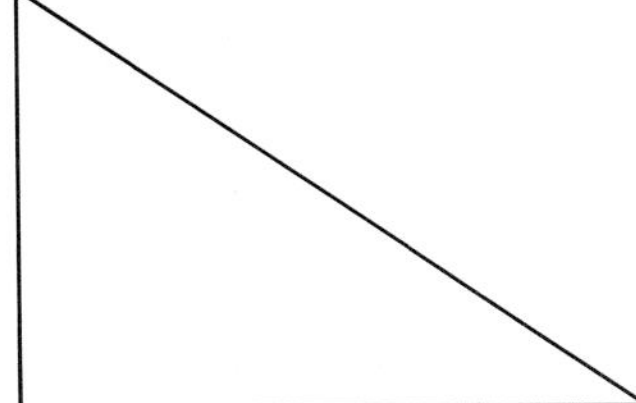

5.

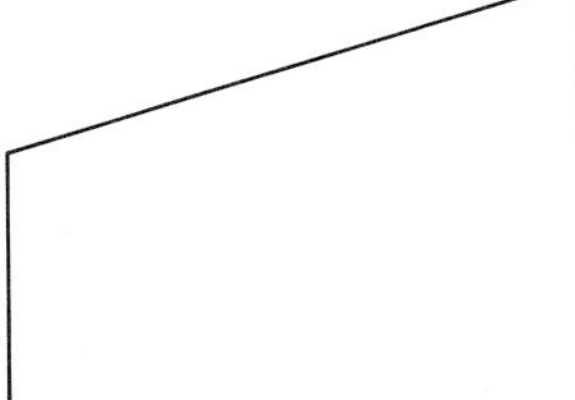

6.

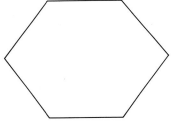

Give the number of segments and angles for each figure.

7.

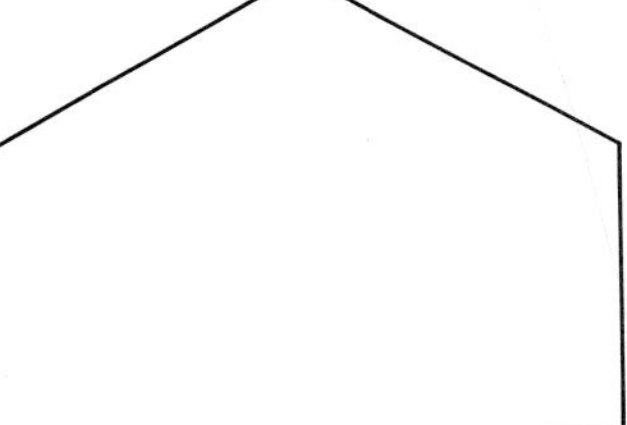

8.

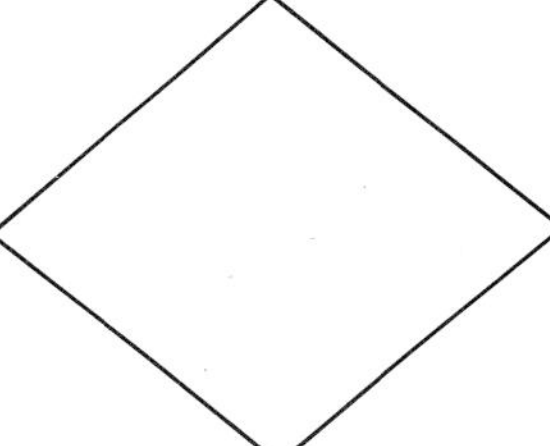

9.

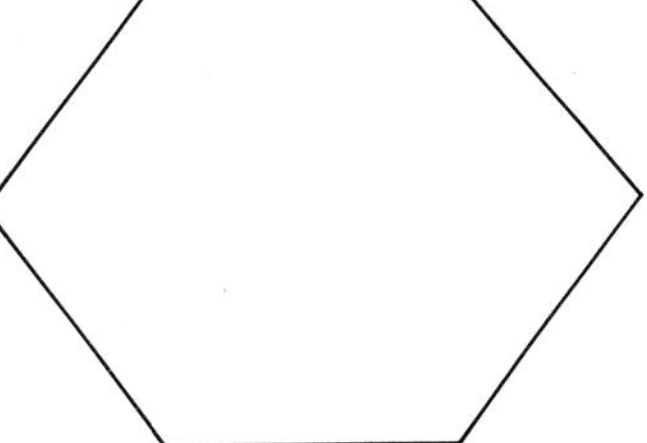

10. Name two different times when the clock hands form a right angle.

THINK

Shape Perception

Fold a piece of paper.

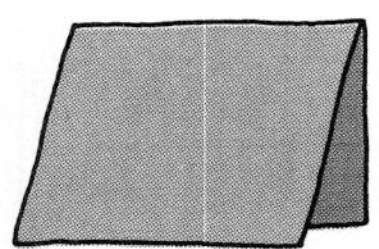

Fold it again so the first fold meets.

Open your paper and find some right angles.

MATH

Congruent Figures

Carmen Reyes is making a blouse. She must cut the material exactly the same size and shape as the pattern.

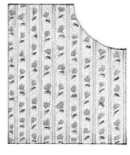

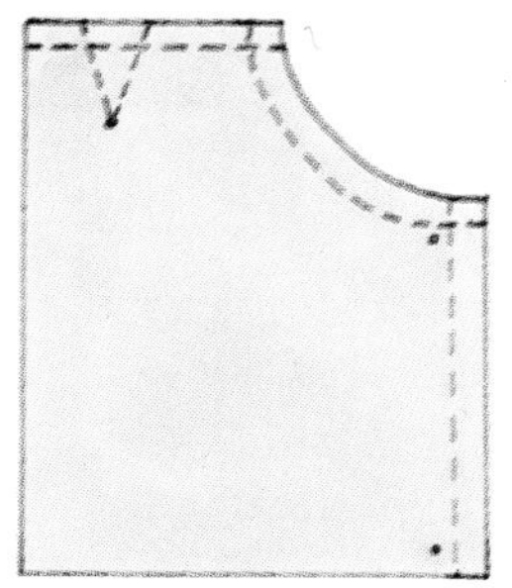

Figures that have the same size and shape are **congruent** to each other. A copy of one will fit exactly on the other.

These two triangles are congruent.

These two triangles are not congruent.

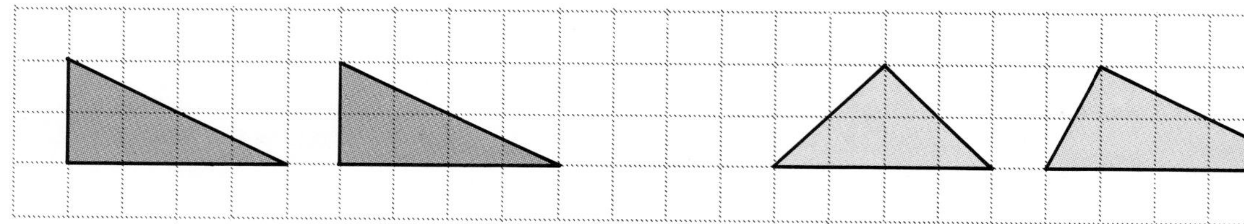

Warm Up Which figure is congruent to the first?

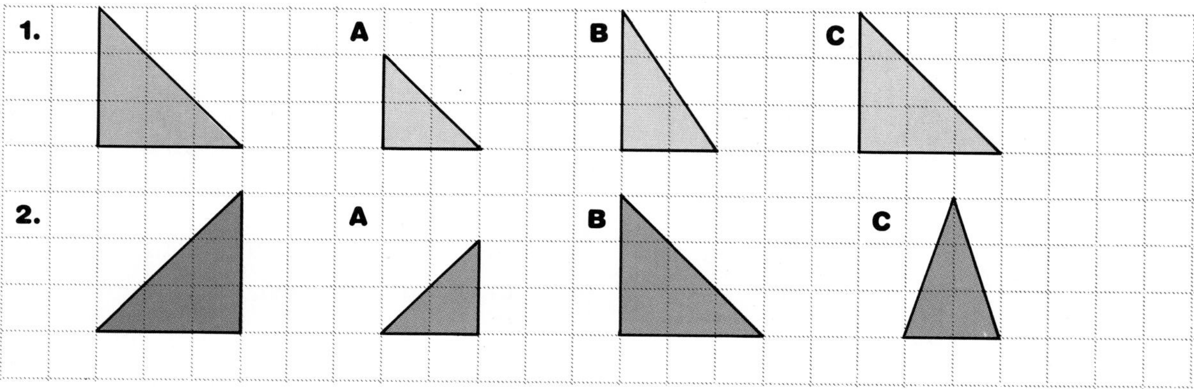

Practice Which figure is congruent to the first?

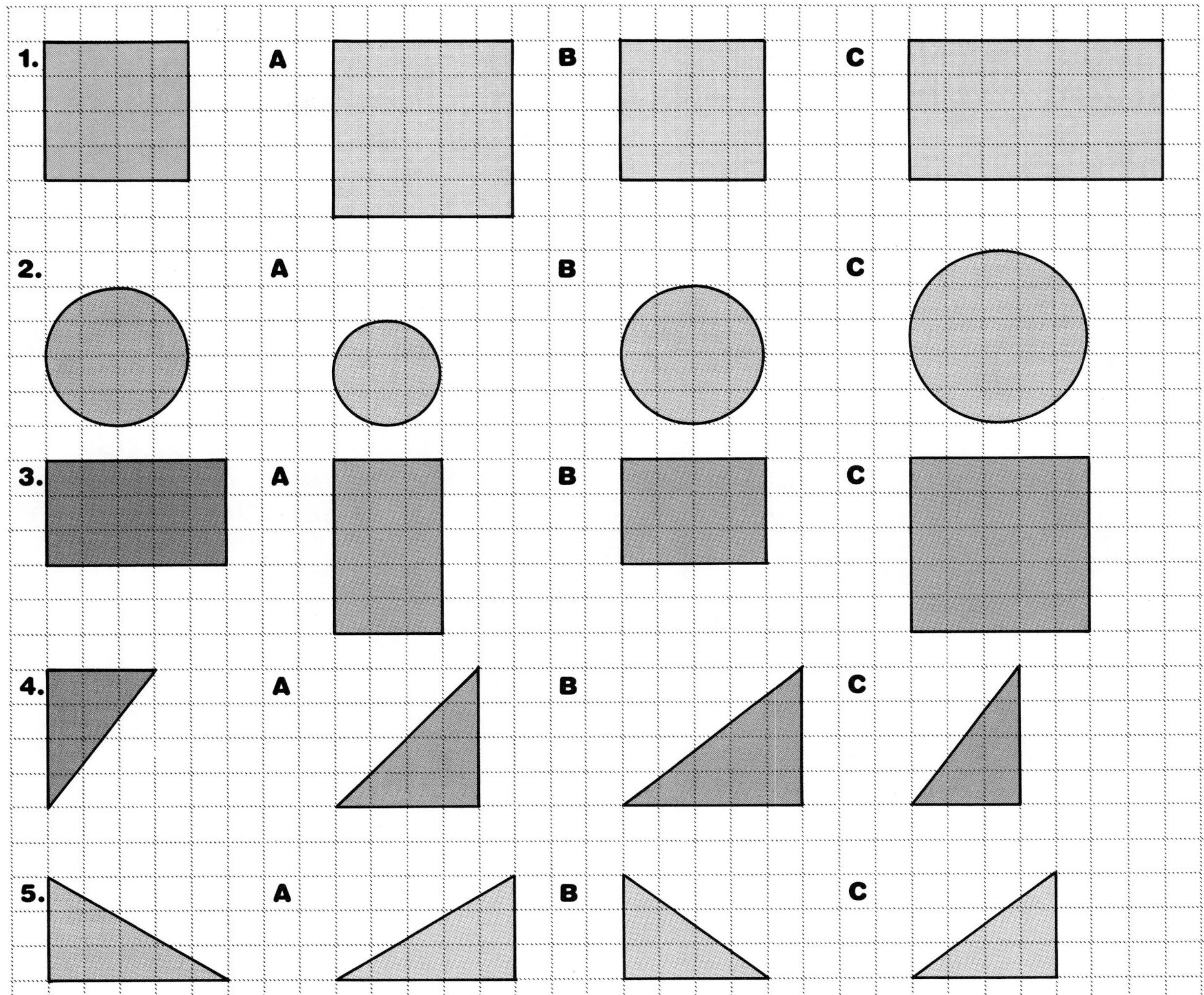

SKILLKEEPER

Estimate by rounding to the nearest hundred or dollar.

1. 306 + 458	**2.** 798 − 332	**3.** 456 − 198	**4.** 235 + 406
5. \$3.08 − 1.96	**6.** \$6.53 + 2.25	**7.** \$9.47 + 3.61	**8.** \$2.84 − 2.06

Lines of Symmetry

A figure has a line of **symmetry** if it can be folded so the two parts fit exactly.

Pictures of real objects sometimes appear to have a line of symmetry.

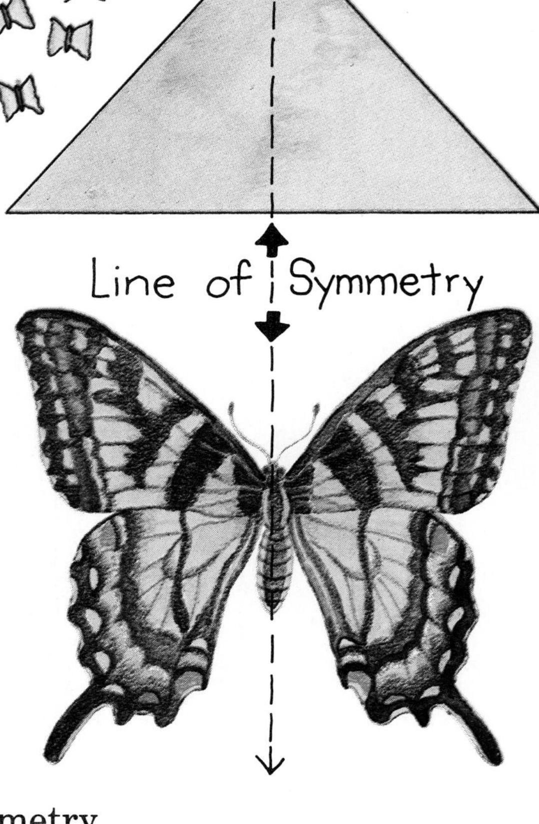

Warm Up Does the dashed line appear to be a line of symmetry? Answer yes or no.

Figures from geometry

1. 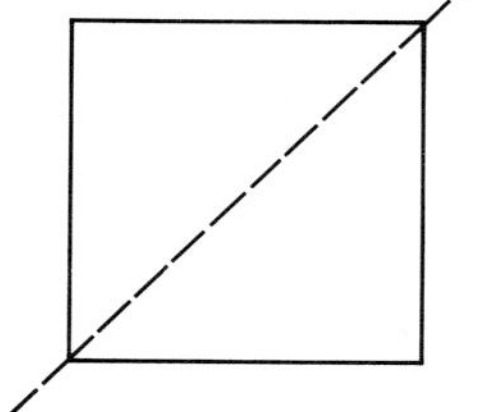

2. 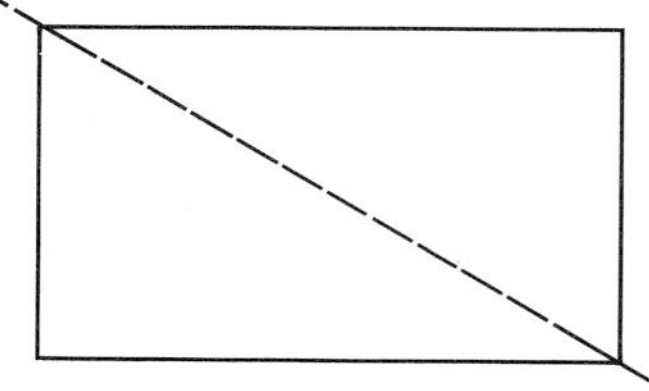

3. 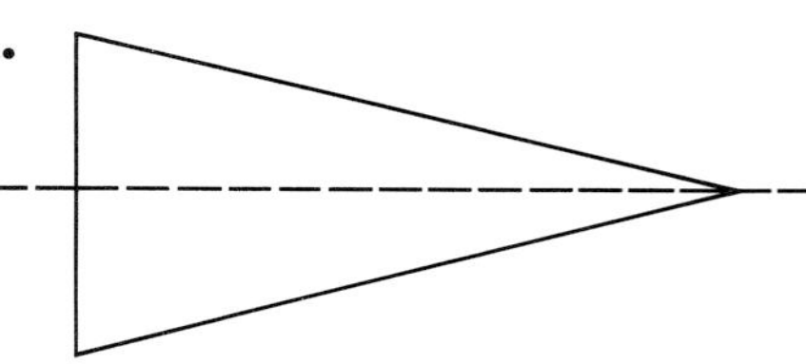

Pictures from nature

4. 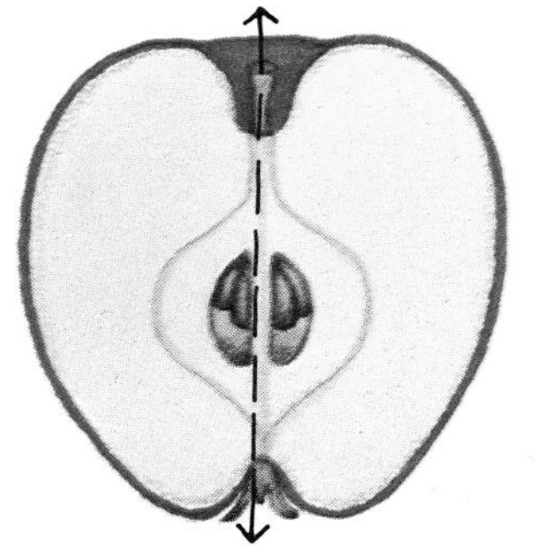

5. 

6. 

Practice Which of these shapes can be folded to make a line of symmetry? Trace and fold if you cannot tell.

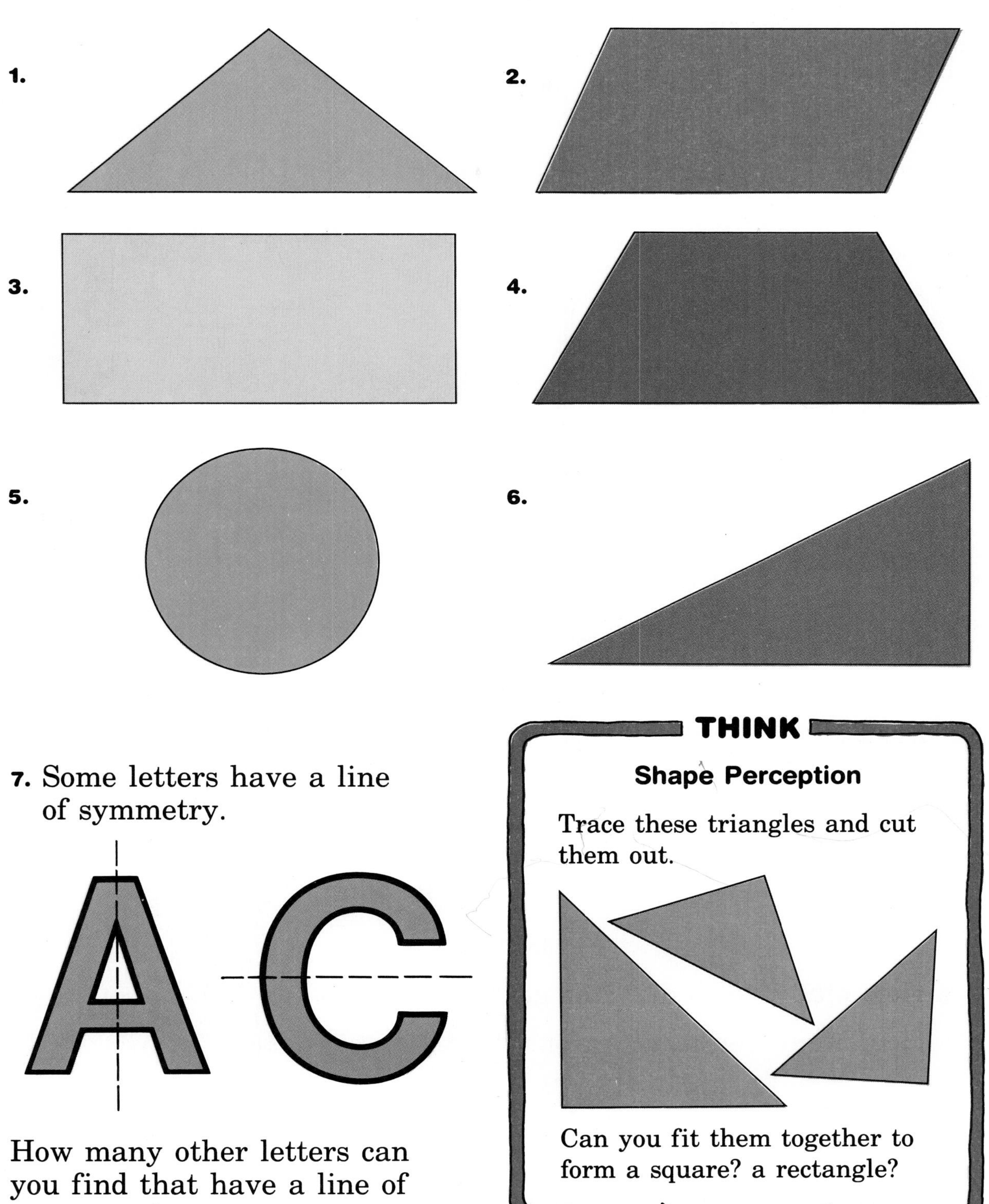

1.

2.

3.

4.

5.

6.

7. Some letters have a line of symmetry.

How many other letters can you find that have a line of symmetry?

THINK

Shape Perception

Trace these triangles and cut them out.

Can you fit them together to form a square? a rectangle?

MATH

Tallies and Bar Graphs

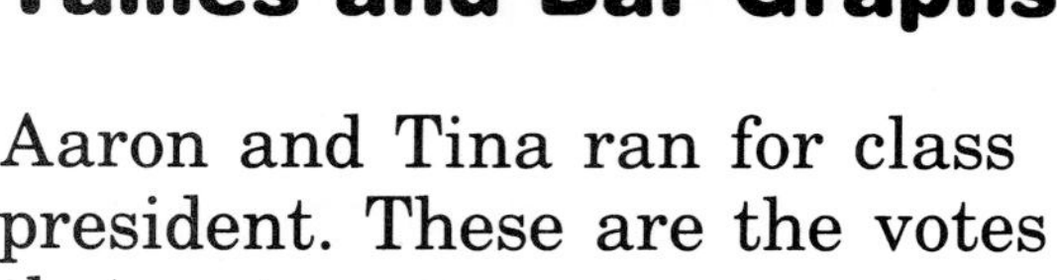

Aaron and Tina ran for class president. These are the votes they got.

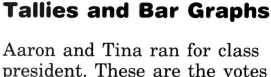

Niki made a **tally chart** to show the votes. He put one mark for each vote. Niki shows 5 votes as 卌 so the votes are easy to count.

Votes for Class President	
Tina	卌 卌 ||
Aaron	卌 |||

Vera made a **bar graph** to show the votes.

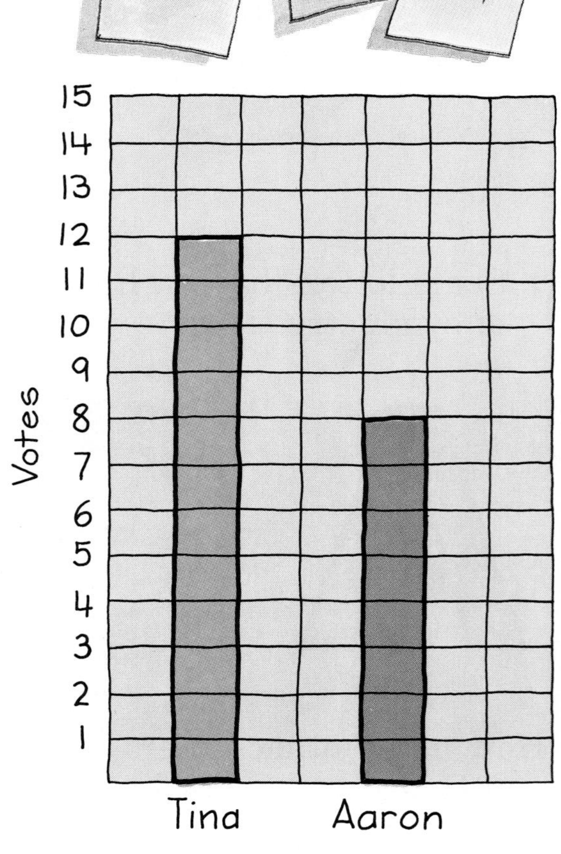

Warm Up

1. How many votes did Tina get?
2. How many votes did Aaron get?
3. Who won the election?
4. Do the numbers on the tally chart agree with the graph?

1. Liz and Ray ran for Vice-President. These are their votes. Count the votes for each person. Make a tally chart to show the votes.

2. Alicia and Tico ran for Secretary. This tally chart shows the votes. Make a graph to show Alicia's and Tico's votes.

Votes for Secretary

Alicia	𝍸 𝍸 |
Tico	𝍸 ||||

3. Trudy and Ian ran for Treasurer. These are the votes they received. Make a tally chart and a bar graph to show their votes.

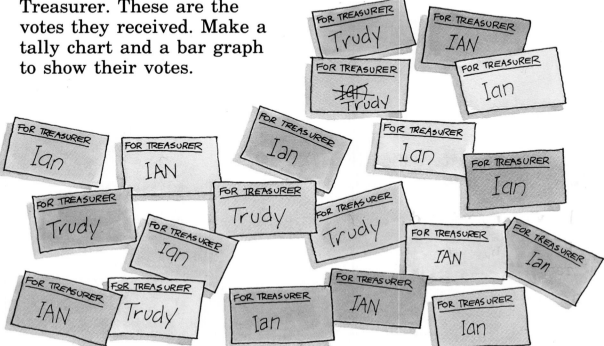

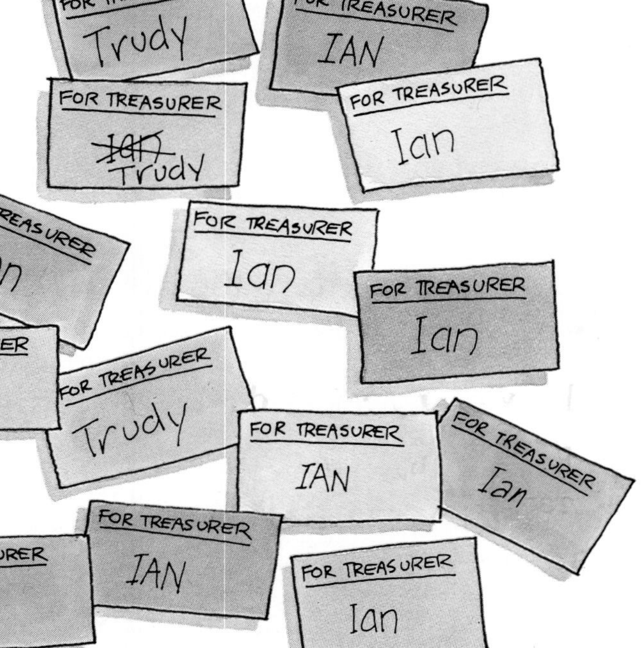

Picture Graphs

Ms. Hall runs her own business. The **picture graph** below shows the mail she got in one week. The graph shows 3 envelopes for Monday. Each envelope means 5 letters. So, Ms. Hall got $\mathbf{3 \times 5}$, or **15** letters, on Monday.

Warm Up

1. How many letters did Ms. Hall get on Tuesday?
2. On what two days did Ms. Hall receive the same amount of mail?
3. How many letters did Ms. Hall get on Wednesday?
4. What is the most letters Ms. Hall got in one day?
5. What is the fewest letters Ms. Hall got in one day?

Practice Use the magazine graph to answer questions 1–5.

1. How many magazines were delivered on Wednesday?
2. On which day were the fewest magazines delivered?
3. What is the most magazines delivered in one day?
4. How many magazines were delivered on Friday?
5. On which two days were the same number of magazines delivered?

Use the new books graph to answer questions 6–10.

6. How many books were received on Friday?
7. What is the fewest number of books received in one day?
8. On what two days were the same number of books received?
9. What is the most books received in one day?
10. How many books were received on Thursday?

Number Pairs on a Graph

Number pairs give the location of a point on a graph. The number pair (3,4) gives you the location of the star ( ). The first number tells you to go 3 spaces to the right ( ). The second number tells you to go 4 spaces up ( ).

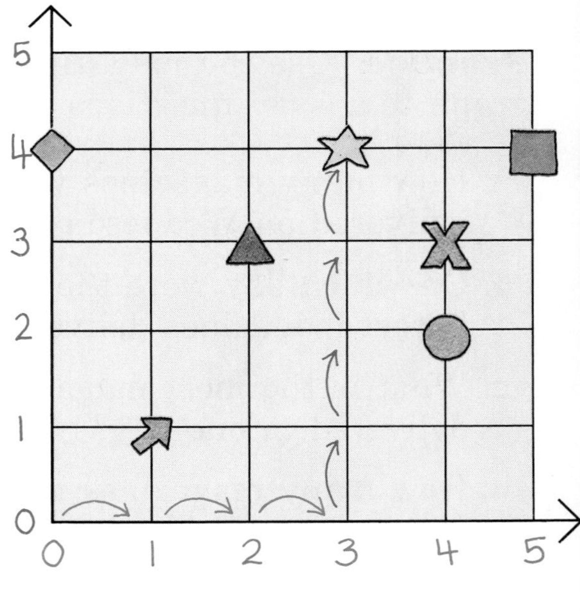

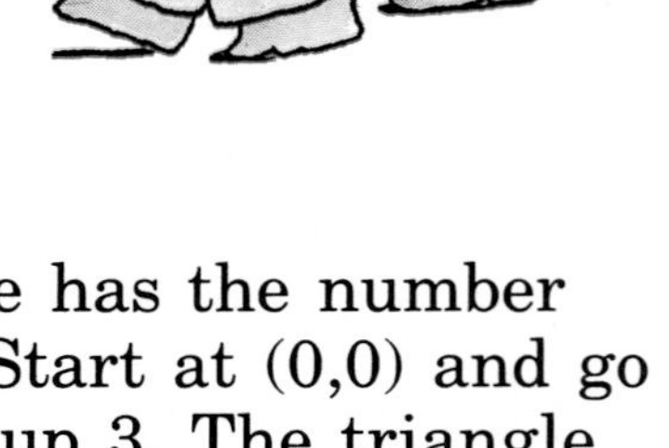

Other Examples

What is the number pair for the circle? The circle is over 4 and up 2. Its number pair is (4,2).

What figure has the number pair (2,3)? Start at (0,0) and go over 2 and up 3. The triangle has the number pair (2,3).

Warm Up Use the graph to answer the questions.

1. What is the number pair for the times sign ( )?
2. What figure has the number pair (5,4)?
3. What is the number pair for the diamond ( )?
4. What figure has the number pair (1,1)?

Practice Use the graph at the right to answer questions 1–4.

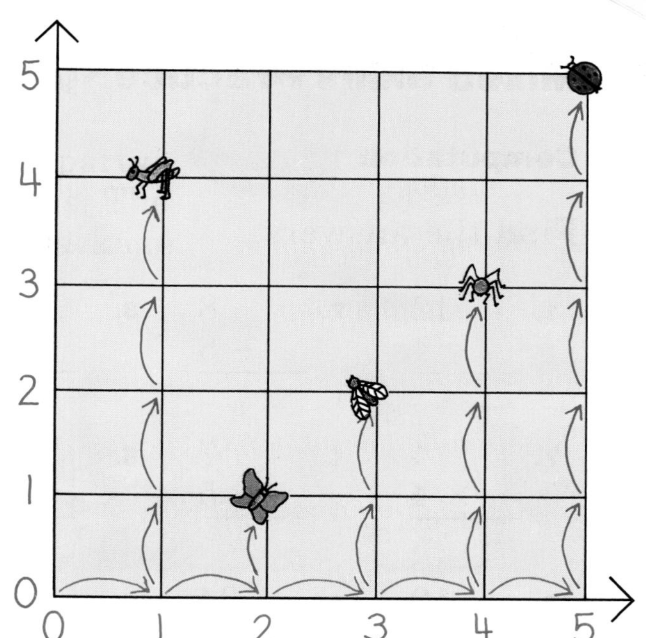

1. The fly is over 3 (⤻) and up 2 (⤴). What is the number pair for the fly?
2. What is the number pair for the grasshopper?
3. What is the number pair for the spider?
4. What is the number pair for the butterfly?

Use the graph at the right to answer questions 5–10.

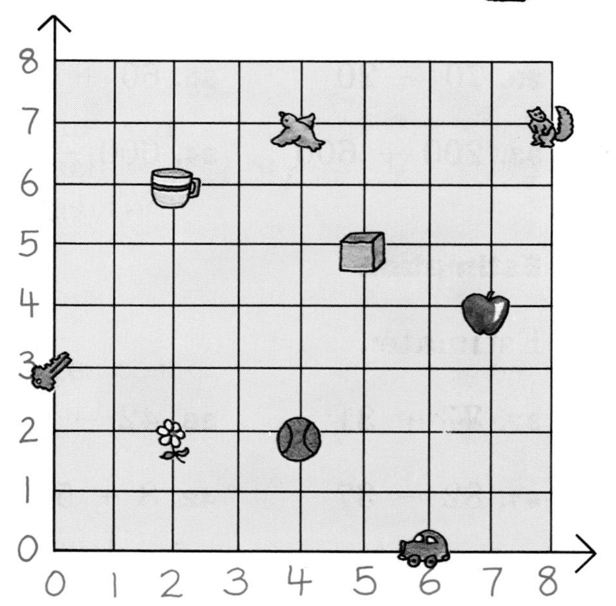

5. Go over 4 (⤻) and up 2 (⤴). What do you find?
6. What has the number pair (2,6)?
7. What has the number pair (7,4)?
8. What has the number pair (0,3)?
9. What has the number pair (4,7)?
10. What has the number pair (2,2)?

QUESTION
DATA
PLAN
ANSWER
CHECK

PROBLEM-SOLVING STRATEGY
Find a Pattern

To solve a problem like this, you may need to do more than just quickly add, subtract, multiply, or divide. A strategy that can help you is given below.

Try This Guy started an exercise program. The first day he did 8 push-ups. The second day he did 10, the third day he did 12, and so on. How many push-ups did he do on the eighth day?

FIND A PATTERN

I will start a table and look for a pattern.

Day	1	2	3		
Push-ups	8	10	12		

I see the pattern! Each day the number of push-ups is 2 more than the day before.

Day	1	2	3	4
Push-ups	8	10	12	14

I'll complete the table using the pattern.

Day	1	2	3	4	5	6	7	8
Push-ups	8	10	12	14	16	18	20	22

Guy did 22 push-ups on the eighth day.

Solve.

1. Guy did 5 sit-ups the first day. The second day he did 6, the third day he did 7, and so on. How many sit-ups did he do on the 18th day?

2. Here is Guy's knee-bend list.

Day	1	2	3	4	5	6
Knee-bends	7	7	9	9	11	11

How many knee-bends did he do on the 14th day?

Name each figure.

1.

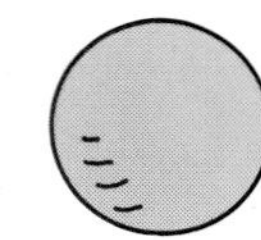

2.

3.

4.

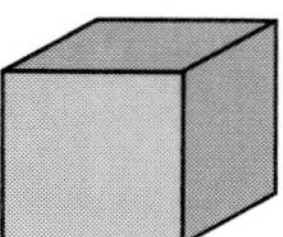

5. Which figure matches these segments?

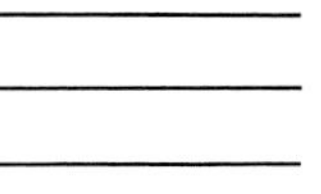

A

B

C

6. How many angles are in this figure?

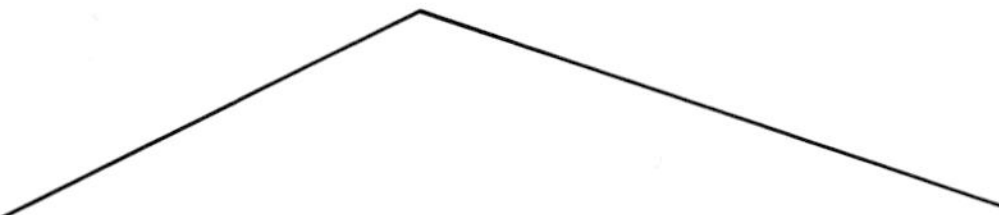

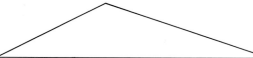

7. How many right angles are in this figure?

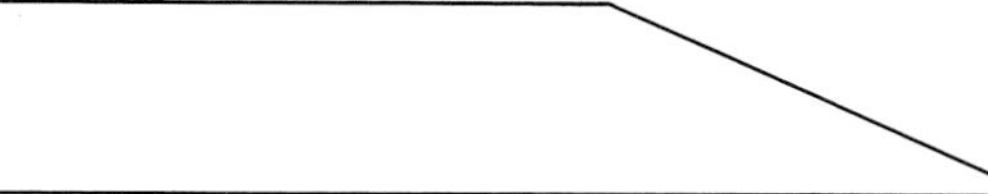

8. Which figure is congruent to the first?

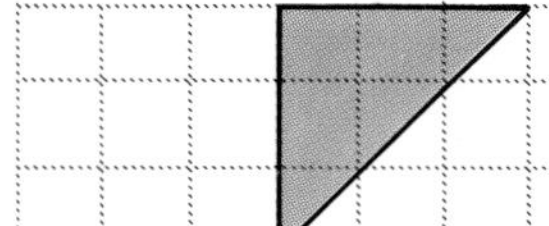

A

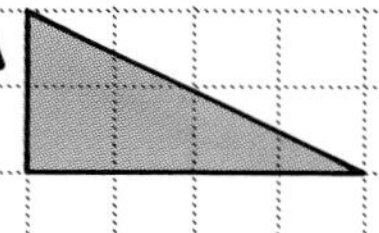

B

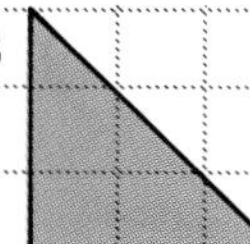

C

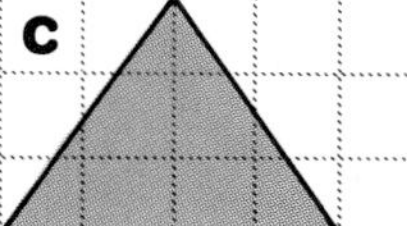

9. Which shape has a line of symmetry?

A

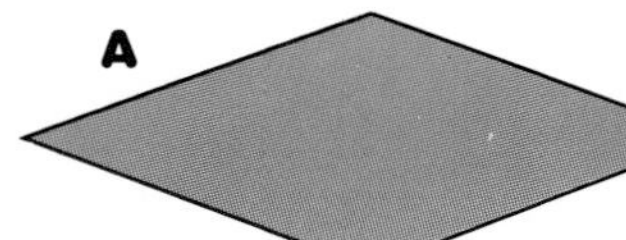

B

C

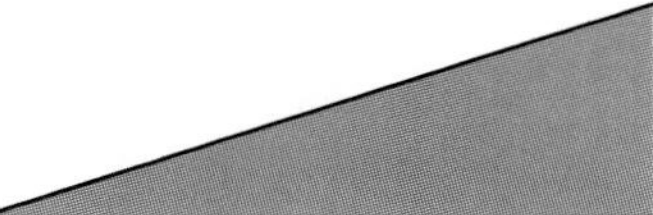

10. Use the graph below. How many votes did Tammy get?

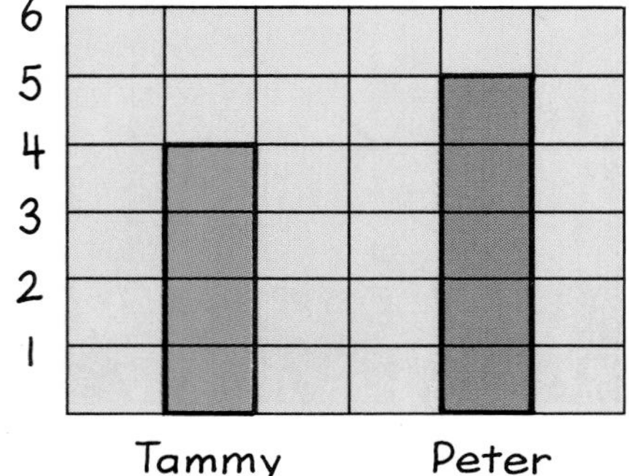

11. Use the graph below. What is the number pair for the bell?

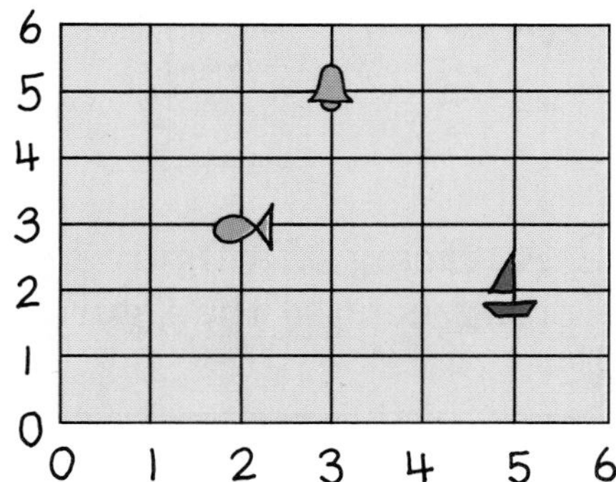

ANOTHER LOOK

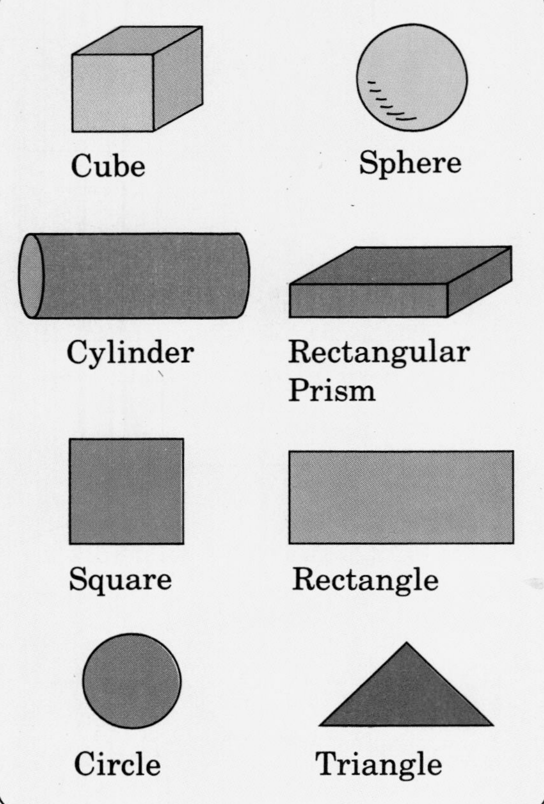

Name each shape.

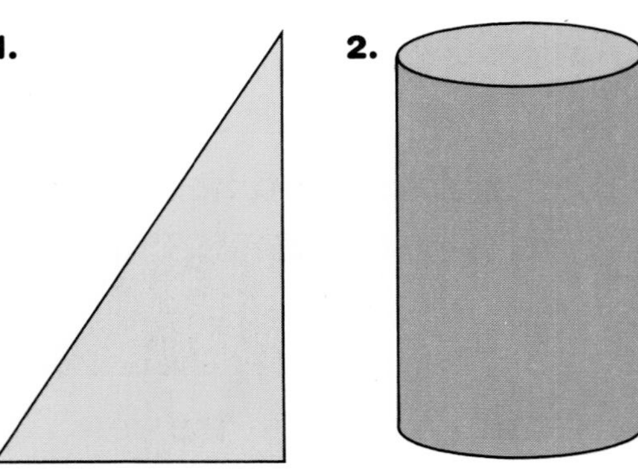

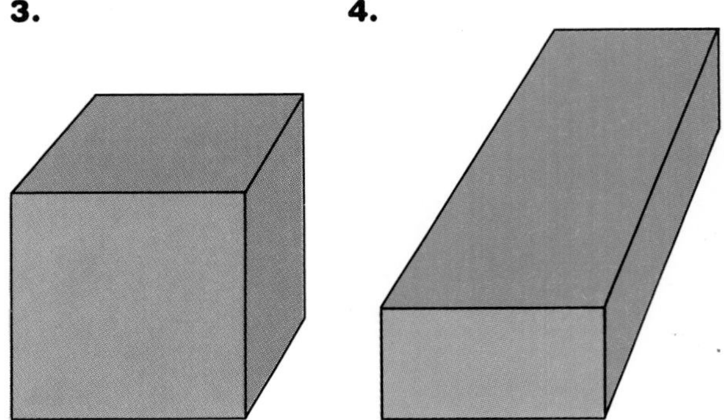

A tracing of a figure is congruent to the figure.

Which figure is congruent to the first?

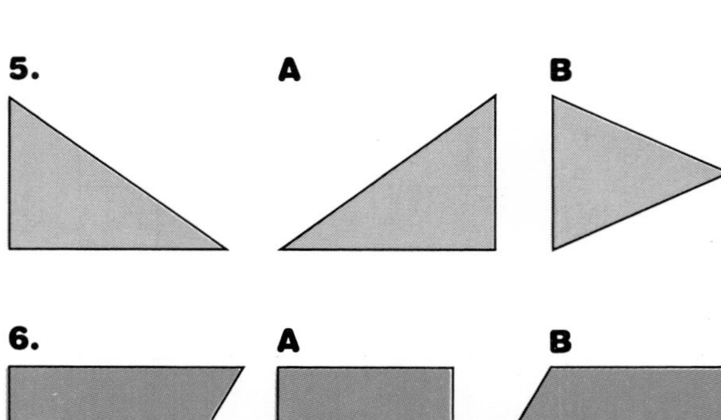

ENRICHMENT

Moving Figures on a Graph

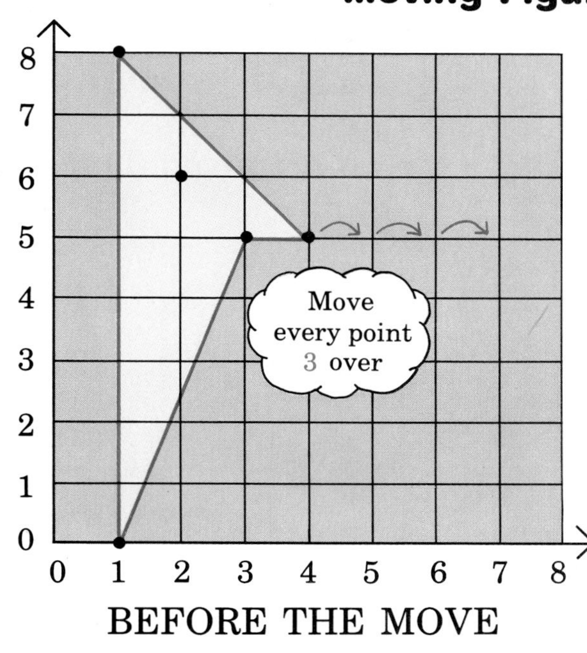

BEFORE THE MOVE

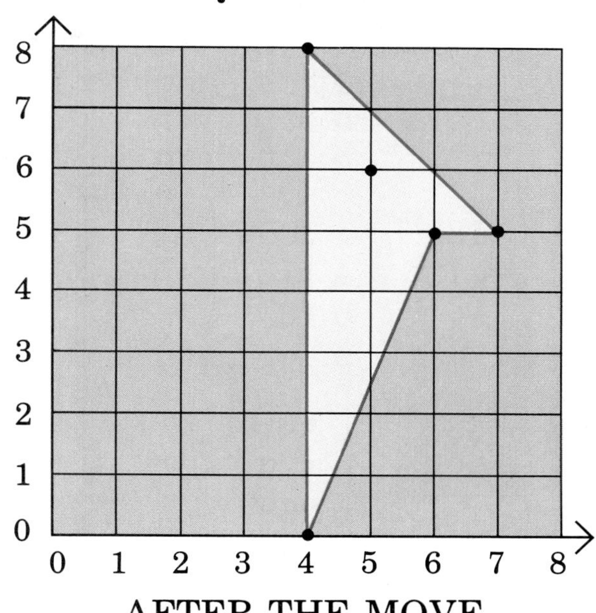

AFTER THE MOVE

Use graph paper. Put the numbers 0–10 on your graph paper as shown below. Show each figure AFTER THE MOVE.

1.

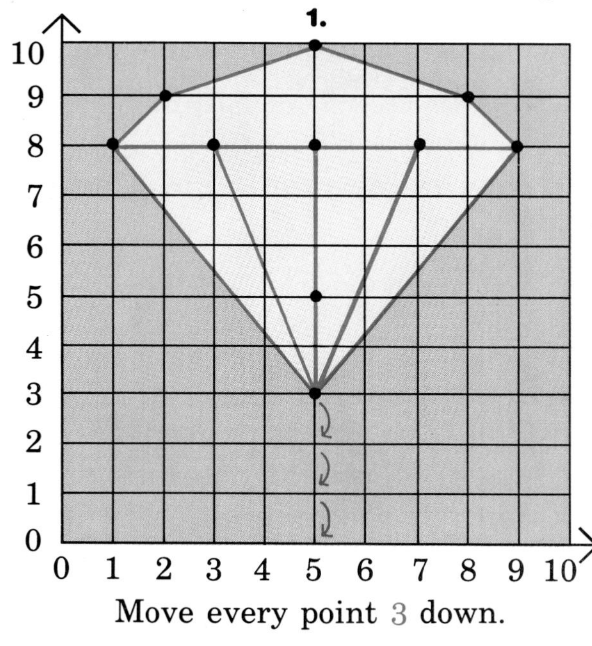

Move every point 3 down.

2.

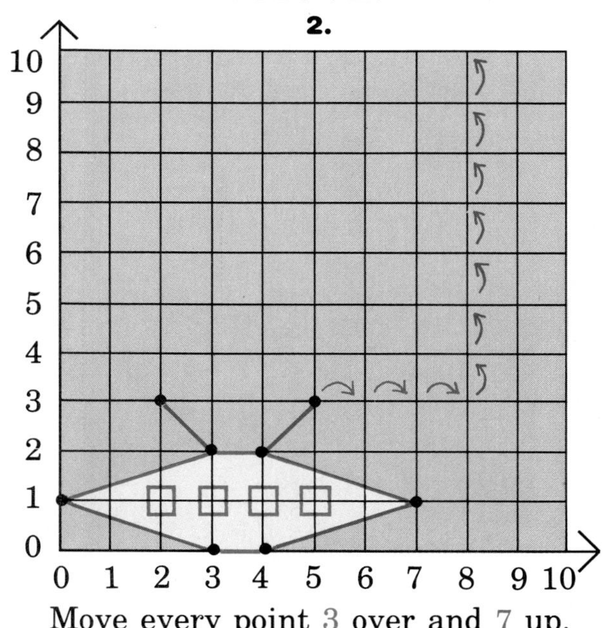

Move every point 3 over and 7 up.

CUMULATIVE REVIEW

Give the letter for the correct answer.

1. $\begin{array}{r} 38 \\ -\ 29 \\ \hline \end{array}$

   A 19
   B 9
   C 8
   D not given

2. $\begin{array}{r} 186 \\ -\ 78 \\ \hline \end{array}$

   A 108
   B 118
   C 109
   D not given

3. $\begin{array}{r} 582 \\ -\ 393 \\ \hline \end{array}$

   A 89
   B 189
   C 289
   D not given

4. $\begin{array}{r} 736 \\ -\ 503 \\ \hline \end{array}$

   A 303
   B 203
   C 223
   D not given

5. $\begin{array}{r} \$7.25 \\ -\ 6.18 \\ \hline \end{array}$

   A $1.07
   B $1.17
   C $1.06
   D not given

6. $\begin{array}{r} \$5.00 \\ -\ 3.79 \\ \hline \end{array}$

   A $2.31
   B $1.31
   C $1.21
   D not given

7. $\begin{array}{r} 2 \\ \times\ 3 \\ \hline \end{array}$

   A 4 B 5
   C 6 D not given

8. $\begin{array}{r} 4 \\ \times\ 2 \\ \hline \end{array}$

   A 6 B 8
   C 10 D not given

9. $\begin{array}{r} 5 \\ \times\ 3 \\ \hline \end{array}$

   A 15
   B 8
   C 12
   D not given

10. $\begin{array}{r} 1 \\ \times\ 6 \\ \hline \end{array}$

    A 5
    B 6
    C 7
    D not given

11. $\begin{array}{r} 4 \\ \times\ 3 \\ \hline \end{array}$

    A 15
    B 12
    C 7
    D not given

12. $\begin{array}{r} 0 \\ \times\ 7 \\ \hline \end{array}$

    A 7
    B 0
    C 70
    D not given

13. Manuel scored 3 field goals in the basketball game. Each field goal was worth 2 points. How many points did Manuel score?

    A 3 B 6
    C 5 D not given

14. Jenny is on a soccer team. Her team plays 3 games each week. How many games does Jenny's soccer team play in 5 weeks?

    A 15 B 8
    C 12 D not given

DIVISION FACTS 9

When Nina goes to the beach with her mother they find seashells. Nina has learned the names of many shells. Some animals live in shells. Nina knows that they like to stay on, under, and between rocks. On her last seashell hunt, Nina found some rocks covered with bluish-purple mussel shells. Nina also found 12 black shells called turban snail shells. She lined up the black shells on the sand with 4 in each row.

Understanding Division

Jay and Carmen are making cakes for the bake sale. Each cake takes 3 eggs. They have 12 eggs. How many cakes can they make?

Find how many threes are in 12.

1 three	2 threes	3 threes	4 threes

There are 4 threes in 12.

Jay and Carmen have enough eggs for 4 cakes.
We write $12 \div 3 = 4 \leftarrow$ Quotient
We read, **"Twelve divided by three equals four."**

Warm Up Answer the questions. Then read the number sentences aloud and give the quotients.

1.

How many 2s are in 6?

$6 \div 2 =$ ____

2.

How many 3s are in 9?

$9 \div 3 =$ ____

3.

How many 2s are in 10?

$10 \div 2 =$ ____

4.

How many 2s are in 4?

$4 \div 2 =$ ____

Practice Answer the questions.

1. 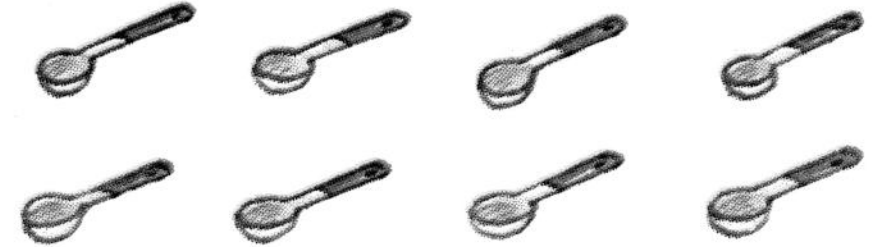

   How many 2s are in 8?

2. 

   How many 3s are in 6?

3. 

   How many 2s are in 12?

4. 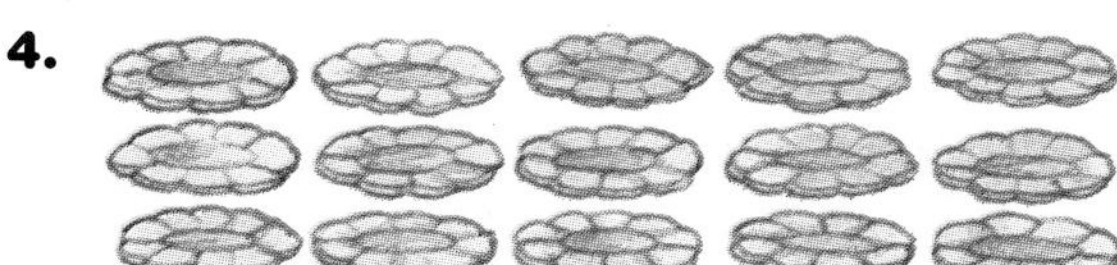

   How many 3s are in 15?

Find the quotients.

5. 

   $8 \div 2 =$ ____

6. 

   $6 \div 3 =$ ____

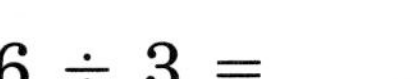

7. 

   $12 \div 2 =$ ____

8. 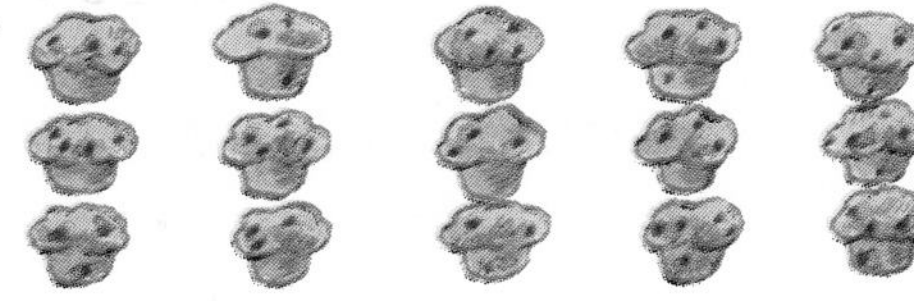

   $15 \div 3 =$ ____

Mixed Applications

9. Dave and Helen made cakes. Each cake took 2 eggs. They had 10 eggs. How many cakes did they make?

10. Ben uses 3 bananas for each loaf of banana bread. How many bananas would he need to make 8 loaves of bread?

THINK

Patterns

Carlos has a music lesson every Friday. Give the dates for his music lessons in February.

MATH

Dividing by 2 and 3

Divide by 2.

1. How many 2s are in 4?

4 ÷ 2 = ___

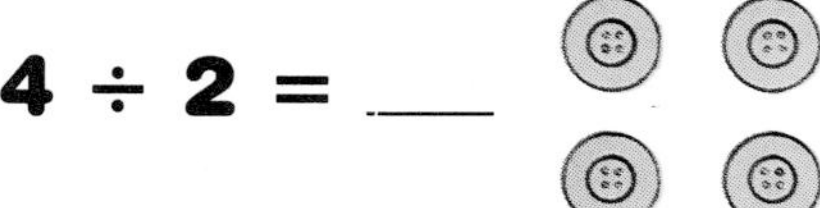

2. How many 2s are in 6?

6 ÷ 2 = ___

Use this picture if you need help.

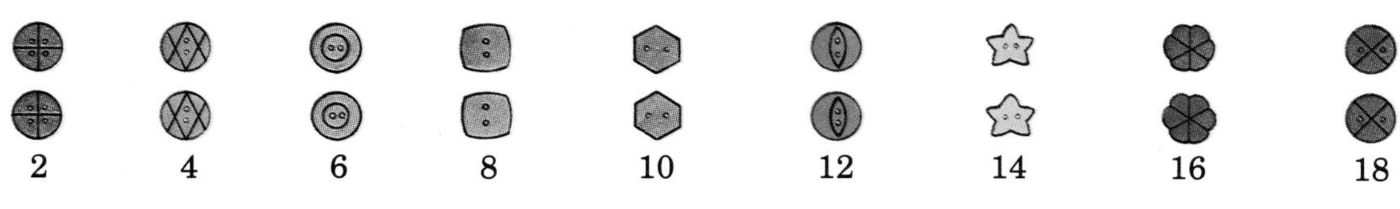

3. 8 ÷ 2 = ___
4. 10 ÷ 2 = ___
5. 12 ÷ 2 = ___
6. 14 ÷ 2 = ___
7. 16 ÷ 2 = ___
8. 18 ÷ 2 = ___

Divide by 3.

9. How many 3s are in 6?

6 ÷ 3 = ___

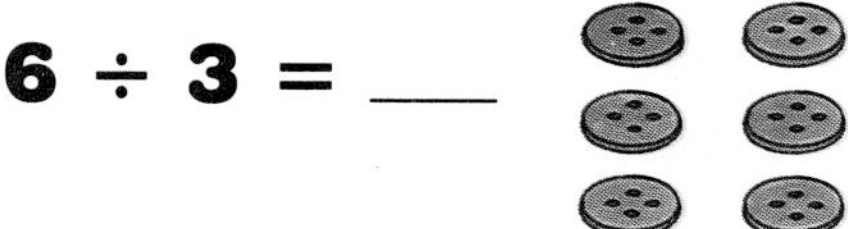

10. How many 3s are in 9?

9 ÷ 3 = ___

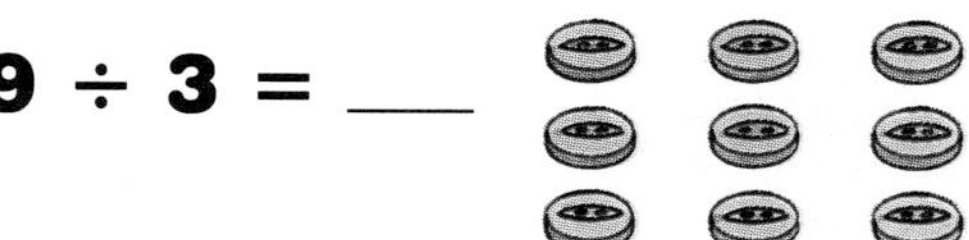

Use this picture if you need help.

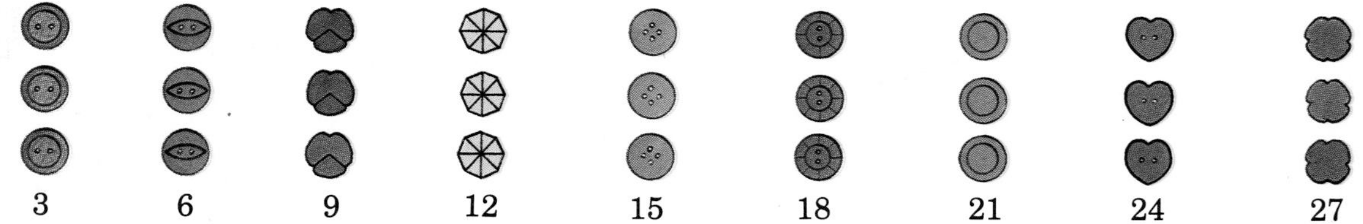

11. 12 ÷ 3 = ___
12. 15 ÷ 3 = ___
13. 18 ÷ 3 = ___
14. 21 ÷ 3 = ___
15. 24 ÷ 3 = ___
16. 27 ÷ 3 = ___

Warm Up Read each number sentence aloud and give the quotient.

17. 14 ÷ 2 = ___
18. 6 ÷ 3 = ___
19. 16 ÷ 2 = ___
20. 27 ÷ 3 = ___
21. 15 ÷ 3 = ___
22. 21 ÷ 3 = ___

Practice Divide.

1. 21 ÷ 3
2. 2 ÷ 2
3. 12 ÷ 2
4. 18 ÷ 3
5. 14 ÷ 2
6. 3 ÷ 3
7. 8 ÷ 2
8. 9 ÷ 3
9. 24 ÷ 3
10. 18 ÷ 2
11. 12 ÷ 3
12. 14 ÷ 2
13. 10 ÷ 2
14. 6 ÷ 2
15. 27 ÷ 3
16. 6 ÷ 3
17. 18 ÷ 3
18. 12 ÷ 2
19. 18 ÷ 2
20. 21 ÷ 3
21. 16 ÷ 2
22. 24 ÷ 3
23. 15 ÷ 3
24. 4 ÷ 2
25. 6 ÷ 2
26. 10 ÷ 2
27. 12 ÷ 3
28. 18 ÷ 2
29. Divide 21 by 3.
30. Divide 8 by 2.
31. Divide 9 by 3.
32. Divide 27 by 3.
33. Divide 16 by 2.
34. Divide 12 by 2.
35. Divide 18 by 3.
36. Divide 24 by 3.
37. Divide 14 by 2.

Give the missing numbers.

	÷2	
	12	6
	18	9
38.	10	▮▮▮
39.	8	▮▮▮
40.	14	▮▮▮
41.	16	▮▮▮

	÷3	
	24	8
	15	5
42.	21	▮▮▮
43.	12	▮▮▮
44.	27	▮▮▮
45.	18	▮▮▮

THINK

Logical Reasoning

Find the sum of

1. the numbers in the red ring.
2. the numbers not in the blue ring.
3. the numbers that are in the blue ring but not the red ring.

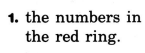

8 5
2 6
4 7

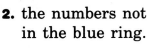

MATH

Multiplication and Division Are Related

5 × 3 = 15
If you know this multiplication fact, you know another multiplication fact and two division facts.
Fact Family
5 × 3 = 15
3 × 5 = 15
15 ÷ 3 = 5
15 ÷ 5 = 3

Warm Up Solve each number sentence.

1. $8 \times 2 =$ ____	**2.** $7 \times 3 =$ ____	**3.** $9 \times 2 =$ ____	**4.** $6 \times 3 =$ ____
$2 \times 8 =$ ____	$3 \times 7 =$ ____	$2 \times 9 =$ ____	$3 \times 6 =$ ____
$16 \div 2 =$ ____	$21 \div 3 =$ ____	$18 \div 2 =$ ____	$18 \div 3 =$ ____
$16 \div 8 =$ ____	$21 \div 7 =$ ____	$18 \div 9 =$ ____	$18 \div 6 =$ ____

You can find quotients by thinking of missing factors.

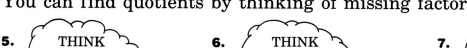

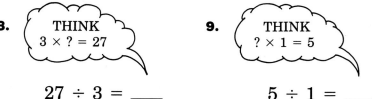

5. THINK ? × 3 = 12

$12 \div 3 =$ ____

6. 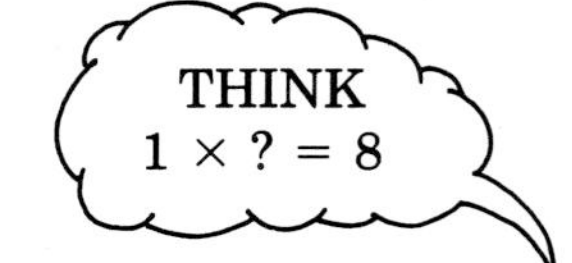

$8 \div 1 =$ ____

7. 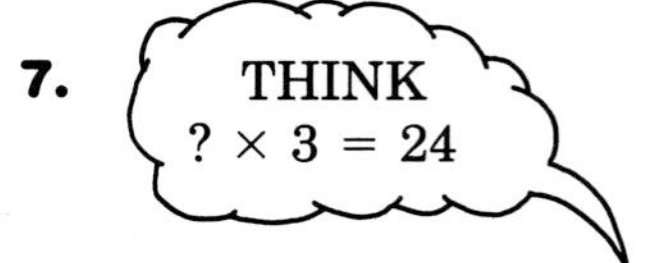

$24 \div 3 =$ ____

8. THINK 3 × ? = 27

$27 \div 3 =$ ____

9. 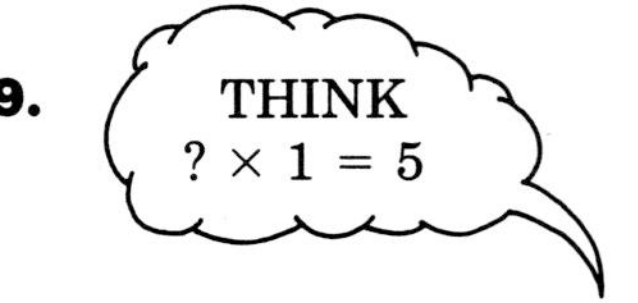

$5 \div 1 =$ ____

10. 

$9 \div 3 =$ ____

Practice Divide. Think about missing factors.

1. $21 \div 3$	2. $15 \div 3$	3. $16 \div 2$	4. $27 \div 3$
5. $9 \div 3$	6. $10 \div 2$	7. $6 \div 3$	8. $14 \div 2$
9. $8 \div 2$	10. $2 \div 1$	11. $24 \div 3$	12. $16 \div 2$
13. $27 \div 3$	14. $3 \div 3$	15. $4 \div 2$	16. $18 \div 3$
17. $6 \div 2$	18. $14 \div 2$	19. $7 \div 1$	20. $2 \div 2$
21. $9 \div 1$	22. $12 \div 3$	23. $12 \div 2$	24. $3 \div 1$

Write a multiplication and a division number sentence for each picture. Example:

25.

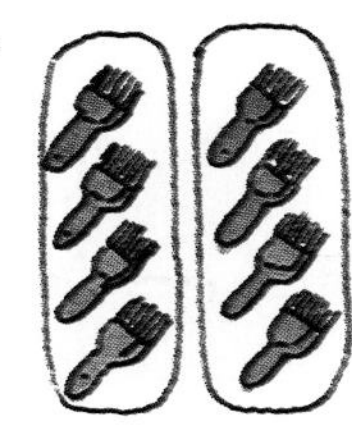

26.

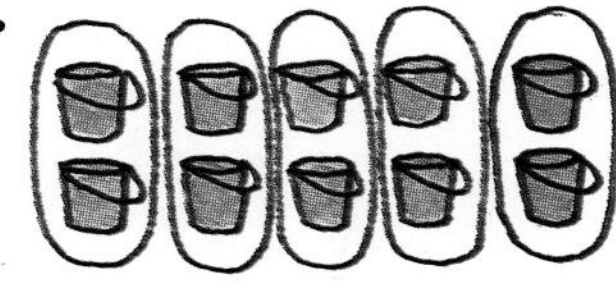

27.

28.

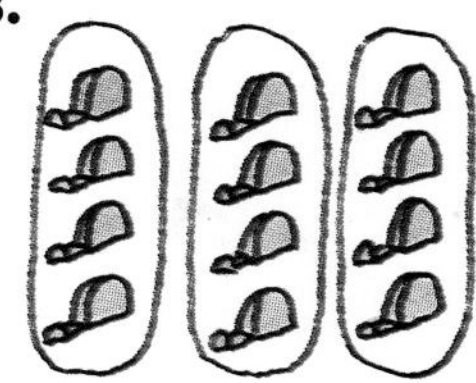

SKILLKEEPER

Multiply.

1. 7×2	2. 3×5	3. 4×1	4. 2×6	5. 8×0	6. 2×3
7. 3×9	8. 6×2	9. 2×4	10. 5×3	11. 9×2	12. 2×2

Dividing by 4

Divide by 4.

1. How many 4s are in 20?

20 ÷ 4 = ___

2. How many 4s are in 8?

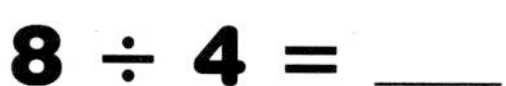

8 ÷ 4 = ___

3. How many 4s are in 12?

12 ÷ 4 = ___

4. How many 4s are in 16?

16 ÷ 4 = ___

Use these pictures if you need help.

4 8 12 16 20 24 28 32 36

5. 28 ÷ 4 = ___
6. 4 ÷ 4 = ___
7. 36 ÷ 4 = ___
8. 20 ÷ 4 = ___
9. 32 ÷ 4 = ___
10. 24 ÷ 4 = ___

Warm Up Give each quotient aloud.

11. 28 ÷ 4 = ___
12. 12 ÷ 4 = ___
13. 18 ÷ 3 = ___
14. 36 ÷ 4 = ___
15. 12 ÷ 2 = ___
16. 32 ÷ 4 = ___
17. 14 ÷ 2 = ___
18. 20 ÷ 4 = ___
19. 24 ÷ 4 = ___
20. 24 ÷ 3 = ___
21. 4 ÷ 4 = ___
22. 18 ÷ 2 = ___
23. 16 ÷ 2 = ___
24. 27 ÷ 3 = ___
25. 16 ÷ 4 = ___
26. 8 ÷ 4 = ___
27. 21 ÷ 3 = ___
28. 15 ÷ 3 = ___

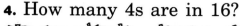

Practice Divide.

1. 16 ÷ 4
2. 21 ÷ 3
3. 32 ÷ 4
4. 18 ÷ 2
5. 20 ÷ 4
6. 8 ÷ 4
7. 10 ÷ 2
8. 24 ÷ 4
9. 14 ÷ 2
10. 36 ÷ 4
11. 9 ÷ 1
12. 24 ÷ 3
13. 28 ÷ 4
14. 18 ÷ 3
15. 12 ÷ 2
16. 36 ÷ 4
17. 16 ÷ 2
18. 28 ÷ 4
19. 24 ÷ 4
20. 32 ÷ 4
21. How many 4s are in 16?
22. How many 4s are in 24?
23. How many 4s are in 32?
24. How many 4s are in 12?
25. How many 4s are in 8?
26. How many 4s are in 36?

27.

How many boxes of 4 can you fill?

28.

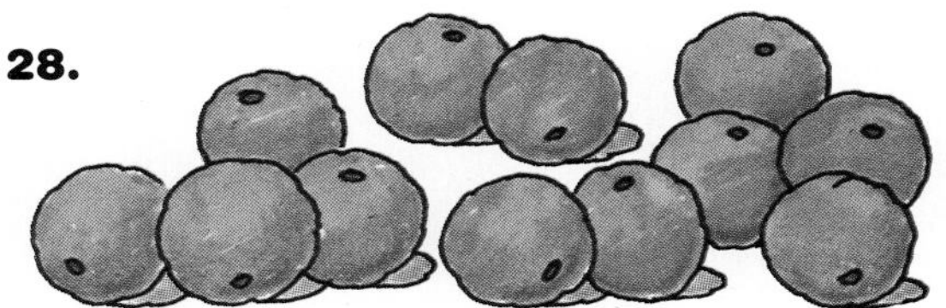

How many boxes of 3 can you fill?

Find the missing numbers.

	X3	
	4	12
	6	18
29.	▥	6
30.	▥	15
31.	▥	9
32.	▥	24

	X4	
	5	20
	7	28
33.	▥	24
34.	▥	36
35.	▥	12
36.	▥	32

THINK MATH

Using a Calculator

Start with ⟶ 162
Subtract ⟶ 27
135
Subtract ⟶ 27
108
Continue ⟶ ⋮

How many times did you subtract to get 0?
How many 27s are in 162?
Find 162 ÷ 27 on your calculator.

More Practice, page 395, Set C

Dividing by 5

Divide by 5.

1. How many 5s are in 20?

20 ÷ 5 = ___

2. How many 5s are in 15?

15 ÷ 5 = ___

3. How many 5s are in 10?

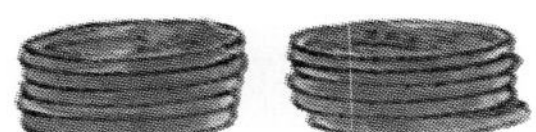

10 ÷ 5 = ___

4. How many 5s are in 25?

25 ÷ 5 = ___

Use this picture if you need help.

5 10 15 20 25 30 35 40 45

5. 40 ÷ 5 = ___
6. 5 ÷ 5 = ___
7. 30 ÷ 5 = ___
8. 25 ÷ 5 = ___
9. 45 ÷ 5 = ___
10. 35 ÷ 5 = ___

Warm Up Give each quotient aloud.

11. 15 ÷ 5 = ___
12. 32 ÷ 4 = ___
13. 35 ÷ 5 = ___
14. 18 ÷ 2 = ___
15. 27 ÷ 3 = ___
16. 25 ÷ 5 = ___
17. 10 ÷ 5 = ___
18. 20 ÷ 4 = ___
19. 45 ÷ 5 = ___
20. 21 ÷ 3 = ___
21. 40 ÷ 5 = ___
22. 16 ÷ 2 = ___
23. 30 ÷ 5 = ___
24. 24 ÷ 4 = ___
25. 5 ÷ 5 = ___
26. 20 ÷ 5 = ___
27. 12 ÷ 2 = ___
28. 28 ÷ 4 = ___

Practice Divide.

1. $10 \div 5$
2. $24 \div 4$
3. $30 \div 5$
4. $10 \div 2$
5. $21 \div 3$
6. $5 \div 5$
7. $40 \div 5$
8. $12 \div 4$
9. $20 \div 5$
10. $35 \div 5$
11. $18 \div 3$
12. $45 \div 5$
13. $12 \div 2$
14. $15 \div 5$
15. $16 \div 4$
16. $40 \div 5$
17. $30 \div 5$
18. $16 \div 2$
19. $35 \div 5$
20. $20 \div 5$
21. $20 \div 4$
22. $25 \div 5$
23. $45 \div 5$
24. $27 \div 3$
25. What is 35 divided by 5?
26. What is 20 divided by 5?
27. What is 40 divided by 5?
28. What is 30 divided by 5?

How many nickels could you get for these pennies?

29. 

20 pennies

30. 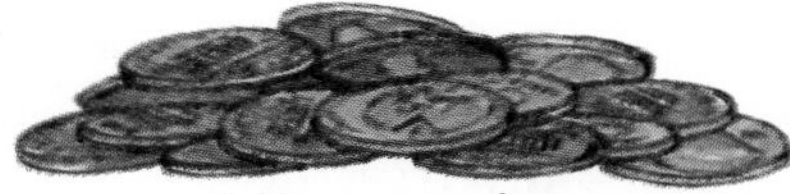

15 pennies

31. How many nickels will it take to buy the two toys?

SKILLKEEPER

Multiply.

1. 9×5
2. 7×6
3. 9×9
4. 6×8
5. 8×8
6. 5×6
7. 3×8
8. 8×7
9. 7×9
10. 6×9
11. 2×8
12. 5×4

More Practice, page 396, Set A

PROBLEM SOLVING
Understanding the Operation

There are 5 boxes of apples.
4 apples are in each box.
There are 20 apples in all.

You can use division two different ways.

Division Problem

Suppose you know:
20 apples, 4 for each box
You can **divide** to find
how many boxes.

$$20 \div 4 = 5$$

There are 5 boxes.

Division tells
how many sets.

Division Problem

Suppose you know:
20 apples, put in 5 boxes
You can **divide** to find
how many in each box.

$$20 \div 5 = 4$$

There are 4 apples in each box.

Division tells
how many in each set.

Solve.

1. There are 12 berries. The berries are shared equally by 4 children. How many berries does each child get?

2. There are 12 berries. Each child gets 3 berries. How many children will get berries?

3. Adam bought 5 tickets. He spent 35 dollars. How much did he pay for each ticket?

4. Rana spent 21 dollars for tickets. Each ticket cost 3 dollars. How many tickets did she buy?

5. ***Strategy Practice*** Rosa had 12 red apples and 8 yellow apples. She divided the apples equally into 5 baskets. How many apples are in each basket? Hint: Choose the operations.

A New Sign for Division

There are 32 marbles.
Each bag holds 4 marbles.
How many bags are there?

32 MARBLES

Two ways to write it

$$32 \div 4 = 8 \qquad 4\overline{)32}$$

Quotient → 8

Divisor → 4

There are 8 bags of marbles.

Practice Find the quotients.

1. $4\overline{)24}$ 2. $3\overline{)18}$ 3. $5\overline{)10}$ 4. $1\overline{)8}$ 5. $5\overline{)30}$

6. $4\overline{)32}$ 7. $3\overline{)24}$ 8. $5\overline{)45}$ 9. $4\overline{)16}$ 10. $2\overline{)14}$

11. $3\overline{)21}$ 12. $5\overline{)25}$ 13. $4\overline{)36}$ 14. $5\overline{)15}$ 15. $4\overline{)12}$

16. $8 \div 2$ 17. $40 \div 5$ 18. $20 \div 4$ 19. $27 \div 3$

20. $15 \div 3$ 21. $35 \div 5$ 22. $28 \div 4$ 23. $20 \div 5$

How many bags of marbles are there?

24. 28 MARBLES

25. 30 MARBLES

PROBLEM SOLVING
Identifying Unneeded Data

Each of these problems has more data than you need. Use only the numbers you need.

Tell what data you do not need. Then solve.

1. There are 15 columns on the first story and 30 columns on the next 6 stories. It takes an hour to clean 5 columns. How long will it take to clean the first story columns?

2. The Tower leans 6 meters. It is 54 meters tall and 16 meters wide. How much taller is it than it is wide?

3. One day 3 workers climbed the 294 steps to the top of the Tower. They cleaned the 12 columns. How many columns did each worker clean if they each cleaned an equal number of columns?

4. A worker sweeps 8 steps a minute for 7 minutes. Then he rests for 15 minutes. How many steps did he sweep?

★ 5. Workers started building the Leaning Tower of Pisa in the year 1173. It began to lean after 3 stories were built. The Tower was finished 199 years after it was started. What year was it finished?

6. ***Strategy Practice*** One day, 30 people went into the Tower the first hour, 35 in the second hour, and 40 in the third hour. At this rate, how many people would go into the Tower in the sixth hour? Hint: Find a pattern.

Practice the Facts

Find the products.

1. $\begin{array}{r}4\\ \times 8\\ \hline\end{array}$ 2. $\begin{array}{r}2\\ \times 7\\ \hline\end{array}$ 3. $\begin{array}{r}3\\ \times 6\\ \hline\end{array}$ 4. $\begin{array}{r}5\\ \times 7\\ \hline\end{array}$ 5. $\begin{array}{r}2\\ \times 9\\ \hline\end{array}$ 6. $\begin{array}{r}3\\ \times 8\\ \hline\end{array}$ 7. $\begin{array}{r}2\\ \times 5\\ \hline\end{array}$

8. $\begin{array}{r}5\\ \times 8\\ \hline\end{array}$ 9. $\begin{array}{r}4\\ \times 9\\ \hline\end{array}$ 10. $\begin{array}{r}2\\ \times 3\\ \hline\end{array}$ 11. $\begin{array}{r}3\\ \times 3\\ \hline\end{array}$ 12. $\begin{array}{r}4\\ \times 4\\ \hline\end{array}$ 13. $\begin{array}{r}5\\ \times 5\\ \hline\end{array}$ 14. $\begin{array}{r}4\\ \times 7\\ \hline\end{array}$

15. $\begin{array}{r}5\\ \times 3\\ \hline\end{array}$ 16. $\begin{array}{r}4\\ \times 5\\ \hline\end{array}$ 17. $\begin{array}{r}5\\ \times 4\\ \hline\end{array}$ 18. $\begin{array}{r}3\\ \times 4\\ \hline\end{array}$ 19. $\begin{array}{r}2\\ \times 4\\ \hline\end{array}$ 20. $\begin{array}{r}3\\ \times 3\\ \hline\end{array}$ 21. $\begin{array}{r}4\\ \times 6\\ \hline\end{array}$

22. 9×5 23. 4×2 24. 4×3 25. 6×2

26. 7×3 27. 6×5 28. 8×2 29. 9×3

Find the quotients.

30. $3\overline{)21}$ 31. $5\overline{)40}$ 32. $2\overline{)16}$ 33. $5\overline{)25}$ 34. $4\overline{)32}$

35. $2\overline{)12}$ 36. $4\overline{)24}$ 37. $5\overline{)10}$ 38. $4\overline{)16}$ 39. $3\overline{)24}$

40. $5\overline{)20}$ 41. $4\overline{)36}$ 42. $3\overline{)27}$ 43. $5\overline{)35}$ 44. $2\overline{)18}$

45. $20 \div 4$ 46. $10 \div 2$ 47. $45 \div 5$ 48. $12 \div 4$

49. $15 \div 3$ 50. $18 \div 3$ 51. $14 \div 2$ 52. $28 \div 4$

53. $8 \div 2$ 54. $32 \div 4$ 55. $18 \div 2$ 56. $18 \div 3$

PROBLEM SOLVING
Estimation

Use estimation or the basic facts to choose the correct answer.

1. The coach divided 45 players into 5 equal teams. Each team had how many players?
   A 50 **B** 40 **C** 9

2. A team scored 48 points the first half and 53 the second. How many points were scored?
   A 101 **B** 5 **C** 51

3. The Jets scored 35 points. The Giants scored 17. The Jets won by how much?
   A 52 **B** 26 **C** 18

4. The Rams scored 52 points. They made 19 points more than the Eagles. How many did the Eagles make?
   A 33 **B** 71 **C** 47

5. There are 9 tennis courts. 4 players are on each court. How many players are there?
   A 13 **B** 5 **C** 36

6. There were 24 teams at the track meet. They were in 4 equal groups. How many teams were in each group?
   A 4 **B** 6 **C** 20

7. Laura's bowling score was 102. Tod's was 85. How much higher was Laura's score?
   A 17 **B** 23 **C** 94

8. ***Strategy Practice*** There were 4 teams A, B, C, and D in the school. Each team played every other team once. How many games were played? Hint: Make a list.

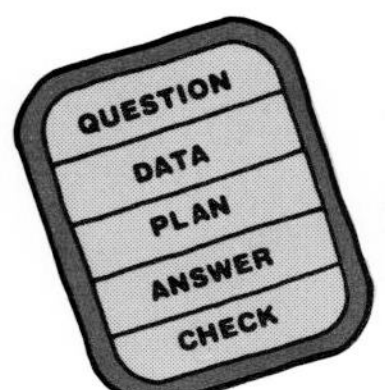

PROBLEM SOLVING
Mixed Practice

Some Hotel Facts
Number of rooms 205
Cost of rooms
single $ 55
double $ 65
Number of employees
kitchen 28
coffee shop 19
dining room 18
front desk 12
housekeeping 32
other 43

Solve. You may need to use the fact sheet.

1. One night only 87 rooms were rented. How many rooms were empty?

2. A family rented a double room and a single room. How much did they pay for both rooms?

3. A housekeeper used 16 sheets. He put 2 on each bed. How many beds did he make?

4. The kitchen workers are divided into 4 equal groups. How many workers are in each group?

5. A group of 32 people checked in. 4 of them stayed in each room. How many rooms were needed?

6. How many people work in the kitchen, the coffee shop, and the dining room of the hotel altogether?

7. **DATA BANK** See page 377. Suppose everyone on a full DC-10 wanted their own room in the hotel. If the hotel were empty, how many could still not have a room?

8. ***Strategy Practice*** Mr. Brown and Mr. Davis checked in. There are 3 rooms, 701, 308, and 512. How many different ways could they be given 2 rooms? Hint: Make a list.

PROBLEM SOLVING
Using the Strategies

Use one or more of the strategies listed to solve each problem below.

PROBLEM-SOLVING STRATEGIES

Guess and Check
Use Logical Reasoning
Draw a Picture
Make a List
Make a Table
Choose the Operations
Find a Pattern

Name	Height
Amy	137 cm
Lee	129 cm
Sam	155 cm
Mary	118 cm
Juan	146 cm

1. Look at the table. Which two children have heights that differ by 17 cm?

2. Maya bought 3 rolls of film. She can take 24 pictures with each roll. The first day Maya took 17 pictures. How many pictures can she still take?

3. Jeff said, "My weight is between 25 kg and 40 kg. It is an even number. The sum of the two digits is 9." How much does Jeff weigh?

4. Sandy had 3 pairs of socks—white, blue, and yellow. The socks were mixed up in her drawer. One morning, without looking, she picked out 2 socks to wear. How many different ways could this "pair" of socks look?

CHAPTER REVIEW/TEST

Answer the questions.

1.

How many 2s are in 12?

2.

How many 3s are in 18?

Find the quotients.

3. 21 ÷ 3 **4.** 25 ÷ 5 **5.** 12 ÷ 4 **6.** 18 ÷ 2

7. 35 ÷ 5 **8.** 32 ÷ 4 **9.** 15 ÷ 3 **10.** 8 ÷ 2

11. 2 ÷ 2 **12.** 9 ÷ 3 **13.** 45 ÷ 5 **14.** 24 ÷ 4

15. 14 ÷ 2 **16.** 20 ÷ 4 **17.** 27 ÷ 3 **18.** 15 ÷ 5

19. $4\overline{)8}$ **20.** $5\overline{)10}$ **21.** $2\overline{)12}$ **22.** $5\overline{)40}$ **23.** $3\overline{)12}$

24. $4\overline{)16}$ **25.** $2\overline{)16}$ **26.** $1\overline{)6}$ **27.** $4\overline{)36}$ **28.** $3\overline{)18}$

29. $5\overline{)30}$ **30.** $3\overline{)24}$ **31.** $5\overline{)20}$ **32.** $2\overline{)10}$ **33.** $4\overline{)28}$

Solve.

34. Luis bought 5 tickets. He spent 30 dollars. How much was each ticket?

36. There were 40 clean towels. Each room needs 5 towels. How many rooms can get clean towels?

35. Trudy bought 8 tickets. Each ticket cost 4 dollars. How much did she spend for the tickets?

37. Jack spent 40 cents for 8 pencils. How much did each pencil cost?

ANOTHER LOOK

Dividing by 2 and 3

1	2	3	4	5	6	7	8	9
2	4	6	8	10	12	14	16	18

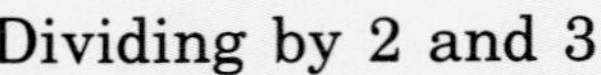

1	2	3	4	5	6	7	8	9
3	6	9	12	15	18	21	24	27

12 ÷ 2 = 6
16 ÷ 2 = 8

15 ÷ 3 = 5
27 ÷ 3 = 9

Using multiplication
to find quotients.

3 × 4 = 12

12 ÷ 4 = 3
12 ÷ 3 = 4

4 × 5 = 20

20 ÷ 5 = 4
20 ÷ 4 = 5

5 × [8] = 40

5)40

4 × [7] = 28

4)28

3 × [9] = 27

3)27

2 × [6] = 12

2)12

Divide.

1. 12 ÷ 2 **2.** 21 ÷ 3

3. 12 ÷ 3 **4.** 10 ÷ 2

5. 16 ÷ 2 **6.** 27 ÷ 3

7. 18 ÷ 3 **8.** 18 ÷ 2

9. 8 ÷ 2 **10.** 14 ÷ 2

11. 15 ÷ 3 **12.** 9 ÷ 3

13. 32 ÷ 4 **14.** 25 ÷ 5

15. 35 ÷ 5 **16.** 24 ÷ 4

17. 16 ÷ 4 **18.** 40 ÷ 5

19. 15 ÷ 5 **20.** 20 ÷ 4

21. 5)35 **22.** 3)18 **23.** 2)18

24. 4)32 **25.** 3)24 **26.** 5)45

27. 4)16 **28.** 4)28 **29.** 2)14

Probability Zoo Game

Use a spinner like the one shown at the right.

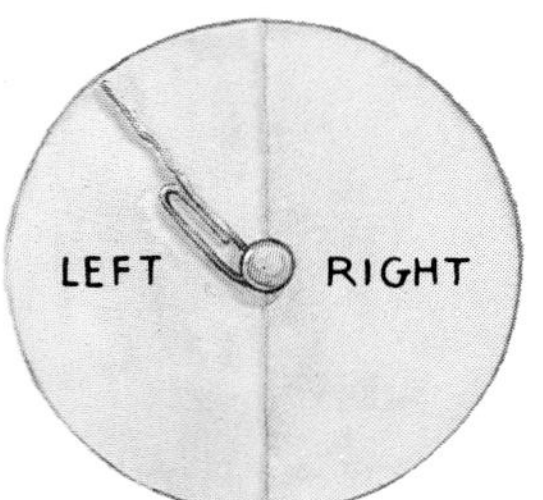

Game Rules

1. Start at Enter. Follow the zoo path until it splits into two paths.
2. Spin to find out which way to turn.
3. Follow the new path.
4. Spin again every time the path splits into two paths.

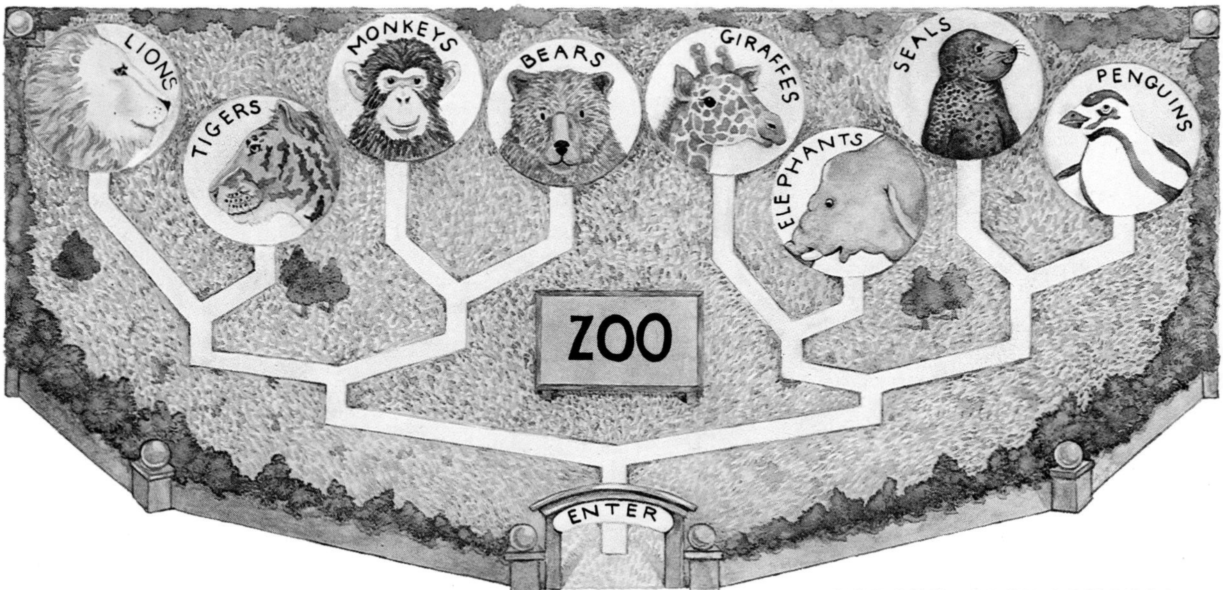

1. How many spins do you think it takes to visit each animal?
2. Do you have an even chance of turning left or right at each spin?
3. Play the game 24 times. Use tally marks to make a record of the animals you visit. Do you visit them all about the same number of times or do you visit some animals more?

NUMBER OF VISITS TO EACH ANIMAL

LIONS
TIGERS
MONKEYS
BEARS
GIRAFFES
ELEPHANTS
SEALS
PENGUINS

CUMULATIVE REVIEW

Give the letter for the correct answer.

1. 9×7
   A 56 B 54
   C 63 D not given

2. 7×7
   A 46 B 49
   C 56 D not given

3. 9×8
   A 72 B 56
   C 64 D not given

4. 8×6
   A 48 B 56
   C 63 D not given

5. 7×8
   A 63 B 64
   C 56 D not given

6. 9×9
   A 49 B 89
   C 84 D not given

7. What time is shown?

   A 10:05
   B 1:52
   C 10:52
   D not given

8. Give the perimeter.

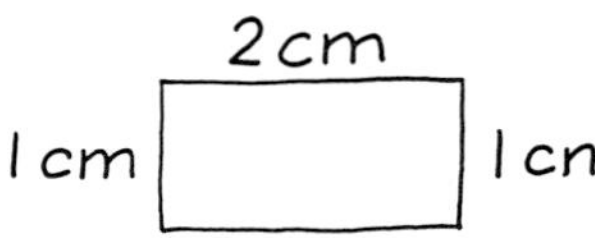

   A 2 cm
   B 4 cm
   C 6 cm
   D not given

9. A kitchen counter is about 1 ____ high.
   A centimeter B meter
   C kilometer D not given

10. Choose the best estimate.

A cup

   A more than a liter
   B less than a liter
   C a liter
   D not given

11. Choose the best estimate.

A banana

   A more than a gram
   B less than a gram
   C a gram
   D not given

12. Read the thermometer.

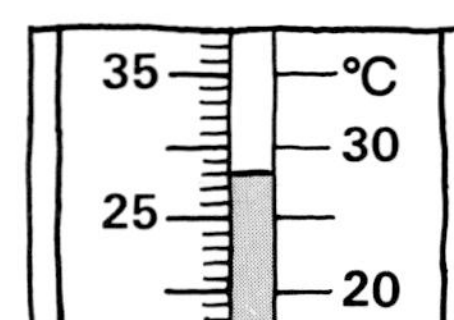

   A 32°C
   B 28°C
   C 23°C
   D not given

13. Timothy gets on the bus at 8:10 a.m. The ride to school takes 25 minutes. What time does he get to school?
   A 8:25 a.m. B 8:35 a.m.
   C 8:45 a.m. D not given

14. Jessica's ride home from school takes 45 minutes. She gets home at 4:00 p.m. What time does she leave school?
   A 4:45 p.m. B 3:45 p.m.
   C 3:15 p.m. D not given

MORE DIVISION FACTS 10

Diane is the mail carrier who delivers mail on Steve's block. One summer day Diane asked Steve if he wanted to come with her for a few hours. First he watched as she opened her truck and filled her mailbag. There is so much mail that Diane often fills her bag 12 times in one day. Her arms must be strong because she carries about 9 kg of mail at a time. Diane works 5 days a week. Each week she walks more than 45 km.

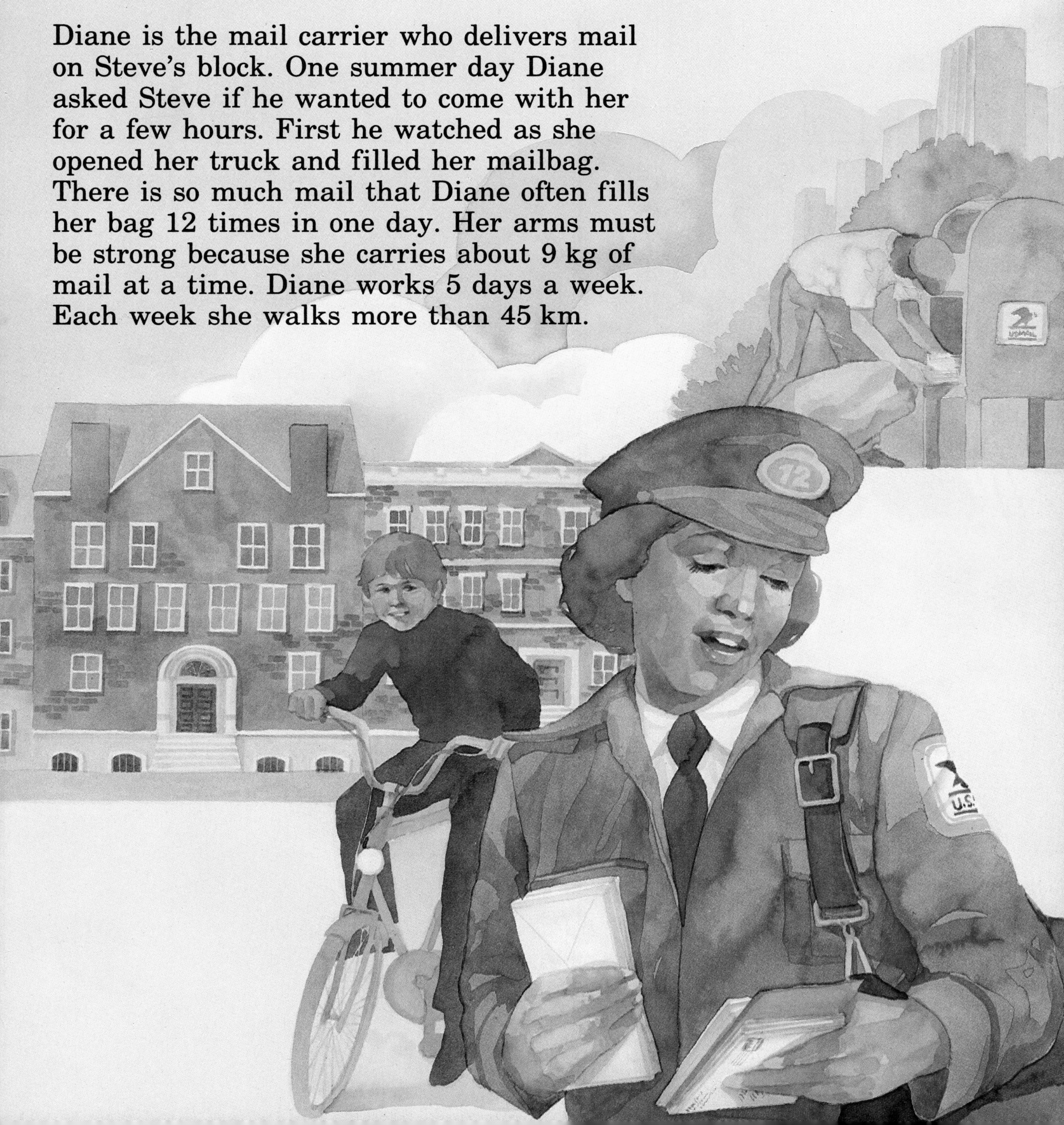

Dividing by 6

Scott bought 30 cans of juice. There were 6 cans in each box. How many boxes of juice did Scott buy?

Betsy bought 42 cans of juice. There were 6 cans in each box. How many boxes of juice did Betsy buy?

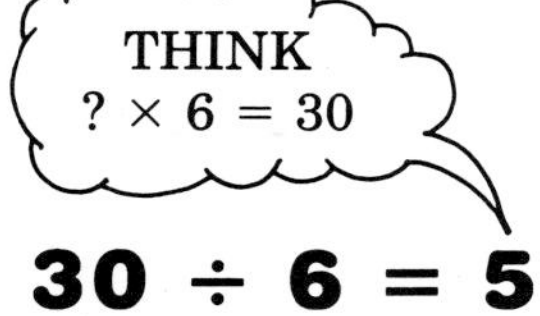

30 ÷ 6 = 5

Scott bought 5 boxes of juice.

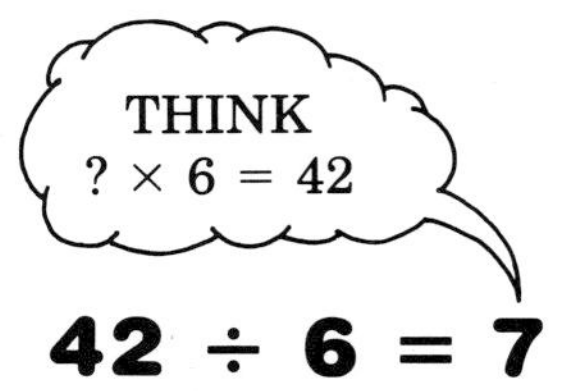

42 ÷ 6 = 7

Betsy bought 7 boxes of juice.

Solve. Think about missing factors.

1. ? × 6 = 36

36 ÷ 6 = ____

2. ? × 6 = 48

48 ÷ 6 = ____

3. ? × 6 = 54

54 ÷ 6 = ____

Warm Up Read each number sentence aloud and give the quotient.

4. 12 ÷ 6 = ____ **5.** 24 ÷ 3 = ____ **6.** 18 ÷ 6 = ____ **7.** 54 ÷ 6 = ____

8. 24 ÷ 6 = ____ **9.** 48 ÷ 6 = ____ **10.** 30 ÷ 5 = ____ **11.** 45 ÷ 5 = ____

Give each quotient aloud.

12. $4\overline{)32}$ **13.** $6\overline{)30}$ **14.** $4\overline{)28}$ **15.** $5\overline{)40}$

16. $6\overline{)54}$ **17.** $3\overline{)27}$ **18.** $6\overline{)24}$ **19.** $2\overline{)16}$

Practice Divide.

1. $6\overline{)12}$
2. $6\overline{)30}$
3. $4\overline{)36}$
4. $6\overline{)24}$
5. $6\overline{)36}$
6. $6\overline{)18}$
7. $6\overline{)48}$
8. $1\overline{)8}$
9. $5\overline{)25}$
10. $6\overline{)42}$
11. $27 \div 3$
12. $24 \div 6$
13. $18 \div 2$
14. $30 \div 6$
15. $42 \div 6$
16. $30 \div 5$
17. $36 \div 6$
18. $6 \div 6$
19. How many 6s are in 24?
20. How many 6s are in 42?
21. How many 6s are in 12?
22. How many 6s are in 30?
23. How many 6s are in 48?
24. How many 6s are in 54?
25. How many 6s are in 36?
26. How many 6s are in 18?

Mixed Applications

27. Pam bought 36 muffins. There were 6 muffins in each package. How many packages did she buy?
28. Ms. Chan bought 9 packages of rolls. There were 6 rolls in each package. How many rolls did she buy?
29. This problem has extra data. Jim packed 42 twelve-ounce bottles in boxes holding 7 each. How many boxes did he use?

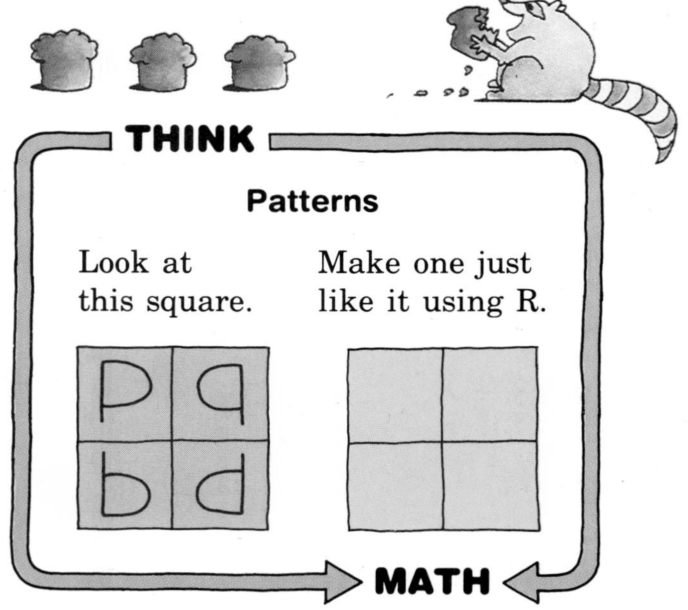

THINK
Patterns
Look at this square.
Make one just like it using R.
MATH

More Practice, page 396, Set B

Dividing by 7

Peg's puppy is 42 days old. There are 7 days in a week. How many weeks old is the puppy?

THINK
$? \times 7 = 42$

42 ÷ 7 = 6

Peg's puppy is 6 weeks old.

Eric's kitten is only 28 days old. There are 7 days in a week. How many weeks old is Eric's kitten?

THINK
$? \times 7 = 28$

28 ÷ 7 = 4

Eric's kitten is 4 weeks old.

Solve. Think about missing factors.

1. $? \times 7 = 49$

$49 \div 7 =$ ____

2. $? \times 7 = 63$

$63 \div 7 =$ ____

3. $? \times 7 = 56$

$56 \div 7 =$ ____

Warm Up Give each quotient aloud.

4. $35 \div 7 =$ ____ **5.** $14 \div 7 =$ ____ **6.** $30 \div 5 =$ ____ **7.** $28 \div 7 =$ ____

8. $28 \div 4 =$ ____ **9.** $63 \div 7 =$ ____ **10.** $42 \div 7 =$ ____ **11.** $36 \div 4 =$ ____

12. $1\overline{)7}$ **13.** $2\overline{)14}$ **14.** $7\overline{)7}$ **15.** $3\overline{)24}$

16. $7\overline{)63}$ **17.** $7\overline{)21}$ **18.** $7\overline{)49}$ **19.** $7\overline{)28}$

Practice Divide.

1. $6\overline{)42}$ 2. $7\overline{)35}$ 3. $7\overline{)49}$ 4. $4\overline{)24}$ 5. $7\overline{)21}$

6. $7\overline{)56}$ 7. $7\overline{)28}$ 8. $7\overline{)7}$ 9. $7\overline{)42}$ 10. $5\overline{)25}$

11. $6\overline{)48}$ 12. $3\overline{)27}$ 13. $7\overline{)56}$ 14. $6\overline{)54}$ 15. $7\overline{)63}$

16. $7\overline{)35}$ 17. $7\overline{)14}$ 18. $5\overline{)40}$ 19. $6\overline{)36}$ 20. $7\overline{)49}$

21. $10 \div 2$ 22. $42 \div 7$ 23. $63 \div 7$ 24. $28 \div 7$

25. Divide 49 by 7.
26. Divide 21 by 7.
27. Divide 56 by 7.
28. Divide 35 by 7.
29. Divide 7 by 7.
30. Divide 63 by 7.
31. Divide 42 by 7.
32. Divide 28 by 7.

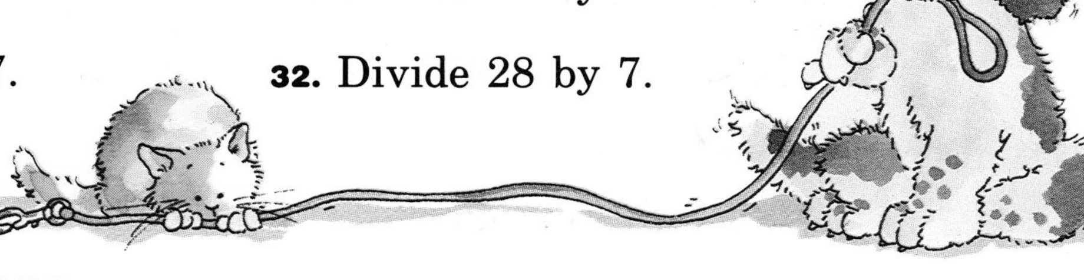

Mixed Applications

33. Steven has had his rabbit, Fred, for exactly 6 weeks. How many days old is Fred?

34. Dora's puppy is 49 days old. How many weeks old is Dora's puppy?

SKILLKEEPER

Add.

1.	2.	3.	4.	5.
$1.58 + 1.21	$7.50 + 3.60	$8.95 + 7.23	$5.39 + 6.56	$1.06 + 2.78

6.	7.	8.	9.	10.
$6.05 + 8.98	$5.50 + 2.25	$3.80 + 7.52	$6.98 + 3.23	$6.86 + 7.54

More Practice, page 396, Set C

Practice the Facts

Division Fact Helpers		
Fact-Family Numbers	Missing Factor	Thinking About Sets
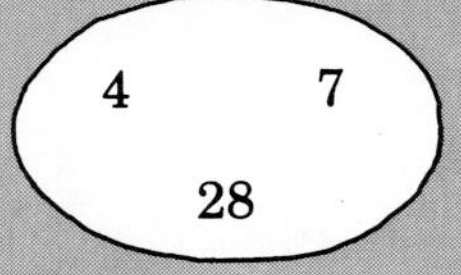	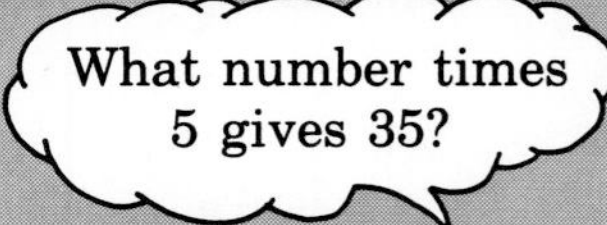	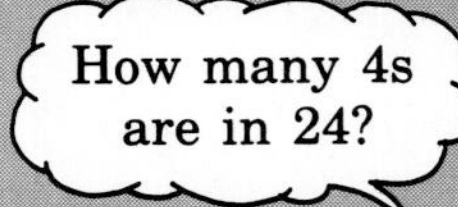
$28 \div 7 = $ ____	$35 \div 5 = $ ____	$24 \div 4 = $ ____

Find the quotients.

1. $36 \div 4$ **2.** $7 \div 7$ **3.** $35 \div 5$ **4.** $54 \div 6$

5. $35 \div 7$ **6.** $16 \div 2$ **7.** $18 \div 3$ **8.** $9 \div 3$

9. $8 \div 4$ **10.** $48 \div 6$ **11.** $10 \div 5$ **12.** $12 \div 6$

13. $56 \div 7$ **14.** $6 \div 3$ **15.** $20 \div 4$ **16.** $4 \div 4$

17. $21 \div 3$ **18.** $14 \div 7$ **19.** $12 \div 2$ **20.** $40 \div 5$

21. $6\overline{)24}$ **22.** $4\overline{)12}$ **23.** $5\overline{)5}$ **24.** $7\overline{)28}$ **25.** $2\overline{)14}$

26. $7\overline{)63}$ **27.** $3\overline{)3}$ **28.** $4\overline{)16}$ **29.** $3\overline{)12}$ **30.** $5\overline{)25}$

31. $6\overline{)18}$ **32.** $5\overline{)20}$ **33.** $2\overline{)18}$ **34.** $7\overline{)49}$ **35.** $6\overline{)42}$

36. $3\overline{)24}$ **37.** $7\overline{)21}$ **38.** $5\overline{)45}$ **39.** $4\overline{)24}$ **40.** $3\overline{)15}$

PROBLEM SOLVING

Multi-step Problems

Solve. Each problem requires more than one step.

1. Dee bought some blue buttons for 12¢ and some red buttons for 20¢. Each one cost 4¢. How many buttons did Dee buy?

2. Paco had \$12. He spent \$4 for a gift for his sister. Then he earned \$5. How much does Paco have now?

3. Lee bought 6 animal books. Each one cost \$3. He bought another book for \$5. What was the total cost?

4. Rita saved \$19. She earned another \$9 for cutting grass. She spent all of her money to buy 7 cans of paint. How much was each can?

5. Luke bought 5 tickets. He paid for them with a 20-dollar bill and a 10-dollar bill. How much was each ticket?

6. Gail had \$43. She bought a gift for \$28. She spent the rest of her money on books that were \$3 each. How many books did she buy?

7. Tony has a 20-dollar bill, a 10-dollar bill, and a 5-dollar bill. How many gifts can he buy for 5 dollars each?

8. ***Strategy Practice*** Jamie saved 1¢ on the first day, 2¢ on the second, 4¢ on the third, 8¢ on the fourth, and so on for 8 days. How much did she save the eighth day?

Dividing by 8

There are 40 arms in all. Each octopus has 8 arms. How many octopuses are there?

40 ÷ 8 = 5

There are 5 octopuses.

There are 64 arms in all. Each octopus has 8 arms. How many octopuses are there?

64 ÷ 8 = 8

There are 8 octopuses.

Solve. Think about missing factors.

1. ? × 8 = 48

48 ÷ 8 = ____

2. ? × 8 = 72

72 ÷ 8 = ____

3. ? × 8 = 56

56 ÷ 8 = ____

Warm Up Give each quotient aloud.

4. 24 ÷ 8 = ____ **5.** 56 ÷ 7 = ____ **6.** 56 ÷ 8 = ____ **7.** 32 ÷ 8 = ____

8. 72 ÷ 8 = ____ **9.** 40 ÷ 8 = ____ **10.** 48 ÷ 6 = ____ **11.** 64 ÷ 8 = ____

12. $8\overline{)32}$ **13.** $4\overline{)32}$ **14.** $6\overline{)54}$ **15.** $8\overline{)24}$

16. $7\overline{)49}$ **17.** $8\overline{)8}$ **18.** $8\overline{)64}$ **19.** $8\overline{)56}$

Practice Divide.

1. $7\overline{)42}$ 2. $8\overline{)48}$ 3. $6\overline{)30}$ 4. $8\overline{)16}$ 5. $8\overline{)64}$

6. $8\overline{)32}$ 7. $8\overline{)72}$ 8. $8\overline{)40}$ 9. $8\overline{)56}$ 10. $4\overline{)36}$

11. $5\overline{)35}$ 12. $6\overline{)54}$ 13. $7\overline{)35}$ 14. $6\overline{)36}$ 15. $8\overline{)24}$

16. $4\overline{)32}$ 17. $8\overline{)64}$ 18. $8\overline{)8}$ 19. $8\overline{)72}$ 20. $8\overline{)48}$

21. $40 \div 8$ 22. $42 \div 6$ 23. $56 \div 8$ 24. $56 \div 7$

25. What is 32 divided by 8?

26. What is 48 divided by 8?

27. What is 64 divided by 8?

Mixed Applications

28. There are 32 arms in all. Each octopus has 8 arms. How many octopuses are there?

29. There were 6 horses in the barn. Each horse had a horseshoe on each foot. How many shoes were there?

30. There are 48 legs in all. Each bug has 6 legs. How many bugs?

31. Make up a question you can answer using this data.

    Each bird has 2 legs. How many birds are there?

THINK

Clock Puzzle

How many minutes will it be until the hands form a straight line?

How many minutes will it be until the hands form a right angle?

MATH

Dividing by 9

36 children wanted to play baseball. There are 9 players on each team. How many teams can be made?

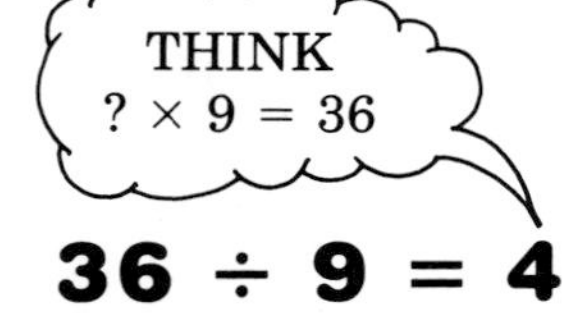

36 ÷ 9 = 4

4 teams can be made.

There were 45 orange slices for the team. The 9 players shared them equally. How many orange slices did each player get?

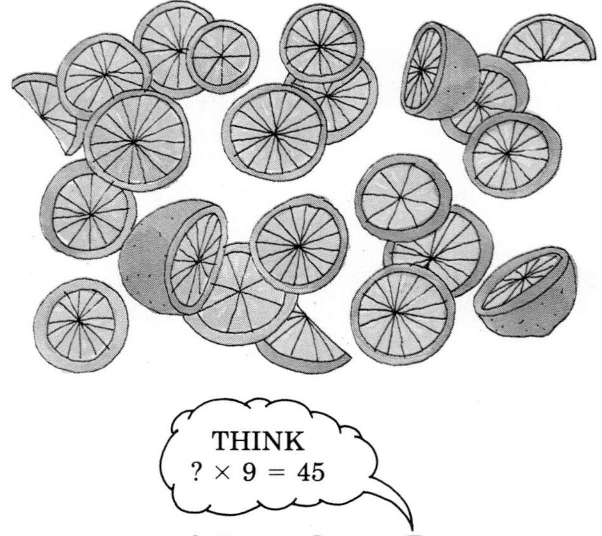

THINK
? × 9 = 45

45 ÷ 9 = 5

Each player gets 5 orange slices.

Solve. Think about missing factors.

1. ? × 9 = 63

63 ÷ 9 = ____

2. ? × 9 = 72

72 ÷ 9 = ____

3. ? × 9 = 81

81 ÷ 9 = ____

Warm Up Give each quotient aloud.

4. 36 ÷ 9 = ____ **5.** 54 ÷ 6 = ____ **6.** 63 ÷ 9 = ____ **7.** 64 ÷ 8 = ____

8. 72 ÷ 9 = ____ **9.** 63 ÷ 7 = ____ **10.** 45 ÷ 9 = ____ **11.** 18 ÷ 9 = ____

12. $8\overline{)40}$ **13.** $9\overline{)9}$ **14.** $8\overline{)72}$ **15.** $9\overline{)63}$

16. $9\overline{)45}$ **17.** $8\overline{)56}$ **18.** $7\overline{)49}$ **19.** $9\overline{)27}$

Practice Divide.

1. $9\overline{)54}$ 2. $8\overline{)56}$ 3. $9\overline{)63}$

4. $9\overline{)36}$ 5. $9\overline{)72}$ 6. $8\overline{)72}$

7. $6\overline{)48}$ 8. $7\overline{)56}$ 9. $9\overline{)9}$ 10. $8\overline{)48}$ 11. $9\overline{)81}$

12. $9\overline{)27}$ 13. $9\overline{)63}$ 14. $6\overline{)54}$ 15. $9\overline{)72}$ 16. $9\overline{)54}$

17. $42 \div 6$ 18. $64 \div 8$ 19. $81 \div 9$ 20. $45 \div 9$

21. How many 9s are in 63?
22. How many 9s are in 54?
23. How many 9s are in 72?
24. How many 9s are in 18?
25. How many 9s are in 45?
26. How many 9s are in 81?

Mixed Applications

27. There are 9 players on each baseball team. How many teams can be made from 54 players?
28. There were 7 teams with 9 players on each team. How many players were there altogether?

SKILLKEEPER

Find the missing factors.

1. $7 \times \square = 49$ 2. $\square \times 3 = 24$ 3. $8 \times \square = 72$

4. $7 \times \square = 56$ 5. $9 \times \square = 54$ 6. $\square \times 5 = 40$

7. $\square \times 4 = 28$ 8. $9 \times \square = 81$ 9. $8 \times \square = 48$

More Practice, page 397, Set B

More about Division

Kirk planned to give all the fish he caught to 2 friends. But Kirk did not catch any fish. How many fish did his friends get?

$$0 \div 2 = 0$$

His friends got 0 fish.

Zero divided by any number (not 0) is zero.

Joni caught 6 fish. She gave 0 fish to each of her friends. How many friends could she give 0 fish to?

$$6 \div 0 = \underline{\quad}$$

This does not make sense!

Never divide by zero.

Practice Divide.

1. $5\overline{)45}$	**2.** $6\overline{)36}$	**3.** $1\overline{)9}$	**4.** $5\overline{)0}$	**5.** $7\overline{)49}$
6. $3\overline{)27}$	**7.** $9\overline{)72}$	**8.** $2\overline{)18}$	**9.** $4\overline{)12}$	**10.** $6\overline{)54}$
11. $8\overline{)64}$	**12.** $5\overline{)40}$	**13.** $9\overline{)0}$	**14.** $8\overline{)48}$	**15.** $5\overline{)30}$
16. $6\overline{)42}$	**17.** $4\overline{)16}$	**18.** $9\overline{)81}$	**19.** $4\overline{)0}$	**20.** $1\overline{)3}$

21. $42 \div 6$	**22.** $16 \div 4$	**23.** $81 \div 9$	**24.** $0 \div 4$
25. $3 \div 1$	**26.** $16 \div 2$	**27.** $28 \div 7$	**28.** $35 \div 7$
29. $56 \div 8$	**30.** $0 \div 7$	**31.** $63 \div 9$	**32.** $12 \div 2$

PROBLEM SOLVING
Choosing a Calculation Method

Your choice!

Pencil-Paper • Mental Math • Estimation • Calculator

You may use any of these methods to solve the problems, but use each method at least once.

1. Jamie paid $1.95 for a pen and $1.98 for paper. She had $5. Was that enough?
2. Mike bought a package of 6 file folders. He paid 54¢ for the package. How much did each file folder cost?
3. Donna Smith bought 27 art books for her class. Each book cost $4.95. How much did all the books cost?
4. Lori bought a pencil for 25¢ and an eraser for 12¢. How much was this in all?
5. Jim had a 5-dollar bill. He spent $3.95. How much change did he get back?
6. Vicki bought an eraser for $0.39. She also bought a box of crayons for $1.29 and a pad of paper for $0.79. How much did she spend?
7. Dick had a 10-dollar bill. He spent $3.95 for a book. Will he get more or less than 6 dollars in change?
8. ***Strategy Practice*** Lois saw some books on sale. The prices were $3, $5, $6, and $7. She bought two books for $9. What were the prices of her books?

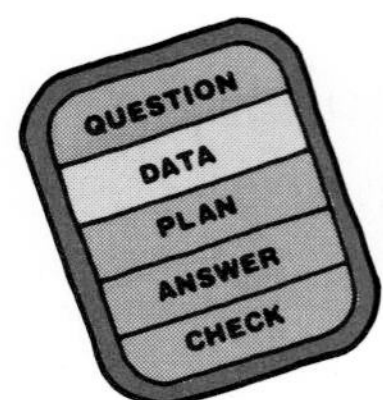

PROBLEM SOLVING
Using Data from a Table

Supermarket Jobs	
Jobs	Number of People
Manager	5
Check-out	32
Baggers	15
Stock	11
Produce	5
Meat	7
Other	9
TOTAL	84

Many people are needed to run a supermarket. The table shows the different jobs and the number of people in each job.

Decide whether you need to use the data from the table. Then solve the problems.

1. Mr. Thomas is the head manager. How many other managers are there?
2. How many more check-out people are there than baggers?
3. A produce worker counted 32 kinds of vegetables and 14 kinds of fruit. How many more kinds of vegetables were there?
4. The meat workers worked a total of 56 hours on Friday. Each person worked the same number of hours. How many hours did each person work?
5. A worker put 56 packages of ground meat into 7 equal stacks. How many packages were in each stack?
6. Each person in meats worked 6 hours on Friday. What was the total amount of hours they worked?
7. How many people work at the supermarket other than the managers?
8. Oranges are sacked 8 to a bag. How many bags can be filled with 72 oranges?

9. The baggers are divided into 3 equal groups. How many are in each group?

10. Mrs. Clark bought 6 bunches of carrots. Each bunch had 7 carrots. How many carrots did she buy?

11. In July, 7 check-out people went on vacation. How many check-out people were left?

12. A produce worker opened a box of apples. She put 8 apples in each of 9 bags. There were 19 apples left in the box. How many were in the box when she opened it?

13. On Monday, all the baggers, stock, produce, and meat people worked in the stock room. How many people worked in the stock room?

14. **DATA BANK** Look at page 376. What is the total number of stores for the first three supermarkets?

15. **DATA HUNT** Go to a supermarket. Count the different kinds of fresh vegetables and fresh fruits. What is the difference in the number of vegetables and fruits?

16. ***Strategy Practice*** Linda and Steve are checkers. Joshua, Meg, and Nate are baggers. How many checker-bagger pairs can they make? Hint: Make a list.

PROBLEM SOLVING
Using the Strategies

Use one or more of the strategies listed to solve each problem below.

PROBLEM-SOLVING STRATEGIES

Guess and Check
Use Logical Reasoning
Draw a Picture
Make a List
Make a Table
Choose the Operations
Find a Pattern

1. Chuy can ride his bicycle 6 miles in 1 hour. Ross can ride 5 miles in 1 hour. They start riding at the same time. How far has Ross gone when Chuy has ridden 36 miles?

Chuy	6	12	18	
Ross	5	10	15	

2. Celia's grandmother lives farther from Celia than her uncle does. Her aunt lives between Celia's grandmother and uncle. Celia's friend lives closer than Celia's uncle. Who lives farthest from Celia?

3. Mr. Abrams drove from home to the park one way. He drove back home another way. He traveled 23 km. What two roads did he take?

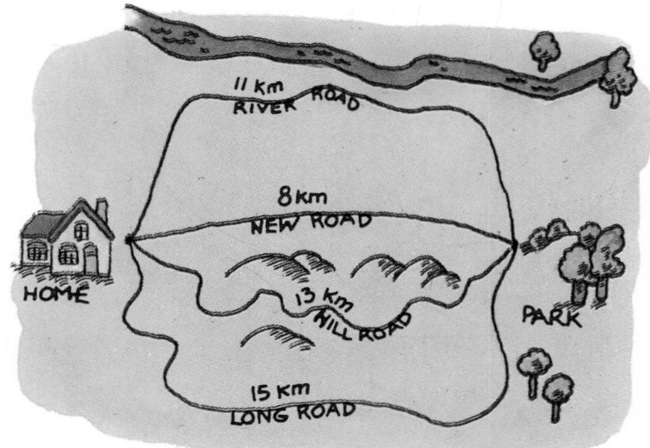

4. There are 17 girls and 19 boys going to the park. Each car can hold 4 children. How many cars are needed?

CHAPTER REVIEW/TEST

Find the quotients.

1. $6\overline{)36}$	**2.** $7\overline{)56}$	**3.** $6\overline{)42}$	**4.** $6\overline{)30}$	**5.** $7\overline{)49}$
6. $6\overline{)48}$	**7.** $7\overline{)63}$	**8.** $7\overline{)42}$	**9.** $6\overline{)54}$	**10.** $7\overline{)35}$
11. $8\overline{)64}$	**12.** $9\overline{)63}$	**13.** $8\overline{)40}$	**14.** $8\overline{)72}$	**15.** $9\overline{)36}$
16. $8\overline{)56}$	**17.** $9\overline{)81}$	**18.** $9\overline{)27}$	**19.** $7\overline{)49}$	**20.** $9\overline{)54}$
21. $8\overline{)72}$	**22.** $6\overline{)42}$	**23.** $7\overline{)14}$	**24.** $8\overline{)40}$	**25.** $6\overline{)18}$
26. $9\overline{)27}$	**27.** $9\overline{)72}$	**28.** $8\overline{)24}$	**29.** $7\overline{)0}$	**30.** $9\overline{)45}$
31. $8\overline{)48}$	**32.** $6\overline{)24}$	**33.** $9\overline{)63}$	**34.** $7\overline{)56}$	**35.** $8\overline{)48}$

Solve.

36. There were 36 check-out people. 19 baggers were helping them. How many workers were there in all?

37. There were 8 bunches of bananas. Each bunch had 7 bananas. How many bananas were there?

38. Ted spent 48 cents for 6 plums. How much did each plum cost?

39. Laura had \$9.00. She spent a total of \$6.95 on school supplies. How much was left?

ANOTHER LOOK

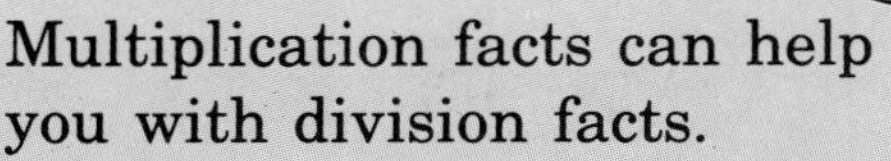

Multiplication facts can help you with division facts.

$$\begin{array}{r}6\\ \times 6\\ \hline 36\end{array}\quad \begin{array}{r}6\\ \times 7\\ \hline 42\end{array}\quad \begin{array}{r}6\\ \times 8\\ \hline 48\end{array}\quad \begin{array}{r}6\\ \times 9\\ \hline 54\end{array}$$

$$6\overline{)42}\ \text{answer } \mathbf{7} \qquad 6\overline{)54}\ \text{answer } \mathbf{9}$$

Divide.

1. $6\overline{)36}$ 2. $6\overline{)30}$ 3. $6\overline{)48}$

4. $6\overline{)24}$ 5. $6\overline{)54}$ 6. $6\overline{)42}$

$$\begin{array}{r}7\\ \times 6\\ \hline 42\end{array}\quad \begin{array}{r}7\\ \times 7\\ \hline 49\end{array}\quad \begin{array}{r}7\\ \times 8\\ \hline 56\end{array}\quad \begin{array}{r}7\\ \times 9\\ \hline 63\end{array}$$

$$7\overline{)42}\ \text{answer } \mathbf{6} \qquad 7\overline{)56}\ \text{answer } \mathbf{8}$$

7. $7\overline{)63}$ 8. $7\overline{)35}$ 9. $7\overline{)49}$

10. $7\overline{)28}$ 11. $7\overline{)56}$ 12. $7\overline{)42}$

$$\begin{array}{r}8\\ \times 6\\ \hline 48\end{array}\quad \begin{array}{r}8\\ \times 7\\ \hline 56\end{array}\quad \begin{array}{r}8\\ \times 8\\ \hline 64\end{array}\quad \begin{array}{r}8\\ \times 9\\ \hline 72\end{array}$$

$$8\overline{)56}\ \text{answer } \mathbf{7} \qquad 8\overline{)64}\ \text{answer } \mathbf{8}$$

13. $8\overline{)48}$ 14. $8\overline{)72}$ 15. $8\overline{)56}$

16. $8\overline{)64}$ 17. $8\overline{)40}$ 18. $8\overline{)32}$

$$\begin{array}{r}9\\ \times 6\\ \hline 54\end{array}\quad \begin{array}{r}9\\ \times 7\\ \hline 63\end{array}\quad \begin{array}{r}9\\ \times 8\\ \hline 72\end{array}\quad \begin{array}{r}9\\ \times 9\\ \hline 81\end{array}$$

$$9\overline{)54}\ \text{answer } \mathbf{6} \qquad 9\overline{)81}\ \text{answer } \mathbf{9}$$

19. $9\overline{)63}$ 20. $9\overline{)45}$ 21. $9\overline{)81}$

22. $9\overline{)72}$ 23. $9\overline{)54}$ 24. $9\overline{)36}$

ENRICHMENT

Negative Numbers

Elena made this graph to show the temperature from 1:00 a.m. to 8:00 a.m. She used **negative numbers** to show temperatures **below** zero.

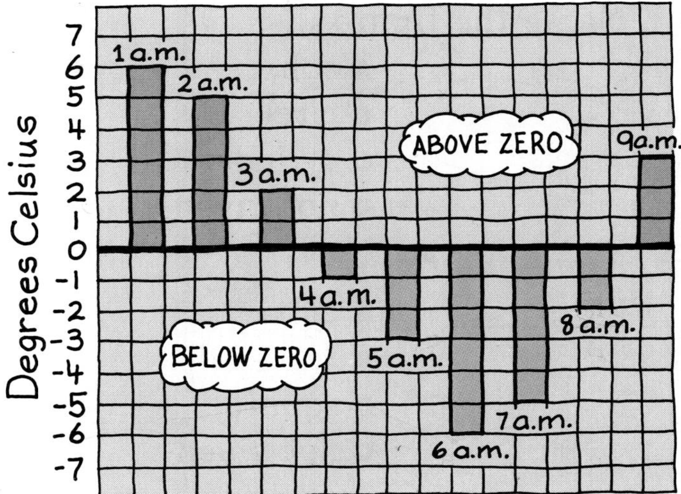

Read negative numbers as:

negative one
negative two
negative three
.
.
.

The temperature at 2:00 a.m. was 5 degrees.
The temperature at 5:00 a.m. was $^{-}3$ degrees.

Use the graph to answer the questions.

1. What was the temperature at 1:00 a.m.?
2. What was the temperature at 7:00 a.m.?
3. At what time was the temperature $^{-}2$ degrees?
4. At what time was the temperature 2 degrees?
5. At what time was it coldest?
6. What was the difference in temperature between 2:00 a.m. and 3:00 a.m.?
7. What was the difference in temperature between 4:00 a.m. and 5:00 a.m.?

CUMULATIVE REVIEW

Give the letter for the correct answer.

1. Name the figure.

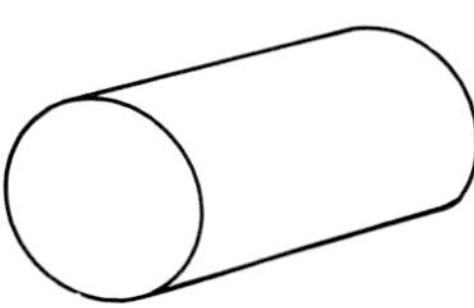

A sphere
B circle
C cylinder
D not given

2. Name the figure.

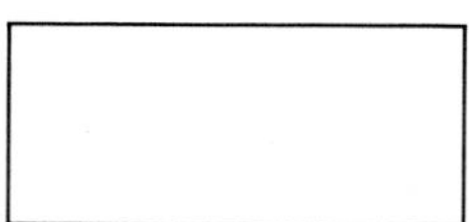

A cube
B rectangle
C square
D not given

3. Name the figure.

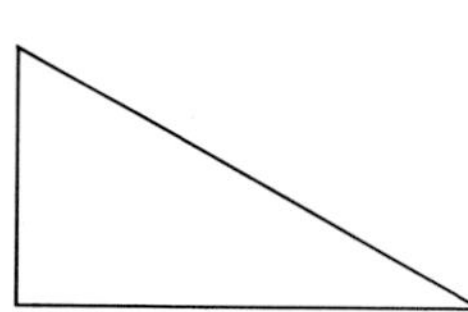

A triangle
B cube
C rectangular prism
D not given

4. Which shape is congruent to this shape?

A 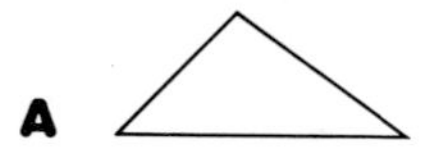
B 
C 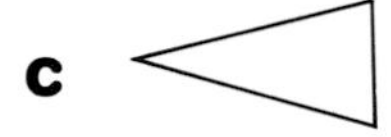
D not given

5. Which shape is congruent to this shape?

A 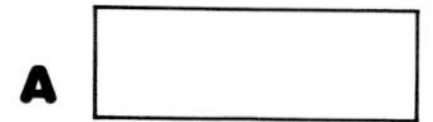
B 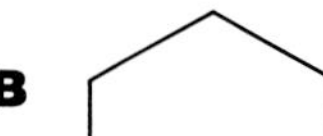
C
D not given

6. Which is a line of symmetry?

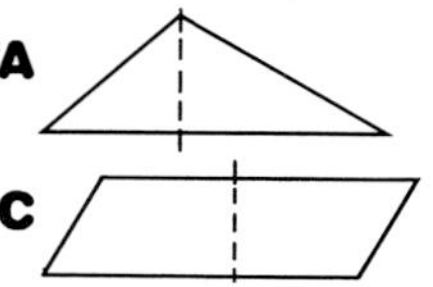

A
B
C
D not given

7. 2×8 A 10   B 16   C 21   D not given

8. 3×7 A 24   B 28   C 21   D not given

9. 4×9 A 34   B 36   C 38   D not given

10. 5×8 A 40   B 45   C 48   D not given

11. 6×9 A 63   B 48   C 54   D not given

12. 5×7 A 45   B 35   C 30   D not given

13. Dana made 4 field goals. Each one was 2 points. How many points did Dana make?

A 6   B 8
C 2   D not given

14. Wendy baked 2 cakes. Each cake took 3 eggs. How many eggs did she use?

A 6   B 5
C 8   D not given

MULTIPLICATION 11

When Tania turned 11 she took over her brother's paper route. Tania must get up at 5:30 every morning. First she counts the papers to make sure she has enough. It takes her about 10 minutes to fold the papers. Then she delivers the papers to the houses. Once a month Tania collects for the paper from the people on her route.

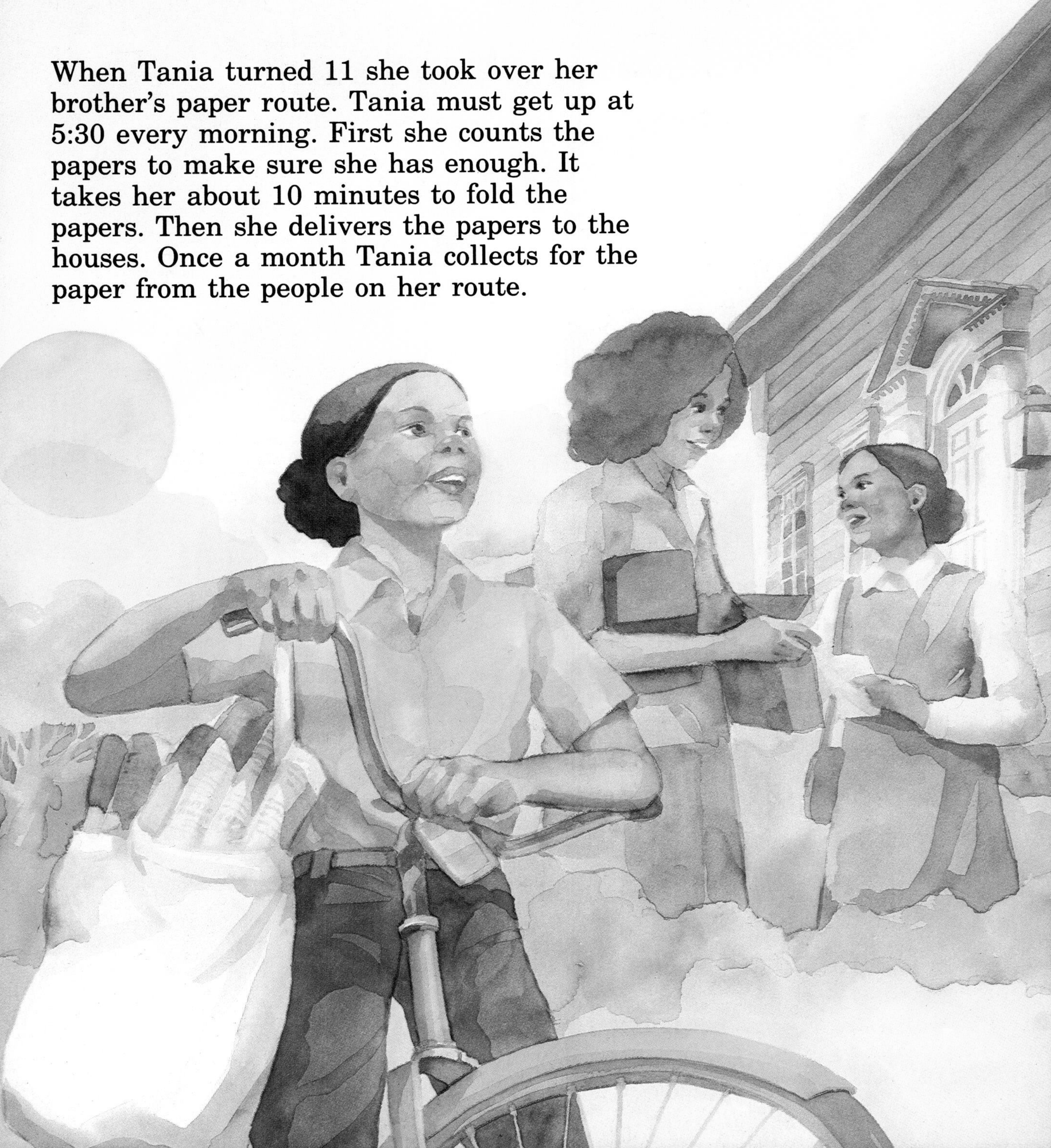

Special Products: Mental Math

Leo bought 6 packages of pencils and 3 cards of tacks. How many pencils and how many tacks did he buy?

Since we want totals for equal sets, we multiply.

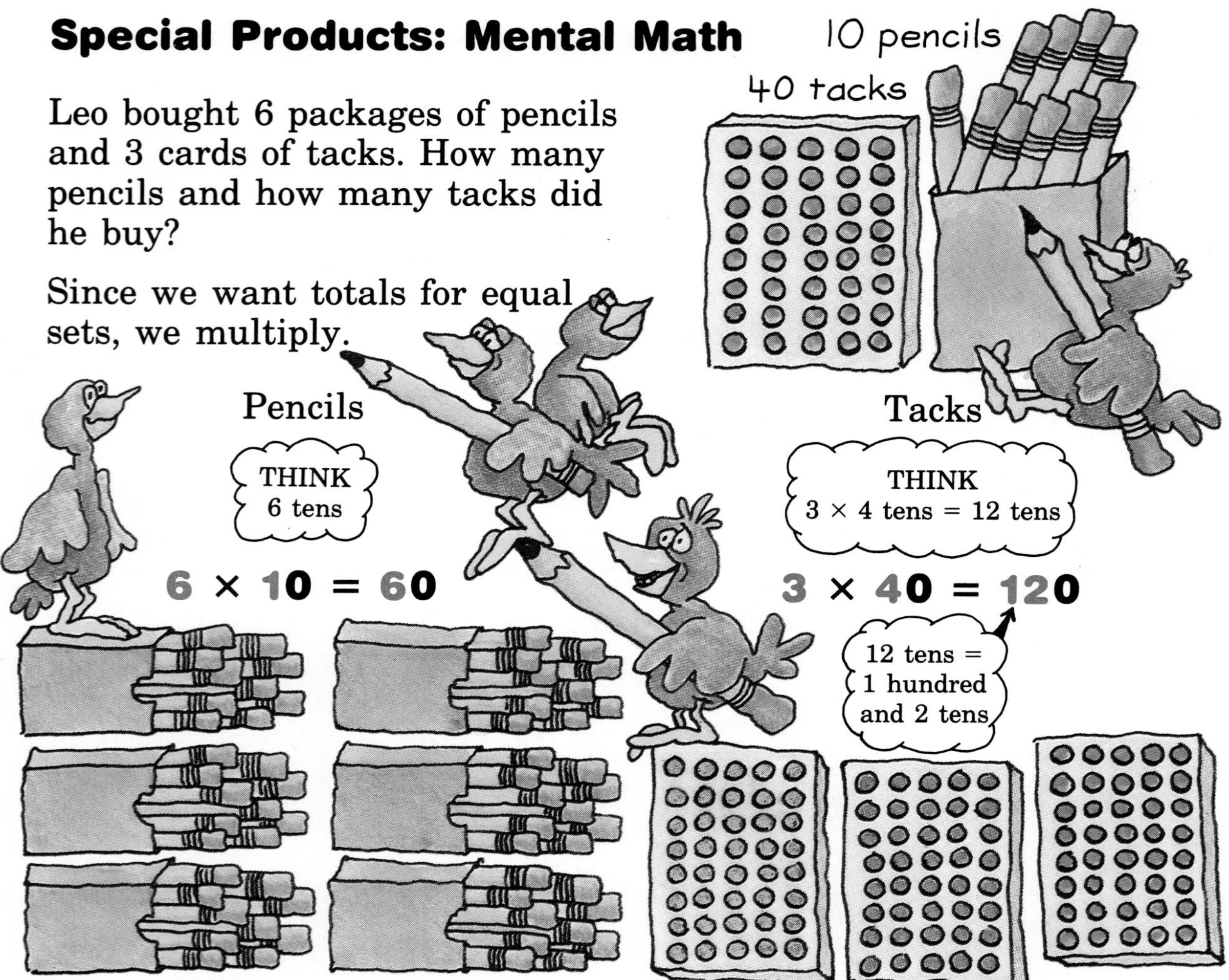

Pencils

$6 \times 10 = 60$

Tacks

$3 \times 40 = 120$

Leo bought 60 pencils and 120 tacks.

Other Examples

$3 \times 10 = 30$ $\qquad$ $4 \times 20 = 80$ $\qquad$ $5 \times 40 = 200$

20 tens = 2 hundred

Warm Up Give each product aloud.

1. 4×10	**2.** 6×10	**3.** 8×10	**4.** 7×10
5. 3×20	**6.** 4×30	**7.** 6×40	**8.** 5×30
9. 2×10	**10.** 2×80	**11.** 5×10	**12.** 4×40
13. 5×80	**14.** 1×10	**15.** 2×50	**16.** 9×10

Practice Find the products.

1. 3×10	2. 6×10	3. 4×10	4. 7×10
5. 8×10	6. 2×10	7. 5×10	8. 9×10
9. 2×40	10. 4×30	11. 6×40	12. 2×90
13. 7×20	14. 5×70	15. 8×30	16. 4×50
17. 7×10	18. 2×30	19. 1×10	20. 6×30
21. 8×20	22. 5×10	23. 3×70	24. 4×90

25. Give the product of 3 and 10.

26. Give the product of 9 and 40.

27. Give the product of 7 and 50.

★ 28. $2 \times 3 \times 10$

★ 29. $4 \times 2 \times 10$

★ 30. $3 \times 3 \times 10$

★ 31. $2 \times 4 \times 20$

Mixed Applications

32. You have 50 tacks. How many groups of 5 is this?

33. You have 5 piles of tacks. There are 6 in each pile. How many tacks altogether?

34. **DATA HUNT** How many crayons in a box? How many crayons in 10 boxes?

THINK

Mental Math

CAT is worth 12 points.

C A T
2 + 2 + 8

1. Find the points for these words.

DOG	SUN	TWO
ONE	SIX	TEN

2. Find the points for your name.
3. Find a 10-point word.

MATH

Multiplication and Addition Mental Math

Mike mailed three packages. He bought a 5¢ stamp and a 40¢ stamp for each package. Here is how the clerk figured out how much Mike had to pay.

THINK 3 fives	$3 \times 5 =$	15
THINK 3 forties	$3 \times 40 =$	120
Add		135

The clerk asked Mike to pay 135¢ ($1.35).

Find the cost.

1. 5 packages

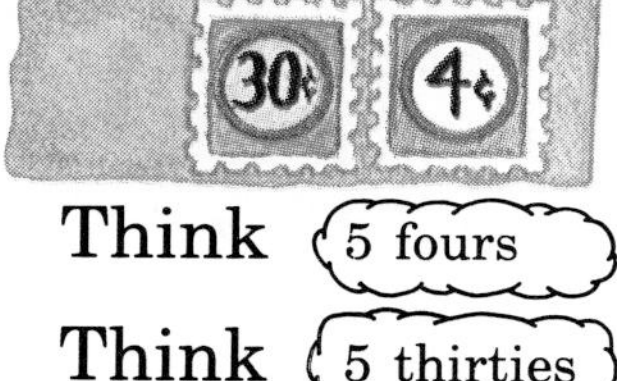

Think (5 fours)

Think (5 thirties)

Then add.

2. 7 packages

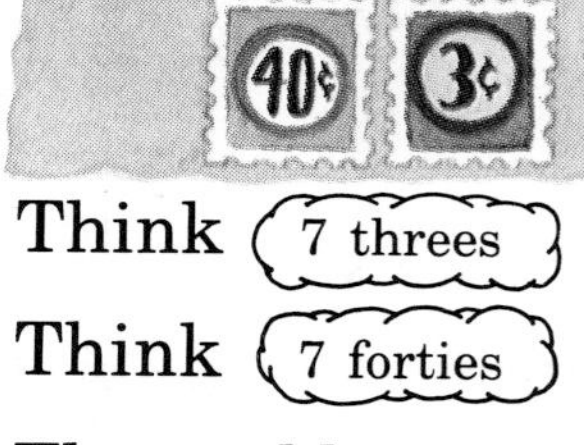

Think (7 threes)

Think (7 forties)

Then add.

3. 4 packages

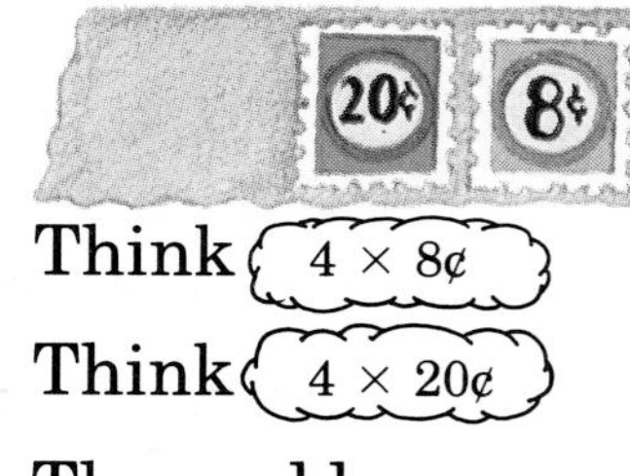

Think (4×8¢)

Think (4×20¢)

Then add.

How much to mail

4. 2 blue packages?

5. 4 blue packages?

6. 5 yellow packages?

7. 3 yellow packages?

8. 4 brown packages?

9. 5 brown packages?

Mixed Applications

★**10.** Doris mailed 6 small packages to her friends. The clerk put stamps worth 32¢ on each package. How much did Doris have to pay?

11. **DATA BANK** See page 375. How much will it cost to mail 5 packages if each package has a First Man on the Moon stamp and a Circus stamp?

PROBLEM SOLVING
Choose the Operations

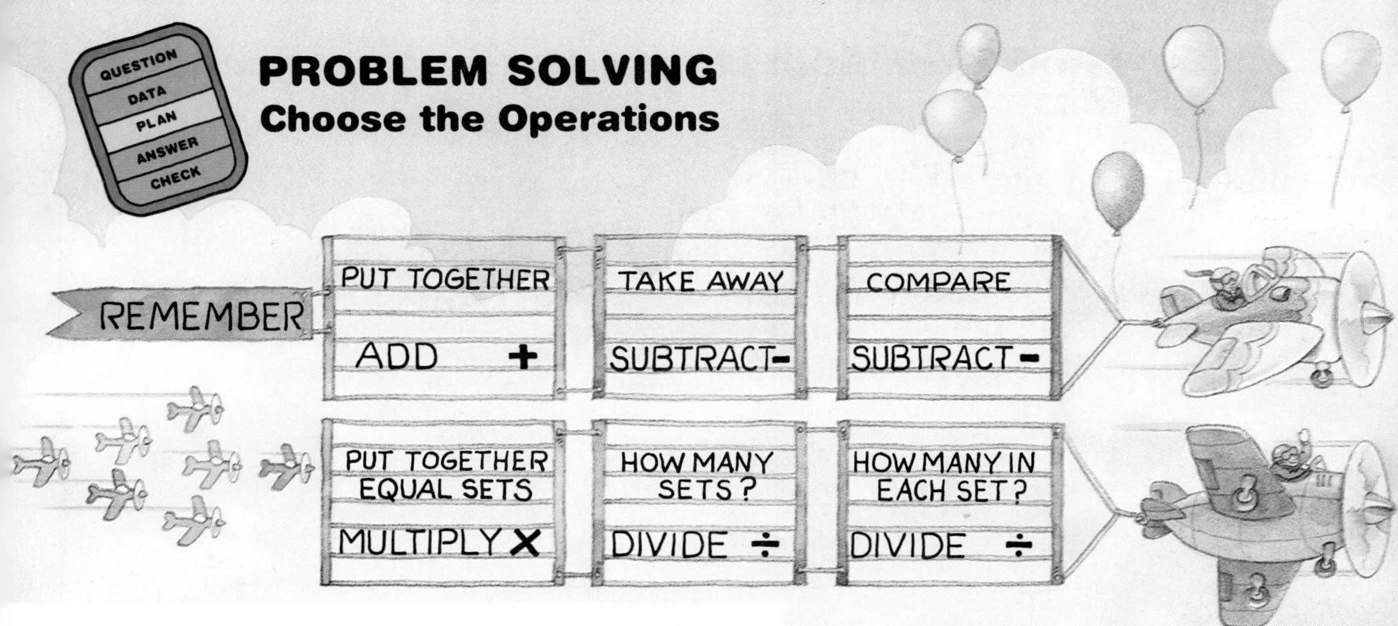

Choose the operation and then solve.

1. Miguel Gonzales bought 7 40¢-stamps and 7 5¢-stamps. How much did he pay in all?

2. On Tuesday Bill paid \$1.76 to mail a package. On Friday he paid \$2.35 to mail another package. How much less did he pay on Tuesday?

3. A clerk sold 8 books of stamps. There are 30 stamps in each book. How many stamps were sold?

4. Don put the same number of stamps on 5 packages. He used 15 stamps. How many stamps are on each package?

5. Matt mailed 3 packages. One cost \$2.85 to mail. The second cost \$0.95. The third cost \$1.33. How much did Matt pay?

6. Liz bought 5 20¢-stamps. How much did she pay? She gave the clerk \$5. How much money did she get back?

7. ***Strategy Practice*** Cindy collects flag stamps and animal stamps. Every time she buys 5 flag stamps, she buys 3 animal stamps. She has 18 animal stamps. How many flag stamps does she have? Hint: Complete the table.

Flag Stamps	5	10	15
Animal Stamps	3	6	9

Multiply and Then Add: Mental Math

Sandy and Jerry are playing a multiply and add game. What are their scores?

To find the scores, multiply the numbers on the red cubes and then add the number on the blue cube.

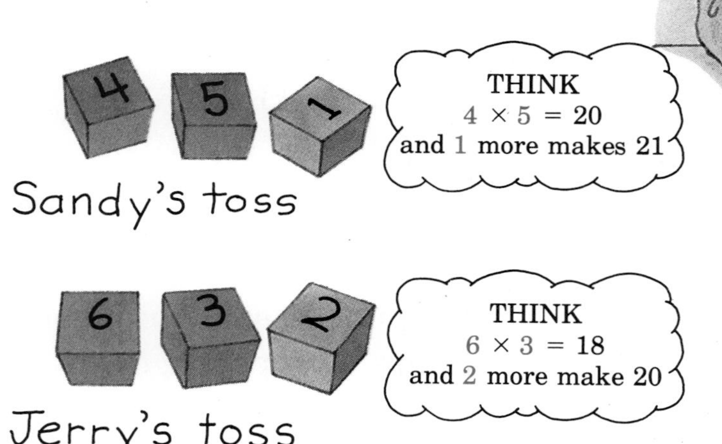

Sandy scored 21 points and Jerry scored 20 points.

Warm Up Give each score aloud.

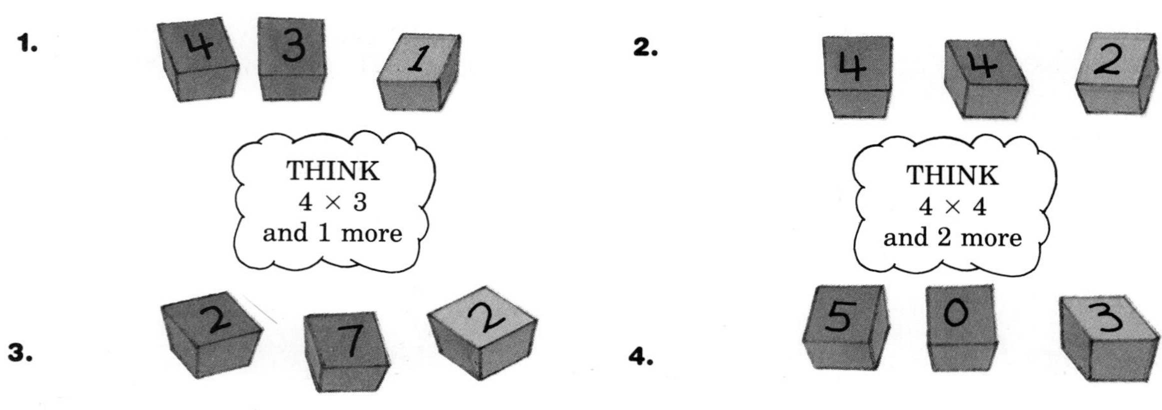

5. 3, 7, 2 **6.** 4, 2, 1 **7.** 5, 3, 3

8. 2, 8, 3 **9.** 9, 0, 1 **10.** 4, 7, 2

11. 2, 4, 3 **12.** 3, 6, 3 **13.** 2, 9, 2

Practice Multiply and then add 1. Write answers only.

1. 2×3 **2.** 7×5 **3.** 4×9 **4.** 8×0

5. 6×2 **6.** 4×1 **7.** 3×8 **8.** 4×2

Multiply and then add 2. Write answers only.

9. 5×2 **10.** 6×1 **11.** 4×5 **12.** 3×3

13. 4×7 **14.** 9×0 **15.** 2×9 **16.** 5×6

Multiply and then add 3. Write answers only.

17. 3×4 **18.** 2×2 **19.** 4×0 **20.** 8×1

21. 3×9 **22.** 9×5 **23.** 7×4 **24.** 4×2

Multiply and then add 4. Write answers only.

25. 3×5 **26.** 4×8 **27.** 8×5 **28.** 2×3

29. 7×0 **30.** 1×7 **31.** 6×3 **32.** 9×4

Find the score for each toss. Write answers only. The first one is done for you.

	Red Cube	Red Cube	Blue Cube	Score
	3	7	2	23
33.	4	6	1	
34.	5	3	3	
35.	8	4	2	
36.	9	3	3	

★ **37.** Pamela scored 28. The blue cube was 3. What numbers showed on the red cubes?

THINK
Logical Reasoning
Find the missing numbers.
1. 3 × ▯ = 120
2. 8 × ▯ = 240
3. ▯ × 50 = 450
MATH

Multiplying: Trading Ones

Joanne collects coins. How many quarters does the coin folder hold?

Since there are the same number on each of 4 pages, we multiply.

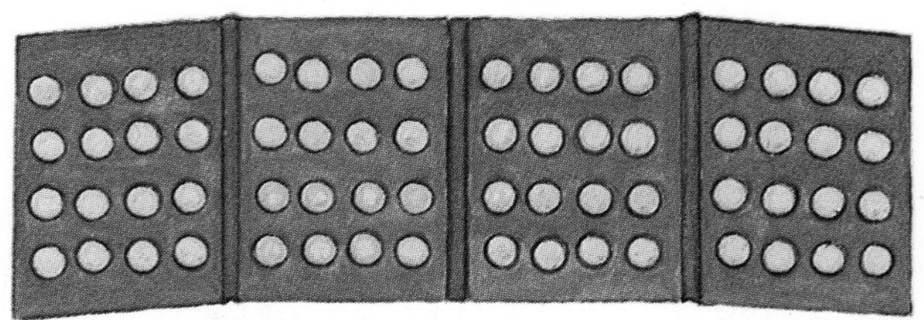

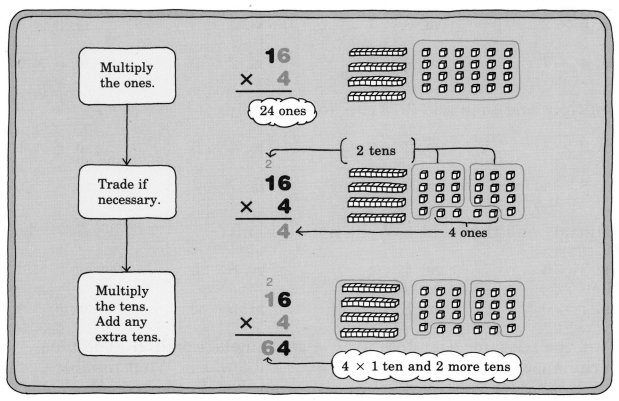

Multiply the ones.

$$\begin{array}{r} 16 \\ \times\ \ 4 \\ \hline \end{array}$$

24 ones

Trade if necessary.

2 tens

$$\begin{array}{r} {\scriptstyle 2} \\ 16 \\ \times\ \ 4 \\ \hline 4 \end{array}$$

4 ones

Multiply the tens. Add any extra tens.

$$\begin{array}{r} {\scriptstyle 2} \\ 16 \\ \times\ \ 4 \\ \hline 64 \end{array}$$

4 × 1 ten and 2 more tens

There are 64 quarters in the coin folder.

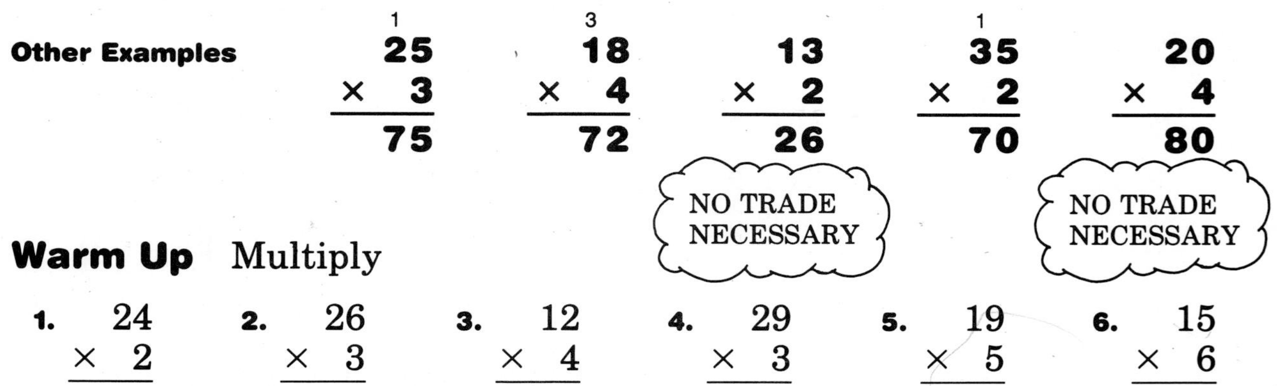

Other Examples

$$\begin{array}{r} {\scriptstyle 1} \\ 25 \\ \times\ \ 3 \\ \hline 75 \end{array} \qquad \begin{array}{r} {\scriptstyle 3} \\ 18 \\ \times\ \ 4 \\ \hline 72 \end{array} \qquad \begin{array}{r} \\ 13 \\ \times\ \ 2 \\ \hline 26 \end{array} \qquad \begin{array}{r} {\scriptstyle 1} \\ 35 \\ \times\ \ 2 \\ \hline 70 \end{array} \qquad \begin{array}{r} \\ 20 \\ \times\ \ 4 \\ \hline 80 \end{array}$$

Warm Up Multiply

1. $\begin{array}{r} 24 \\ \times\ \ 2 \\ \hline \end{array}$ **2.** $\begin{array}{r} 26 \\ \times\ \ 3 \\ \hline \end{array}$ **3.** $\begin{array}{r} 12 \\ \times\ \ 4 \\ \hline \end{array}$ **4.** $\begin{array}{r} 29 \\ \times\ \ 3 \\ \hline \end{array}$ **5.** $\begin{array}{r} 19 \\ \times\ \ 5 \\ \hline \end{array}$ **6.** $\begin{array}{r} 15 \\ \times\ \ 6 \\ \hline \end{array}$

Practice Find the products.

1. $\begin{array}{r} 14 \\ \times\ 2 \\ \hline \end{array}$
2. $\begin{array}{r} 34 \\ \times\ 2 \\ \hline \end{array}$
3. $\begin{array}{r} 16 \\ \times\ 3 \\ \hline \end{array}$
4. $\begin{array}{r} 21 \\ \times\ 4 \\ \hline \end{array}$
5. $\begin{array}{r} 32 \\ \times\ 3 \\ \hline \end{array}$
6. $\begin{array}{r} 12 \\ \times\ 8 \\ \hline \end{array}$
7. $\begin{array}{r} 17 \\ \times\ 3 \\ \hline \end{array}$
8. $\begin{array}{r} 20 \\ \times\ 4 \\ \hline \end{array}$
9. $\begin{array}{r} 19 \\ \times\ 4 \\ \hline \end{array}$
10. $\begin{array}{r} 16 \\ \times\ 5 \\ \hline \end{array}$
11. $\begin{array}{r} 43 \\ \times\ 2 \\ \hline \end{array}$
12. $\begin{array}{r} 12 \\ \times\ 7 \\ \hline \end{array}$
13. $\begin{array}{r} 15 \\ \times\ 6 \\ \hline \end{array}$
14. $\begin{array}{r} 19 \\ \times\ 5 \\ \hline \end{array}$
15. $\begin{array}{r} 13 \\ \times\ 5 \\ \hline \end{array}$
16. $\begin{array}{r} 11 \\ \times\ 9 \\ \hline \end{array}$
17. $\begin{array}{r} 46 \\ \times\ 2 \\ \hline \end{array}$
18. $\begin{array}{r} 28 \\ \times\ 2 \\ \hline \end{array}$
19. $\begin{array}{r} 33 \\ \times\ 3 \\ \hline \end{array}$
20. $\begin{array}{r} 15 \\ \times\ 4 \\ \hline \end{array}$

21. 4×22
22. 2×18
23. 5×12
24. 3×30

25. Multiply 15 by 5.
26. Multiply 42 by 2.

Mixed Applications

27. Carlos has a coin folder for nickels. It has spaces for 21 nickels on each page. There are 3 pages. How many nickels does the folder hold?

28. Janet wants to put 56 coins in a picture frame. The frame holds 6 rows of 9 coins. Can she put all of her coins in the frame?

SKILLKEEPER

Divide.

1. $16 \div 8$
2. $25 \div 5$
3. $48 \div 6$
4. $45 \div 9$
5. $28 \div 4$
6. $36 \div 9$
7. $24 \div 6$
8. $10 \div 5$
9. $18 \div 2$
10. $54 \div 9$
11. $16 \div 2$
12. $36 \div 6$
13. $20 \div 5$
14. $24 \div 8$
15. $12 \div 6$
16. $49 \div 7$

More Practice, page 398, Set A

Multiplying: Trading Ones and Tens

Geri David is putting new tile down. There will be 4 rows of tile with 32 tiles in each row. How many tiles does she need?

Since we want the total and each row has the same number of tiles, we multiply.

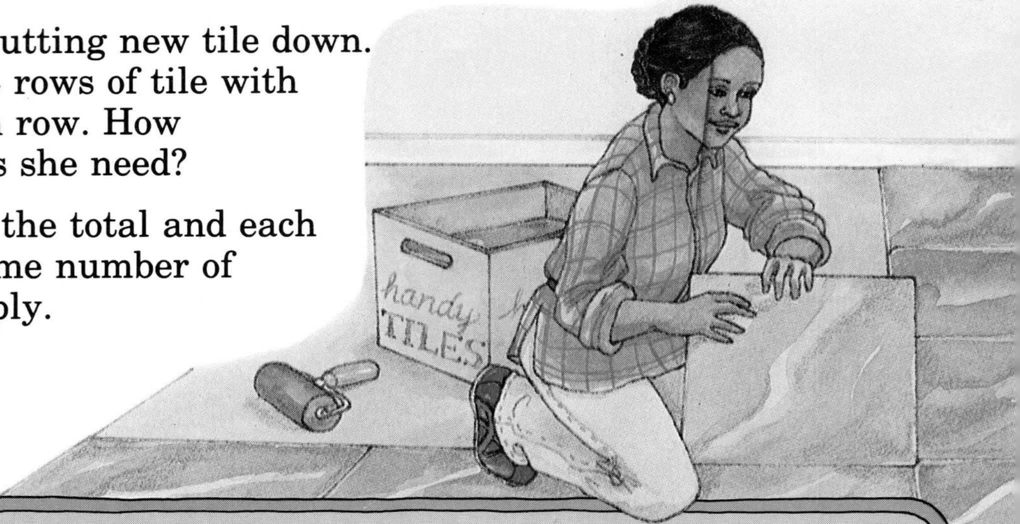

Multiply the ones.
Trade if necessary.

$$\begin{array}{r} 32 \\ \times\ \ 4 \\ \hline 8 \end{array}$$

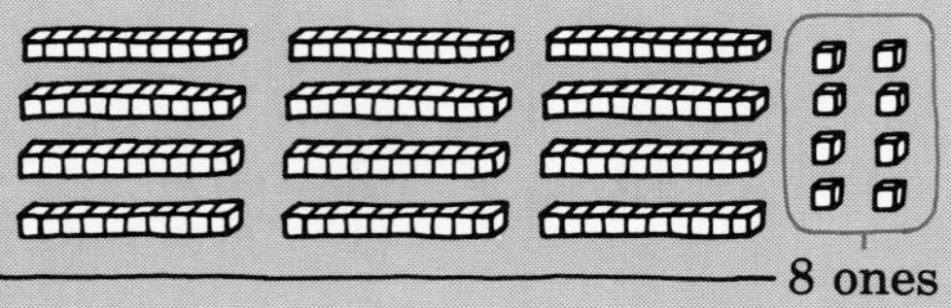

Multiply the tens.
Add any extra tens.

$$\begin{array}{r} 32 \\ \times\ \ 4 \\ \hline 128 \end{array}$$

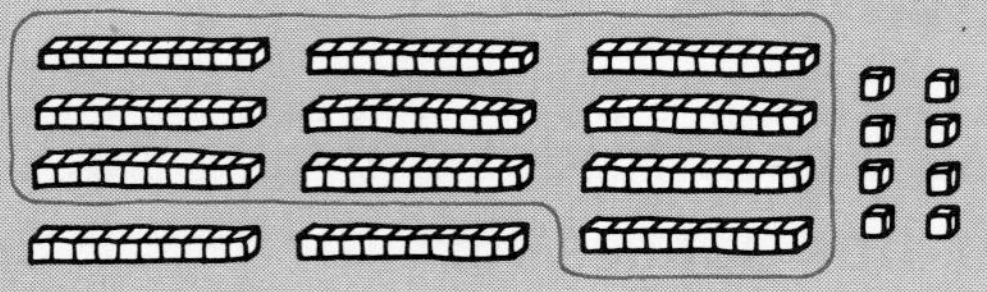

12 tens = 1 hundred and 2 tens

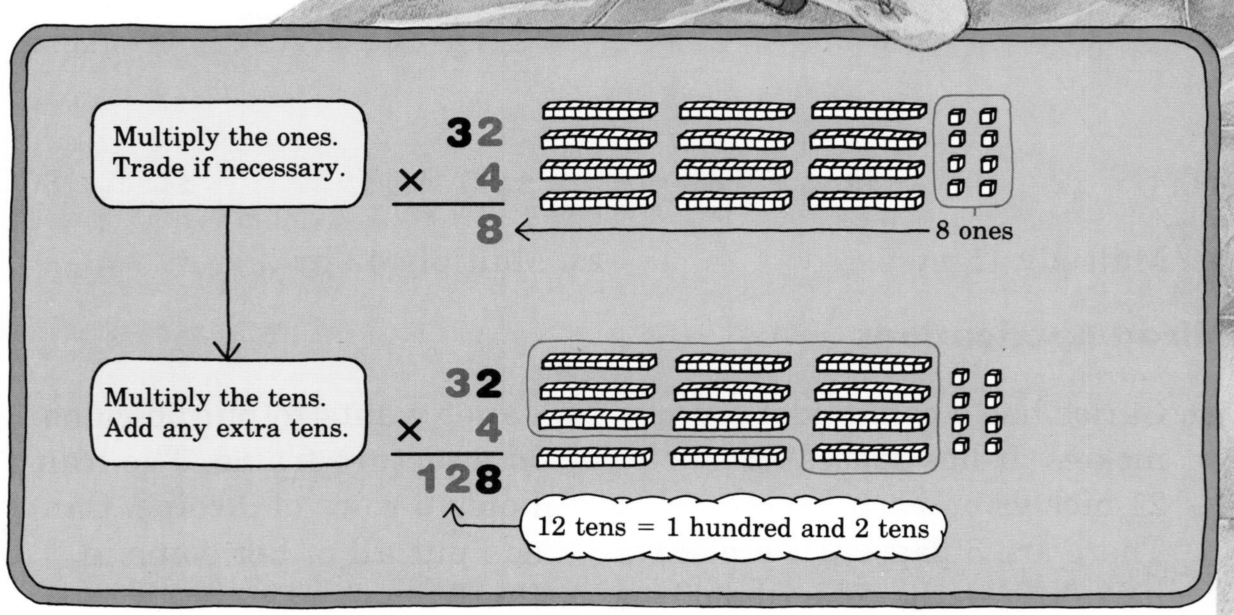

Ms. David needs 128 tiles.

Other Examples

$$\begin{array}{r} 21 \\ \times\ \ 6 \\ \hline 126 \end{array} \qquad \begin{array}{r} \scriptstyle 1 \\ 46 \\ \times\ \ 3 \\ \hline 138 \end{array} \qquad \begin{array}{r} \scriptstyle 4 \\ 35 \\ \times\ \ 8 \\ \hline 280 \end{array} \qquad \begin{array}{r} \scriptstyle 2 \\ 25 \\ \times\ \ 4 \\ \hline 100 \end{array}$$

Warm Up Multiply.

1. $\begin{array}{r} 42 \\ \times\ \ 3 \\ \hline \end{array}$ **2.** $\begin{array}{r} 41 \\ \times\ \ 7 \\ \hline \end{array}$ **3.** $\begin{array}{r} 24 \\ \times\ \ 6 \\ \hline \end{array}$ **4.** $\begin{array}{r} 36 \\ \times\ \ 5 \\ \hline \end{array}$ **5.** $\begin{array}{r} 75 \\ \times\ \ 4 \\ \hline \end{array}$ **6.** $\begin{array}{r} 68 \\ \times\ \ 3 \\ \hline \end{array}$

Practice Find the products.

1. 32 × 4
2. 63 × 2
3. 58 × 3
4. 43 × 5
5. 42 × 6
6. 23 × 3
7. 45 × 8
8. 67 × 5
9. 23 × 7
10. 94 × 2
11. 13 × 7
12. 35 × 6
13. 25 × 7
14. 66 × 3
15. 52 × 6
16. 19 × 4
17. 36 × 5
18. 42 × 8
19. 4 × 49
20. 3 × 83
21. 8 × 25
22. 9 × 23
23. 6 × 14
24. 2 × 52
25. 3 × 29
26. 9 × 15
27. Give the product of 2 and 75.
28. Give the product of 5 and 25.
29. Give the product of 4 and 62.
30. Give the product of 6 and 53.

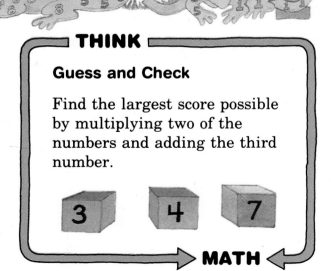

Mixed Applications

31. Mr. Allen tiled an office floor with 9 rows of tile. There were 35 tiles in each row. How many tiles did he use?

32. Make up needed data and then solve.

    Mr. Carl used 38 tiles to cover a floor. How many tiles did he have left?

THINK

Guess and Check

Find the largest score possible by multiplying two of the numbers and adding the third number.

MATH

More Practice, page 398, Set B

Multiplying with Money

Sean needs to buy 6 AA batteries for his radio. How much will they cost?

Since we want the total amounts, we multiply.

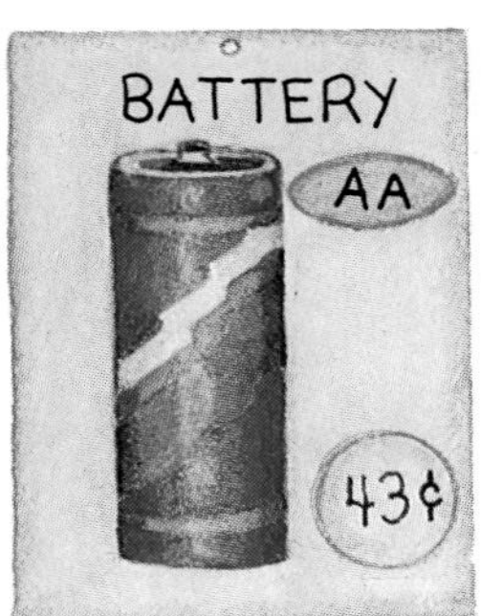

Multiply. → Show cents or dollars and cents.

$$\begin{array}{r} \overset{1}{4}3¢ \\ \times \quad 6 \\ \hline 258 \end{array} \qquad \begin{array}{r} 43¢ \\ \times \quad 6 \\ \hline 258¢ \text{ or } \$2.58 \end{array}$$

The cost of 6 batteries is $2.58.

Other Examples

14¢ (carry 1)	65¢ (carry 2)	34¢ (carry 3)	25¢ (carry 4)
× 4	× 4	× 9	× 8
56¢	260¢	306¢	200¢
$0.56	$2.60	$3.06	$2.00

Warm Up Find the amounts.
Write the answers with dollars and cents.

1. 82¢ × 2 **2.** 54¢ × 5 **3.** 12¢ × 8 **4.** 34¢ × 3 **5.** 75¢ × 4

Practice Find the amounts.
Write the amounts with dollars and cents.

1. 41¢ × 6	2. 23¢ × 3	3. 45¢ × 7	4. 68¢ × 2	5. 56¢ × 4	6. 36¢ × 5
7. 54¢ × 8	8. 81¢ × 5	9. 42¢ × 9	10. 95¢ × 3	11. 15¢ × 6	12. 48¢ × 7
13. 98¢ × 4	14. 34¢ × 7	15. 26¢ × 4	16. 55¢ × 9	17. 77¢ × 3	18. 57¢ × 5

19. 3 × 38¢ **20.** 4 × 49¢ **21.** 9 × 13¢

22. 2 × 52¢ **23.** 5 × 78¢ **24.** 8 × 25¢

25. 3 at 45¢ each **26.** 6 at 53¢ each **27.** 8 at 19¢ each

28. 5 at 92¢ each **29.** 7 at 32¢ each **30.** 4 at 67¢ each

Mixed Applications

Look at page 280.

31. Juanita needs to buy 4 of the AA batteries. How much will they cost?

32. How much more do 3 AAA batteries cost than 3 AA batteries?

33. What is the cost of 7 AA batteries? 43¢ is the same as 0.43.

THINK

Mental Math

3 tens and 3 twos

3 × 12 = 36

Find the products in your head.

4 tens and 4 twos

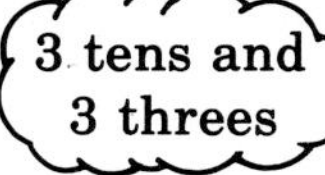

1. 4 × 12 **2.** 3 × 13

3. 4 × 11 **4.** 2 × 14

5. 2 × 13 **6.** 5 × 11

MATH

PROBLEM SOLVING
Using Data from a Picture Graph

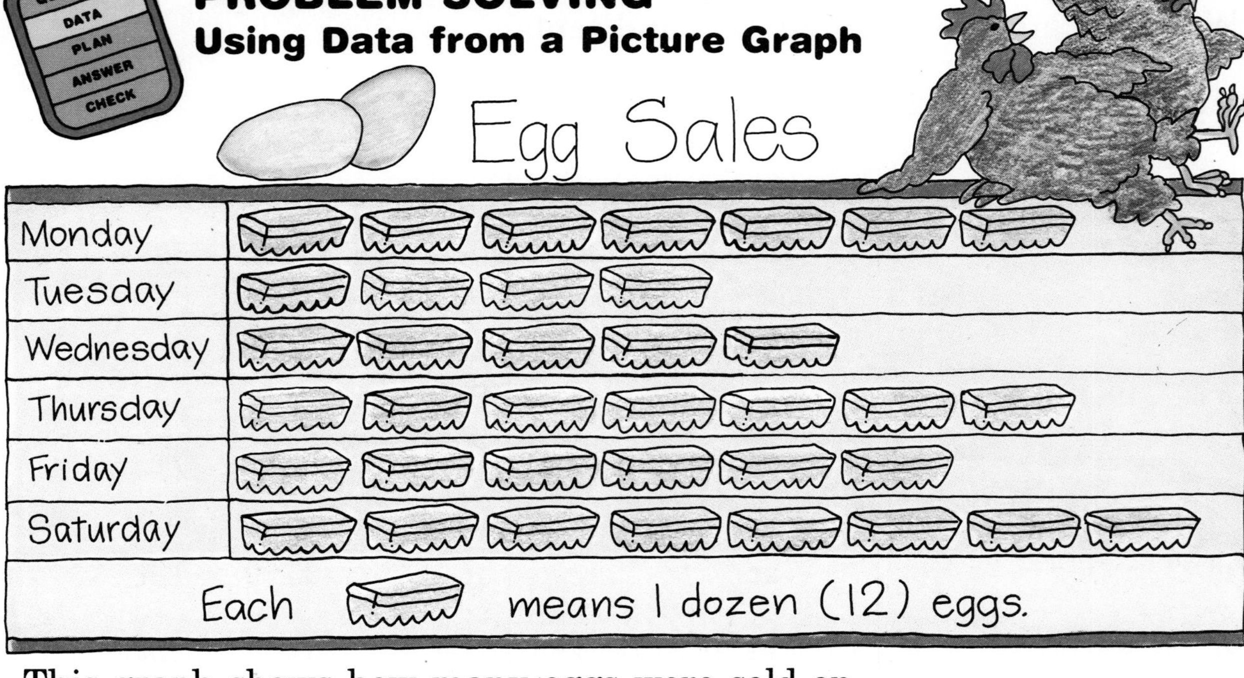

This graph shows how many eggs were sold on the Sanders' farm in one week.

Use the graph to answer the questions.

1. On what day were the most eggs sold?

2. On what day were the fewest eggs sold?

3. How many more dozen were sold on Saturday than on Wednesday?

4. How many dozen were sold in the first 3 days?

5. On Tuesday 4 dozen eggs were sold. How many eggs are there in 4 dozen?

6. How much money did the Sanders make on Wednesday if they sold the eggs at 93¢ a dozen?

★ 7. How much more money would they have made on Wednesday if they had raised the price to 99¢ a dozen?

8. ***Strategy Practice*** There are 4 hens—Lulu, Peck, Red, and Queen. Peck is larger than Red. Lulu is smaller than Red. Peck is smaller than Queen. Which hen is largest?

Multiplication Practice

Find the products.

1. $\begin{array}{r} 31 \\ \times\ 3 \\ \hline \end{array}$ 2. $\begin{array}{r} 35 \\ \times\ 2 \\ \hline \end{array}$ 3. $\begin{array}{r} 11 \\ \times\ 9 \\ \hline \end{array}$ 4. $\begin{array}{r} 24 \\ \times\ 4 \\ \hline \end{array}$ 5. $\begin{array}{r} 13 \\ \times\ 5 \\ \hline \end{array}$ 6. $\begin{array}{r} 23 \\ \times\ 3 \\ \hline \end{array}$

7. $\begin{array}{r} 33 \\ \times\ 8 \\ \hline \end{array}$ 8. $\begin{array}{r} 68 \\ \times\ 4 \\ \hline \end{array}$ 9. $\begin{array}{r} 60 \\ \times\ 3 \\ \hline \end{array}$ 10. $\begin{array}{r} 75 \\ \times\ 4 \\ \hline \end{array}$ 11. $\begin{array}{r} 14 \\ \times\ 2 \\ \hline \end{array}$ 12. $\begin{array}{r} 29 \\ \times\ 3 \\ \hline \end{array}$

13. $\begin{array}{r} 34¢ \\ \times\ 6 \\ \hline \end{array}$ 14. $\begin{array}{r} 19¢ \\ \times\ 4 \\ \hline \end{array}$ 15. $\begin{array}{r} 52¢ \\ \times\ 7 \\ \hline \end{array}$ 16. $\begin{array}{r} 62¢ \\ \times\ 2 \\ \hline \end{array}$ 17. $\begin{array}{r} 55¢ \\ \times\ 3 \\ \hline \end{array}$ 18. $\begin{array}{r} 29¢ \\ \times\ 5 \\ \hline \end{array}$

19. $\begin{array}{r} 12¢ \\ \times\ 5 \\ \hline \end{array}$ 20. $\begin{array}{r} 20¢ \\ \times\ 5 \\ \hline \end{array}$ 21. $\begin{array}{r} 75¢ \\ \times\ 2 \\ \hline \end{array}$ 22. $\begin{array}{r} 49¢ \\ \times\ 4 \\ \hline \end{array}$ 23. $\begin{array}{r} 53¢ \\ \times\ 5 \\ \hline \end{array}$ 24. $\begin{array}{r} 63¢ \\ \times\ 5 \\ \hline \end{array}$

25. 8×24 26. 5×37 27. 2×76

28. $3 \times 47¢$ 29. $4 \times 52¢$ 30. $6 \times 13¢$

SKILLKEEPER

Subtract.

1. $\begin{array}{r} 95 \\ -\ 73 \\ \hline \end{array}$ 2. $\begin{array}{r} 82 \\ -\ 79 \\ \hline \end{array}$ 3. $\begin{array}{r} 30 \\ -\ 16 \\ \hline \end{array}$ 4. $\begin{array}{r} 67 \\ -\ 48 \\ \hline \end{array}$

5. $\begin{array}{r} \$2.05 \\ -\ 1.69 \\ \hline \end{array}$ 6. $\begin{array}{r} \$3.52 \\ -\ 0.71 \\ \hline \end{array}$ 7. $\begin{array}{r} \$5.13 \\ -\ 4.07 \\ \hline \end{array}$ 8. $\begin{array}{r} \$8.21 \\ -\ 7.89 \\ \hline \end{array}$

Estimating Products with Money Using Rounding

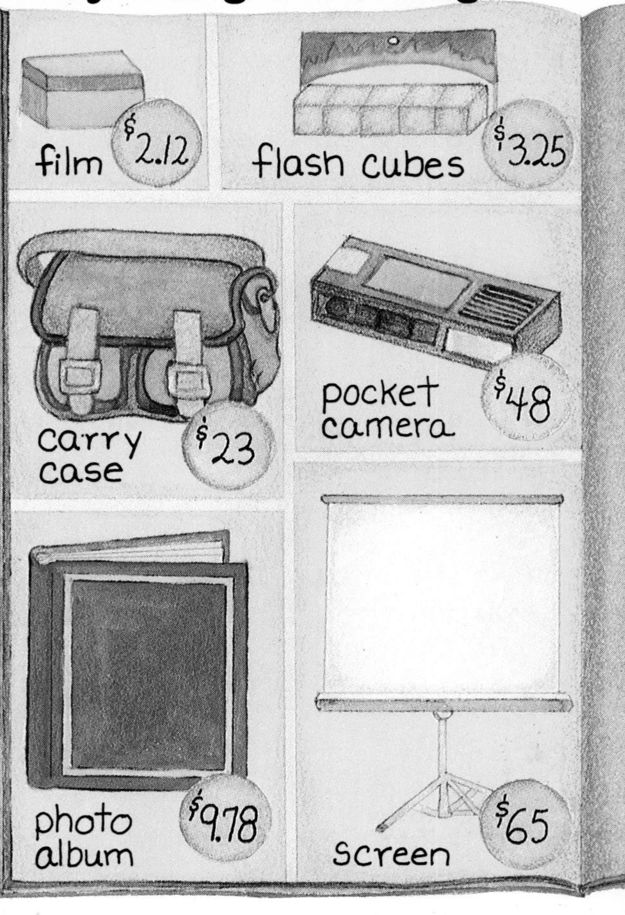

About how many dollars do 3 rolls of film cost?

Since you want an answer that is only **close** to the exact answer, you **estimate** by rounding to the nearest dollar and multiplying in your head.

3 × $2.12

THINK
3 × $2 = $6

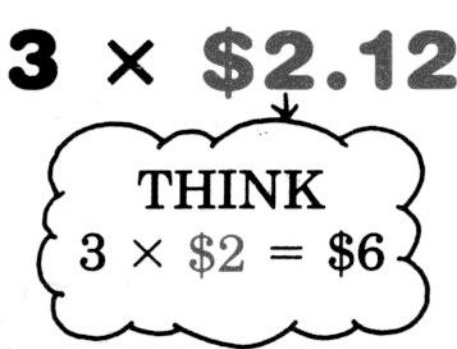

Film costs about $6 for 3 rolls.

Other Examples

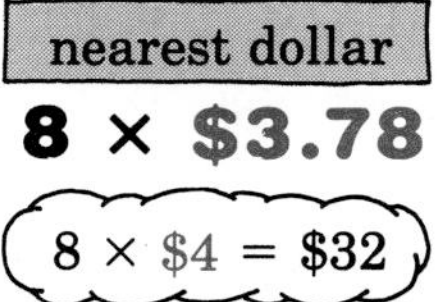

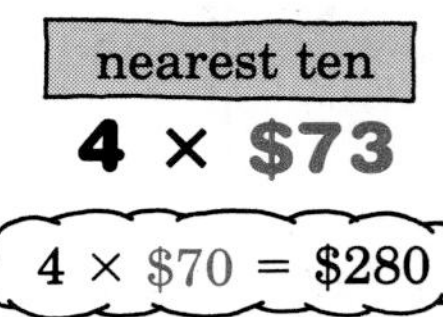

nearest dollar	nearest ten
8 × $3.78	**4 × $73**
8 × $4 = $32	4 × $70 = $280

Estimate by rounding to the nearest dollar. Write answers only.

1. 4 × $4.34 **2.** 3 × $6.92 **3.** 7 × $3.50

4. 5 × $8.07 **5.** 8 × $2.03 **6.** 3 × $5.82

7. 5 × $3.26 **8.** 2 × $9.15 **9.** 4 × $3.50

Estimate by rounding to the nearest ten. Write answers only.

10. 3 × $27 **11.** 8 × $33 **12.** 4 × $85

13. 2 × $66 **14.** 4 × $21 **15.** 3 × $68

16. 6 × $53 **17.** 7 × $25 **18.** 9 × $36

PROBLEM SOLVING
Estimating to Check Answers

Jean and Dan used estimation to check the totals on their sales slips.

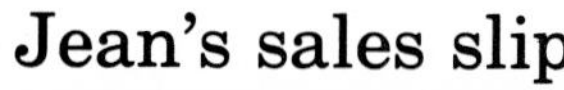

Jean's sales slip

3 × $10 = $30

The total should be about $30. It is. The sales slip seems to be right.

Dan's sales slip

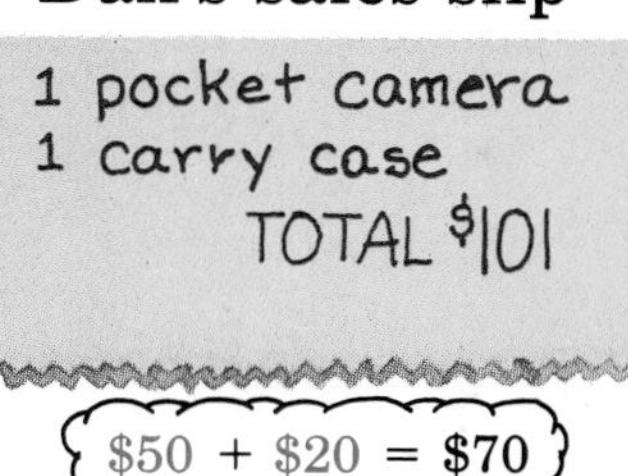

$50 + $20 = $70

The total should be about $70. It is not. The sales slip seems to be wrong. The total should be $71.

Use the pictures on page 284.
Write an estimate for each purchase. If a sales slip seems to be wrong, find the actual total and write it next to your estimate.

1. 1 roll of film
1 photo album
TOTAL $11.90

2. 4 pocket cameras
TOTAL $38.40

3. 1 package of flash cubes
1 roll of film
TOTAL $4.37

4. 8 rolls of film
TOTAL $6.96

5. 5 screens
TOTAL $385

★ 6. 1 screen
2 carry cases
1 pocket camera
TOTAL $250

7. ***Strategy Practice*** Dan wants to take a picture of his friends, Alex, Bess, and Connie. How many different ways can he line them up?

PROBLEM SOLVING
Mixed Practice

Penny Patterson studies how gorillas think. She has been teaching Koko and Michael to talk using sign language.

Solve. You may need to use the table on page 287.

1. In one year, Koko learned 5 signs each month. There are 12 months in a year. How many signs did Koko learn that year?

2. Michael learned 24 signs in 6 months. He learned the same number of signs each month. How many did he learn each month?

3. Koko knows 210 more signs than Michael. Michael knows 190 signs. How many signs does Koko know?

4. When Koko becomes an adult gorilla, she will weigh about 110 kg. How much weight does she have to gain?

5. How much weight will Michael have to gain to weigh 110 kg?

6. How much taller is Michael than Koko?

	Koko	Michael
Weight	93 kg	86 kg
Height	145 cm	152 cm
Wrist	25 cm	27 cm
Hand	24 cm	26 cm
Foot	28 cm	30 cm
Eats	4 kg of food each day	5 kg of food each day

7. How many kilograms of food does Koko eat in 2 weeks (14 days)?

8. How many kilograms of food does Michael eat in one month (31 days)?

9. Koko's chest measurement is 30 cm less than her height. What is Koko's chest measurement?

10. Michael's chest measurement is 73 cm greater than his wrist measurement. What is Michael's chest measurement?

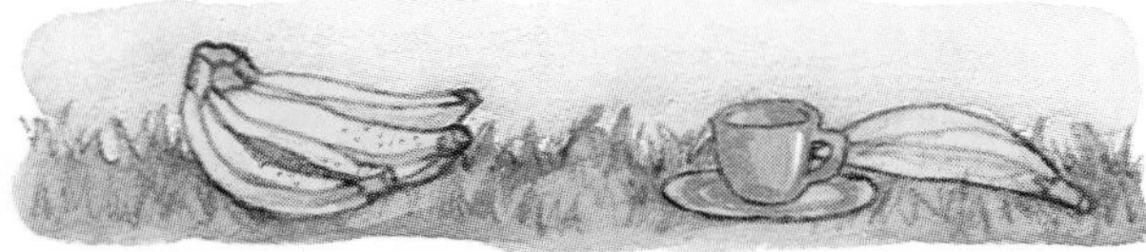

11. Michael's neck measurement is 2 times the measurement of his foot. What is his neck measurement?

★ 12. Koko's neck measurement is 2 cm more than twice her foot measurement. What is her neck measurement?

13. **DATA HUNT** Each gorilla has the same number of teeth as an adult human. How many teeth do Koko and Michael have together?

14. ***Strategy Practice*** Koko is 13 years old. Michael is 15 years younger than twice Koko's age. How old is Michael?

Mixed Skills Practice

Computation

Find the answers.

1. $\begin{array}{r} 38 \\ +\ 29 \\ \hline \end{array}$ **2.** $\begin{array}{r} 156 \\ -\ 98 \\ \hline \end{array}$ **3.** $\begin{array}{r} 258 \\ +\ 175 \\ \hline \end{array}$ **4.** $\begin{array}{r} 369 \\ +\ 985 \\ \hline \end{array}$ **5.** $\begin{array}{r} 624 \\ -\ 275 \\ \hline \end{array}$ **6.** $\begin{array}{r} 804 \\ -\ 178 \\ \hline \end{array}$

7. $\begin{array}{r} 6 \\ \times\ 7 \\ \hline \end{array}$ **8.** $\begin{array}{r} 8 \\ \times\ 9 \\ \hline \end{array}$ **9.** $\begin{array}{r} 7 \\ \times\ 5 \\ \hline \end{array}$ **10.** $\begin{array}{r} 6 \\ \times\ 8 \\ \hline \end{array}$ **11.** $\begin{array}{r} 7 \\ \times\ 7 \\ \hline \end{array}$ **12.** $\begin{array}{r} 9 \\ \times\ 6 \\ \hline \end{array}$

13. $6\overline{)54}$ **14.** $3\overline{)54}$ **15.** $5\overline{)60}$ **16.** $9\overline{)81}$ **17.** $4\overline{)36}$ **18.** $7\overline{)42}$

19. $\begin{array}{r} 35 \\ \times\ 6 \\ \hline \end{array}$ **20.** $\begin{array}{r} 24 \\ \times\ 8 \\ \hline \end{array}$ **21.** $\begin{array}{r} 69 \\ \times\ 4 \\ \hline \end{array}$ **22.** $\begin{array}{r} 98 \\ \times\ 3 \\ \hline \end{array}$ **23.** $\begin{array}{r} 32 \\ \times\ 7 \\ \hline \end{array}$ **24.** $\begin{array}{r} 63 \\ \times\ 5 \\ \hline \end{array}$

Mental Math

Write only the answers.

25. $38 - 5$ **26.** $23 + 5$ **27.** $57 - 6$ **28.** $82 + 7$

29. $400 + 500$ **30.** $700 - 200$ **31.** $600 + 300$ **32.** $800 - 600$

33. 4×80 **34.** 3×70 **35.** 6×50 **36.** 9×20

Estimation

Estimate.

37. $49 + 23$ **38.** $62 + 19$ **39.** $395 + 408$ **40.** \$6.95 + \$1.98

41. $63 - 29$ **42.** $79 - 32$ **43.** $496 - 118$ **44.** \$7.12 − \$2.89

45. 3 × \$1.95 **46.** 2 × \$4.98 **47.** 5 × \$1.98 **48.** 4 × \$6.95

APPLIED PROBLEM SOLVING

You are going shopping to buy gifts for Tyler, Monica, and Trisha. You have $20. You want to choose from these gifts:

Some Things to Consider

- You do not want to spend all of your money.
- Trisha is your best friend.
- You do not want to hurt anyone's feelings by spending too much or too little.

Some Questions to Answer

1. If you bought A, C, and F, how much would you spend?
2. Should you buy all 3 friends a C? How much money would you have left over?
3. Should you buy all 3 friends the same gift?
4. If you bought a B and a D, how much would you have left for the other gift?

What Is Your Decision?

What did you buy for Tyler, Monica, and Trisha?
Do you have any money left over?

PROBLEM SOLVING
Using the Strategies

Use one or more of the strategies listed to solve each problem below.

PROBLEM-SOLVING STRATEGIES
Guess and Check
Use Logical Reasoning
Draw a Picture
Make a List
Make a Table
Choose the Operations
Find a Pattern

1. Socks cost $5 for 3 pairs. On Friday, 21 pairs were sold. What was the total cost?

Pairs of Socks	3	6	9
Cost	$5	$10	$15

2. Jack is first in line. Ann is between Jack and Sue. Sue is between Ann and Bob. Who is last in line?

3. Jay collected 6 cans the first day, 10 cans the second day, 14 cans the third, and so on. How many cans did he collect on the seventh day?

4. Kay bought 2 books for $10.40. Which books did she buy?

Book	Cost
Training Puppies	$4.35
Fruit Trees	$6.95
Health Foods	$5.55
Model Cars	$6.05

CHAPTER REVIEW/TEST

Multiply.

1. 3×30
2. 4×60
3. 2×30
4. 8×40
5. 5×70

6. $\begin{array}{r} 28 \\ \times\ 3 \\ \hline \end{array}$
7. $\begin{array}{r} 46 \\ \times\ 2 \\ \hline \end{array}$
8. $\begin{array}{r} 21 \\ \times\ 4 \\ \hline \end{array}$
9. $\begin{array}{r} 16 \\ \times\ 3 \\ \hline \end{array}$
10. $\begin{array}{r} 35 \\ \times\ 2 \\ \hline \end{array}$

11. $\begin{array}{r} 61 \\ \times\ 5 \\ \hline \end{array}$
12. $\begin{array}{r} 43 \\ \times\ 7 \\ \hline \end{array}$
13. $\begin{array}{r} 82 \\ \times\ 4 \\ \hline \end{array}$
14. $\begin{array}{r} 78 \\ \times\ 5 \\ \hline \end{array}$
15. $\begin{array}{r} 34 \\ \times\ 9 \\ \hline \end{array}$

16. $\begin{array}{r} 32¢ \\ \times\ 6 \\ \hline \end{array}$
17. $\begin{array}{r} 12¢ \\ \times\ 8 \\ \hline \end{array}$
18. $\begin{array}{r} 62¢ \\ \times\ 3 \\ \hline \end{array}$
19. $\begin{array}{r} 74¢ \\ \times\ 2 \\ \hline \end{array}$
20. $\begin{array}{r} 50¢ \\ \times\ 6 \\ \hline \end{array}$

Estimate the product by rounding to the nearest dollar or ten.

21. $4 \times \$2.75$
22. $8 \times \$4.02$
23. $5 \times \$3.50$
24. $2 \times \$53$
25. $6 \times \$35$
26. $3 \times \$62$

Solve. Use the graph for problems 27–29.

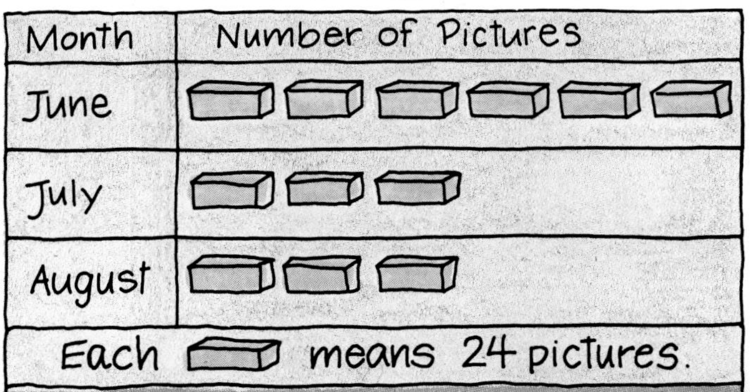

Month
Number of Pictures
June
July
August
Each means 24 pictures.

27. How much more film was used in June than in July?

28. How many pictures were taken in June?

29. How many pictures were taken in July?

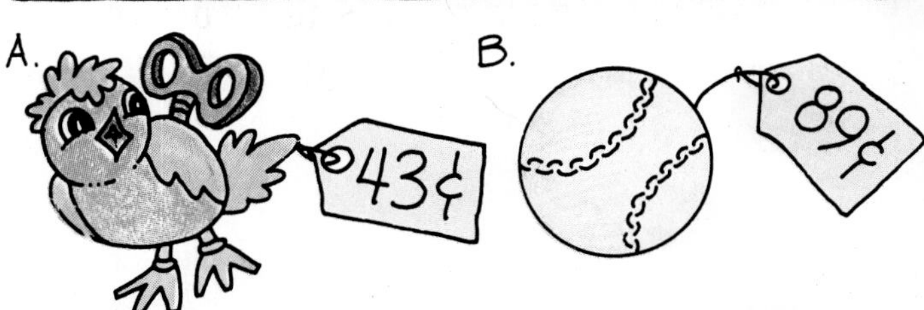

30. How much for 9 A?

31. How much for 4 B?

ANOTHER LOOK

Step 1

$$\begin{array}{r} {}^{1}\\ 26 \\ \times\ 3 \\ \hline 8 \end{array}$$

THINK
3 × 6 = 18
That is 1 ten
and 8 ones.

Step 2

$$\begin{array}{r} {}^{1}\\ 26 \\ \times\ 3 \\ \hline 78 \end{array}$$

THINK
2 × 3 = 6
and 1 more
makes 7.

Step 1

$$\begin{array}{r} {}^{2}\\ 37 \\ \times\ 4 \\ \hline 8 \end{array}$$

THINK
4 × 7 = 28
That is 2 tens
and 8 ones.

Step 2

$$\begin{array}{r} {}^{2}\\ 37 \\ \times\ 4 \\ \hline 148 \end{array}$$

THINK
4 × 3 = 12
and 2 more
make 14.

$$\begin{array}{r} {}^{3}\\ 54¢ \\ \times\ 8 \\ \hline 4\ 32¢ \\ \$4.32 \end{array}$$

Multiply.

1. 24×3
2. 16×4
3. 45×2
4. 12×4
5. 19×5
6. 17×3
7. 15×5
8. 13×5
9. 25×3
10. 76×2
11. 25×7
12. 43×7
13. 63×3
14. 57×5
15. 34×6
16. 64×5
17. 43×4
18. 35×5
19. 82¢ × 2
20. 23¢ × 9
21. 79¢ × 4
22. 83¢ × 5
23. 25¢ × 8
24. 15¢ × 6

ENRICHMENT

Estimating by Clustering

Jan's basketball team played 4 games. In the games, Jan scored 19, 24, 23, and 18 points. About how many points did Jan score?

Since all of the scores are close to 20, you can multiply to estimate the sum.

Jan scored about 80 points.

19 + 24 + 23 + 18

4×20

estimate

80

Estimate each sum. Use multiplication when you can.

All of the numbers are close to 20. THINK: 3×20

1. 19 + 22 + 17

All of the numbers are close to 50. THINK: 4×50

2. 46 + 54 + 49 + 53

All of the numbers are close to 40. THINK: 4×40

3. 44 + 39 + 38 + 41

All of the numbers are close to 30. THINK: 5×30

4. 27 + 29 + 31 + 28 + 30

All of the numbers are close to 90. THINK: 3×90

5. 89 + 93 + 88

All of the numbers are close to 60. THINK: 5×60

6. 59 + 56 + 62 + 61 + 58

7. 17 + 22 + 24

8. 32 + 29 + 33 + 28

9. 41 + 36 + 39 + 38

10. 69 + 72 + 67

11. 49 + 54 + 52 + 53 + 48

12. 21 + 18 + 19 + 17 + 22

CUMULATIVE REVIEW

Give the letter for the correct answer.

1. $\begin{array}{r} 6 \\ \times 7 \\ \hline \end{array}$

   A 48
   B 42
   C 49
   D not given

2. $\begin{array}{r} 8 \\ \times 8 \\ \hline \end{array}$

   A 48
   B 64
   C 56
   D not given

3. $\begin{array}{r} 9 \\ \times 6 \\ \hline \end{array}$

   A 56
   B 64
   C 53
   D not given

4. $\begin{array}{r} 9 \\ \times 0 \\ \hline \end{array}$

   A 9
   B 0
   C 8
   D not given

5. $\begin{array}{r} 6 \\ \times 6 \\ \hline \end{array}$

   A 32
   B 30
   C 36
   D not given

6. $\begin{array}{r} 8 \\ \times 5 \\ \hline \end{array}$

   A 40
   B 48
   C 45
   D not given

7. $9 \div 3$

   A 2
   B 3
   C 4
   D not given

8. $18 \div 2$

   A 6
   B 8
   C 9
   D not given

9. $35 \div 5$

   A 6
   B 7
   C 5
   D not given

10. $8\overline{)48}$

    A 6 B 5
    C 4 D not given

11. $9\overline{)63}$

    A 8 B 6
    C 7 D not given

12. $6\overline{)54}$

    A 9 B 8
    C 7 D not given

13. Paul needs 9 buttons. Each card has 3 buttons. How many cards of buttons must Paul buy?

    A 2 B 3
    C 27 D not given

14. Alice needs 3 bananas to make a loaf of banana bread. How many bananas will Alice need to make 4 loaves?

    A 3 B 12
    C 8 D not given

DIVISION 12

John started piano lessons when he was 9 years old. The first year he learned how to read music. He also learned about rhythm. Rhythm is the beat of the music. Here is one of the first pieces John learned to play:

Hey did-dle,
did-dle, the
cat and the
fid-dle the

This part of the song has 12 notes divided into 4 groups. Now John plays music written by famous composers. He plays one piece written by Mozart at the age of five.

Checking Division

You can check a division problem by multiplying the **quotient** by the **divisor** and then adding the **remainder**.

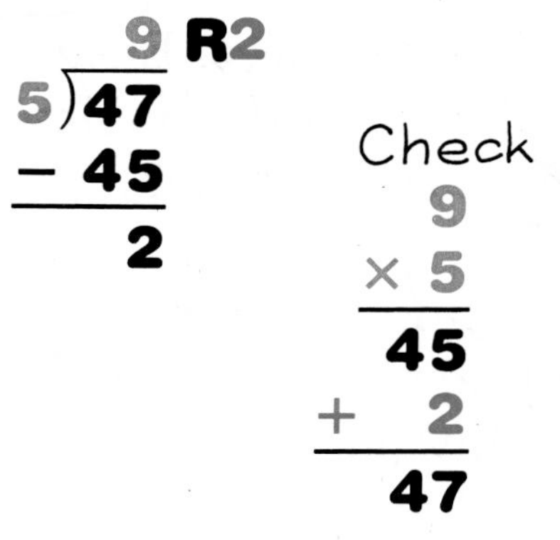

Barry missed two division problems on his paper. Check his problems. Which ones did he miss?

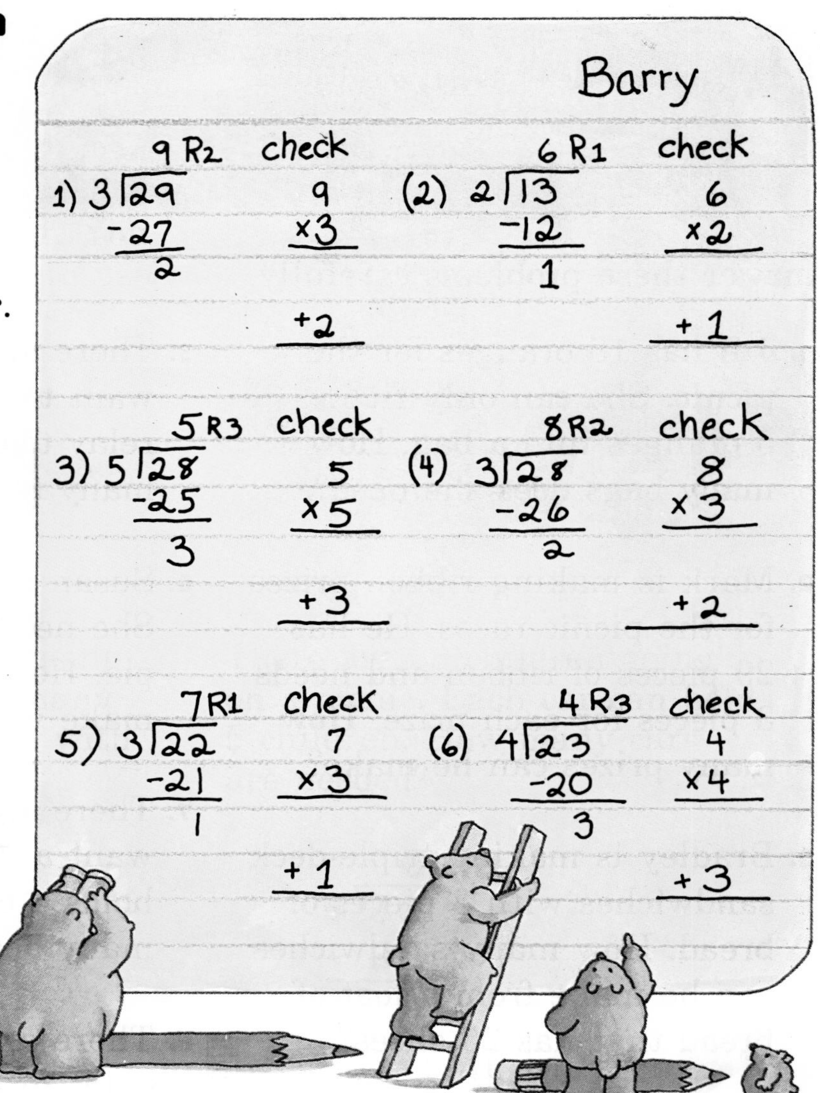

Find the quotients. Use Barry's method to check each answer.

1. 2)11 **2.** 5)14 **3.** 3)26 **4.** 2)15 **5.** 4)25

6. 3)20 **7.** 2)19 **8.** 3)13 **9.** 5)18 **10.** 4)22

11. 5)48 **12.** 4)19 **13.** 2)17 **14.** 5)45 **15.** 5)33

16. Check this problem by multiplying and then adding. Is it correct?

964 R1
4)3853

PROBLEM SOLVING
Multi-step Problems

Solve.

1. The roller rink charges $3 a ticket. Brian has $25 for skating. How many tickets can he buy? How much money would be left?

2. The roller rink rents skates for 75¢. How much do Kristi, Roberto, and Daryl have to pay in all to rent skates? How much change will they get back from a $5 bill?

3. The roller rink sold 583 tickets on Friday night. They sold 398 on Saturday afternoon and 716 on Saturday night. How many more tickets were sold on Saturday than on Friday?

4. Knee pads cost $32 for 4 pads. How much does it cost for 2 pads?

5. Janet has $25 in the bank. She will get $6 more today. How much more will she need to buy skates that cost $44?

6. Tom has $8 in the bank. He will get $3 more today. How much more will he need to buy a skate helmet that costs $17?

7. **DATA BANK** See page 378. How many more skaters does the Jellibeans skating rink hold than the Happy Wheels and Roller City skating rinks together?

8. ***Strategy Practice*** The Yellow Rink is larger than the Blue Rink. The Red Rink is the largest. The Green Rink is larger than the Yellow Rink. Give the order of these four rinks, starting with the largest.

2-Digit Quotients

Dan has 36 blocks. He wants to put them in 2 equal sets. How many should he put in each set?

Since we want to know how many in each set, we divide.

Dividing Tens

- Divide
- Multiply
- Subtract
- Compare

1
2)36
− 2
1
Used 2 tens so 1 ten is left.

Dividing Ones

- Bring down the ones next to the tens.

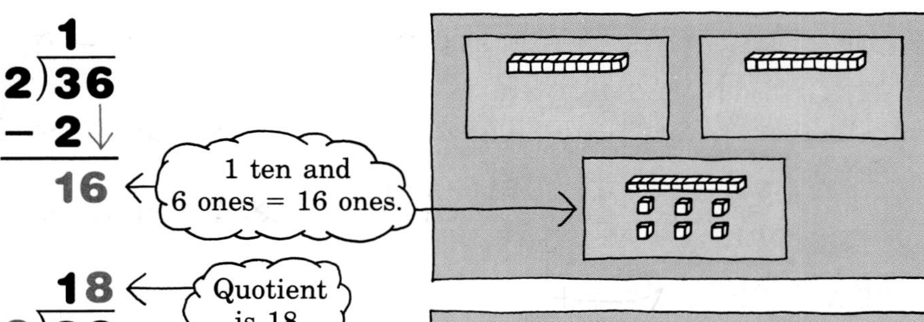

- Divide
- Multiply
- Subtract
- Compare

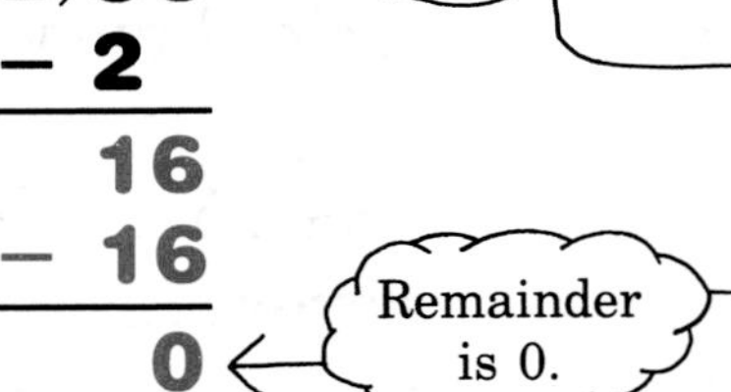

− 2
16
− 16
0

Remainder is 0.

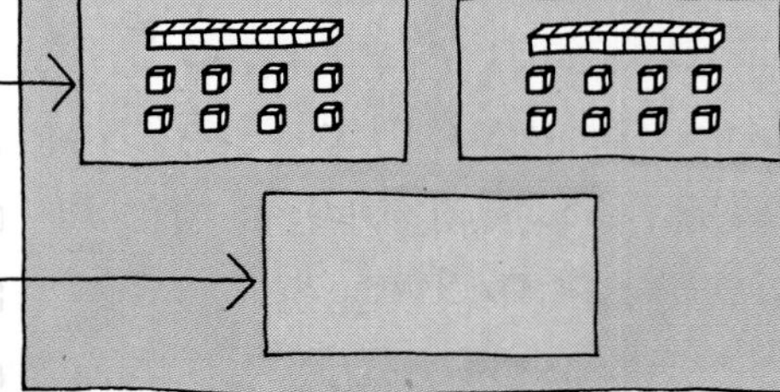

Dan should put 18 blocks in each set.

Other Examples

19	45	31	10
4)76	2)90	3)93	5)50
− 4	− 8	− 9	− 5
36	10	03	00
− 36	− 10	− 3	− 0
0	0	0	0

Warm Up Find the quotients. Check your answers.

1. 3)42 **2.** 5)60 **3.** 4)64 **4.** 3)69 **5.** 2)80

Practice Find the quotients.

1. $2\overline{)32}$ 2. $5\overline{)80}$ 3. $4\overline{)96}$

4. $5\overline{)65}$ 5. $2\overline{)86}$ 6. $3\overline{)84}$

7. $4\overline{)84}$ 8. $3\overline{)78}$ 9. $2\overline{)50}$ 10. $2\overline{)40}$ 11. $3\overline{)51}$

12. $3\overline{)27}$ 13. $2\overline{)44}$ 14. $3\overline{)63}$ 15. $3\overline{)60}$ 16. $4\overline{)72}$

17. $3\overline{)63}$ 18. $2\overline{)72}$ 19. $2\overline{)38}$ 20. $4\overline{)32}$ 21. $4\overline{)44}$

22. $76 \div 2$ 23. $60 \div 4$ 24. $85 \div 5$ 25. $96 \div 6$

26. $56 \div 4$ 27. $72 \div 3$ 28. $46 \div 2$ 29. $52 \div 4$

30. What is 70 divided by 5?

31. What is 86 divided by 2?

32. What is 60 divided by 3?

33. What is 68 divided by 4?

Mixed Applications

34. Four children are playing a card game with 52 cards. Each person gets the same number of cards. How many cards does each person get?

35. Eric, Larry, and Lucy are playing cards. Each person has 15 cards. There are 7 cards on the table. How many cards altogether?

SKILLKEEPER

Add or subtract.

1. $8 + 5$ 2. $9 - 3$ 3. $9 + 8$ 4. $4 + 7$ 5. $11 - 6$ 6. $8 + 8$

7. $13 - 6$ 8. $12 - 4$ 9. $5 + 9$ 10. $15 - 8$ 11. $6 + 4$ 12. $9 + 6$

More Practice, page 399, Set C

2-Digit Quotients and Remainders

Sharon has 67¢. How many Pony Express stamps can she buy? How much money would she have left?

Pony Express 4¢

Johnny Appleseed 5¢

Since we want to know how many fours are in 67, we divide.

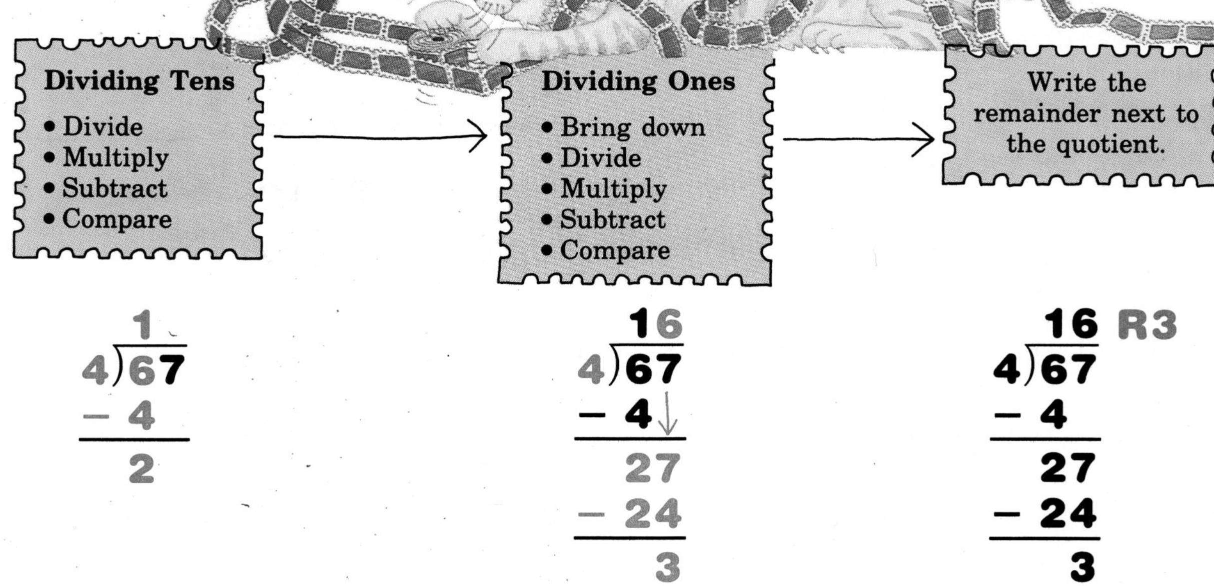

Dividing Tens

- Divide
- Multiply
- Subtract
- Compare

→

Dividing Ones

- Bring down
- Divide
- Multiply
- Subtract
- Compare

→

Write the remainder next to the quotient.

```
   1          16         16 R3
4)67        4)67        4)67
 -4          -4↓         -4
  2           27          27
             -24         -24
               3           3
```

Sharon can buy 16 Pony Express stamps. She would have 3¢ left.

Other Examples

```
  23 R1      21 R2      10 R4       45
4)93       3)65       5)54       2)90
 -8         -6         -5         -8
  13         05         04         10
 -12        - 3        - 0        -10
   1          2          4          0
```

Warm Up Find the quotients and remainders.

1. $3\overline{)43}$ **2.** $5\overline{)62}$ **3.** $2\overline{)21}$ **4.** $3\overline{)54}$ **5.** $4\overline{)55}$

Practice Find the quotients and remainders.

1. $2\overline{)71}$	2. $4\overline{)62}$	3. $3\overline{)85}$	4. $2\overline{)58}$	5. $3\overline{)74}$
6. $4\overline{)76}$	7. $5\overline{)91}$	8. $2\overline{)34}$	9. $4\overline{)92}$	10. $3\overline{)92}$
11. $5\overline{)82}$	12. $4\overline{)35}$	13. $3\overline{)50}$	14. $4\overline{)83}$	15. $5\overline{)60}$

16. $38 \div 3$
17. $70 \div 4$
18. $53 \div 2$
19. $59 \div 5$
20. $75 \div 5$
21. $88 \div 3$
22. Divide 83 by 4.
23. Divide 78 by 2.

Mixed Applications

24. Look at the picture on page 306. How many Johnny Appleseed stamps can Gina buy with 91¢? How much money would she have left?

25. Jake has 58 stamps. He needs 4 stamps on each package. How many packages could get 4 stamps? How many stamps would be left?

26. **DATA BANK** See page 375. How much change would you get from a quarter if you bought 3 Crane Stamps?

THINK

Patterns

Jack's birthday is October 15.

OCTOBER						
SUN	MON	TUES	WED	THURS	FRI	SAT
				1	2	3
4	5	6	7	8	9	10
11	12	13	14	(15)	16	17
18	19	20	21	22	23	24
25	26	27	28	29	30	31

1. Add the numbers on each side of his birthday (14 + 16). Divide the sum by 2.
2. Add the numbers above and below his birthday. Divide the sum by 2.

What is special about Jack's birthday?

Find out what is special about Mindy's and Karl's birthdays by doing the same. Mindy's birthday is October 9. Karl's birthday is October 20.

MATH

More Practice, page 400, Set A

Estimating Quotients with Money Using Rounding

About how many dollars does 1 package of marking pens cost?

Marking Pens 3 for $5.96

Since you want an answer that is only close to the exact answer, you **estimate** by rounding and dividing in your head.

$5.96 ÷ 3

THINK
$6 ÷ 3 = $2

The cost of 1 package of pens is about $2.

Other Examples

$8.10 ÷ 2

$8 ÷ 2 = $4

$35.95 ÷ 4

$36 ÷ 4 = $9

Estimate the quotients. Give answers aloud.

Round to the nearest dollar and divide.

1. $3.12 ÷ 3 **2.** $3.96 ÷ 4 **3.** $7.95 ÷ 2 **4.** $1.88 ÷ 2

5. $5.25 ÷ 5 **6.** $8.30 ÷ 4 **7.** $5.90 ÷ 3 **8.** $8.88 ÷ 3

9. $10.05 ÷ 2 **10.** $14.95 ÷ 3 **11.** $20.25 ÷ 4 **12.** $17.75 ÷ 3

Estimate the quotients. Write answers only.

13. $6.30 ÷ 2 **14.** $7.96 ÷ 4 **15.** $5.70 ÷ 3 **16.** $4.05 ÷ 4

17. $23.95 ÷ 3 **18.** $16.10 ÷ 4 **19.** $9.95 ÷ 2 **20.** $34.95 ÷ 5

21. $27.15 ÷ 3 **22.** $4.10 ÷ 2 **23.** $27.95 ÷ 4 **24.** $4.95 ÷ 5

PROBLEM SOLVING
Choosing a Calculation Method

Your choice!
Pencil-Paper • Mental Math
Estimation • Calculator

You may use any of these methods to solve the problems, but use each method at least once.

1. Sharon bought a paint set and a ruler. Can she pay with a $5 bill?

2. Randy bought a calculator, 2 pairs of scissors, and a stapler. What was the total cost?

3. Ron bought 2 jars of glue. How much did they cost?

4. How much more does the paint set cost than the ruler?

5. Does 1 box of clay cost more or less than 2 dollars?

6. Mr. Jones bought 25 calculators for his class. How much did they cost?

7. Diane bought a paint set and a jar of glue. How much were they?

8. Can Jerry pay for 6 boxes of clay with a $10 bill?

9. Can Jerry get 2 calculators with his $10?

10. How much will it cost to buy a calculator and a stapler?

11. **DATA HUNT** Find a newspaper advertisement for three things that you would like to have. Estimate the cost for all three.

12. ***Strategy Practice*** Anthony wanted to buy the calculator, the ruler, the paint set, and the stapler. He bought only two of them and spent $9.04. What did he buy?

APPLIED PROBLEM SOLVING

QUESTION
DATA
PLAN
ANSWER
CHECK

You live in Green Hill, and you want to spend the day at the park. You can walk or ride a bicycle. There are 3 roads to the park. Plan your trip.

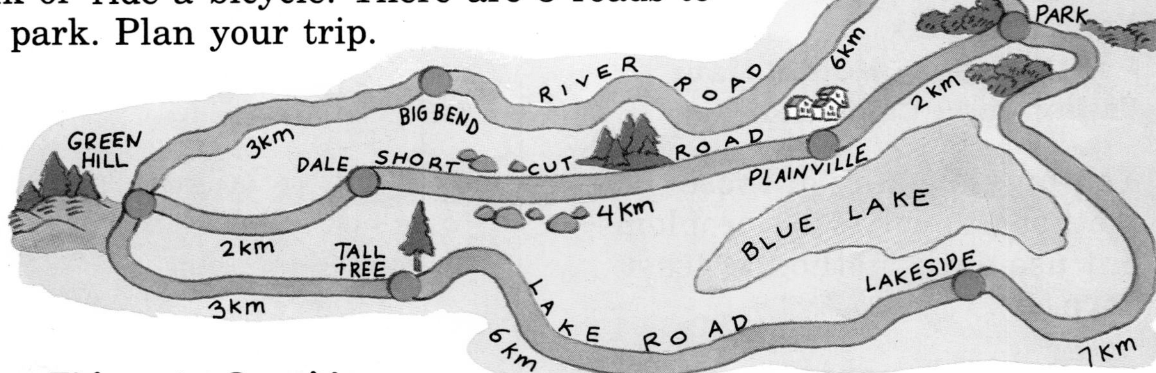

Some Things to Consider

- River Road has steep hills. The shortcut is not good for bikes. Lake Road is smooth and even.
- You can ride twice as fast on level ground as you can walk. Lake Road is twice as long as the shortcut.
- River Road is the most scenic.
- You want to get to the park quickly, but also see some scenery.
- The morning is supposed to be sunny. There is a chance of rain in the afternoon.

Some Questions to Answer

1. How many kilometers is the River Road trip? Would you walk it or ride it? Why?
2. How many kilometers is the shortcut trip? Would you walk it or ride it? Why?
3. How many kilometers is the Lake Road trip? Would you walk it or ride it? Why?
4. Could you take one road to get to the park and a different one back?

What Is Your Decision?

Would you walk or ride?
Would you take River Road, shortcut, or Lake Road? A combination?

CHAPTER REVIEW/TEST

Divide.

1. $3\overline{)7}$
2. $2\overline{)9}$
3. $5\overline{)3}$
4. $4\overline{)7}$
5. $4\overline{)2}$
6. $4\overline{)30}$
7. $3\overline{)19}$
8. $5\overline{)24}$
9. $2\overline{)19}$
10. $4\overline{)14}$
11. $2\overline{)42}$
12. $3\overline{)96}$
13. $4\overline{)80}$
14. $3\overline{)39}$
15. $2\overline{)68}$
16. $2\overline{)56}$
17. $4\overline{)92}$
18. $5\overline{)90}$
19. $2\overline{)74}$
20. $3\overline{)48}$
21. $4\overline{)78}$
22. $3\overline{)46}$
23. $2\overline{)85}$
24. $4\overline{)67}$
25. $5\overline{)53}$

Estimate the quotient by rounding to the nearest dollar.

26. $4.23 ÷ 2
27. $9.50 ÷ 5
28. $14.82 ÷ 3

Solve. Use the newspaper ad for problems 29–32.

29. How much does it cost to buy 2 kg of bananas?
30. How much does 1 pineapple and 1 kg of grapes cost in all?
31. How much does a 4-kg watermelon cost?
32. How many boxes of oranges can you buy with $35?

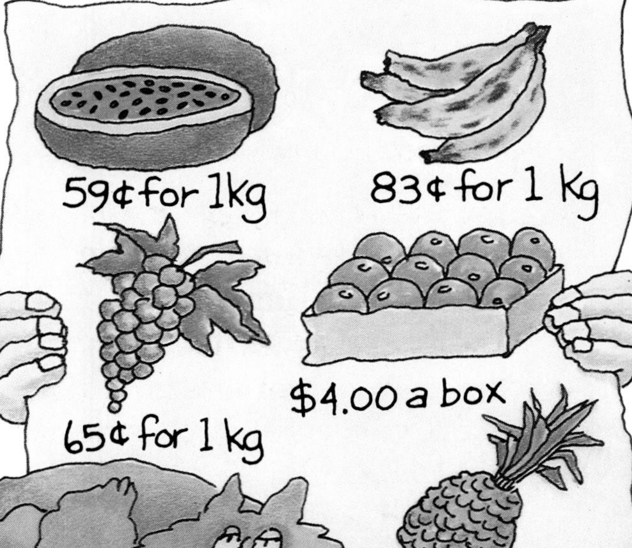

ANOTHER LOOK

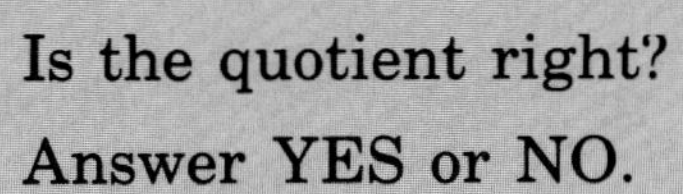

Is the quotient right?

Answer YES or NO.

8	**4**	**9**
3)28	**5)17**	**4)37**
− 24	**20**	**− 36**
4		**1**
No. 8 is too small	No. 4 is too large	Yes.

Find the right quotient.

4)27

5 is too small.

$$\begin{array}{r} 5 \\ 4\overline{)27} \\ -\ 20 \\ \hline 7 \end{array}$$

7 is too large.

$$\begin{array}{r} 7 \\ 4\overline{)27} \\ 28 \end{array}$$

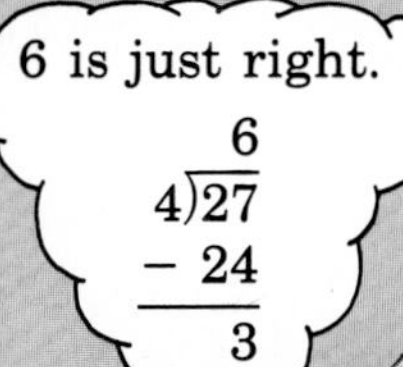

6 is just right.

$$\begin{array}{r} 6 \\ 4\overline{)27} \\ -\ 24 \\ \hline 3 \end{array}$$

Is the quotient right? Answer YES or NO.

1. $\begin{array}{r} 3 \\ 4\overline{)10} \\ 12 \\ \hline \end{array}$

2. $\begin{array}{r} 6 \\ 3\overline{)22} \\ -\ 18 \\ \hline 4 \end{array}$

3. $\begin{array}{r} 7 \\ 5\overline{)39} \\ -\ 35 \\ \hline 4 \end{array}$

4. $\begin{array}{r} 4 \\ 4\overline{)17} \\ -\ 16 \\ \hline 1 \end{array}$

5. $\begin{array}{r} 7 \\ 3\overline{)25} \\ -\ 21 \\ \hline 4 \end{array}$

6. $\begin{array}{r} 9 \\ 5\overline{)42} \\ 45 \\ \hline \end{array}$

Find the quotients and remainders.

7. $4\overline{)15}$
8. $3\overline{)23}$
9. $4\overline{)33}$
10. $5\overline{)28}$
11. $2\overline{)13}$
12. $3\overline{)14}$
13. $4\overline{)34}$
14. $3\overline{)28}$
15. $5\overline{)49}$

ENRICHMENT

Logical Reasoning

Make these pieces.
There are 2 colors, 2 sizes, and 3 shapes.

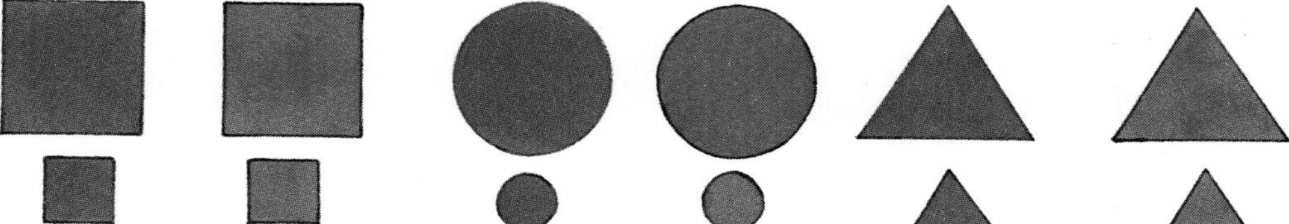

Play a One Difference game with a friend.

1. Pass out six pieces to each player.
2. The first player puts down a piece to start.
3. Take turns placing the pieces next to each other in a row.

   To play a piece, it must be different from the one next to it in one and only one way. It can be different in color, or shape, or size.

   If you cannot play a piece, skip your turn.
4. The first player to use up all six pieces wins.

Now play a Two Difference game. Each piece played must have exactly two differences from the one next to it.

CUMULATIVE REVIEW

Give the letter for the correct answer.

1. Name the figure.

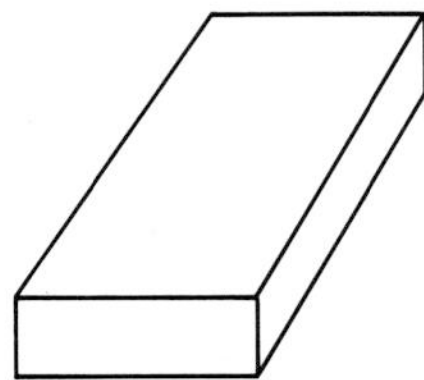

A square
B rectangular prism
C rectangle
D not given

2. Name the figure.

A sphere
B circle
C cylinder
D not given

3. Name the figure.

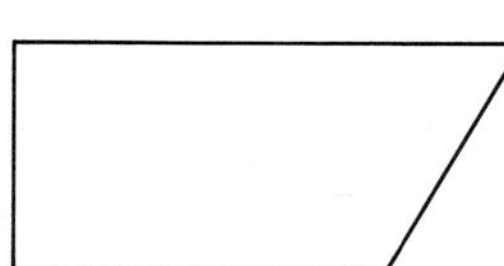

A rectangle
B square
C circle
D not given

4. Which figure is congruent to this figure?

A
B
C

D not given

5. Which figure is congruent to this figure?

A
B
C
D not given

6. Which shape has a line of symmetry?

A
B
C
D not given

7. $\begin{array}{r} 30 \\ \times\ 5 \\ \hline \end{array}$
A 15 B 150
C 1,500 D not given

8. $\begin{array}{r} 34 \\ \times\ 2 \\ \hline \end{array}$
A 14 B 86
C 68 D not given

9. $\begin{array}{r} 27 \\ \times\ 3 \\ \hline \end{array}$
A 81 B 61
C 621 D not given

10. $\begin{array}{r} 74 \\ \times\ 5 \\ \hline \end{array}$
A 370 B 350
C 3,520 D not given

11. $\begin{array}{r} 68 \\ \times\ 4 \\ \hline \end{array}$
A 274 B 242
C 272 D not given

12. $\begin{array}{r} 56¢ \\ \times\ 7 \\ \hline \end{array}$
A \$3.92 B \$35.2
C \$35.42 D not given

13. Martin wants to buy 4 rolls of film. A roll of film costs \$2.12. Estimate the cost of 4 rolls of film to the nearest dollar.
A \$12 B \$6
C \$8 D not given

14. Loni's vacation lasted 12 days. She took 4 pictures each day. How many pictures did she take?
A 3 B 46
C 48 D not given

FRACTIONS AND DECIMALS 13

One day Moriko showed Tina how to do "origami." Origami is the Japanese art of folding colored paper. Tina picked a red paper. Moriko told Tina to fold the paper into 2 equal parts. In three more steps Tina had made a red sailboat. Tina also learned how to make a bird. She started by folding a blue paper into 4 equal parts. When Tina was finished she had a beautiful blue crane.

Naming Parts of a Whole

Give the missing word.

Halves
Each piece is one half of the whole.

1. Ned and Philip shared the sandwich equally. Each boy had one _____ of it.

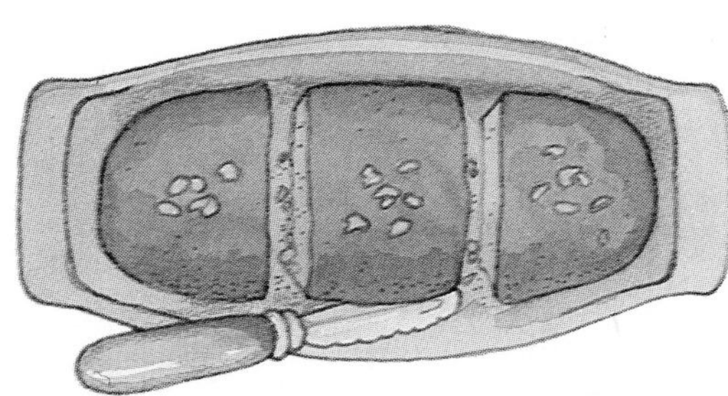

Thirds
Each piece is one third of the whole.

2. Patty, Marianne, and Nora shared the nut bread equally. Each girl had one _____ of it.

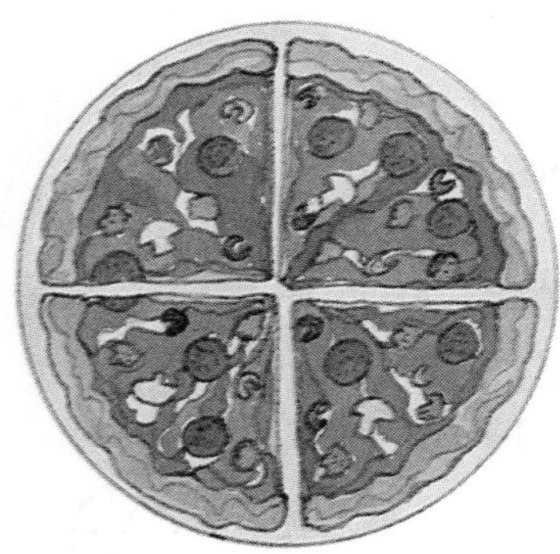

Fourths
Each piece is one fourth of the whole.

3. Rodney, Kris, Tomas, and Janice shared the pizza equally. Each child had one _____ of the pizza.

Here are some other names of parts of a whole.

5 Equal Parts	6 Equal Parts	8 Equal Parts	10 Equal Parts	100 Equal Parts
Fifths	Sixths	Eighths	Tenths	Hundredths

Practice Choose the correct letter.

1. 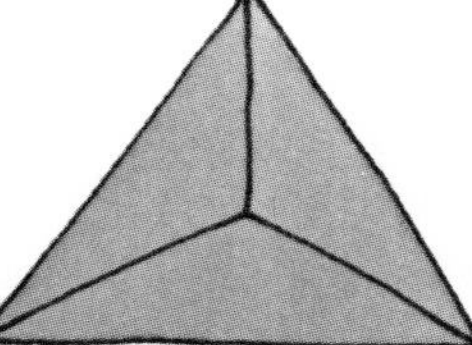

   A halves
   B thirds
   C fourths
   D not given

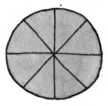

2. **A** fourths
   B sixths
   C eighths
   D not given

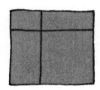

3. **A** halves
   B thirds
   C fourths
   D not given

4. 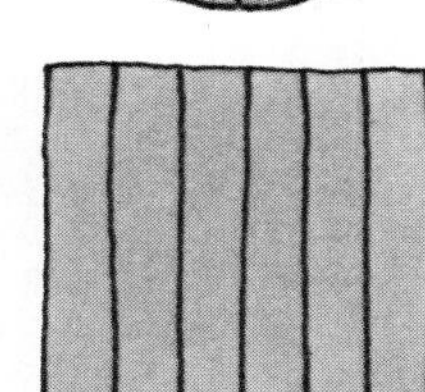
   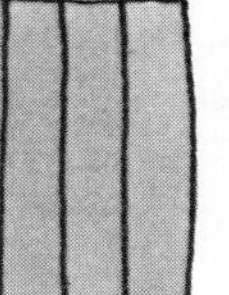

   A sixths
   B eighths
   C tenths
   D not given

5. 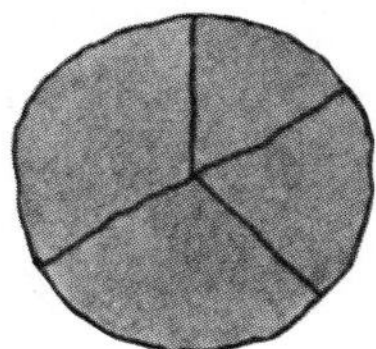

   A fifths
   B sixths
   C eighths
   D not given

6. 

   A eighths
   B tenths
   C hundredths
   D not given

7. Kenneth cut a pizza into 2 equal pieces. Then he cut each of those pieces into 2 equal pieces. How was the pizza divided?

THINK

Space Perception

Read the problem all the way through. First guess the answer. Then do the folding to check your guess.

1. Start with a paper strip.
2. Fold it once.
3. Fold it again.
4. Fold it once more. How do the folds divide the paper?

MATH

Finding Fractions of a Whole

Diane cut a pizza into **fourths**. She and two friends ate 3 of the pieces. What part of the pizza did they eat?

Fourths

Three pieces were eaten. → $\mathbf{3}$
Each piece was a fourth. → $\mathbf{4}$

We use the **fraction** $\frac{3}{4}$ (three fourths) to answer the question.

The children ate $\frac{3}{4}$ of the pizza.

Warm Up Choose the fraction that tells how much pizza is left on the tray.

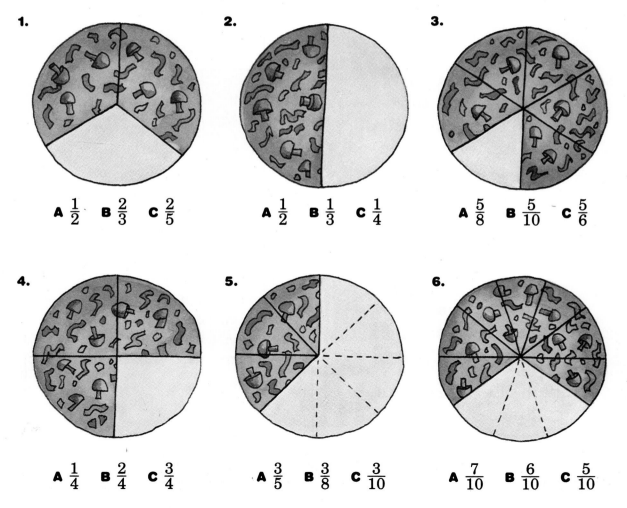

1. **A** $\frac{1}{2}$ **B** $\frac{2}{3}$ **C** $\frac{2}{5}$

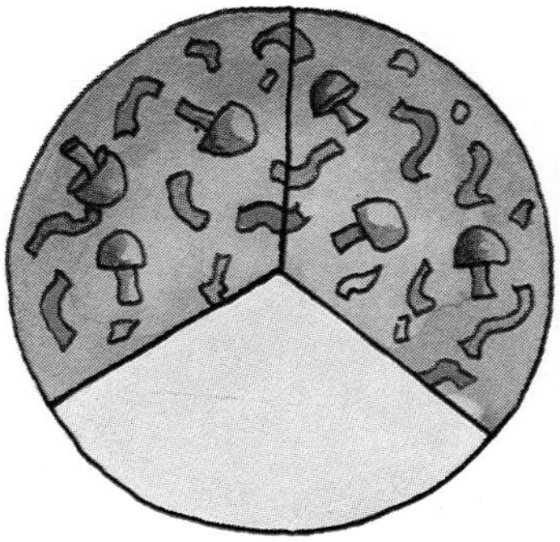

2. **A** $\frac{1}{2}$ **B** $\frac{1}{3}$ **C** $\frac{1}{4}$

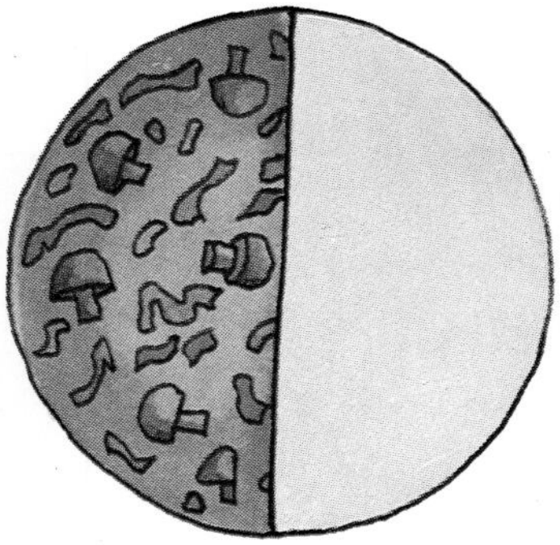

3. **A** $\frac{5}{8}$ **B** $\frac{5}{10}$ **C** $\frac{5}{6}$

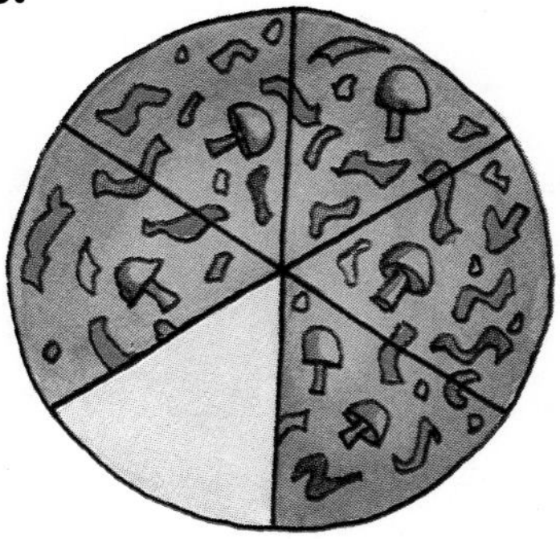

4. **A** $\frac{1}{4}$ **B** $\frac{2}{4}$ **C** $\frac{3}{4}$

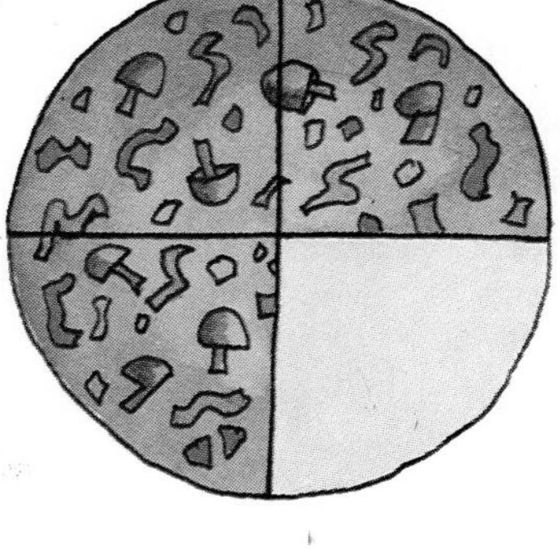

5. **A** $\frac{3}{5}$ **B** $\frac{3}{8}$ **C** $\frac{3}{10}$

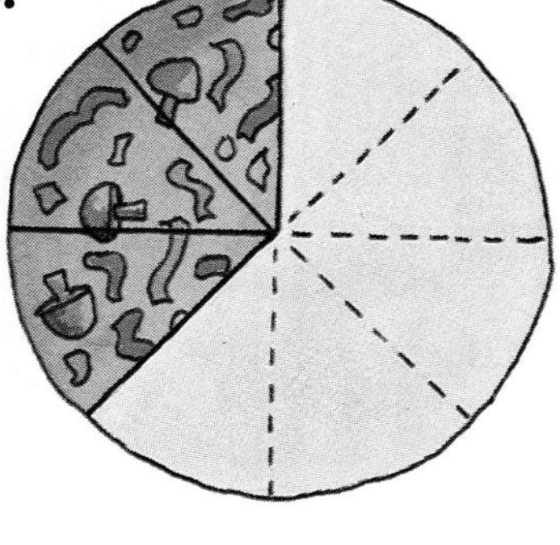

6. **A** $\frac{7}{10}$ **B** $\frac{6}{10}$ **C** $\frac{5}{10}$

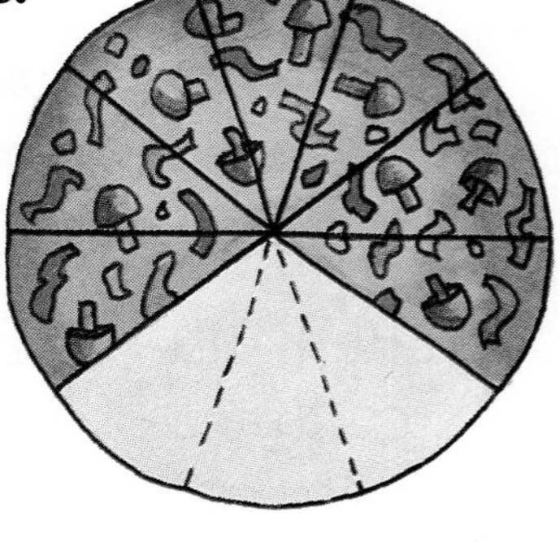

Practice Write the fraction that tells what part is yellow.

1. 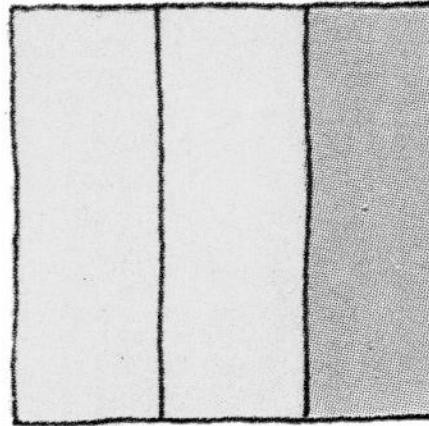

2. 

3. 

4. 

5. 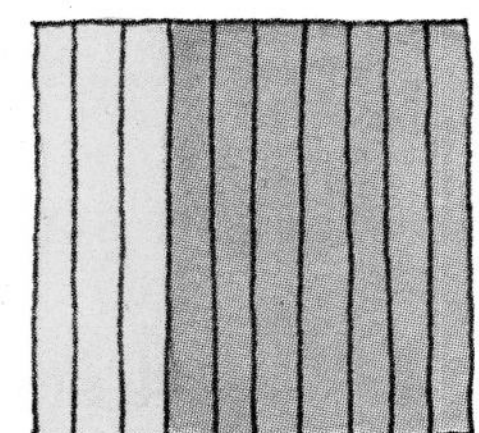

6. 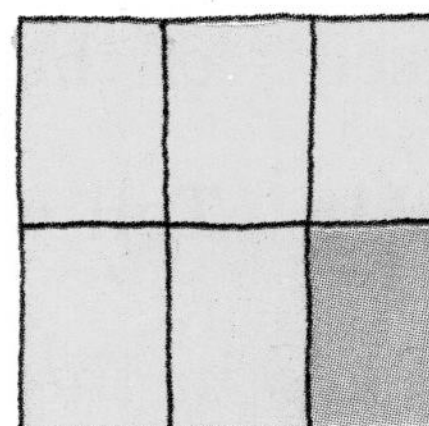

7. 

8. 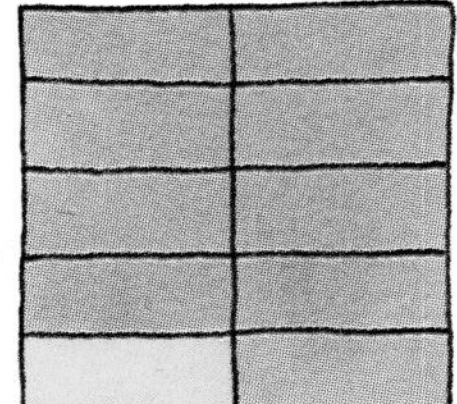

9. 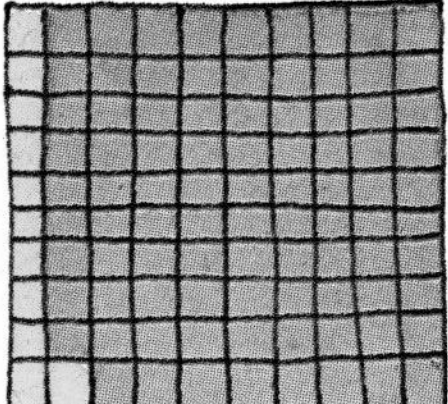

10. This is how William cut his pizza. 7 pieces of the pizza were eaten. What fraction of the pizza was left?

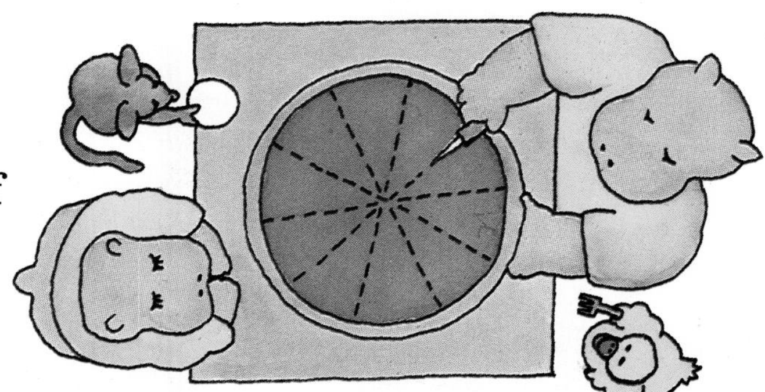

SKILLKEEPER

Find the quotients and remainders.

1. $3\overline{)7}$ **2.** $4\overline{)9}$ **3.** $4\overline{)14}$ **4.** $2\overline{)17}$

5. $3\overline{)13}$ **6.** $5\overline{)17}$ **7.** $4\overline{)11}$ **8.** $3\overline{)14}$

Finding Fractional Parts of a Set

There were 8 stamps in a strip. Kent used 3 of them to mail some letters. What fraction of the strip did Kent use?

Three stamps were used. ⟶ **3**
Each stamp was an eighth. ⟶ **8**

Kent used $\frac{3}{8}$ of the strip.

Warm Up Tell what fraction of each strip of stamps is used.

1. 5 stamps in the strip

2. 4 stamps in the strip

3. 6 stamps in the strip

4. 3 stamps in the strip

Practice What fractions of the stamps are used?

1.

Answer $\frac{4}{5}$

2.

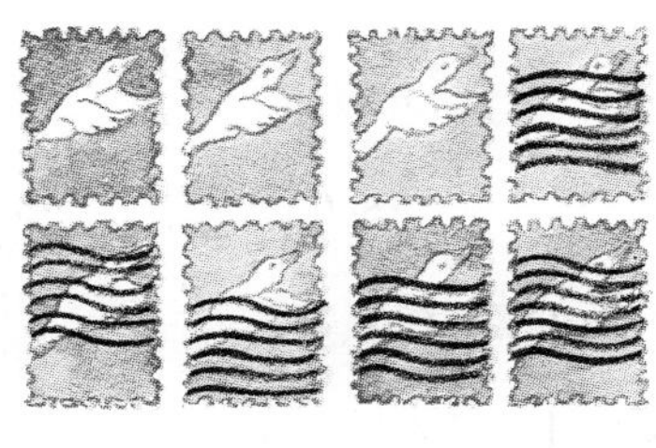

3.

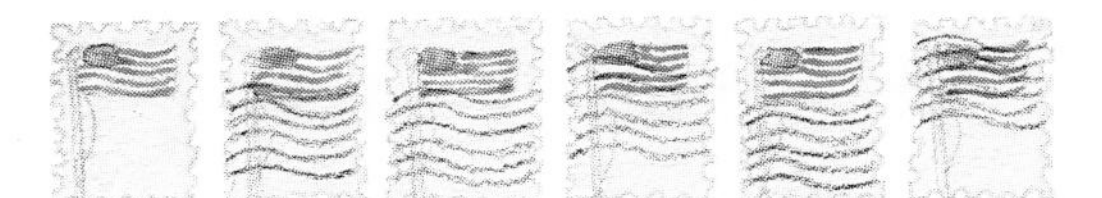

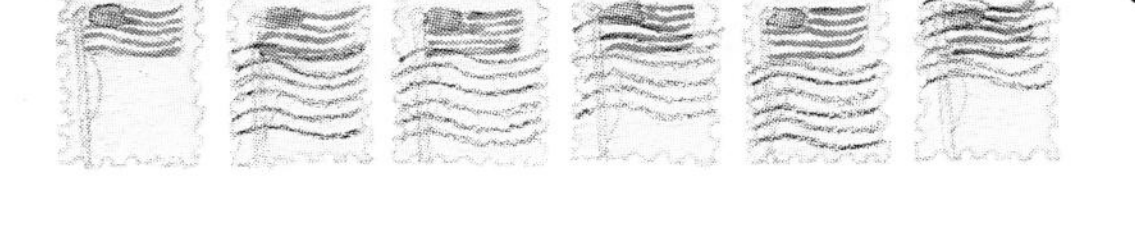

4.

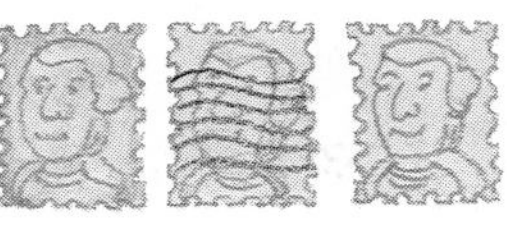

5.

6.

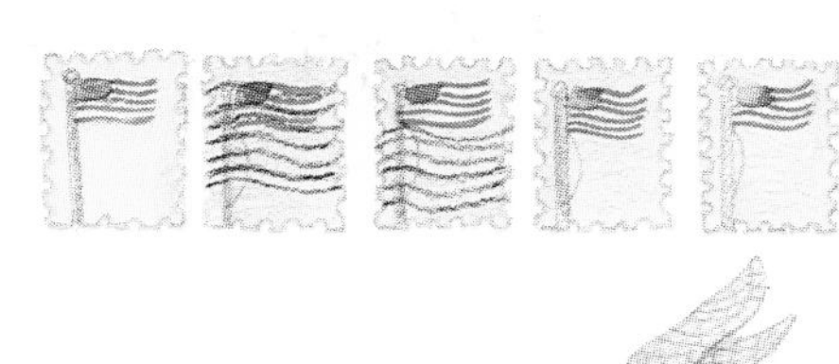

7.

8.

9. Kevin has 8 stamps. He used 5 of the stamps to mail some letters. What fraction of the stamps did he use?

★ 10. Cindy has 10 stamps. She used 7 of the stamps on a package. What fraction of the stamps does she have left?

THINK

Shape Perception

How many different ways can you tear 3 stamps from a large sheet of stamps?

Example

Draw pictures on a sheet of paper to show your answers.

MATH

Fractions of a Set

Jack had 8 toy boats. He painted $\frac{1}{2}$ of them blue.

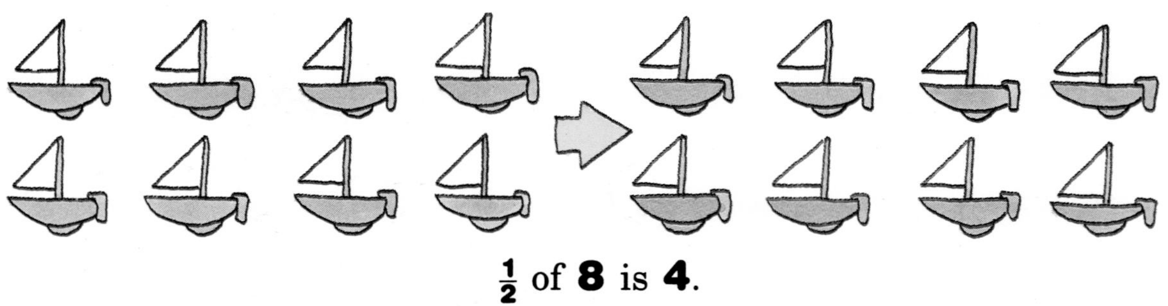

$\frac{1}{2}$ of 8 is 4.

To find $\frac{1}{2}$ of a number, divide by 2.

Other Examples

Marcia painted $\frac{1}{3}$ of the cars red.

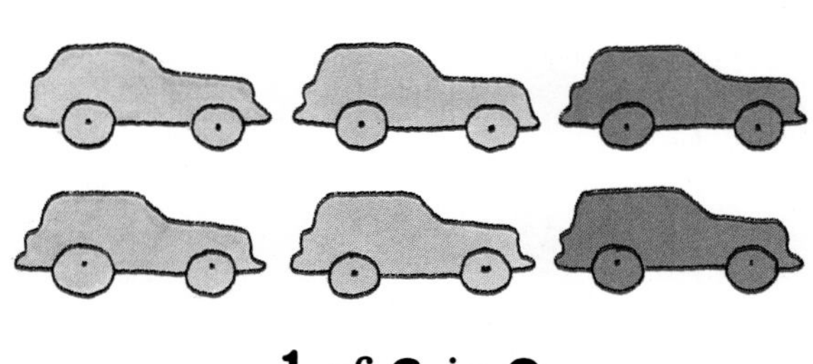

$\frac{1}{3}$ of 6 is 2.

To find $\frac{1}{3}$ of a number, divide by 3.

Brad painted $\frac{1}{4}$ of the trucks green.

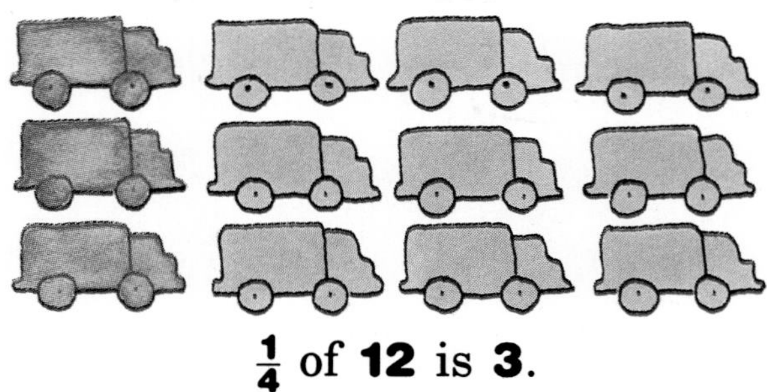

$\frac{1}{4}$ of 12 is 3.

To find $\frac{1}{4}$ of a number, divide by 4.

Solve.

1. Sara had 10 toy boats. She painted $\frac{1}{2}$ of them yellow. How many did she paint yellow?

2. Tony had 6 toy airplanes. He painted $\frac{1}{3}$ of them blue. How many did he paint blue?

PROBLEM SOLVING: Mixed Practice

Solve.

1. Dick has 8 toy cars. Each car has 4 wheels. How many wheels are there?

2. Larry had 12 balloons. He popped $\frac{1}{3}$ of them. How many balloons did Larry pop?

3. Peggy had 24 marbles. She gave away 9 of them. How many marbles does Peggy have left?

4. June has 6 toy horses. She painted $\frac{1}{2}$ of them brown. How many of June's horses are brown?

5. Isabel had 10 pennies. She spent $\frac{1}{2}$ of them. How many pennies did Isabel spend?

6. Marie saw a toy train pulling 18 cars. $\frac{1}{3}$ of the cars were boxcars. How many of the cars were boxcars?

7. Rick has 16 fish in his tank. $\frac{1}{2}$ of the fish are goldfish. How many goldfish does Rick have in his tank?

8. Ron has 16 red balloons and 17 yellow balloons. How many balloons does Ron have?

9. Dave had 15 pennies. He spent $\frac{1}{3}$ of them. How many pennies did Dave spend?

★ 10. Javier had 32 baseball cards. He gave away $\frac{1}{4}$ of them. How many baseball cards did Javier keep?

11. ***Strategy Practice*** Corey sold between 15 and 20 toy trains on Saturday. He sold an even number of trains. Corey has never sold 18 trains in one day. How many toy trains did Corey sell?

Equivalent Fractions

Brenda and Tim each colored part of a paper strip.

I colored $\frac{1}{2}$ of my strip.
I colored $\frac{2}{4}$ of my strip.

The children colored the **same amount** of the strips. Fractions that name the same amount are **equivalent fractions**.

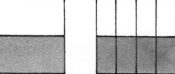

We write $\mathbf{\frac{1}{2} = \frac{2}{4}}$

Many fractions are equivalent to $\frac{1}{2}$.

Warm Up Give the missing fractions.

1.

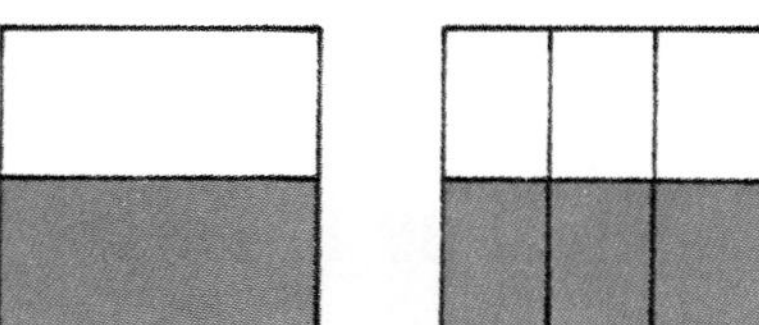

$\frac{1}{2}$ = ____

2.

$\frac{1}{2}$ = ____

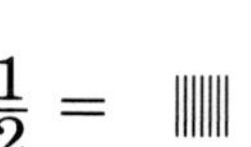

3.

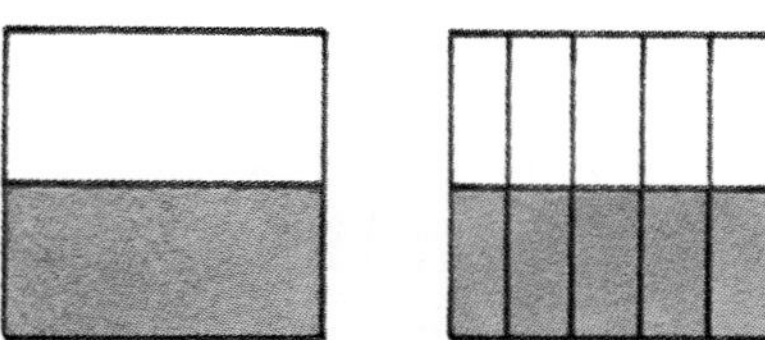

$\frac{1}{2}$ = ____

4.

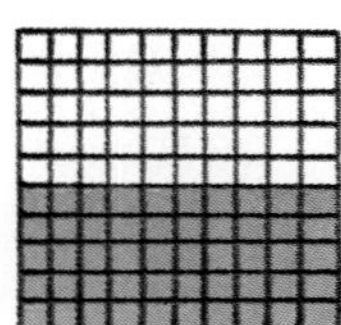

$\frac{1}{2}$ = ____

Practice Write the missing fractions.

1. 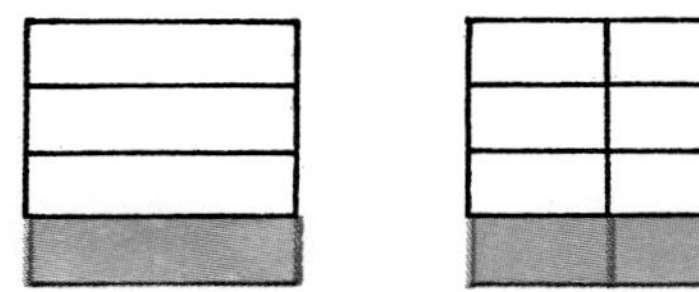

$\frac{1}{4} = $ ____

2. 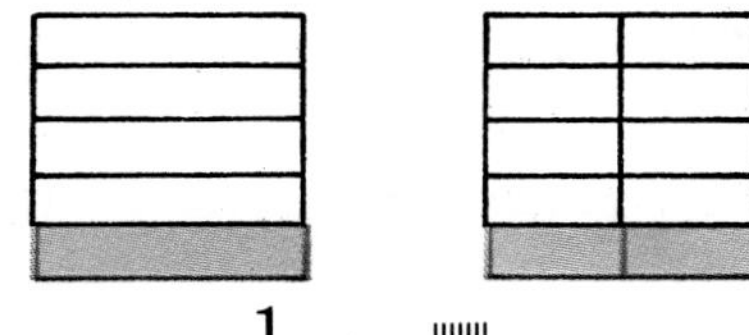

$\frac{1}{5} = $ ____

3. 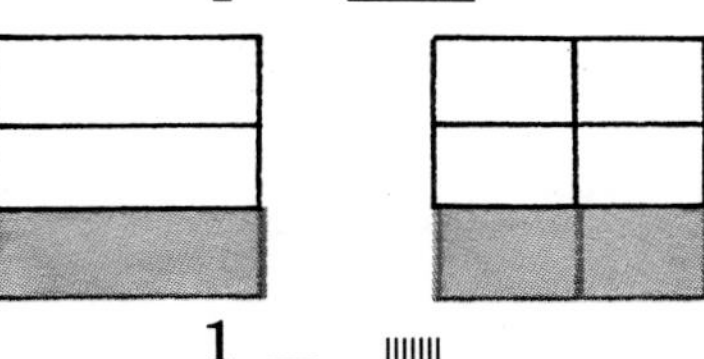

$\frac{1}{3} = $ ____

4. 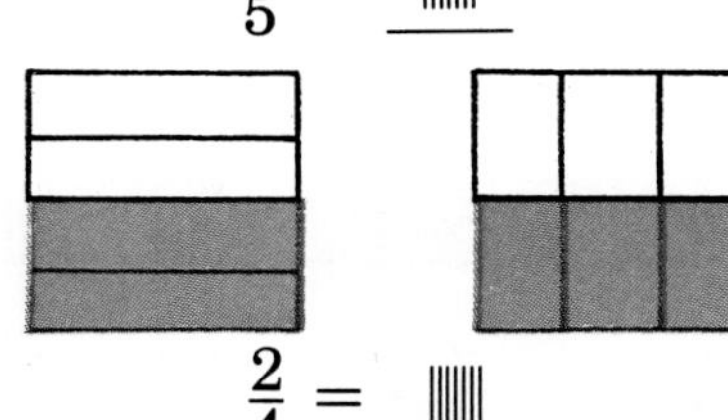

$\frac{2}{4} = $ ____

5. 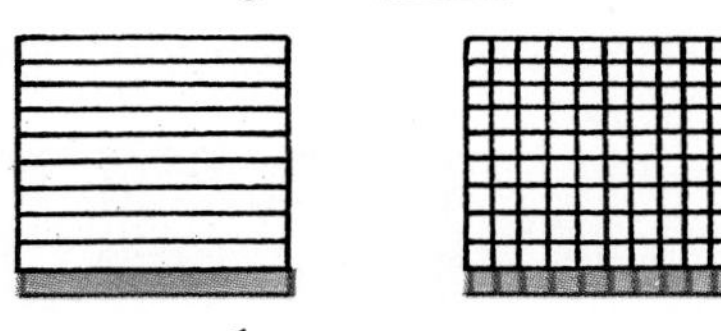

$\frac{1}{10} = $ ____

6. 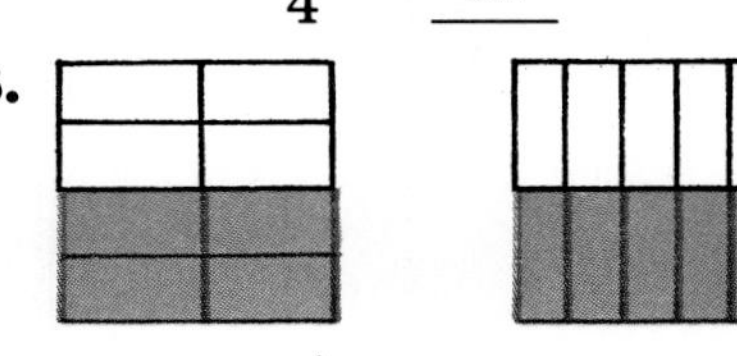

$\frac{4}{8} = $ ____

7. 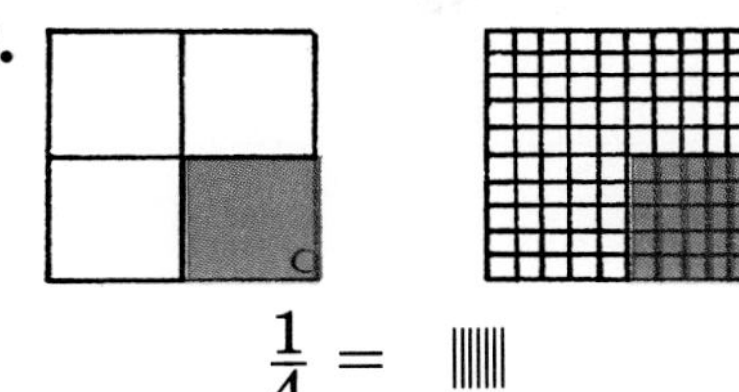

$\frac{1}{4} = $ ____

8. 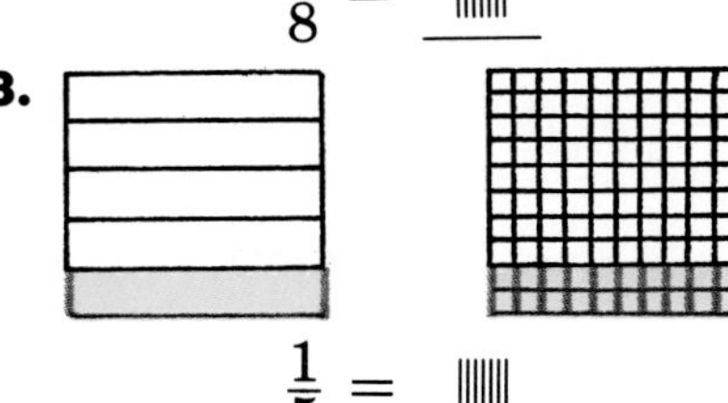

$\frac{1}{5} = $ ____

9. Janet's sandwich was cut into fourths. She ate half of it. How many pieces did she eat?

THINK

Estimation

Give a fraction to tell how much gasoline is in the tank.

Example

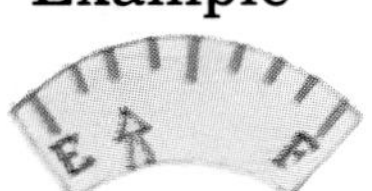

Answer $\frac{1}{4}$

1. 

2. 

3. 

MATH

Comparing Fractions

The colored strips will help you compare fractions.

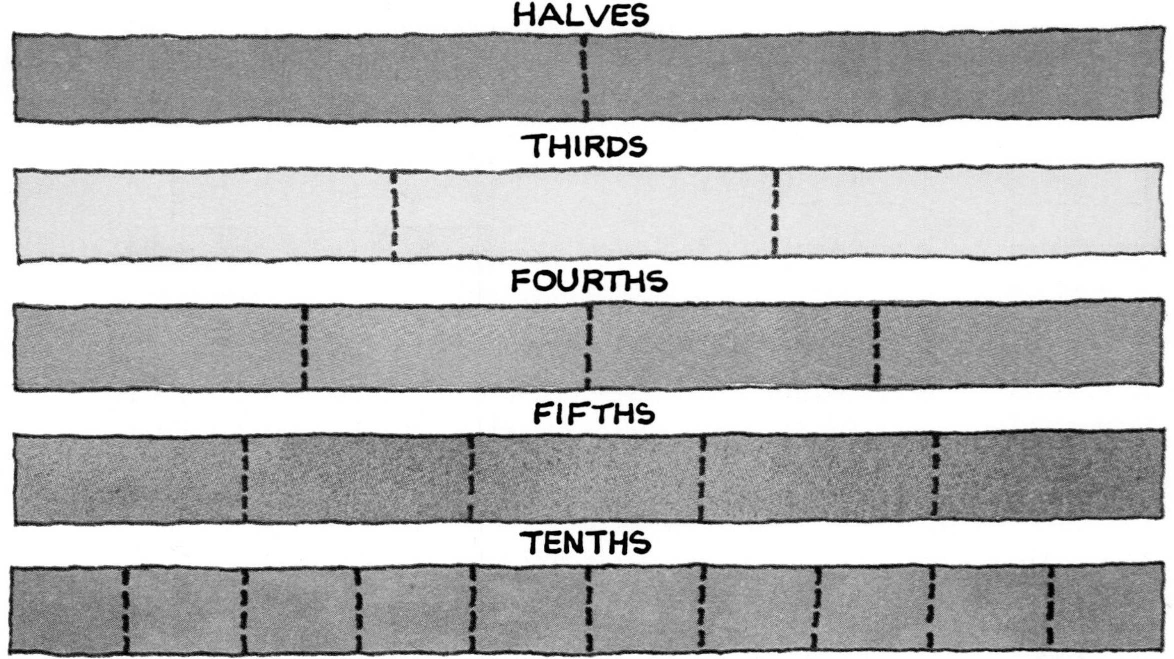

Examples

$\frac{1}{3}$ is greater than $\frac{1}{4} \longrightarrow \frac{1}{3} > \frac{1}{4}$

$\frac{1}{4}$ is less than $\frac{2}{5} \longrightarrow \frac{1}{4} < \frac{2}{5}$

$\frac{1}{2}$ is equal to $\frac{2}{4} \longrightarrow \frac{1}{2} = \frac{2}{4}$

Practice Write the sign >, <, or = for each ●.

1. $\frac{1}{2}$ ● $\frac{1}{3}$	**2.** $\frac{1}{5}$ ● $\frac{1}{3}$	**3.** $\frac{1}{10}$ ● $\frac{1}{5}$	**4.** $\frac{1}{4}$ ● $\frac{1}{5}$	**5.** $\frac{2}{4}$ ● $\frac{5}{10}$
6. $\frac{1}{3}$ ● $\frac{1}{10}$	**7.** $\frac{2}{5}$ ● $\frac{1}{2}$	**8.** $\frac{1}{5}$ ● $\frac{3}{10}$	**9.** $\frac{1}{5}$ ● $\frac{2}{10}$	**10.** $\frac{3}{4}$ ● $\frac{2}{3}$
11. $\frac{3}{5}$ ● $\frac{6}{10}$	**12.** $\frac{7}{10}$ ● $\frac{4}{5}$	**13.** $\frac{5}{10}$ ● $\frac{4}{5}$	**14.** $\frac{8}{10}$ ● $\frac{4}{5}$	**15.** $\frac{1}{2}$ ● $\frac{2}{3}$
16. $\frac{2}{3}$ ● $\frac{2}{5}$	**17.** $\frac{4}{10}$ ● $\frac{3}{5}$	**18.** $\frac{2}{5}$ ● $\frac{1}{4}$	**19.** $\frac{1}{5}$ ● $\frac{1}{4}$	**20.** $\frac{9}{10}$ ● $\frac{4}{5}$

QUESTION
DATA
PLAN
ANSWER
CHECK

PROBLEM SOLVING
Mixed Practice

Solve.

1. Marie ate $\frac{1}{2}$ of her sandwich. Tod ate $\frac{1}{4}$ of his sandwich. Who ate more, Marie or Tod?

2. Sheri bought 4 packages of lunch meat. Each package weighed 14 ounces. How many ounces of lunch meat did Sheri buy?

3. Salvador ran $\frac{3}{4}$ of a mile. Drew ran $\frac{1}{2}$ of a mile. Who ran farther?

4. Karl practiced the piano for $\frac{1}{2}$ of an hour. Brandon practiced for $\frac{1}{3}$ of an hour. Who practiced longer?

5. Tess ate 42 raisins. Joyce ate 19 raisins. How many more raisins did Tess eat?

6. Lana had 24 grapes. Lana ate $\frac{1}{3}$ of her grapes. How many grapes did Lana eat?

7. Alex and Jon each had 20 raisins. Alex ate 6 of his raisins. Jon ate $\frac{1}{4}$ of his raisins. Who ate more raisins?

8. ***Strategy Practice*** Keiko and Robert each got a pizza. Keiko's was cut into sixths. Robert's was cut into eighths. They ate half of their pizzas. How many more pieces did Robert eat?

Fractions and Decimals

There are 10 books on the shelf. **3** of the **10** books are red. Three tenths of the books are red. For three tenths, you can write a fraction or a **decimal**.

Fraction	Decimal
$\frac{3}{10}$	**0.3** (↑ Decimal point)

We read, "**three tenths**."

Other Examples

$\frac{6}{10}$ **0.6** $\frac{7}{10}$ **0.7**

Warm Up Read each decimal.

1. 0.4 **2.** 0.9 **3.** 0.2 **4.** 0.5 **5.** 0.4 **6.** 0.8

Write a fraction in tenths and a decimal for the red part of each set or figure.

7.

8.

9.

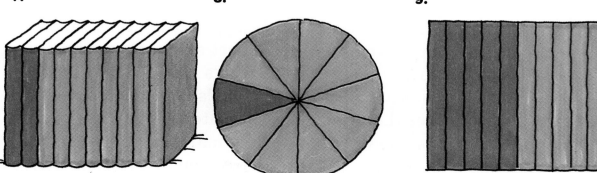

Practice Write a decimal for the red part of each set or figure.

SKILLKEEPER

Multiply.

1. $\begin{array}{r} 17 \\ \times\ 3 \\ \hline \end{array}$

2. $\begin{array}{r} 22 \\ \times\ 4 \\ \hline \end{array}$

3. $\begin{array}{r} 26 \\ \times\ 3 \\ \hline \end{array}$

4. $\begin{array}{r} 12 \\ \times\ 4 \\ \hline \end{array}$

5. $\begin{array}{r} 35 \\ \times\ 2 \\ \hline \end{array}$

6. $\begin{array}{r} 32¢ \\ \times\ 4 \\ \hline \end{array}$

7. $\begin{array}{r} 58¢ \\ \times\ 2 \\ \hline \end{array}$

8. $\begin{array}{r} 43¢ \\ \times\ 3 \\ \hline \end{array}$

9. $\begin{array}{r} 38¢ \\ \times\ 5 \\ \hline \end{array}$

10. $\begin{array}{r} 76¢ \\ \times\ 4 \\ \hline \end{array}$

Larger Decimals

The class had enough art papers to fill 1 whole bulletin board and 0.7 of another. For one and seven tenths, you can write a **mixed number** or a decimal.

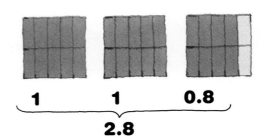

0.7

Mixed Number	Decimal
$1\frac{7}{10}$	**1.7**

We read, "**one and seven tenths**."

Other Examples

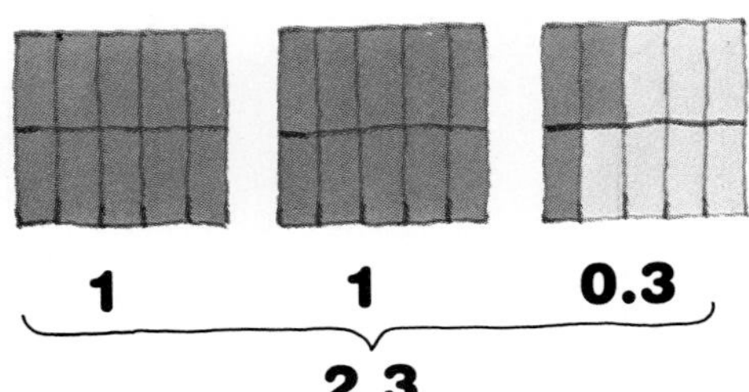

1 1 0.8

2.8

Warm Up Read each decimal.

1. 6.8 **2.** 4.5 **3.** 23.6 **4.** 75.2 **5.** 38.1 **6.** 49.7

Write a decimal for each part.

7. **8.**

Practice Write a decimal for each part.

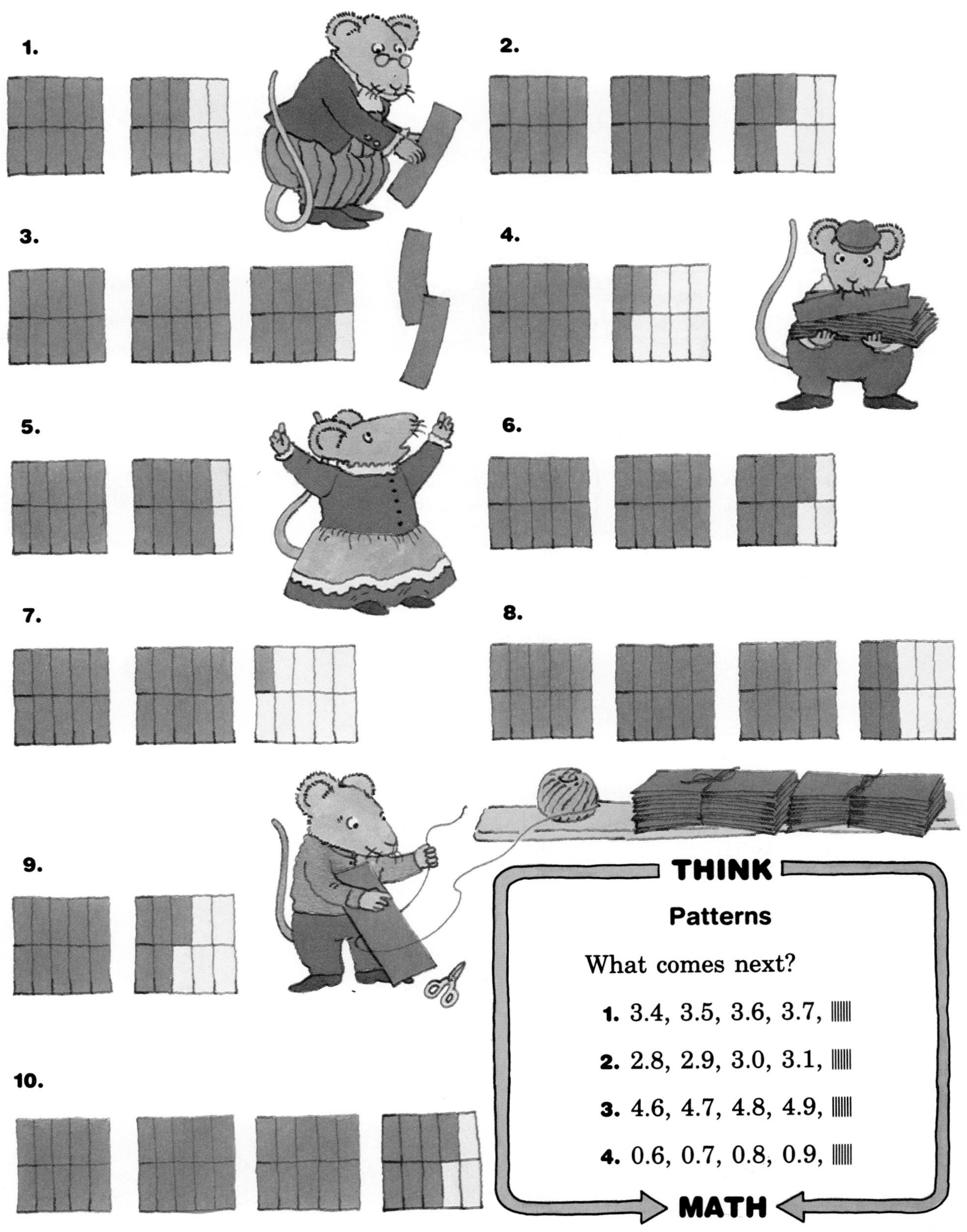

1.

2.

3.

4.

5.

6.

7.

8.

9.

10.

THINK

Patterns

What comes next?

1. 3.4, 3.5, 3.6, 3.7, ▒

2. 2.8, 2.9, 3.0, 3.1, ▒

3. 4.6, 4.7, 4.8, 4.9, ▒

4. 0.6, 0.7, 0.8, 0.9, ▒

MATH

Adding Decimals

How much juice is used in the recipe?

Orange-Pineapple Punch
Mix these:
Serves 12
Orange juice 2.6 liters
Pineapple juice 1.7 liters
before serving, add
Ginger ale 1.0 liter
Ice cubes 2 trays

Since we want the total, we add.

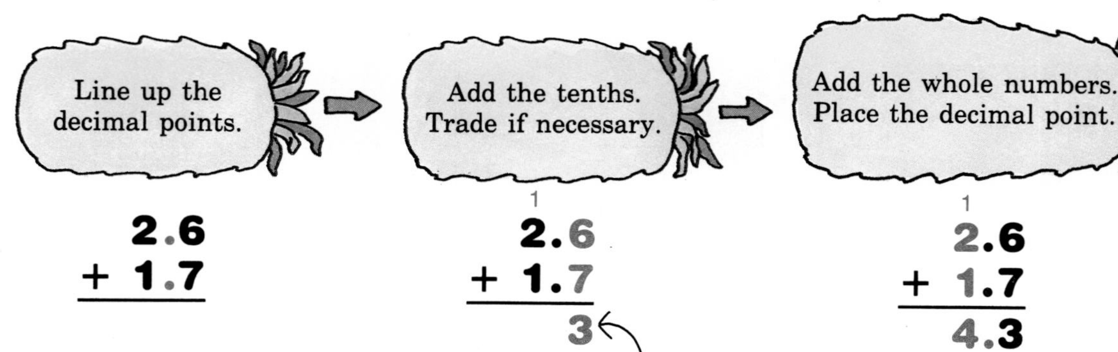

Line up the decimal points.
Add the tenths. Trade if necessary.
Add the whole numbers. Place the decimal point.

$$\begin{array}{r} 2.6 \\ +\ 1.7 \\ \hline \end{array} \qquad \begin{array}{r} {}^{1} \\ 2.6 \\ +\ 1.7 \\ \hline 3 \end{array} \qquad \begin{array}{r} {}^{1} \\ 2.6 \\ +\ 1.7 \\ \hline 4.3 \end{array}$$

13 tenths is 1 whole and 3 tenths

There are 4.3 liters of juice.

Other Examples

$$\begin{array}{r} {}^{1} \\ 8.4 \\ +\ 6.9 \\ \hline 15.3 \end{array} \qquad \begin{array}{r} {}^{1\,1} \\ 27.6 \\ +\ 39.8 \\ \hline 67.4 \end{array} \qquad \begin{array}{r} {}^{1} \\ 43.2 \\ +\ 9.5 \\ \hline 52.7 \end{array}$$

Warm Up Add.

1. $\begin{array}{r} 3.6 \\ +\ 1.9 \\ \hline \end{array}$ **2.** $\begin{array}{r} 8.7 \\ +\ 9.6 \\ \hline \end{array}$ **3.** $\begin{array}{r} 6.2 \\ +\ 7.3 \\ \hline \end{array}$ **4.** $\begin{array}{r} 35.4 \\ +\ 27.8 \\ \hline \end{array}$ **5.** $\begin{array}{r} 56.7 \\ +\ 9.8 \\ \hline \end{array}$

Practice Find the sums.

1. $\begin{array}{r} 2.8 \\ +\ 1.3 \\ \hline \end{array}$	**2.** $\begin{array}{r} 5.6 \\ +\ 1.8 \\ \hline \end{array}$	**3.** $\begin{array}{r} 7.9 \\ +\ 6.7 \\ \hline \end{array}$	**4.** $\begin{array}{r} 25.8 \\ +\ \ 7.6 \\ \hline \end{array}$	**5.** $\begin{array}{r} 32.0 \\ +\ \ 7.6 \\ \hline \end{array}$
6. $\begin{array}{r} 32.8 \\ +\ \ 6.5 \\ \hline \end{array}$	**7.** $\begin{array}{r} 54.7 \\ +\ 12.9 \\ \hline \end{array}$	**8.** $\begin{array}{r} 65.3 \\ +\ 18.2 \\ \hline \end{array}$	**9.** $\begin{array}{r} 76.7 \\ +\ 14.8 \\ \hline \end{array}$	**10.** $\begin{array}{r} 85.3 \\ +\ 12.9 \\ \hline \end{array}$
11. $\begin{array}{r} 46.3 \\ +\ \ 8.9 \\ \hline \end{array}$	**12.** $\begin{array}{r} 75.4 \\ +\ \ 6.8 \\ \hline \end{array}$	**13.** $\begin{array}{r} 80.6 \\ +\ 18.7 \\ \hline \end{array}$	**14.** $\begin{array}{r} 16.2 \\ +\ 75.3 \\ \hline \end{array}$	**15.** $\begin{array}{r} 38.7 \\ +\ 19.6 \\ \hline \end{array}$

16. 4.7 + 2.8 **17.** 6.9 + 3.5 **18.** 7.3 + 2.6 **19.** 37.2 + 46.5

20. Add 5.6 to 1.8. **21.** Find the sum of 16.7 and 17.8.

Mixed Applications

Use the recipe to solve 22-24.

22. How much lemonade and limeade is there altogether?

23. An ice cube tray holds 16 cubes. How many cubes to make Lemon-Lime Cooler?

★ **24.** Each ice cube tray had 0.5 liters of water. How much Lemon-Lime Cooler will there be when the ice melts?

Lemon-Lime Cooler	
Lemonade	2.5 liters
Limeade	1.8 liters
Ginger ale	1.0 liter
Ice	2 trays

THINK

Mental Math

Find the sums in your head.

1. 0.5 + 0.5 **2.** 0.7 + 0.3 **3.** 0.2 + 0.8 **4.** 0.6 + 0.4
5. 3.5 + 5.5 **6.** 2.7 + 1.3 **7.** 3.2 + 4.8 **8.** 2.6 + 2.4

MATH

More Practice, page 400, Set B

Subtracting Decimals

When Jill had the flu, her temperature was 40.1°C. After taking medicine for one day, her temperature dropped to 37.3°C. How much did it drop?

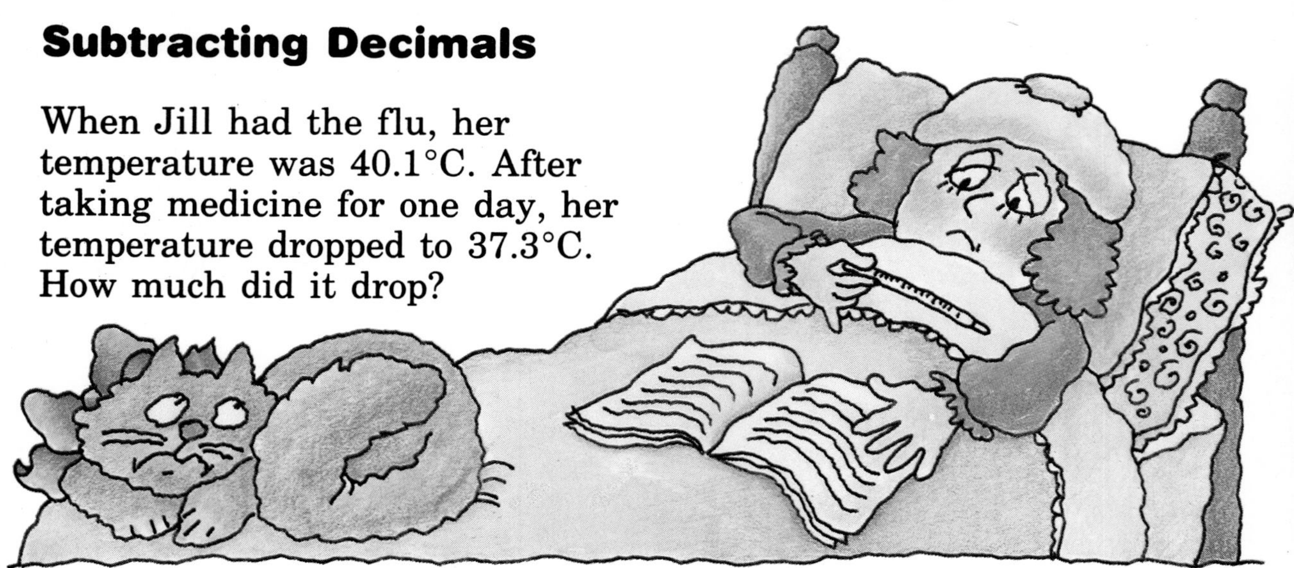

Since we want to find how much less, we subtract.

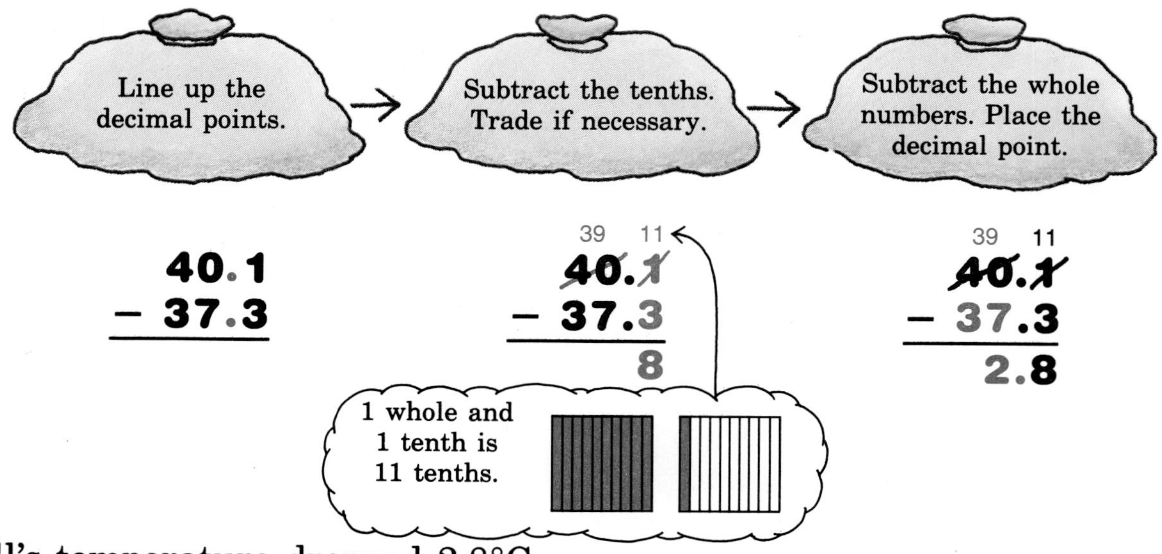

Line up the decimal points.
Subtract the tenths. Trade if necessary.
Subtract the whole numbers. Place the decimal point.
40.1
− 37.3
39 11
40.1
− 37.3
8
39 11
40.1
− 37.3
2.8
1 whole and 1 tenth is 11 tenths.

Jill's temperature dropped 2.8°C.

Other Examples

7 13 8.3 − 2.7 5.6	1 13 12.3 − 11.9 0.4	4 12 52.6 − 17.2 35.4	4 10 75.0 − 21.3 53.7

Warm Up Subtract.

1. 7.4 − 2.6	**2.** 59.5 − 21.8	**3.** 30.2 − 17.9	**4.** 78.0 − 35.6	**5.** 54.3 − 53.6

Practice Find the differences.

1. $\begin{array}{r} 9.2 \\ -\ 1.6 \\ \hline \end{array}$

2. $\begin{array}{r} 3.1 \\ -\ 1.7 \\ \hline \end{array}$

3. $\begin{array}{r} 6.4 \\ -\ 2.9 \\ \hline \end{array}$

4. $\begin{array}{r} 7.3 \\ -\ 3.8 \\ \hline \end{array}$

5. $\begin{array}{r} 8.4 \\ -\ 2.1 \\ \hline \end{array}$

6. $\begin{array}{r} 57.3 \\ -\ 14.6 \\ \hline \end{array}$

7. $\begin{array}{r} 65.4 \\ -\ 38.1 \\ \hline \end{array}$

8. $\begin{array}{r} 56.0 \\ -\ 10.4 \\ \hline \end{array}$

9. $\begin{array}{r} 16.2 \\ -\ 15.9 \\ \hline \end{array}$

10. $\begin{array}{r} 32.7 \\ -\ 6.9 \\ \hline \end{array}$

11. $\begin{array}{r} 52.1 \\ -\ 24.3 \\ \hline \end{array}$

12. $\begin{array}{r} 34.6 \\ -\ 16.0 \\ \hline \end{array}$

13. $\begin{array}{r} 45.2 \\ -\ 17.8 \\ \hline \end{array}$

14. $\begin{array}{r} 57.1 \\ -\ 56.9 \\ \hline \end{array}$

15. $\begin{array}{r} 62.0 \\ -\ 30.4 \\ \hline \end{array}$

16. 12.2 − 0.4

17. 9.3 − 8.6

18. 7.1 − 3.3

19. 1.9 − 0.8

20. 14.5 − 9.8

21. 6.7 − 4.2

22. 17.3 − 9.6

23. 5.0 − 2.7

24. 6.8 − 3.5

25. Subtract 7.8 from 9.3.

26. Subtract 54.6 from 92.3.

Mixed Applications

27. Lou's temperature was 39.6°C when he was sick. After he took medicine, his temperature dropped to 37.9°C. How much did it drop?

28. At 8:00 a.m. the temperature was 25.1°C. In the next hour it went up 1.5°C. In the second hour it went up 2.8°C. What was the temperature after the second hour?

29. Pia had a temperature of 40.2°C when she was sick. It dropped 1.7°C the first day and 1.5°C the second. What was it then?

30. Make up a question you can answer using the data below. Then answer the question. Laurie's temperature was 37.7°C. In 3 hours it went up 1.4°C.

More Practice, page 400, Set C

PROBLEM SOLVING
Using Data from a Map

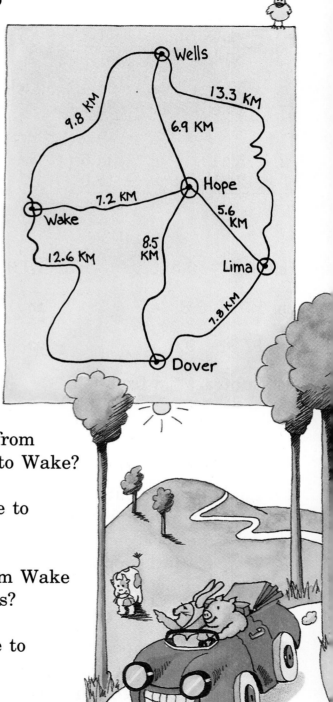

Use the map to answer the following questions.

1. How far is it from Lima to Hope to Wells?

2. How much farther is it from Dover to Hope than from Dover to Lima?

3. How much closer is Wake to Hope than Dover to Hope?

4. How far is it from Dover to Wake to Wells?

5. How much shorter is the drive from Wells to Hope than from Wells to Wake?

6. How long is the drive from Hope to Wake to Wells?

7. How much longer is the trip from Wake to Hope than from Hope to Wells?

★ 8. How far is it from Lima to Hope to Dover to Wake?

9. ***Strategy Practice*** Jenny and Jay started at Wake. They drove 16.7 km. What two cities did they visit? Hint: Guess and check.

PROBLEM SOLVING
Using a Calculator

Try these calculator activities.

To enter 372.4 on your calculator, press 3 7 2 . 4

To enter $48.65 on your calculator, press 4 8 . 6 5

To divide 230.4 by 4, press 2 3 0 . 4 ÷ 4 =

1. Ben bought 4 sacks of flour. Each sack weighed 2.3 kg. How many kilograms of flour did Ben buy?
Hint: Press 2 . 3 X 4 =

2. Debra has 4.8 kg of peanuts. She divides them equally into 3 bags. How many kilograms of peanuts are in each bag?
Hint: Press 4 . 8 ÷ 3 =

3. The total cost of one car was $8,275.56. Another car was $9,049.79. What was the difference in price?

4. Mona bought 5 pairs of socks. Each pair cost $1.79. How much did she pay for the socks?

5. Ms. Moore paid $7,875.45 for a new car. Taxes and license were $767.75 more. How much did she spend?

6. There is a total of 11.4 L in 6 cans of juice. How much juice is in each can?

7. ***Strategy Practice*** These are the prices of four TV sets. Mr. Wu bought two of them for $624.20. Which two did he buy?

Set A $287.95
Set B $349.55
Set C $298.75
Set D $325.45

Mixed Skills Practice

Computation

Find the answers.

1. $\begin{array}{r} 356 \\ +\ 188 \\ \hline \end{array}$ **2.** $\begin{array}{r} 629 \\ -\ 154 \\ \hline \end{array}$ **3.** $\begin{array}{r} 465 \\ +\ 289 \\ \hline \end{array}$ **4.** $\begin{array}{r} 302 \\ -\ 168 \\ \hline \end{array}$ **5.** $\begin{array}{r} 4{,}276 \\ +\ 1{,}384 \\ \hline \end{array}$

6. $\begin{array}{r} 4{,}387 \\ +\ 1{,}460 \\ \hline \end{array}$ **7.** $\begin{array}{r} 5{,}276 \\ -\ 1{,}834 \\ \hline \end{array}$ **8.** $\begin{array}{r} 4{,}207 \\ -\ 1{,}562 \\ \hline \end{array}$ **9.** $\begin{array}{r} 3{,}827 \\ +\ 1{,}943 \\ \hline \end{array}$ **10.** $\begin{array}{r} 6{,}238 \\ -\ 4{,}099 \\ \hline \end{array}$

11. $\begin{array}{r} 26 \\ \times\ 3 \\ \hline \end{array}$ **12.** $\begin{array}{r} 54 \\ \times\ 4 \\ \hline \end{array}$ **13.** $\begin{array}{r} 27 \\ \times\ 5 \\ \hline \end{array}$ **14.** $\begin{array}{r} 38 \\ \times\ 4 \\ \hline \end{array}$ **15.** $\begin{array}{r} 42 \\ \times\ 3 \\ \hline \end{array}$

16. $4\overline{)128}$ **17.** $3\overline{)168}$ **18.** $5\overline{)117}$ **19.** $4\overline{)330}$ **20.** $2\overline{)129}$

Mental Math

Write only the answers.

21. 28 + 5 **22.** 18 + 7 **23.** 37 + 4 **24.** 29 + 6

25. 70 − 40 **26.** 60 + 30 **27.** 700 + 200 **28.** 800 − 400

29. 6 × 10 **30.** 7 × 20 **31.** 3 × 80 **32.** 4 × 50

Estimation

Estimate.

33. 39 + 18 **34.** 72 − 39 **35.** 59 + 19 **36.** 47 − 21

37. 3 × \$2.95 **38.** 17 + 58 **39.** 2 × \$6.12 **40.** 91 − 79

41. 4 × \$4.98 **42.** 83 − 27 **43.** 5 × \$3.89 **44.** 58 + 18

APPLIED PROBLEM SOLVING

You want to have a dog. Your parents will let you have it if you take care of it. Can you afford it?

Some Things to Consider

- Your dog must be fed twice a day, and it needs fresh water every day.
- The dog needs about 650 grams of food each day.
- A large can of dog food (666 grams) costs 73¢.
- You must buy the food.
- Your parents will pay for the dog's shots and veterinary care.
- A leash, collar, and 2 dog bowls cost about $16.00.
- You earn $7.00 a week working around the house.
- You like to buy a record album every month or two. An album costs about $7.00 or $8.00.

Some Questions to Answer

1. How many cans of food will the dog eat in 1 week? How much money is this each week?
2. About how many weeks must you save to buy the leash, collar, and 2 dog bowls?
3. How much will you have left from $7.00 if you buy food for one week?

What Is Your Decision?

Can you afford the dog? Can you still buy an album every month or two?

PROBLEM SOLVING
Using the Strategies

Use one or more of the strategies listed to solve each problem below.

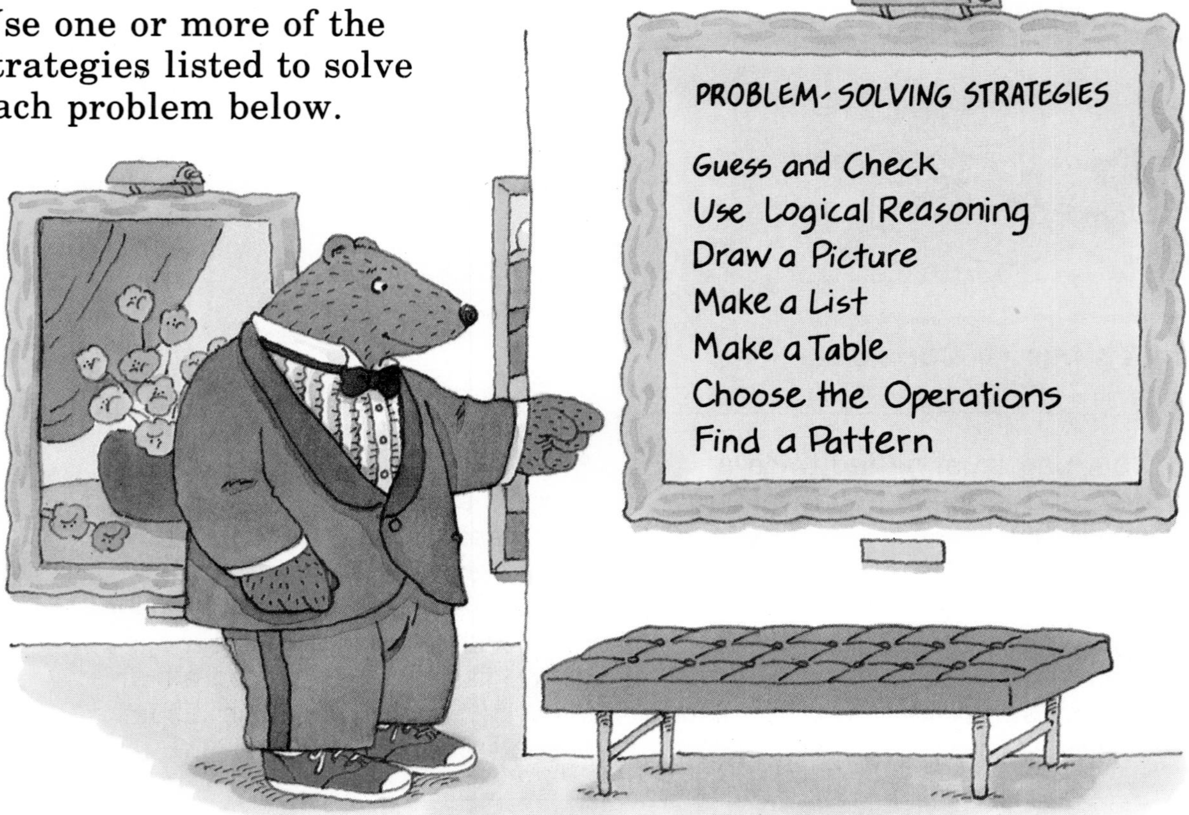

PROBLEM-SOLVING STRATEGIES

Guess and Check
Use Logical Reasoning
Draw a Picture
Make a List
Make a Table
Choose the Operations
Find a Pattern

1. Pat's teacher said, "I'm not 30 yet but I'm more than 25. If you can count by 3s, you'll say it." How old is Pat's teacher?

2. The vases are red, blue, and green. The flowers are pink, yellow, and white. How many ways can you choose a vase with a flower?

3. Dan is older than Lyn and younger than Jane. Jane is younger than Tom. Who is the oldest?

4. The ages of the three math teachers are 36, 37, and 38. The sum of two of the ages is 75. How old is the other teacher?

CHAPTER REVIEW/TEST

Give the correct letter.

1. How is the square divided?

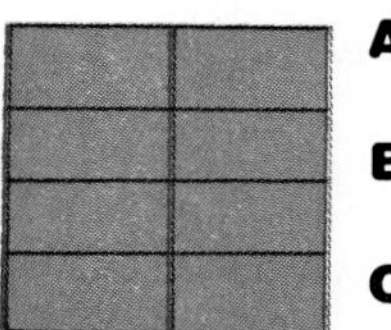

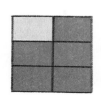

A sixths
B eighths
C tenths
D hundredths

2. What fraction is shaded?

A $\frac{2}{3}$
B $\frac{3}{4}$
C $\frac{5}{6}$
D $\frac{7}{8}$

3. What fraction is used?

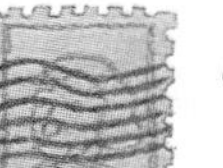
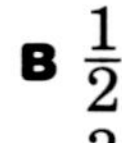
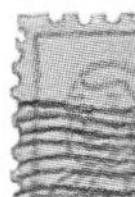

A $\frac{2}{3}$
B $\frac{1}{2}$
C $\frac{3}{4}$
D $\frac{1}{4}$

4. Jean had 6 balloons. She popped $\frac{1}{2}$ of them. How many balloons did Jean pop?

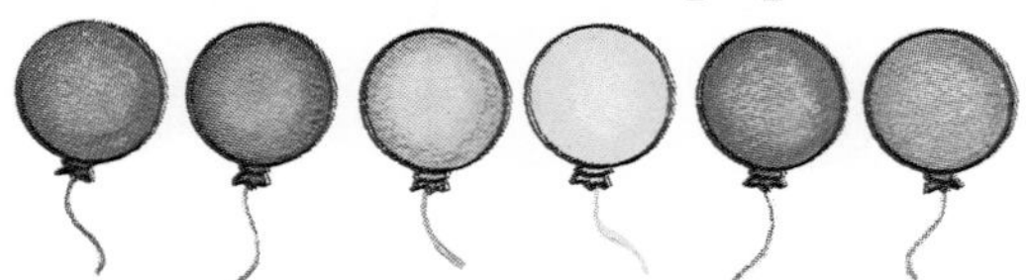

5. Write the missing fraction.

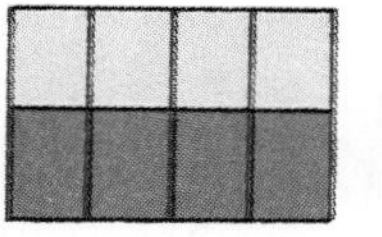
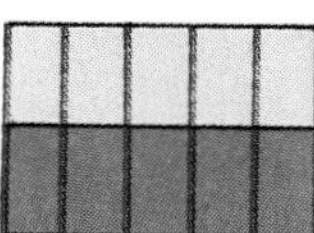

$\frac{4}{8}$ = ▥ ____

Write the sign > or < for each ▥.

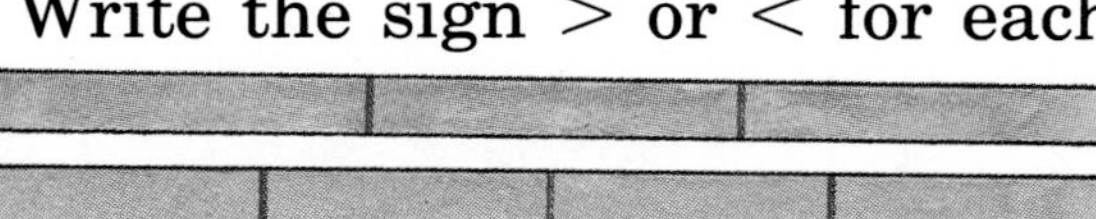

6. $\frac{1}{3}$ ▥ $\frac{1}{4}$

7. $\frac{2}{3}$ ▥ $\frac{3}{4}$

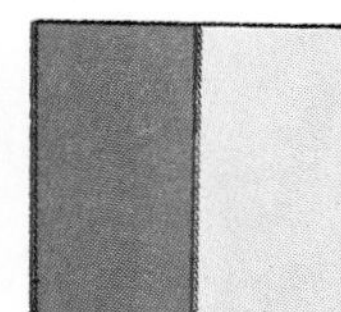

8. Write a decimal for the picture.

Add or subtract.

9. $\begin{array}{r} 3.7 \\ +\ 2.8 \\ \hline \end{array}$

10. $\begin{array}{r} 14.6 \\ +\ 18.9 \\ \hline \end{array}$

11. $\begin{array}{r} 7.2 \\ -\ 3.5 \\ \hline \end{array}$

12. $\begin{array}{r} 24.3 \\ -\ 11.6 \\ \hline \end{array}$

Solve.

13. Geri drove 7.8 km. Then she drove 6.9 km. How far did she drive in all?

14. Al drove 9.4 km Sunday and 5.8 km Monday. How much farther did he drive Sunday?

ANOTHER LOOK

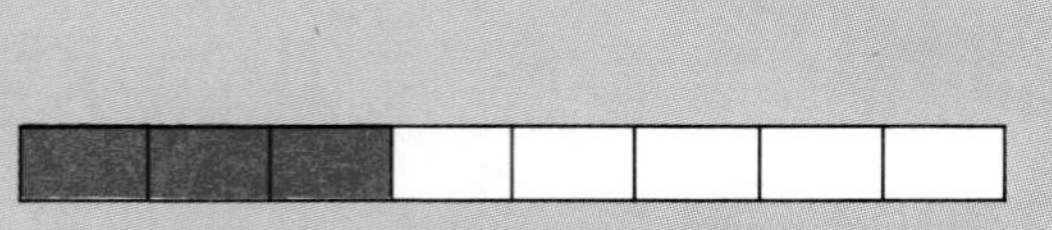

3 parts shaded

8 parts in all

$\frac{3}{8}$ of the strip is shaded.

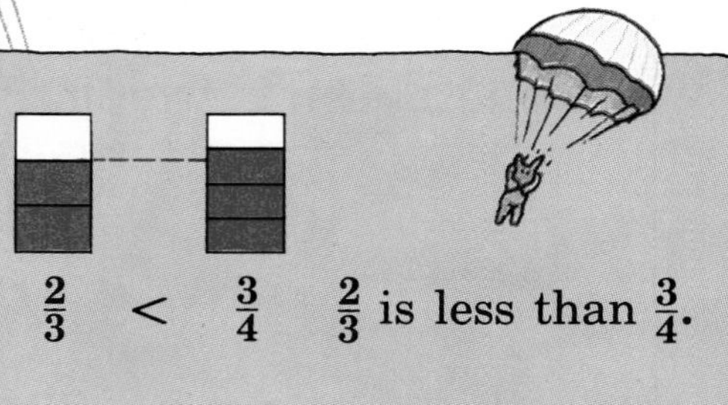

$\frac{2}{3} < \frac{3}{4}$ $\frac{2}{3}$ is less than $\frac{3}{4}$.

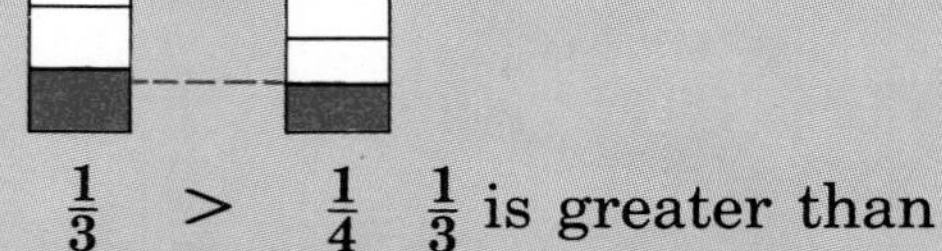

$\frac{1}{3} > \frac{1}{4}$ $\frac{1}{3}$ is greater than $\frac{1}{4}$.

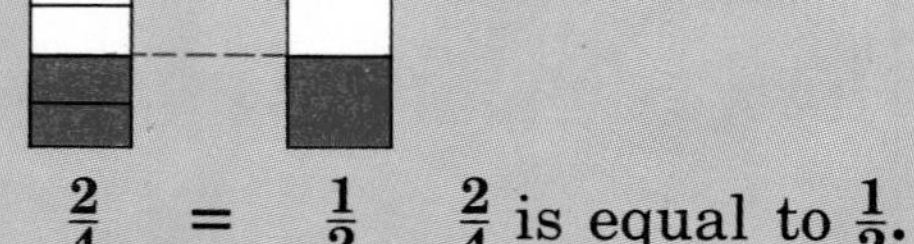

$\frac{2}{4} = \frac{1}{2}$ $\frac{2}{4}$ is equal to $\frac{1}{2}$.

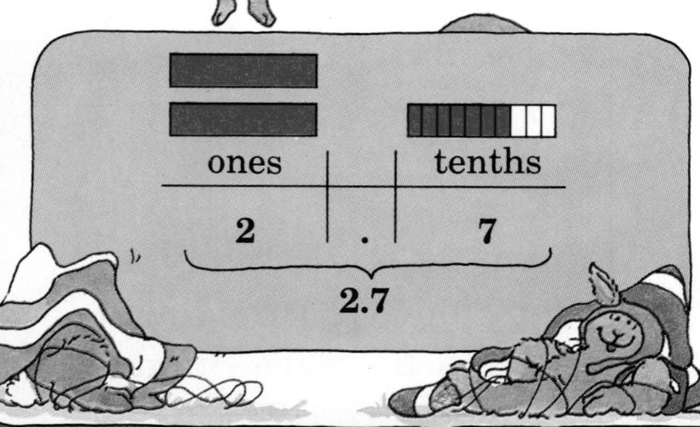

Write a fraction for the shaded parts.

1. 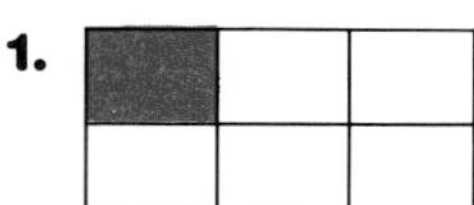

2. 

3. 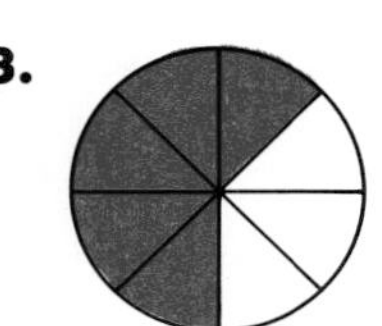

4. 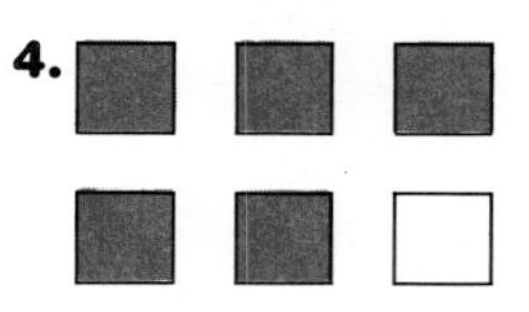

Give the sign >, <, or = for each ◍.

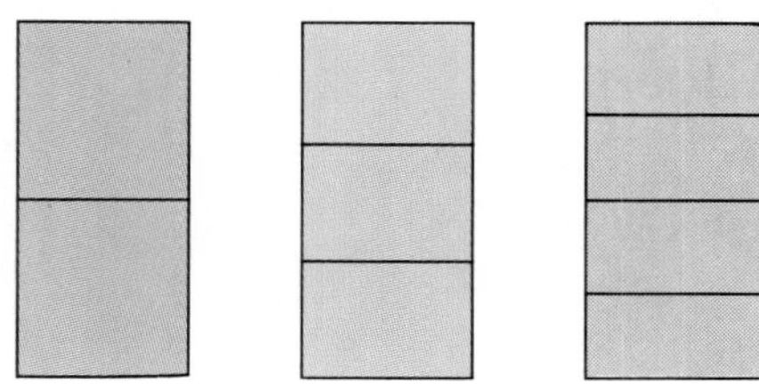

5. $\frac{1}{2}$ ◍ $\frac{1}{3}$

6. $\frac{1}{4}$ ◍ $\frac{2}{3}$

7. $\frac{1}{4}$ ◍ $\frac{1}{2}$

8. $\frac{3}{4}$ ◍ $\frac{1}{2}$

9. $\frac{2}{3}$ ◍ $\frac{1}{2}$

10. $\frac{1}{2}$ ◍ $\frac{2}{4}$

Write a decimal for the shaded parts.

ENRICHMENT

Magic Squares with Your Calculator

Look at the square at the right. It is a **magic square**.

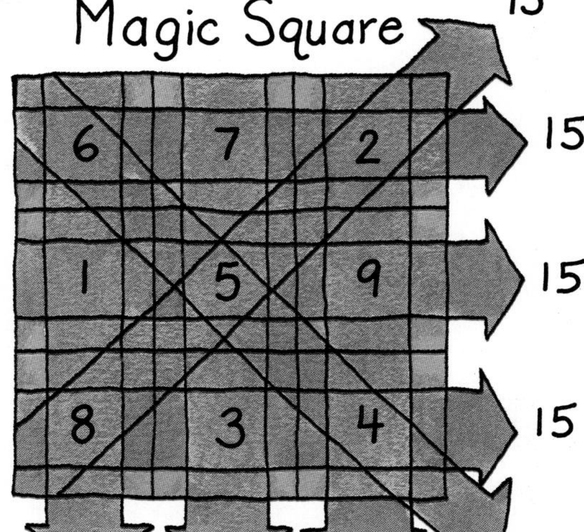

The sum along each

ROW →

COLUMN ↓

DIAGONAL ↗↘

is the same.

In the square, the **magic sum** is 15. Check it.

Copy this square. Fill in the missing numbers so it is a magic square.

9	2	7
		8
	10	

Row sum: 18. Middle column sum: 18.

Hint 1: Add the numbers in the top row to find the **magic sum**.

Hint 2: Then find the number in the middle box. The sum for the middle column should be 18.

Use your **calculator** to make this a magic square.

160	105	116
		171
	149	

Now try this one.

7.3	15.0	
12.8		
11.7		13.9

CUMULATIVE REVIEW

Give the letter for the correct answer.

1. $1\overline{)3}$
   - A 1
   - B 3
   - C 0
   - D not given

2. $4\overline{)28}$
   - A 8
   - B 7
   - C 6
   - D not given

3. $3\overline{)24}$
   - A 8
   - B 9
   - C 7
   - D not given

4. $9\overline{)54}$
   - A 4
   - B 5
   - C 6
   - D not given

5. $7\overline{)35}$
   - A 5
   - B 6
   - C 7
   - D not given

6. $8\overline{)40}$
   - A 4
   - B 5
   - C 6
   - D not given

7. $3\overline{)8}$
   - A 1 R5
   - B 2 R2
   - C 3 R1
   - D not given

8. $5\overline{)36}$
   - A 7 R2
   - B 6 R6
   - C 8 R4
   - D not given

9. $26 \div 4$
   - A 6 R2
   - B 6 R1
   - C 6
   - D not given

10. $17 \div 5$
    - A 3 R1
    - B 3 R2
    - C 2 R4
    - D not given

11. $29 \div 3$
    - A 9 R2
    - B 9 R3
    - C 9
    - D not given

12. $27 \div 4$
    - A 6 R8
    - B 6
    - C 6 R3
    - D not given

13. One pie is enough for 6 people. How many pies are needed for 12 people?
    - A 72
    - B 18
    - C 2
    - D not given

14. Paul needs 4 apples to make a pie. He picked 38 apples. How many pies can he make?
    - A 8 pies
    - B 9 pies, 2 apples left over
    - C 5 pies, 3 apples left over
    - D not given

MEASUREMENT: Customary Units

14

One day Jamie found a baby raccoon in the woods behind her house. Its eyes were closed and it was no bigger than her mother's fist. Jamie named her new pet "Bandit." At first Jamie fed Bandit from a baby bottle. After a few months Bandit was drinking milk and mashed bread from a bowl. After about nine months the raccoon was almost full-grown. Its tail alone was as long as this math book. Jamie had lots of fun taking care of Bandit.

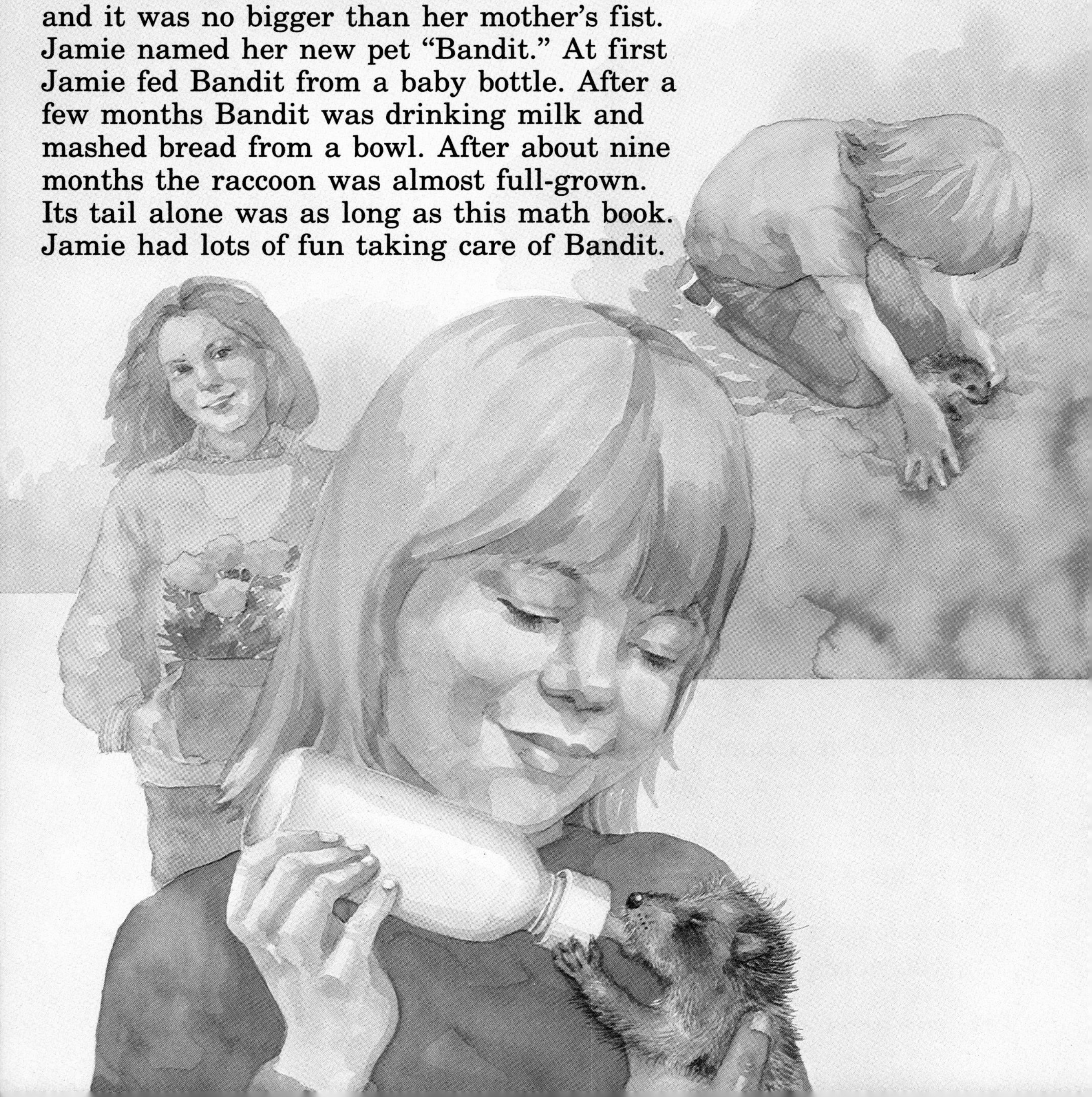

Estimating Length with Customary Units

The pictures below help you think about different **customary** units for measuring length.

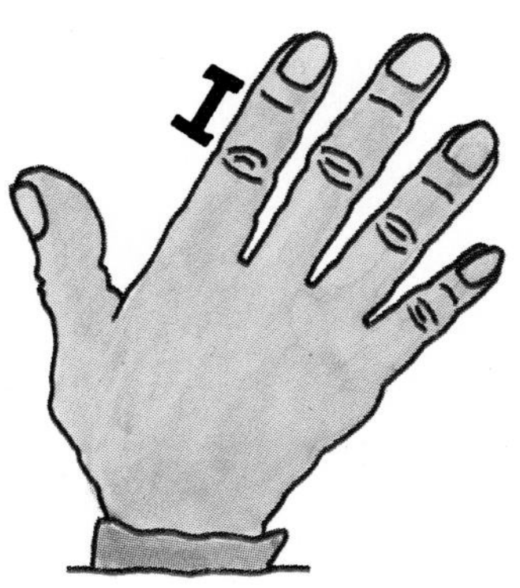

1 inch

1 foot
12 inches

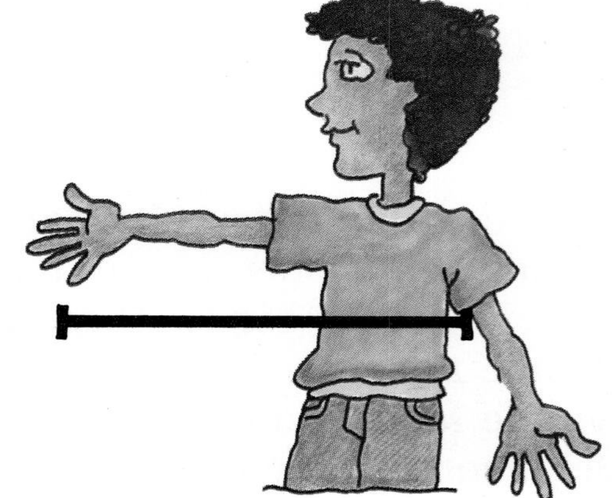

1 yard
3 feet or 36 inches

1 mile = 1,760 yards.
1 mile = 5,280 feet.

Warm Up Choose the better estimate.

1. How high is a door?
   A 8 feet **B** 8 yards
2. How long is a train?
   A 1 yard **B** 1 mile
3. How tall is a man?
   A 2 feet **B** 2 yards
4. How long is a pencil?
   A 7 inches **B** 7 feet
5. How wide is a chalkboard?
   A 8 inches **B** 8 feet
6. How high is an airplane?
   A 5 yards **B** 5 miles
7. How long is a football field?
   A 100 yards **B** 100 miles
8. How far is it across a lake?
   A 3 yards **B** 3 miles

Practice Choose the better estimate.

1. How wide is a classroom door?
   A 1 yard **B** 1 foot

2. How far can a car go in an hour?
   A 50 yards **B** 50 miles

3. How long is a room?
   A 35 inches **B** 35 feet

4. How high is a ceiling?
   A 3 yards **B** 3 feet

5. How far did the batter hit a ball?
   A 100 yards **B** 100 miles

6. How wide is a person's hand?
   A 3 feet **B** 3 inches

7. How high is your desk top?
   A 1 foot **B** 1 yard

8. How long is a car?
   A 10 feet **B** 10 yards

9. The length of a pencil is
   A less than 1 foot.
   B more than 1 foot.

10. The height of an adult is
    A less than 1 yard.
    B more than 1 yard.

11. An hour bike ride is
    A less than 1 mile.
    B more than 1 mile.

12. The width of a fingernail is
    A less than an inch.
    B more than an inch.

THINK

Estimation

The map shows two distances. Estimate each of these distances.

1. Jackson to Union City
2. Kent to Lake
3. Lake to Kane
4. Union City to Kane

MATH

Measuring with Inch Units

The piece of ribbon is 5 inches (in.) long.

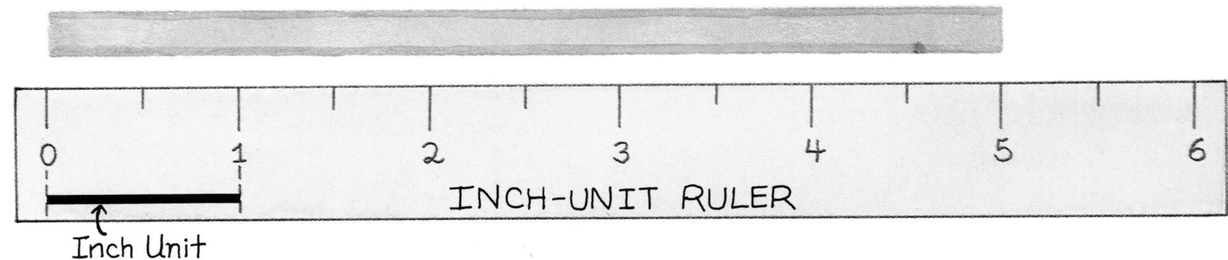

Other Examples

Fractions may be used when you measure with inch units.

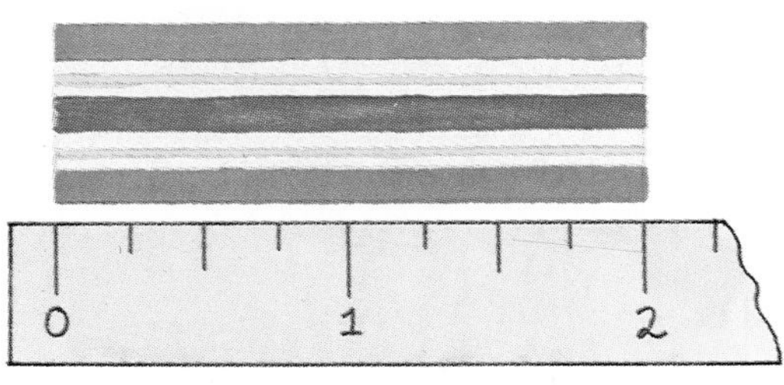

This ribbon is 2 inches long.

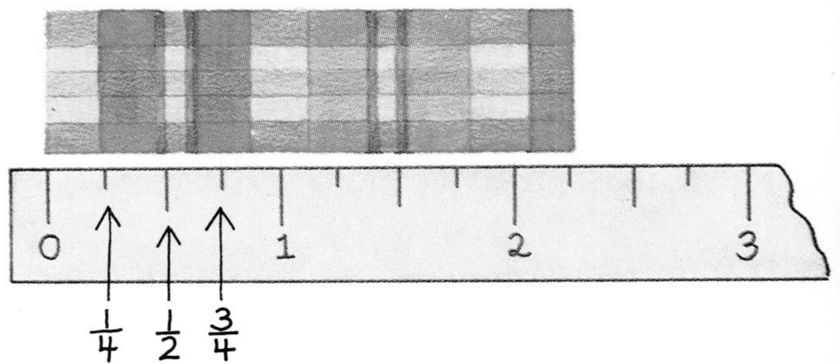

This ribbon is $2\frac{1}{4}$ (2 and $\frac{1}{4}$) inches long.

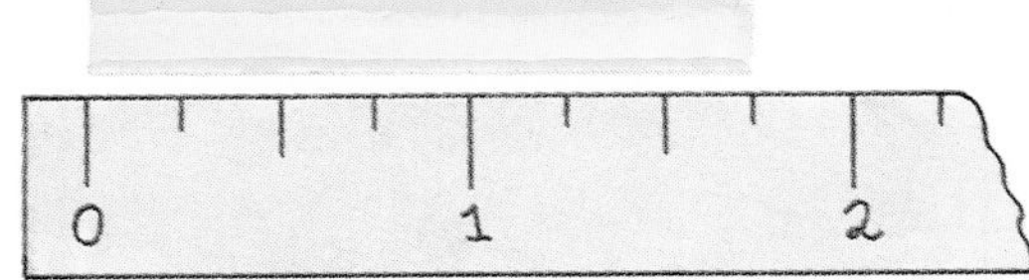

This ribbon is $1\frac{3}{4}$ inches long.

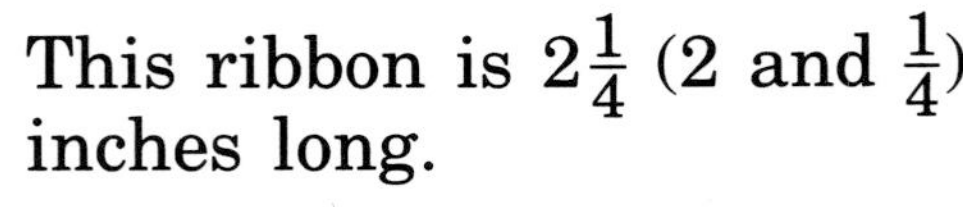

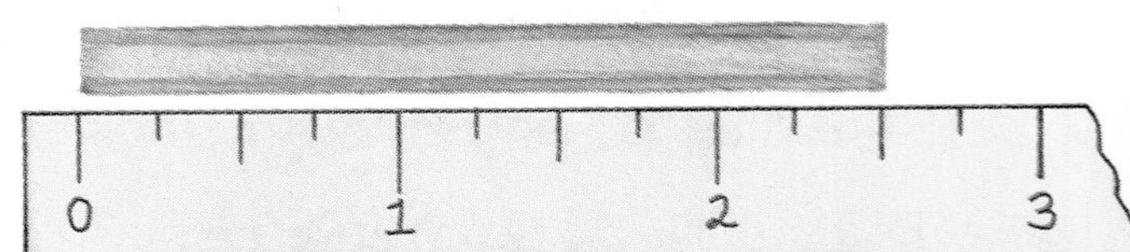

This ribbon is $2\frac{1}{2}$ inches long.

Warm Up Use your inch ruler. Give each length.

1.

2.

3.

4.

ENRICHMENT

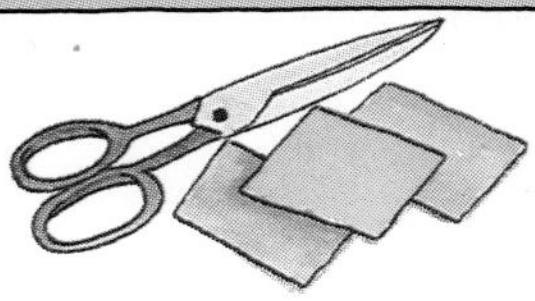

Area Using Half Units

Find the area of each figure.

Example

Figure	Cut apart.	How many unit squares?

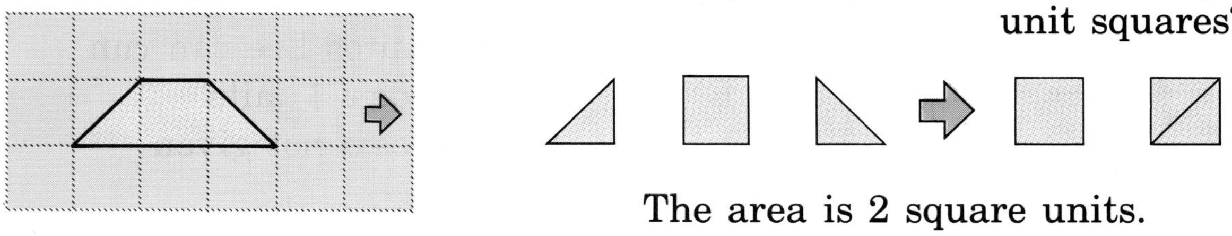

The area is 2 square units.

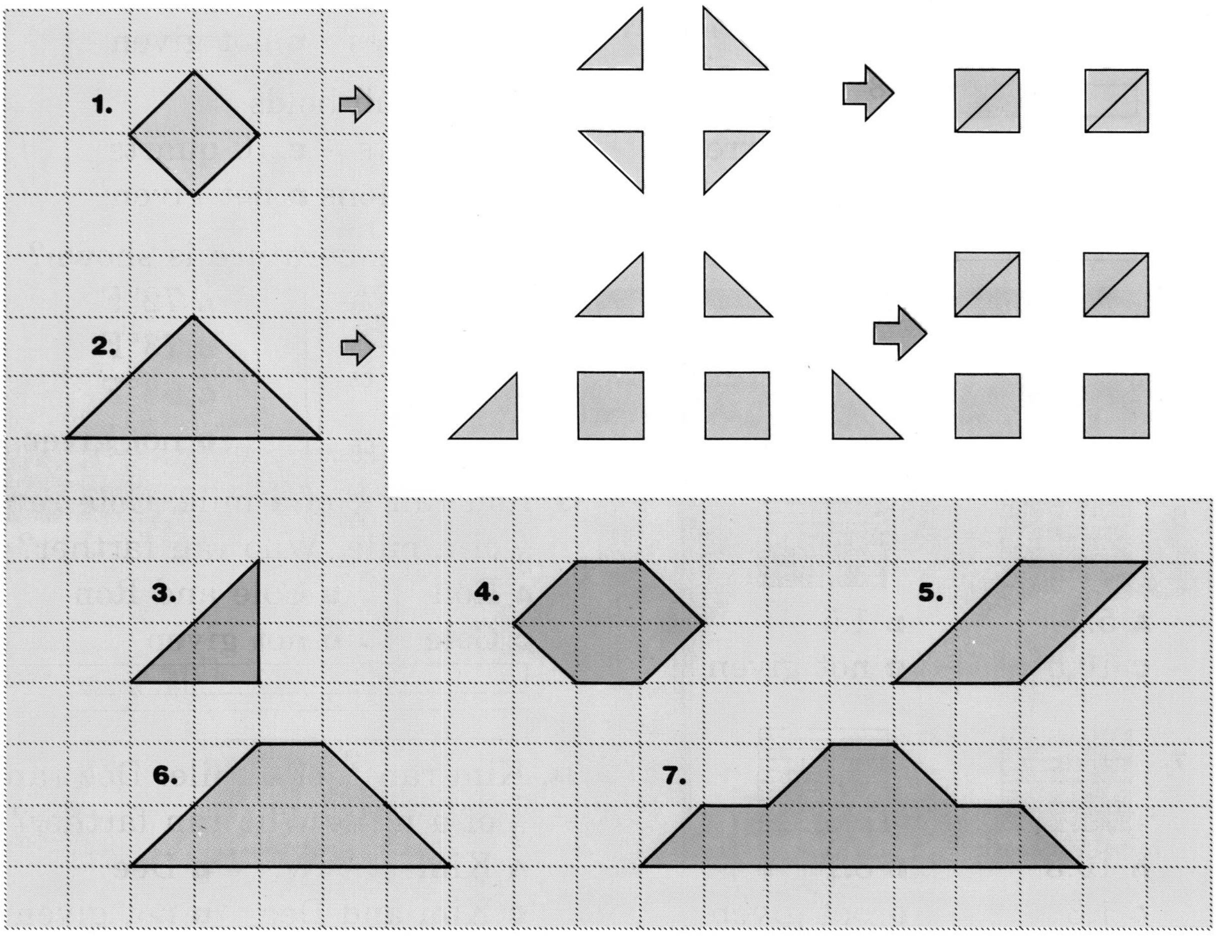

1\.

2\.

3\.

4\.

5\.

6\.

7\.

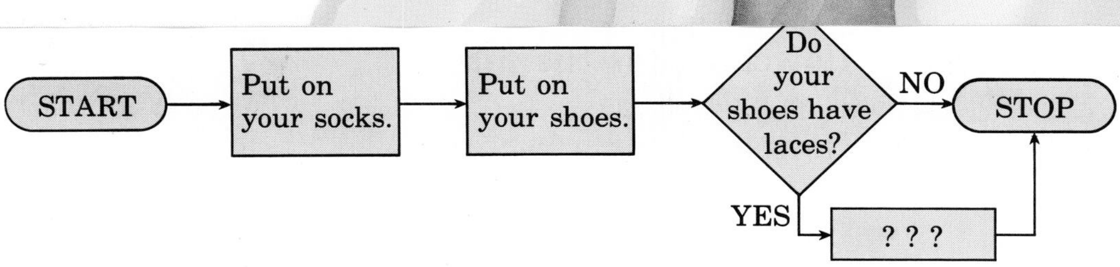

START → Put on your socks. → Put on your shoes. → Do your shoes have laces? NO → STOP

YES → ? ? ? → STOP

CUMULATIVE REVIEW

Give the letter for the correct answer.

Computer Instruction

Flowcharts

Flowcharts show a step-by-step way of doing something. Flowcharts are used to plan instructions for computers. Special shapes are used to show each step.

Computer Instruction

Using Flowcharts

Copy this grid on your paper.

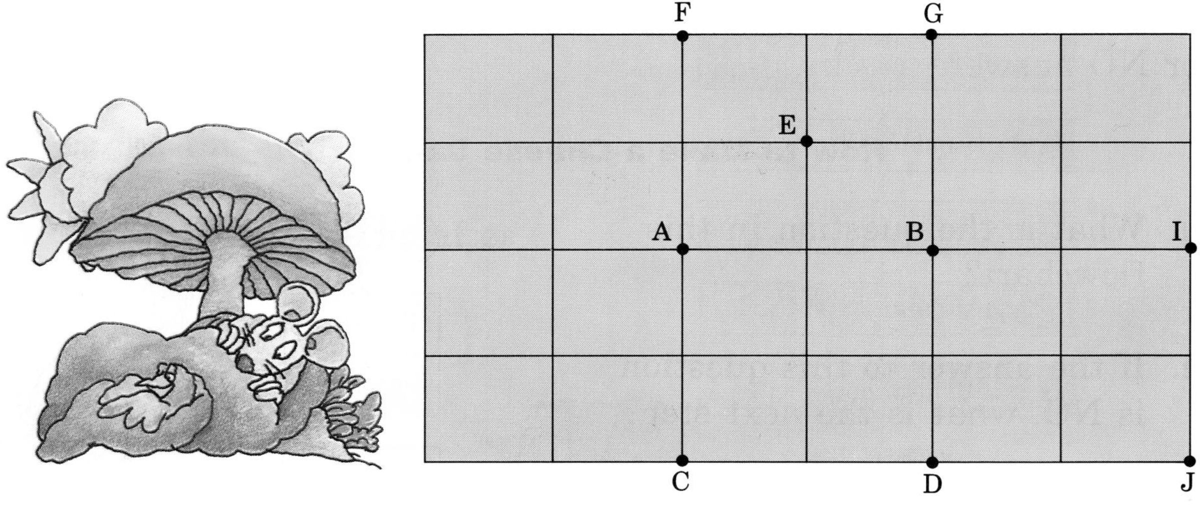

1. This flowchart will make a letter on the figure. What is it?

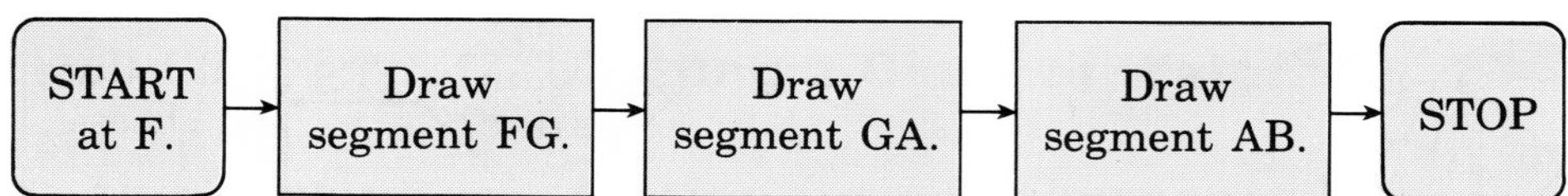

What shapes will you make if you follow these flowcharts?

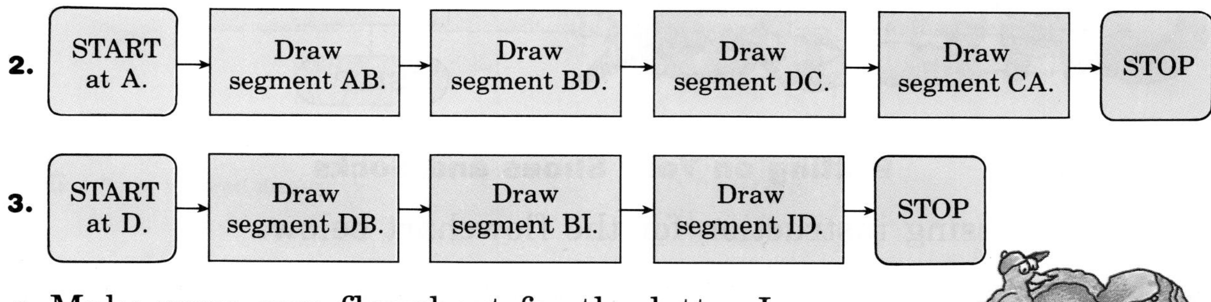

4. Make your own flowchart for the letter L.

5. Make your own flowchart for a rectangle.

The flowcharts below give directions for the map.

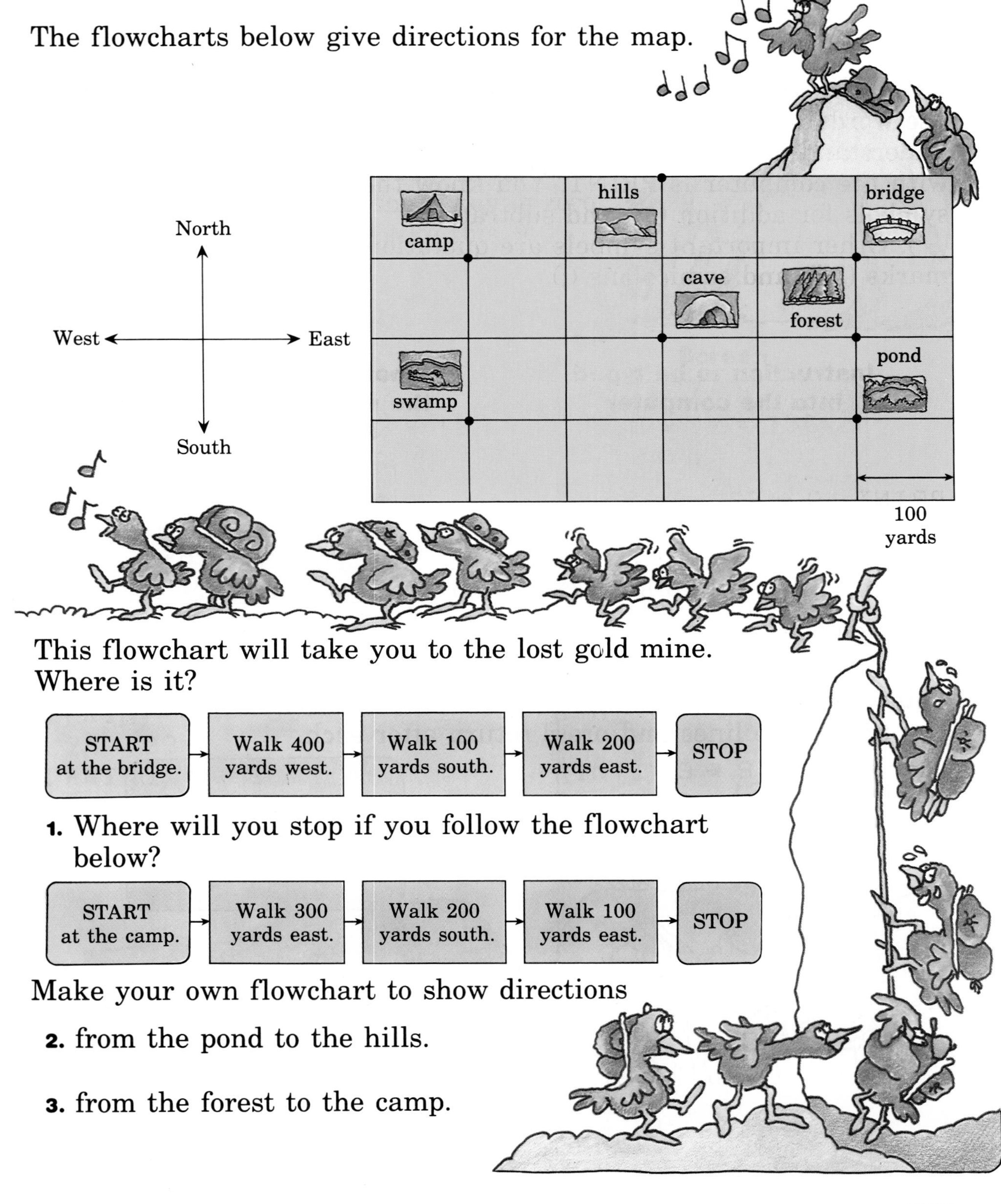

This flowchart will take you to the lost gold mine. Where is it?

START at the bridge. → Walk 400 yards west. → Walk 100 yards south. → Walk 200 yards east. → STOP

1. Where will you stop if you follow the flowchart below?

START at the camp. → Walk 300 yards east. → Walk 200 yards south. → Walk 100 yards east. → STOP

Make your own flowchart to show directions

2. from the pond to the hills.

3. from the forest to the camp.

Computer Drawings

Logo is a special computer language. You can use it to draw pictures on a computer screen. A small triangle ▲, called a *turtle,* can move around to draw pictures. But you must tell the turtle what to do. The pictures show you how to make the turtle move and draw.

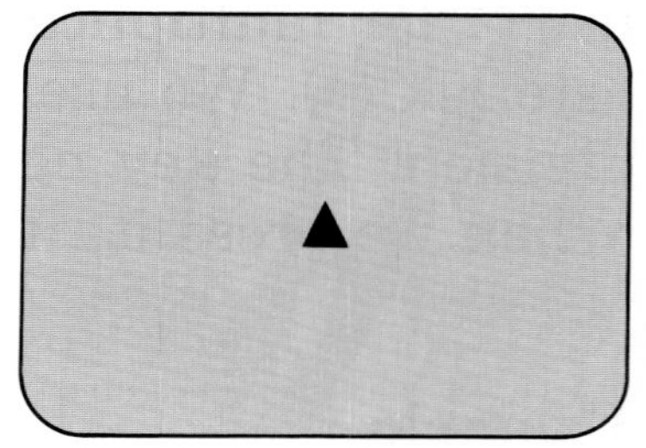

The turtle

Commands:

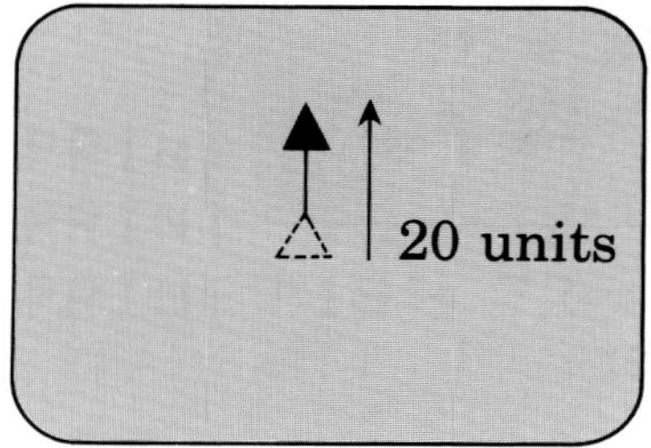

FORWARD 20

Turtle moves forward 20 units in the direction pointed.

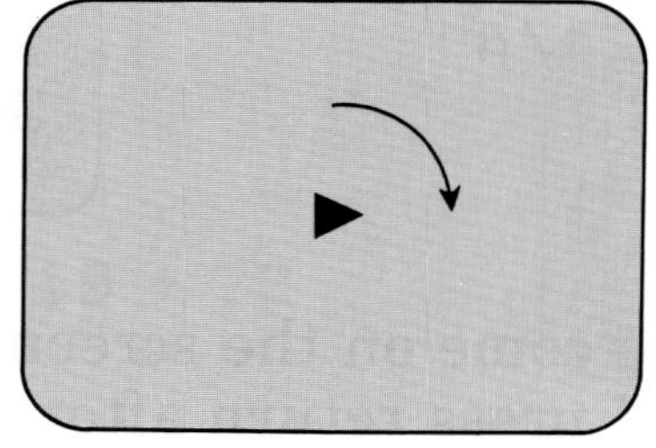

RIGHT 90

Turtle turns right. (15 minutes the way the minute hand turns)

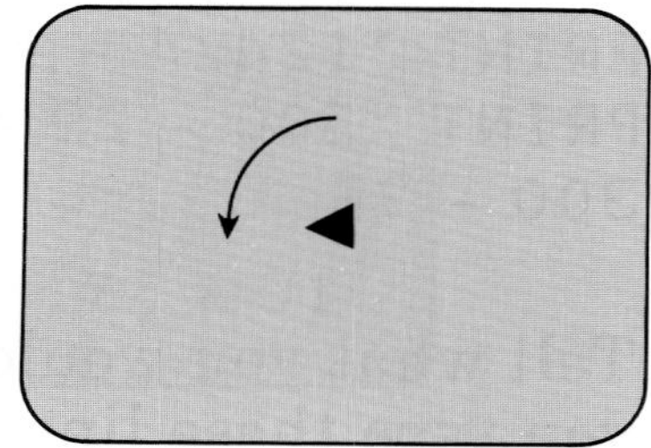

LEFT 90

Turtle turns left. (15 minutes the other way from the minute hand)

Examples:

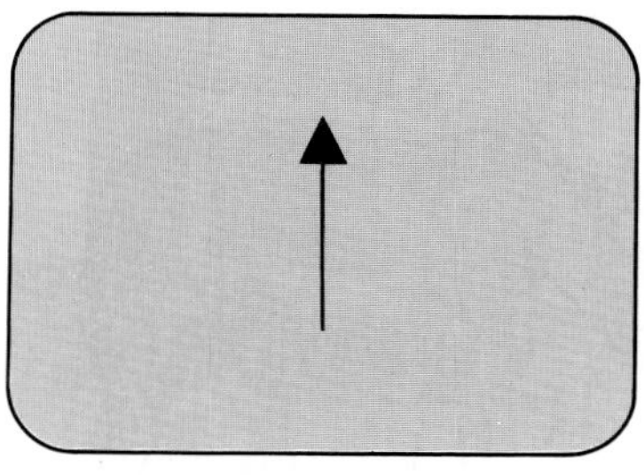

```
FORWARD 30
```

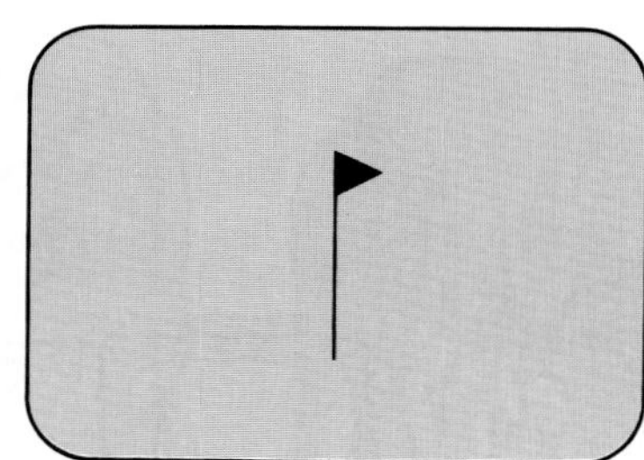

```
FORWARD 30
RIGHT 90
```

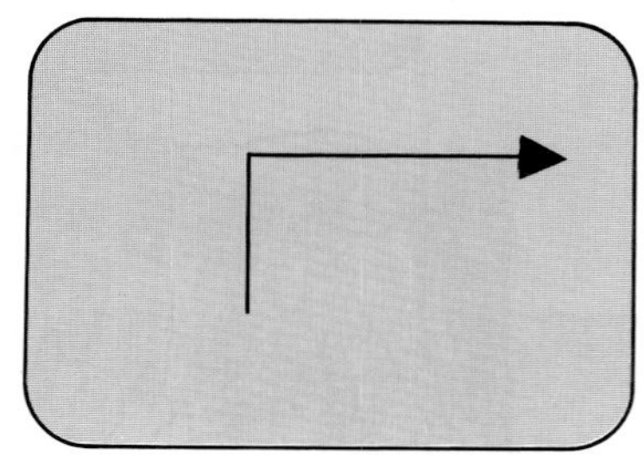

```
FORWARD 30
RIGHT 90
FORWARD 50
```

Give the missing word or number.

1.

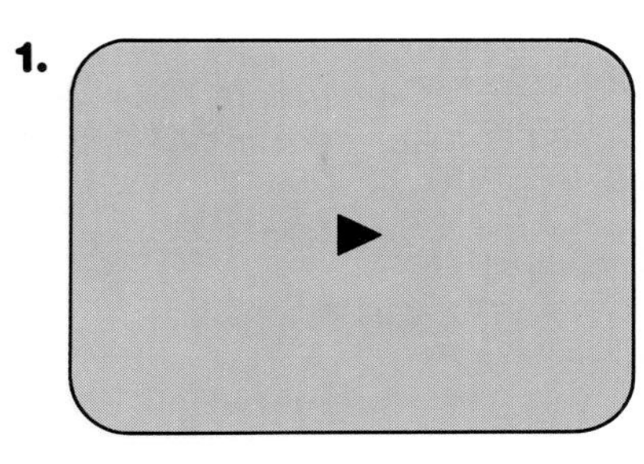

RIGHT ___?___

2.

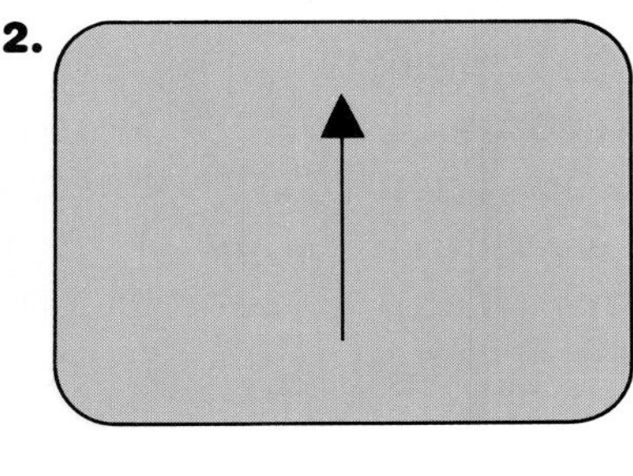

___?___ 40

3.

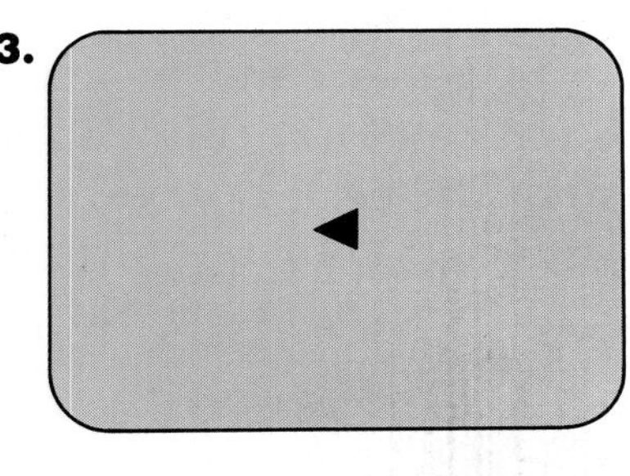

___?___ 90

4.

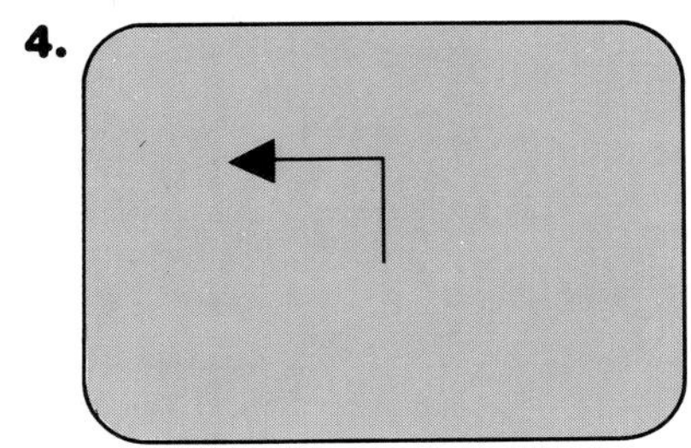

FORWARD 20
LEFT 90
___?___ 20 FORWARD

5.

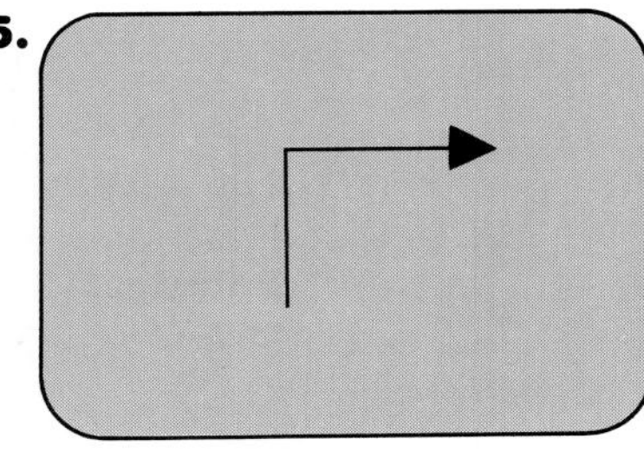

___?___ 30 FORWARD
RIGHT 90
FORWARD 30

6.

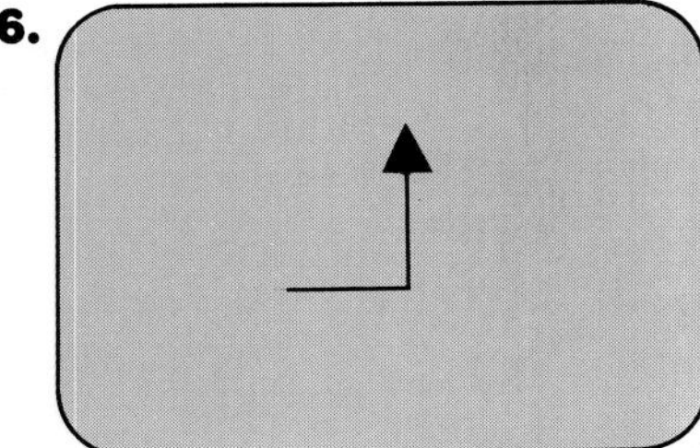

RIGHT 90
FORWARD 20
___?___ 90 LEFT
FORWARD 20

Draw and name a figure for each of these.

7.
FORWARD 30
RIGHT 90
FORWARD 30
RIGHT 90
FORWARD 30
RIGHT 90
FORWARD 30

8.
FORWARD 20
LEFT 90
FORWARD 40
LEFT 90
FORWARD 20
LEFT 90
FORWARD 40

Problem 1 (For use after page 265)
You are helping to set up a baseball team. You need at least 9 players: 1 pitcher, 1 catcher, 4 infielders, and 3 outfielders. You also need some substitutes. 12 players sign up. Then you might have 2 pitchers, 2 catchers, 4 infielders, and 4 outfielders. What are some other ways you could form a team with 12 players? How many different ways are possible?

Program 1

```
 10 REM BASEBALL TEAMS
 20 INPUT "HOW MANY PLAYERS SIGNED
    UP FOR THE TEAM? "; T
 30 PRINT "CATCH. ", "PITCH. ",
    "INF. ", "OUT. ", "TOTAL "
 40 FOR C = 1 TO T - 8
 50 FOR P = 1 TO T - 8
 60 FOR I = 4 TO T - 4
 70 O = T - (P+C+I): IF O<3 THEN 100
 80 PRINT C,P,I,O,C+P+I+O
 90 N = N+1
100 NEXT I
110 NEXT P
120 NEXT C:PRINT:PRINT
130 PRINT "THERE ARE "N" WAYS TO
    DIVIDE THE "T" PLAYERS INTO
    TEAMS. "
140 END
```

Problem 2 (For use after page 177)
How well can the computer predict? Put 2 red and 8 blue counters in a box. Take one out. Is it red or blue? Replace it. Guess how many blue and red you will get if you do this 50 times. Do it and record the results. Have the computer do it. How close were you and the computer?

Program 2

```
 10 REM PREDICTING
 20 INPUT "HOW MANY RED MARBLES? "
    ;R
 30 PRINT : INPUT "HOW MANY BLUE
    MARBLES? ";B
 40 T = R + B:B1 = 0:R1 = 0
 50 PRINT : INPUT "HOW MANY
    PICKS? ";P
 60 FOR X = 1 TO P
 70 Y = INT (T * RND (1) + 1)
 80 IF Y < = R THEN R1 = R1 + 1
 90 IF Y > R THEN B1 = B1 + 1
100 NEXT X
110 PRINT "RED ", "BLUE ": PRINT
    R1,B1
120 END
```

Problem 3 (For use after page 21)
Play the Nim Game. Use 21 counters. Pick up 1, 2, or 3 counters. To win, your friend must pick up the last counter.

Program 3

```
 10 REM NIM GAME
 20 S = 21
 30 FOR N = 1 TO S: PRINT "* "; : NEXT
    N: PRINT S "STARS "
 40 PRINT: FOR K = 1 TO 2: GOSUB 70:
    NEXT K
 50 IF S > 0 THEN 40
 60 END
 70 PRINT "PLAYER ";K: INPUT
    "CHOOSE 1, 2, OR 3 STARS. ";C
 80 IF C < 1 OR C > 3 THEN 70
 90 S = S - C
100 PRINT: IF S < 1 THEN PRINT
    "PLAYER "K " LOSES. ": GOTO 60
110 PRINT: FOR N=1 TO S: PRINT "* ";
120 NEXT N: PRINT S " STARS LEFT "
130 RETURN
```

Problem 4 (For use after page 85)
Pretend you walk into a store. The computer will tell you the price of two things you want to buy. Estimate their total cost by rounding to the nearest dollar. Then check your estimate with the computer.

Program 4

```
10  REM ESTIMATING SUMS
20  A = INT(995*RND(1))/100
30  IF A < 1.1 THEN 20
40  B = INT(995*RND(1))/100
50  IF B < 1.1 THEN 40
60  PRINT, "$"A: PRINT
70  PRINT, "+ "B: PRINT, "______"
80  PRINT: INPUT "ESTIMATE BY
    ROUNDING TO THE NEAREST DOLLAR
    (OMIT '$') ";E
90  A = INT(A + .5): B = INT(B + .5)
100 S = A + B: IF E = S THEN PRINT
    "YOUR ESTIMATE IS CORRECT."
    :GOTO 120
110 PRINT "CORRECT ESTIMATE IS
    $"S"."
120 INPUT "TRY AGAIN?(Y/N) ";Y$
130 IF LEFT$(Y$,1) = "Y" THEN 20
140 END
```

Problem 5 (For use after page 197)
You decide to open a lemonade stand. It costs you 3 cents to make a glass of lemonade. You plan to charge 15 cents a glass. You hope to sell 20 glasses of lemonade a day. Estimate how much money you will make in a day. In 5 days? How close were your estimates to the answers given on the computer?

Program 5

```
10  REM LEMONADE STAND
20  INPUT "HOW MANY CENTS WILL YOU
    CHARGE FOR A GLASS OF LEMONADE?
    ";S
30  PRINT: INPUT "WHAT IS THE COST
    IN CENTS TO MAKE A GLASS OF
    LEMONADE?";C
40  PRINT: INPUT "HOW MANY GLASSES
    WILL YOU SELL EACH DAY? ";G
50  PRINT: INPUT "HOW MANY DAYS WILL
    YOU SELL LEMONADE? ";D
60  P = S - C: T = P * G * D/100
70  PRINT: PRINT "YOUR PROFIT FOR
    "D" DAY(S) WILL BE $ " T/100
80  END
```

Problem 6 (For use after page 311)
You are giving a pizza party. You plan to have 4 tables. When the pizza comes, you find you have 69 pieces. How many will you have for each table and how many will be left?

Program 6

```
10  REM PIZZA
20  INPUT "HOW MANY TABLES? ";T
30  PRINT : INPUT "HOW MANY PIECES OF
    PIZZA? ";Z
40  Q = INT (Z / T):L = Z - (T * Q)
50  PRINT : INPUT "EACH TABLE WILL
    GET HOW MANY PIECES OF PIZZA? ";
    Q1: IF Q1 < > Q THEN PRINT "EACH
    TABLE GETS "Q" PIECE(S)."
60  PRINT : INPUT "HOW MANY PIECES
    ARE LEFT? ";L1: IF L1 < > L THEN
    PRINT L " PIECES(S) ARE LEFT":
    GOTO 80
70  PRINT "CORRECT! "
80  END
```

Problem 7 (For use after page 239)
What is the value of your first name using telephone digits? Can you find a 20-cent name? Example: Each letter (except q and z) has a number value from 2 to 9 on a telephone dial. Using these values, the word CAT is worth 2 + 2 + 8, or 12.

Program 7

```
 10  REM TELEPHONE COUNT
 20  INPUT "WHAT IS THE WORD WHOSE
     VALUE YOU WANT TO FIND? ";A$
 30  FOR X = 1 TO LEN(A$)
 40  Q$ = MID$(A$,X,1): GOSUB 80
 50  A = A + Q: NEXT X
 60  PRINT: PRINT "TOTAL IS "A*100
     "CENTS."
 70  END
 80  IF Q$ = "A" OR Q$ = "B" OR Q$ =
     "C" THEN Q = .02
 90  IF Q$ = "D" OR Q$ = "E" OR Q$ =
     "F" THEN Q = .03
100  IF Q$ = "G" OR Q$ = "H" OR Q$ =
     "I" THEN Q = .04
110  IF Q$ = "J" OR Q$ = "K" OR Q$ =
     "L" THEN Q = .05
120  IF Q$ = "M" OR Q$ = "N" OR Q$ =
     "O" THEN Q = .06
130  IF Q$ = "P" OR Q$ = "R" OR Q$ =
     "S" THEN Q = .07
140  IF Q$ = "T" OR Q$ = "U" OR Q$ =
     "V" THEN Q = .08
150  IF Q$ = "W" OR Q$ = "X" OR Q$ =
     "Y" THEN Q = .09
160  RETURN
```

Problem 8 (For use after page 245)
The computer will give you a number and three possible divisors. You must decide which number or numbers are divisors and find the quotient.

Program 8

```
 10  REM FINDING QUOTIENTS
 20  FOR L = 1 TO 3
 30  D(L) = INT(4*RND(1) + 2)
 40  FOR J = L TO 1 STEP - 1
 50  IF D(L) = D(J) AND L<> J THEN 30
 60  NEXT J : NEXT L
 70  T = INT(3*RND(1) + 1)
 80  M = D(T)*INT(7*RND(1) + 3)
 90  FOR L = 1 TO 3
100  PRINT "DOES ";D(L);" DIVIDE
     ";M;" ?(Y/N) ";
110  INPUT Y$: Y$ = LEFT$(Y$,1):F=0
120  IF M/D(L) = INT(M/D(L)) THEN
     140
130  A$ = "N" : GOTO 150
140  A$ = "Y" : F = 1
150  IF A$ <> Y$ THEN PRINT "IN";
160  PRINT "CORRECT": PRINT: IF F=0
     THEN 200
170  PRINT "WHAT IS ";M;" DIVIDED
     BY ";D(L);
180  INPUT W : IF W <> M/D(L) THEN
     PRINT "IN";
190  PRINT "CORRECT, ";M/D(L);" IS
     THE QUOTIENT": PRINT
200  NEXT L
210  END
```

Problem 9 (For use after page 221)
Find the 5-letter hidden word in the computer. The computer will give you 5 number pairs and a graph. The number pairs show which letters on the graph spell the word.

Fred's Famous Zoo

Average Weights of Animals

Animal	Weight
Buffalo	804 kg
Camel	561 kg
Deer	125 kg
Elk	676 kg
Rhinoceros	2,290 kg
Lion	158 kg
Tiger	182 kg
Hippopotamus	3,563 kg
Bear	376 kg
Elephant	4,093 kg

Some U.S. Stamps

Stamps	Price
Buffalo	6¢
Polar Bears	8¢
First Man on the Moon	10¢
Butterfly	13¢
Owl	15¢
Crane	3¢
Circus	5¢
Windmill	15¢

DAILY DRY DOG FOOD NEEDS

Dog	Daily Need
Chihuahua	45 grams
Yorkshire terrier	100 grams
Dachshund	156 grams
Poodle	198 grams
Beagle	255 grams
Cocker spaniel	355 grams
Bulldog	481 grams
Collie	596 grams
German shepherd	719 grams

LEADING U.S. SUPERMARKETS IN A RECENT YEAR

Supermarkets	Number of Stores
Safeway	2,416
Kroger	1,245
A&P	1,542
Lucky	530
Winn-Dixie	1,192
American	749
Jewel	345
Southland	6,895
Food Fair	203
Albertson's	396

TALL BUILDINGS

BUILDING	CITY	ROOF HEIGHT (IN METERS)	STORIES
SEARS TOWER	CHICAGO, IL	443	110
WORLD TRADE CENTER	NEW YORK CITY, NY	411	110
EMPIRE STATE	NEW YORK CITY, NY	381	102
STANDARD OIL	CHICAGO, IL	346	80
JOHN HANCOCK	CHICAGO, IL	337	100
FIRST BANK TOWER	TORONTO, ON	285	70
CHRYSLER	NEW YORK CITY, NY	264	77
FIRST INTERSTATE TOWER	LOS ANGELES, CA	262	62
40 WALL STREET	NEW YORK CITY, NY	259	71
RCA	NEW YORK CITY, NY	259	70

JET AIRPLANE SEATING CAPACITIES

AIRPLANE	NUMBER OF PERSONS
McDONNELL-DOUGLAS DC-9	155
McDONNELL-DOUGLAS DC-10	380
LOCKHEED L1011	400
CONCORDE	100
BOEING 707	219
BOEING 727	189
BOEING 747	550

• SKATERS' QUARTERLY •

SKATING RINK CAPACITIES

NAME OF RINK	NUMBER OF SKATERS RINK CAN HOLD
Circle K State Ranch, Fresno, CA	500
Happy Wheels, Portland, ME	750
Jellibeans, Atlanta, GA	1,200
Red Wing Rollerway, Columbia, SC	2,500
Roll-on-America, Groton, CT	800
Roller City, Cheyenne, WY	400
Roller Dome South, Ft. Wayne, IN	1,435
Riverdale Roller World, Warwick, RI	1,650
Spinning Wheels, Concordville, PA	2,500
Stars Roller Rink, Bronx, NY	1,500

FLAGS of the UNITED STATES

Date	Stars	Stripes
1777	13	13
1795	15	15
1818	20	13
1861	34	13
1912	48	13
1959	49	13
1960	50	13

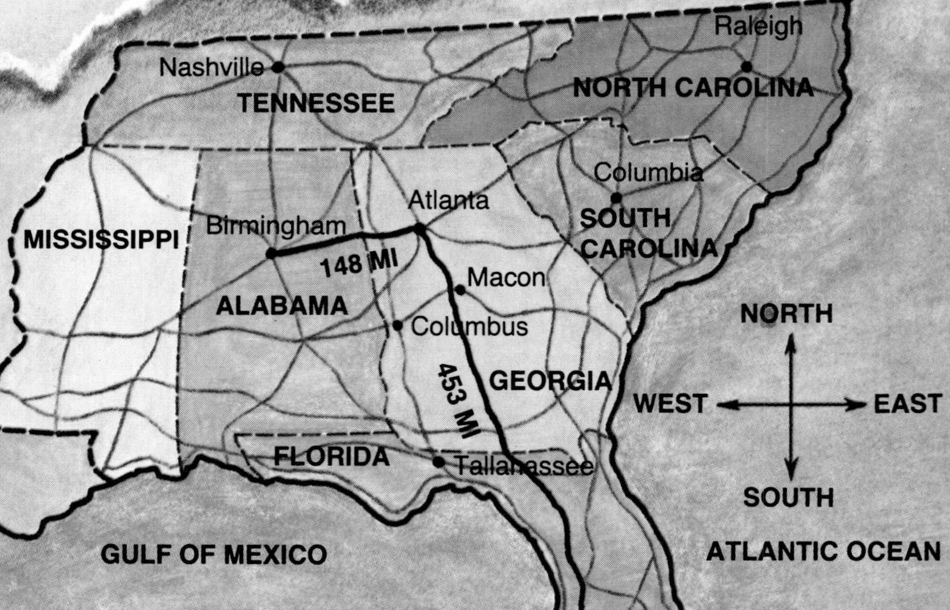

HIGHWAY DISTANCES

More Practice

Set A **For use after page 3**

Add.

1. 3 + 1	**2.** 2 + 5	**3.** 3 + 6	**4.** 1 + 7	**5.** 2 + 1	**6.** 5 + 5	**7.** 9 + 0
8. 2 + 6	**9.** 4 + 5	**10.** 3 + 7	**11.** 5 + 2	**12.** 1 + 8	**13.** 0 + 4	**14.** 5 + 3
15. 7 + 2	**16.** 3 + 5	**17.** 7 + 3	**18.** 3 + 5	**19.** 6 + 1	**20.** 4 + 2	**21.** 8 + 1
22. 4 + 6	**23.** 6 + 2	**24.** 4 + 1	**25.** 6 + 3	**26.** 2 + 7	**27.** 3 + 4	**28.** 4 + 4

Set B **For use after page 5**

Subtract.

1. 8 − 5	**2.** 8 − 4	**3.** 10 − 3	**4.** 3 − 1	**5.** 7 − 6	**6.** 5 − 1	**7.** 10 − 4
8. 7 − 3	**9.** 8 − 6	**10.** 5 − 2	**11.** 9 − 4	**12.** 4 − 4	**13.** 9 − 6	**14.** 6 − 2
15. 9 − 3	**16.** 7 − 4	**17.** 10 − 8	**18.** 6 − 1	**19.** 8 − 7	**20.** 10 − 5	**21.** 7 − 5
22. 10 − 2	**23.** 9 − 8	**24.** 5 − 0	**25.** 8 − 2	**26.** 9 − 0	**27.** 8 − 1	**28.** 9 − 2

Set A **For use after page 7**

Add.

1. $7 + 4$	**2.** $8 + 7$	**3.** $5 + 9$	**4.** $9 + 8$	**5.** $8 + 5$	**6.** $4 + 7$	**7.** $9 + 9$
8. $7 + 6$	**9.** $8 + 3$	**10.** $5 + 7$	**11.** $6 + 8$	**12.** $4 + 9$	**13.** $7 + 5$	**14.** $3 + 9$
15. $8 + 9$	**16.** $6 + 6$	**17.** $9 + 4$	**18.** $7 + 8$	**19.** $2 + 9$	**20.** $5 + 8$	**21.** $9 + 7$
22. $6 + 5$	**23.** $7 + 7$	**24.** $9 + 2$	**25.** $8 + 8$	**26.** $9 + 5$	**27.** $7 + 9$	**28.** $4 + 8$

Set B **For use after page 9**

Subtract.

1. $12 - 9$	**2.** $14 - 8$	**3.** $12 - 7$	**4.** $11 - 6$	**5.** $15 - 9$	**6.** $12 - 3$	**7.** $17 - 9$
8. $16 - 9$	**9.** $14 - 6$	**10.** $12 - 5$	**11.** $16 - 8$	**12.** $13 - 5$	**13.** $13 - 4$	**14.** $11 - 7$
15. $13 - 8$	**16.** $14 - 9$	**17.** $17 - 8$	**18.** $11 - 3$	**19.** $14 - 7$	**20.** $14 - 5$	**21.** $13 - 7$
22. $11 - 2$	**23.** $12 - 8$	**24.** $13 - 9$	**25.** $13 - 6$	**26.** $11 - 5$	**27.** $11 - 9$	**28.** $16 - 7$

Set A **For use after page 17**

Add.

1.	2.	3.	4.	5.	6.	7.
2	4	8	3	6	7	2
4	2	2	1	1	1	5
+ 5	+ 3	+ 5	+ 6	+ 2	+ 6	+ 3

8.	9.	10.	11.	12.	13.	14.
5	4	5	3	1	3	4
3	1	4	3	5	5	1
+ 6	+ 5	+ 6	+ 4	+ 2	+ 3	+ 7

Set B **For use after page 31**

Give the number that comes after.

1. 108 **2.** 60 **3.** 111 **4.** 69 **5.** 18 **6.** 633

Give the number that comes before.

7. 181 **8.** 222 **9.** 100 **10.** 812 **11.** 600 **12.** 88

Give the number that is between.

13. 543 and 545 **14.** 229 and 231 **15.** 699 and 701

Set C **For use after page 32**

Count by twos. Give the next four numbers.

1. 10, 12, 14, 16, ____, ____, ____, ____ **2.** 25, 27, 29, 31, ____, ____, ____, ____

Count by fives. Give the next four numbers.

3. 20, 25, 30, 35, ____, ____, ____, ____ **4.** 110, 115, 120, 125, ____, ____, ____, ____

Count by tens. Give the next four numbers.

5. 120, 130, 140, ____, ____, ____, ____ **6.** 340, 350, 360, ____, ____, ____, ____

Set A **For use after page 37**

Write each amount.

1. 4 dollars, 3 dimes
2. 6 dollars, 2 dimes, 2 pennies
3. 8 dollars
4. 9 dollars and 56 cents
5. 2 dollars, 1 dime, 3 pennies
6. 7 dollars and 98 cents
7. 5 dollars, 5 dimes
8. 3 dollars and 4 cents

Set B **For use after page 39**

Round to the nearest ten.

1. 24 → ||||||	2. 37 → ||||||	3. 83 → ||||||	4. 64 → ||||||
5. 17 → ||||||	6. 35 → ||||||	7. 89 → ||||||	8. 42 → ||||||
9. 14 → ||||||	10. 84 → ||||||	11. 57 → ||||||	12. 62 → ||||||

Set C **For use after page 41**

Round to the nearest hundred.

1. 538 → ||||||	2. 281 → ||||||	3. 108 → ||||||	4. 152 → ||||||
5. 198 → ||||||	6. 663 → ||||||	7. 948 → ||||||	8. 328 → ||||||

Round to the nearest dollar.

9. \$3.48 → ||||||	10. \$8.88 → ||||||	11. \$7.23 → ||||||	12. \$8.69 → ||||||
13. \$8.05 → ||||||	14. \$7.53 → ||||||	15. \$6.85 → ||||||	16. \$8.91 → ||||||

Set A **For use after page 45**

Write > or < for each ●.

1. 90 ● 60	**2.** 200 ● 400	**3.** 1,000 ● 6,000
4. 28 ● 30	**5.** 847 ● 837	**6.** 8,064 ● 8,062
7. 40 ● 60	**8.** 265 ● 295	**9.** 5,232 ● 5,832

Set B **For use after page 47**

Write the number. Use a comma to separate thousands.

1. twenty-six thousand

2. nine hundred twenty-seven thousand

3. eighty-one thousand, two hundred twenty-six

4. thirty-three thousand, eight hundred eight

Set C **For use after page 61**

Find the sums.

1. 12 + 29	**2.** 37 + 43	**3.** 12 + 27	**4.** 80 + 16	**5.** 58 + 24	**6.** 44 + 29
7. 15 + 25	**8.** 34 + 27	**9.** 55 + 12	**10.** 26 + 57	**11.** 49 + 49	**12.** 36 + 9
13. 75 + 19	**14.** 22 + 48	**15.** 13 + 43	**16.** 2 + 69	**17.** 12 + 46	**18.** 46 + 17

Set A   **For use after page 63**

Find the sums.

1. 49 + 61	**2.** 84 + 62	**3.** 98 + 17	**4.** 63 + 27	**5.** 88 + 28	**6.** 37 + 75
7. 85 + 79	**8.** 58 + 83	**9.** 27 + 95	**10.** 66 + 67	**11.** 80 + 52	**12.** 45 + 39
13. 66 + 89	**14.** 73 + 41	**15.** 36 + 96	**16.** 87 + 43	**17.** 22 + 98	**18.** 48 + 73
19. 33 + 73	**20.** 85 + 65	**21.** 20 + 68	**22.** 27 + 96	**23.** 77 + 75	**24.** 82 + 91

Set B   **For use after page 67**

Find the sums.

1. 648 + 104	**2.** 291 + 464	**3.** 260 + 917	**4.** 418 + 750	**5.** 386 + 452	**6.** 605 + 327
7. 123 + 94	**8.** 685 + 812	**9.** 228 + 517	**10.** 625 + 962	**11.** 38 + 180	**12.** 285 + 483
13. 329 + 480	**14.** 605 + 821	**15.** 243 + 747	**16.** 802 + 993	**17.** 208 + 67	**18.** 473 + 518
19. 230 + 589	**20.** 266 + 451	**21.** 805 + 621	**22.** 632 + 241	**23.** 200 + 947	**24.** 628 + 54

Set A **For use after page 69**

Find the sums.

1. $\begin{array}{r} 652 \\ +\ 189 \\ \hline \end{array}$ 2. $\begin{array}{r} 805 \\ +\ 929 \\ \hline \end{array}$ 3. $\begin{array}{r} 472 \\ +\ 687 \\ \hline \end{array}$ 4. $\begin{array}{r} 226 \\ +\ 98 \\ \hline \end{array}$ 5. $\begin{array}{r} 753 \\ +\ 685 \\ \hline \end{array}$ 6. $\begin{array}{r} 764 \\ +\ 187 \\ \hline \end{array}$

7. $\begin{array}{r} 375 \\ +\ 687 \\ \hline \end{array}$ 8. $\begin{array}{r} 457 \\ +\ 382 \\ \hline \end{array}$ 9. $\begin{array}{r} 607 \\ +\ 798 \\ \hline \end{array}$ 10. $\begin{array}{r} 263 \\ +\ 88 \\ \hline \end{array}$ 11. $\begin{array}{r} 486 \\ +\ 978 \\ \hline \end{array}$ 12. $\begin{array}{r} 362 \\ +\ 805 \\ \hline \end{array}$

13. $\begin{array}{r} 288 \\ +\ 554 \\ \hline \end{array}$ 14. $\begin{array}{r} 702 \\ +\ 859 \\ \hline \end{array}$ 15. $\begin{array}{r} 729 \\ +\ 928 \\ \hline \end{array}$ 16. $\begin{array}{r} 447 \\ +\ 285 \\ \hline \end{array}$ 17. $\begin{array}{r} 221 \\ +\ 918 \\ \hline \end{array}$ 18. $\begin{array}{r} 605 \\ +\ 98 \\ \hline \end{array}$

19. $\begin{array}{r} 685 \\ +\ 873 \\ \hline \end{array}$ 20. $\begin{array}{r} 843 \\ +\ 97 \\ \hline \end{array}$ 21. $\begin{array}{r} 782 \\ +\ 507 \\ \hline \end{array}$ 22. $\begin{array}{r} 485 \\ +\ 608 \\ \hline \end{array}$ 23. $\begin{array}{r} 212 \\ +\ 484 \\ \hline \end{array}$ 24. $\begin{array}{r} 375 \\ +\ 829 \\ \hline \end{array}$

Set B **For use after page 70**

Add.

1. $\begin{array}{r} \$3.46 \\ +\ 0.75 \\ \hline \end{array}$ 2. $\begin{array}{r} \$2.57 \\ +\ 8.26 \\ \hline \end{array}$ 3. $\begin{array}{r} \$5.04 \\ +\ 2.57 \\ \hline \end{array}$ 4. $\begin{array}{r} \$9.52 \\ +\ 3.75 \\ \hline \end{array}$ 5. $\begin{array}{r} \$7.39 \\ +\ 2.26 \\ \hline \end{array}$

6. $\begin{array}{r} \$0.87 \\ +\ 3.34 \\ \hline \end{array}$ 7. $\begin{array}{r} \$6.20 \\ +\ 8.99 \\ \hline \end{array}$ 8. $\begin{array}{r} \$4.65 \\ +\ 6.35 \\ \hline \end{array}$ 9. $\begin{array}{r} \$8.16 \\ +\ 0.55 \\ \hline \end{array}$ 10. $\begin{array}{r} \$1.32 \\ +\ 7.87 \\ \hline \end{array}$

11. $\begin{array}{r} \$9.05 \\ +\ 0.36 \\ \hline \end{array}$ 12. $\begin{array}{r} \$5.25 \\ +\ 3.83 \\ \hline \end{array}$ 13. $\begin{array}{r} \$2.17 \\ +\ 6.84 \\ \hline \end{array}$ 14. $\begin{array}{r} \$3.42 \\ +\ 2.95 \\ \hline \end{array}$ 15. $\begin{array}{r} \$8.20 \\ +\ 0.98 \\ \hline \end{array}$

16. $\begin{array}{r} \$5.56 \\ +\ 8.67 \\ \hline \end{array}$ 17. $\begin{array}{r} \$2.65 \\ +\ 4.92 \\ \hline \end{array}$ 18. $\begin{array}{r} \$3.12 \\ +\ 0.94 \\ \hline \end{array}$ 19. $\begin{array}{r} \$4.85 \\ +\ 2.62 \\ \hline \end{array}$ 20. $\begin{array}{r} \$2.82 \\ +\ 8.54 \\ \hline \end{array}$

Set A **For use after page 72**

Find the sums. Write answers only.

1. 60 + 80
2. 70 + 30
3. 90 + 40
4. 30 + 30
5. 900 + 200
6. 500 + 400
7. 300 + 500
8. 900 + 800

9. 20 + 80	10. 70 + 70	11. 60 + 30	12. 80 + 50	13. 90 + 10	14. 20 + 50
15. 500 + 800	16. 400 + 300	17. 800 + 200	18. 600 + 600	19. 100 + 500	20. 700 + 800
21. 200 + 500	22. 300 + 800	23. 200 + 200	24. 700 + 500	25. 600 + 800	26. 800 + 100

Set B **For use after page 75**

Estimate by rounding to the nearest ten.

1. 32 + 49
2. 86 + 43
3. 25 + 28
4. 66 + 47
5. 82 + 34

Estimate by rounding to the nearest hundred.

6. 480 + 520
7. 638 + 402
8. 476 + 154
9. 880 + 321

Estimate by rounding to the nearest dollar.

10. \$6.11 + 4.95
11. \$4.00 + 9.00
12. \$2.95 + 6.12

Set A **For use after page 79**

Find the sums.

1.	2.	3.	4.	5.	6.
23 46 + 17	28 42 + 23	66 43 + 40	57 83 + 8	16 74 + 37	53 4 + 69

7.	8.	9.	10.	11.	12.
25 43 18 + 77	45 62 19 + 33	28 48 31 + 84	54 29 71 + 15	62 85 47 + 41	35 49 20 + 74

13.	14.	15.	16.	17.	18.
315 416 + 207	151 74 + 607	423 185 + 359	512 372 + 429	114 183 + 620	641 88 + 745

Set B **For use after page 81**

Find the sums.

1.	2.	3.	4.	5.
3,059 + 2,717	2,964 + 5,682	1,429 + 6,507	6,781 + 2,657	4,812 + 3,968

6.	7.	8.	9.	10.
7,811 + 1,829	1,854 + 643	5,584 + 3,145	3,808 + 6,137	4,125 + 4,992

11.	12.	13.	14.	15.
6,815 + 2,376	2,964 + 3,071	4,615 + 4,607	2,976 + 4,192	3,804 + 1,562

16.	17.	18.	19.	20.
1,247 + 5,086	3,358 + 3,692	4,532 + 1,607	7,729 + 1,805	3,643 + 5,818

Set A **For use after page 93**

Find the differences.

1. $\begin{array}{r}64\\-27\\\hline\end{array}$	**2.** $\begin{array}{r}81\\-14\\\hline\end{array}$	**3.** $\begin{array}{r}66\\-59\\\hline\end{array}$	**4.** $\begin{array}{r}44\\-23\\\hline\end{array}$	**5.** $\begin{array}{r}30\\-19\\\hline\end{array}$	**6.** $\begin{array}{r}64\\-38\\\hline\end{array}$
7. $\begin{array}{r}85\\-37\\\hline\end{array}$	**8.** $\begin{array}{r}42\\-8\\\hline\end{array}$	**9.** $\begin{array}{r}61\\-54\\\hline\end{array}$	**10.** $\begin{array}{r}99\\-66\\\hline\end{array}$	**11.** $\begin{array}{r}34\\-18\\\hline\end{array}$	**12.** $\begin{array}{r}50\\-36\\\hline\end{array}$
13. $\begin{array}{r}62\\-48\\\hline\end{array}$	**14.** $\begin{array}{r}45\\-19\\\hline\end{array}$	**15.** $\begin{array}{r}63\\-58\\\hline\end{array}$	**16.** $\begin{array}{r}44\\-27\\\hline\end{array}$	**17.** $\begin{array}{r}39\\-25\\\hline\end{array}$	**18.** $\begin{array}{r}82\\-46\\\hline\end{array}$
19. $\begin{array}{r}65\\-29\\\hline\end{array}$	**20.** $\begin{array}{r}45\\-6\\\hline\end{array}$	**21.** $\begin{array}{r}34\\-17\\\hline\end{array}$	**22.** $\begin{array}{r}68\\-34\\\hline\end{array}$	**23.** $\begin{array}{r}73\\-15\\\hline\end{array}$	**24.** $\begin{array}{r}67\\-48\\\hline\end{array}$

Set B **For use after page 97**

Find the differences.

1. $\begin{array}{r}408\\-297\\\hline\end{array}$	**2.** $\begin{array}{r}364\\-182\\\hline\end{array}$	**3.** $\begin{array}{r}512\\-190\\\hline\end{array}$	**4.** $\begin{array}{r}648\\-294\\\hline\end{array}$	**5.** $\begin{array}{r}355\\-72\\\hline\end{array}$	**6.** $\begin{array}{r}411\\-270\\\hline\end{array}$
7. $\begin{array}{r}353\\-181\\\hline\end{array}$	**8.** $\begin{array}{r}859\\-284\\\hline\end{array}$	**9.** $\begin{array}{r}314\\-181\\\hline\end{array}$	**10.** $\begin{array}{r}487\\-391\\\hline\end{array}$	**11.** $\begin{array}{r}405\\-124\\\hline\end{array}$	**12.** $\begin{array}{r}687\\-196\\\hline\end{array}$
13. $\begin{array}{r}559\\-167\\\hline\end{array}$	**14.** $\begin{array}{r}348\\-295\\\hline\end{array}$	**15.** $\begin{array}{r}442\\-180\\\hline\end{array}$	**16.** $\begin{array}{r}312\\-91\\\hline\end{array}$	**17.** $\begin{array}{r}559\\-168\\\hline\end{array}$	**18.** $\begin{array}{r}607\\-234\\\hline\end{array}$
19. $\begin{array}{r}344\\-161\\\hline\end{array}$	**20.** $\begin{array}{r}581\\-390\\\hline\end{array}$	**21.** $\begin{array}{r}650\\-460\\\hline\end{array}$	**22.** $\begin{array}{r}327\\-84\\\hline\end{array}$	**23.** $\begin{array}{r}659\\-167\\\hline\end{array}$	**24.** $\begin{array}{r}526\\-375\\\hline\end{array}$

Set A **For use after page 99**

Find the differences.

1. 423 − 187	2. 154 − 89	3. 865 − 467	4. 312 − 140	5. 568 − 179	6. 205 − 97
7. 439 − 281	8. 644 − 356	9. 212 − 144	10. 761 − 395	11. 366 − 287	12. 391 − 105
13. 604 − 196	14. 227 − 154	15. 364 − 185	16. 228 − 149	17. 361 − 184	18. 641 − 397
19. 322 − 195	20. 612 − 184	21. 351 − 267	22. 885 − 693	23. 904 − 689	24. 326 − 148

Set B **For use after page 105**

Find the differences.

1. 307 − 158	2. 511 − 299	3. 305 − 166	4. 200 − 96	5. 405 − 168	6. 508 − 145
7. 805 − 467	8. 500 − 186	9. 805 − 298	10. 601 − 486	11. 305 − 297	12. 400 − 161
13. 201 − 84	14. 308 − 169	15. 702 − 246	16. 805 − 361	17. 100 − 67	18. 203 − 186
19. 208 − 159	20. 804 − 366	21. 201 − 89	22. 607 − 358	23. 405 − 269	24. 307 − 148

Set A **For use after page 107**

Find the differences in the amounts.

1. $7.00 − 0.98	2. $8.25 − 4.00	3. $4.00 − 1.98	4. $7.50 − 0.75	5. $6.95 − 4.50
6. $3.25 − 1.40	7. $8.00 − 0.79	8. $2.50 − 0.75	9. $6.65 − 4.80	10. $9.00 − 7.25
11. $6.00 − 5.25	12. $4.00 − 1.98	13. $6.25 − 2.75	14. $4.50 − 1.75	15. $6.60 − 1.75
16. $8.25 − 1.50	17. $9.75 − 4.25	18. $8.35 − 4.50	19. $7.25 − 3.98	20. $6.75 − 3.00

Set B **For use after page 109**

Find the differences. Write answers only.

1. 60 – 40 **2.** 800 – 300 **3.** 40 – 10 **4.** 1,300 – 600

5. 1,800 – 900 **6.** 90 – 70 **7.** 600 – 500 **8.** 130 – 80

9. 1,000 − 300	10. 170 − 60	11. 300 − 100	12. 1,300 − 800	13. 80 − 70	14. 600 − 100
15. 1,400 − 600	16. 50 − 10	17. 600 − 300	18. 90 − 20	19. 400 − 300	20. 1,200 − 800
21. 1,100 − 100	22. 180 − 90	23. 600 − 400	24. 120 − 70	25. 1,000 − 200	26. 150 − 70

Set A **For use after page 111**

Estimate by rounding to the nearest ten.

1. $\begin{array}{r} 36 \\ -\ 19 \\ \hline \end{array}$ **2.** $\begin{array}{r} 84 \\ -\ 26 \\ \hline \end{array}$ **3.** $\begin{array}{r} 22 \\ -\ 14 \\ \hline \end{array}$ **4.** $\begin{array}{r} 69 \\ -\ 28 \\ \hline \end{array}$ **5.** $\begin{array}{r} 42 \\ -\ 33 \\ \hline \end{array}$

Estimate by rounding to the nearest hundred.

6. $\begin{array}{r} 418 \\ -\ 297 \\ \hline \end{array}$ **7.** $\begin{array}{r} 630 \\ -\ 149 \\ \hline \end{array}$ **8.** $\begin{array}{r} 850 \\ -\ 429 \\ \hline \end{array}$ **9.** $\begin{array}{r} 645 \\ -\ 168 \\ \hline \end{array}$

Estimate by rounding to the nearest dollar.

10. $\begin{array}{r} \$6.84 \\ -\ 3.20 \\ \hline \end{array}$ **11.** $\begin{array}{r} \$5.50 \\ -\ 3.50 \\ \hline \end{array}$ **12.** $\begin{array}{r} \$8.71 \\ -\ 2.56 \\ \hline \end{array}$ **13.** $\begin{array}{r} \$6.89 \\ -\ 1.35 \\ \hline \end{array}$

Set B **For use after page 113**

Find the differences.

1. $\begin{array}{r} 4{,}077 \\ -\ 2{,}165 \\ \hline \end{array}$ **2.** $\begin{array}{r} 9{,}624 \\ -\ 4{,}312 \\ \hline \end{array}$ **3.** $\begin{array}{r} 1{,}026 \\ -\ 647 \\ \hline \end{array}$ **4.** $\begin{array}{r} 3{,}855 \\ -\ 1{,}862 \\ \hline \end{array}$ **5.** $\begin{array}{r} 6{,}338 \\ -\ 4{,}290 \\ \hline \end{array}$

6. $\begin{array}{r} 7{,}529 \\ -\ 6{,}188 \\ \hline \end{array}$ **7.** $\begin{array}{r} 4{,}036 \\ -\ 2{,}154 \\ \hline \end{array}$ **8.** $\begin{array}{r} 3{,}624 \\ -\ 1{,}518 \\ \hline \end{array}$ **9.** $\begin{array}{r} 9{,}165 \\ -\ 2{,}618 \\ \hline \end{array}$ **10.** $\begin{array}{r} 3{,}277 \\ -\ 1{,}484 \\ \hline \end{array}$

11. $\begin{array}{r} 8{,}826 \\ -\ 5{,}471 \\ \hline \end{array}$ **12.** $\begin{array}{r} 3{,}061 \\ -\ 1{,}890 \\ \hline \end{array}$ **13.** $\begin{array}{r} 6{,}429 \\ -\ 5{,}161 \\ \hline \end{array}$ **14.** $\begin{array}{r} 2{,}436 \\ -\ 1{,}085 \\ \hline \end{array}$ **15.** $\begin{array}{r} 6{,}009 \\ -\ 2{,}324 \\ \hline \end{array}$

16. $\begin{array}{r} 6{,}514 \\ -\ 91 \\ \hline \end{array}$ **17.** $\begin{array}{r} 7{,}268 \\ -\ 4{,}517 \\ \hline \end{array}$ **18.** $\begin{array}{r} 3{,}664 \\ -\ 836 \\ \hline \end{array}$ **19.** $\begin{array}{r} 9{,}258 \\ -\ 5{,}064 \\ \hline \end{array}$ **20.** $\begin{array}{r} 7{,}228 \\ -\ 1{,}416 \\ \hline \end{array}$

Set A **For use after page 159**

Multiply.

1. 2×6
2. 4×2
3. 7×2
4. 2×3
5. 2×5
6. 2×2
7. 8×2
8. 9×2
9. 6×2
10. 2×2
11. 2×4
12. 2×8
13. 5×2
14. 2×9
15. 3×2
16. 2×7
17. 4×2
18. 9×2
19. 6×2
20. 2×3
21. 2×5

Set B **For use after page 161**

Multiply.

1. 3×5
2. 3×3
3. 2×5
4. 6×3
5. 2×3
6. 3×7
7. 4×3
8. 9×3
9. 3×6
10. 3×4
11. 7×3
12. 8×3
13. 3×7
14. 5×3

Set C **For use after page 165**

Multiply.

1. 7×4
2. 4×4
3. 4×9
4. 5×4
5. 2×7
6. 2×4
7. 8×4
8. 4×3
9. 6×4
10. 2×9
11. 3×4
12. 3×5
13. 4×7
14. 4×5

Set A **For use after page 167**

Multiply.

1. 5×2	2. 5×5	3. 4×6	4. 6×5	5. 8×5	6. 4×4	7. 3×5
8. 9×5	9. 5×4	10. 3×3	11. 3×5	12. 4×5	13. 3×9	14. 5×7
15. 5×6	16. 5×2	17. 3×8	18. 4×6	19. 7×5	20. 5×4	21. 2×6

Set B **For use after page 170**

Multiply.

1. 1×7	2. 0×1	3. 1×0	4. 0×4	5. 1×3	6. 0×9	7. 1×9
8. 1×8	9. 0×8	10. 1×6	11. 0×2	12. 1×4	13. 0×5	14. 0×6

Set C **For use after page 183**

Multiply.

1. 9×5	2. 8×9	3. 7×9	4. 5×7	5. 9×3	6. 1×9	7. 9×0
8. 9×9	9. 4×9	10. 9×6	11. 8×8	12. 2×9	13. 5×9	14. 9×7

Set A **For use after page 185**

Multiply.

1. 7×7
2. 3×3
3. 8×8
4. 9×6
5. 4×4
6. 2×5
7. 5×5
8. 2×2
9. 6×6
10. 8×5
11. 9×9
12. 1×1
13. 0×0
14. 9×2

Set B **For use after page 187**

Multiply.

1. 9×9
2. 8×5
3. 9×6
4. 5×7
5. 9×2
6. 4×8
7. 5×9
8. 4×7
9. 3×9
10. 6×8
11. 2×8
12. 6×4
13. 8×7
14. 9×8

Set C **For use after page 190**

Use the grouping shown. Find the products.

1. $(3 \times 1) \times 5 =$ ____
2. $(2 \times 3) \times 3 =$ ____
3. $2 \times (1 \times 4) =$ ____
4. $5 \times (2 \times 3) =$ ____
5. $4 \times (2 \times 4) =$ ____
6. $5 \times (4 \times 2) =$ ____

Use any grouping you want. Find the products.

7. $7 \times 1 \times 5 =$ ____
8. $8 \times 0 \times 6 =$ ____
9. $4 \times 2 \times 2 =$ ____
10. $3 \times 2 \times 4 =$ ____
11. $5 \times 1 \times 9 =$ ____
12. $3 \times 3 \times 2 =$ ____

Set A **For use after page 191**

Find these factors.

1. $6 \times \square = 42$
2. $\square \times 2 = 16$
3. $7 \times \square = 56$
4. $\square \times 7 = 63$
5. $9 \times \square = 45$
6. $\square \times 8 = 64$
7. $4 \times \square = 16$
8. $\square \times 9 = 36$
9. $8 \times \square = 72$
10. $\square \times 7 = 21$
11. $8 \times \square = 32$
12. $2 \times \square = 18$
13. $\square \times 8 = 48$
14. $6 \times \square = 54$
15. $\square \times 9 = 81$
16. $3 \times \square = 21$

Set B **For use after page 231**

Divide.

1. $12 \div 3 =$
2. $10 \div 2 =$
3. $6 \div 3 =$
4. $14 \div 2 =$
5. $16 \div 2 =$
6. $6 \div 2 =$
7. $18 \div 3 =$
8. $6 \div 2 =$
9. $27 \div 3 =$
10. $2 \div 2 =$
11. $18 \div 2 =$
12. $9 \div 3 =$
13. $8 \div 2 =$
14. $6 \div 3 =$
15. $24 \div 3 =$
16. $12 \div 2 =$
17. $15 \div 3 =$
18. $3 \div 3 =$
19. $18 \div 2 =$
20. $21 \div 3 =$

Set C **For use after page 235**

Divide.

1. $16 \div 4 =$
2. $6 \div 3 =$
3. $32 \div 4 =$
4. $12 \div 4 =$
5. $18 \div 2 =$
6. $4 \div 4 =$
7. $14 \div 2 =$
8. $24 \div 3 =$
9. $8 \div 2 =$
10. $28 \div 4 =$
11. $18 \div 3 =$
12. $20 \div 4 =$
13. $24 \div 4 =$
14. $15 \div 3 =$
15. $8 \div 4 =$
16. $36 \div 4 =$
17. $12 \div 3 =$
18. $6 \div 2 =$
19. $21 \div 3 =$
20. $4 \div 2 =$

Set A **For use after page 237**

Divide.

1. $15 \div 5 =$	**2.** $35 \div 5 =$	**3.** $16 \div 4 =$	**4.** $20 \div 5 =$
5. $45 \div 5 =$	**6.** $9 \div 3 =$	**7.** $5 \div 5 =$	**8.** $8 \div 2 =$
9. $27 \div 3 =$	**10.** $10 \div 2 =$	**11.** $30 \div 5 =$	**12.** $36 \div 4 =$
13. $10 \div 5 =$	**14.** $40 \div 5 =$	**15.** $20 \div 4 =$	**16.** $25 \div 5 =$
17. $12 \div 4 =$	**18.** $16 \div 2 =$	**19.** $18 \div 3 =$	**20.** $32 \div 4 =$

Set B **For use after page 251**

Divide.

1. $6\overline{)12}$	**2.** $4\overline{)20}$	**3.** $6\overline{)54}$	**4.** $6\overline{)36}$	**5.** $3\overline{)18}$
6. $2\overline{)18}$	**7.** $6\overline{)42}$	**8.** $6\overline{)6}$	**9.** $2\overline{)16}$	**10.** $3\overline{)21}$
11. $5\overline{)25}$	**12.** $3\overline{)6}$	**13.** $3\overline{)27}$	**14.** $4\overline{)24}$	**15.** $6\overline{)24}$
16. $6\overline{)18}$	**17.** $5\overline{)30}$	**18.** $4\overline{)16}$	**19.** $6\overline{)30}$	**20.** $7\overline{)56}$

Set C **For use after page 253**

Divide.

1. $7\overline{)28}$	**2.** $2\overline{)10}$	**3.** $7\overline{)49}$	**4.** $3\overline{)6}$	**5.** $7\overline{)63}$
6. $5\overline{)40}$	**7.** $7\overline{)7}$	**8.** $6\overline{)42}$	**9.** $7\overline{)21}$	**10.** $7\overline{)42}$
11. $5\overline{)30}$	**12.** $3\overline{)21}$	**13.** $7\overline{)14}$	**14.** $3\overline{)27}$	**15.** $7\overline{)21}$
16. $7\overline{)35}$	**17.** $6\overline{)24}$	**18.** $7\overline{)56}$	**19.** $4\overline{)36}$	**20.** $5\overline{)35}$

Set A **For use after page 257**

Divide.

1. $8\overline{)24}$ 2. $4\overline{)32}$ 3. $8\overline{)72}$ 4. $8\overline{)8}$ 5. $7\overline{)49}$

6. $6\overline{)36}$ 7. $8\overline{)56}$ 8. $3\overline{)21}$ 9. $6\overline{)12}$ 10. $8\overline{)40}$

11. $8\overline{)16}$ 12. $5\overline{)40}$ 13. $8\overline{)64}$ 14. $7\overline{)28}$ 15. $3\overline{)24}$

16. $5\overline{)35}$ 17. $8\overline{)32}$ 18. $7\overline{)49}$ 19. $5\overline{)45}$ 20. $8\overline{)48}$

21. $8\overline{)48}$ 22. $7\overline{)63}$ 23. $8\overline{)16}$ 24. $5\overline{)45}$ 25. $8\overline{)40}$

26. $3\overline{)24}$ 27. $8\overline{)56}$ 28. $4\overline{)36}$ 29. $6\overline{)18}$ 30. $8\overline{)72}$

31. $6\overline{)42}$ 32. $6\overline{)18}$ 33. $2\overline{)12}$ 34. $6\overline{)6}$ 35. $3\overline{)27}$

Set B **For use after page 259**

Divide.

1. $9\overline{)18}$ 2. $9\overline{)81}$ 3. $3\overline{)24}$ 4. $9\overline{)54}$ 5. $4\overline{)36}$

6. $8\overline{)72}$ 7. $9\overline{)27}$ 8. $4\overline{)20}$ 9. $5\overline{)30}$ 10. $9\overline{)72}$

11. $6\overline{)36}$ 12. $7\overline{)56}$ 13. $9\overline{)45}$ 14. $9\overline{)9}$ 15. $2\overline{)18}$

16. $9\overline{)36}$ 17. $3\overline{)18}$ 18. $8\overline{)24}$ 19. $9\overline{)63}$ 20. $6\overline{)54}$

21. $9\overline{)63}$ 22. $3\overline{)12}$ 23. $9\overline{)18}$ 24. $3\overline{)27}$ 25. $9\overline{)45}$

26. $5\overline{)45}$ 27. $9\overline{)9}$ 28. $4\overline{)24}$ 29. $9\overline{)72}$ 30. $5\overline{)40}$

31. $8\overline{)8}$ 32. $7\overline{)21}$ 33. $6\overline{)42}$ 34. $3\overline{)15}$ 35. $2\overline{)16}$

36. $8\overline{)48}$ 37. $6\overline{)24}$ 38. $5\overline{)25}$ 39. $7\overline{)63}$ 40. $4\overline{)16}$

Set A **For use after page 277**

Find the products.

1. $\begin{array}{r} 14 \\ \times\ 5 \\ \hline \end{array}$ 2. $\begin{array}{r} 32 \\ \times\ 3 \\ \hline \end{array}$ 3. $\begin{array}{r} 25 \\ \times\ 3 \\ \hline \end{array}$ 4. $\begin{array}{r} 18 \\ \times\ 5 \\ \hline \end{array}$ 5. $\begin{array}{r} 14 \\ \times\ 2 \\ \hline \end{array}$ 6. $\begin{array}{r} 12 \\ \times\ 7 \\ \hline \end{array}$

7. $\begin{array}{r} 46 \\ \times\ 2 \\ \hline \end{array}$ 8. $\begin{array}{r} 24 \\ \times\ 3 \\ \hline \end{array}$ 9. $\begin{array}{r} 12 \\ \times\ 8 \\ \hline \end{array}$ 10. $\begin{array}{r} 14 \\ \times\ 4 \\ \hline \end{array}$ 11. $\begin{array}{r} 17 \\ \times\ 5 \\ \hline \end{array}$ 12. $\begin{array}{r} 21 \\ \times\ 4 \\ \hline \end{array}$

Set B **For use after page 279**

Find the products.

1. $\begin{array}{r} 42 \\ \times\ 4 \\ \hline \end{array}$ 2. $\begin{array}{r} 34 \\ \times\ 5 \\ \hline \end{array}$ 3. $\begin{array}{r} 61 \\ \times\ 3 \\ \hline \end{array}$ 4. $\begin{array}{r} 12 \\ \times\ 9 \\ \hline \end{array}$ 5. $\begin{array}{r} 44 \\ \times\ 6 \\ \hline \end{array}$ 6. $\begin{array}{r} 38 \\ \times\ 3 \\ \hline \end{array}$

7. $\begin{array}{r} 22 \\ \times\ 3 \\ \hline \end{array}$ 8. $\begin{array}{r} 17 \\ \times\ 8 \\ \hline \end{array}$ 9. $\begin{array}{r} 44 \\ \times\ 5 \\ \hline \end{array}$ 10. $\begin{array}{r} 39 \\ \times\ 2 \\ \hline \end{array}$ 11. $\begin{array}{r} 63 \\ \times\ 3 \\ \hline \end{array}$ 12. $\begin{array}{r} 24 \\ \times\ 4 \\ \hline \end{array}$

Set C **For use after page 281**

Write the amounts with dollars and cents.

1. $\begin{array}{r} 48¢ \\ \times\ 3 \\ \hline \end{array}$ 2. $\begin{array}{r} 65¢ \\ \times\ 4 \\ \hline \end{array}$ 3. $\begin{array}{r} 36¢ \\ \times\ 7 \\ \hline \end{array}$ 4. $\begin{array}{r} 87¢ \\ \times\ 5 \\ \hline \end{array}$ 5. $\begin{array}{r} 22¢ \\ \times\ 8 \\ \hline \end{array}$

6. $\begin{array}{r} 39¢ \\ \times\ 5 \\ \hline \end{array}$ 7. $\begin{array}{r} 18¢ \\ \times\ 8 \\ \hline \end{array}$ 8. $\begin{array}{r} 62¢ \\ \times\ 4 \\ \hline \end{array}$ 9. $\begin{array}{r} 33¢ \\ \times\ 6 \\ \hline \end{array}$ 10. $\begin{array}{r} 25¢ \\ \times\ 2 \\ \hline \end{array}$

11. $\begin{array}{r} 36¢ \\ \times\ 3 \\ \hline \end{array}$ 12. $\begin{array}{r} 42¢ \\ \times\ 8 \\ \hline \end{array}$ 13. $\begin{array}{r} 63¢ \\ \times\ 3 \\ \hline \end{array}$ 14. $\begin{array}{r} 24¢ \\ \times\ 9 \\ \hline \end{array}$ 15. $\begin{array}{r} 35¢ \\ \times\ 4 \\ \hline \end{array}$

Set A **For use after page 297**

Divide. Find the quotients and remainders.

1. $3\overline{)5}$ **2.** $2\overline{)9}$ **3.** $3\overline{)6}$ **4.** $5\overline{)5}$ **5.** $4\overline{)0}$

6. $4\overline{)3}$ **7.** $4\overline{)9}$ **8.** $3\overline{)7}$ **9.** $5\overline{)4}$ **10.** $5\overline{)7}$

11. $3\overline{)9}$ **12.** $2\overline{)3}$ **13.** $3\overline{)2}$ **14.** $4\overline{)7}$ **15.** $5\overline{)6}$

16. $3\overline{)4}$ **17.** $2\overline{)4}$ **18.** $2\overline{)0}$ **19.** $4\overline{)4}$ **20.** $3\overline{)8}$

Set B **For use after page 299**

Divide. Find the quotients and remainders.

1. $5\overline{)14}$ **2.** $3\overline{)26}$ **3.** $5\overline{)18}$ **4.** $5\overline{)34}$ **5.** $4\overline{)21}$

6. $6\overline{)0}$ **7.** $6\overline{)30}$ **8.** $3\overline{)22}$ **9.** $4\overline{)18}$ **10.** $6\overline{)29}$

11. $3\overline{)16}$ **12.** $5\overline{)36}$ **13.** $4\overline{)22}$ **14.** $2\overline{)19}$ **15.** $4\overline{)30}$

16. $4\overline{)0}$ **17.** $5\overline{)18}$ **18.** $3\overline{)23}$ **19.** $3\overline{)11}$ **20.** $2\overline{)18}$

Set C **For use after page 305**

Find the quotients.

1. $2\overline{)46}$ **2.** $4\overline{)56}$ **3.** $5\overline{)55}$ **4.** $2\overline{)82}$ **5.** $4\overline{)36}$

6. $2\overline{)74}$ **7.** $3\overline{)66}$ **8.** $2\overline{)36}$ **9.** $3\overline{)39}$ **10.** $4\overline{)64}$

11. $4\overline{)76}$ **12.** $5\overline{)40}$ **13.** $3\overline{)72}$ **14.** $2\overline{)52}$ **15.** $4\overline{)80}$

16. $5\overline{)70}$ **17.** $2\overline{)54}$ **18.** $3\overline{)24}$ **19.** $5\overline{)95}$ **20.** $3\overline{)96}$

Set A **For use after page 307**

Find the quotients and remainders.

1. $5\overline{)62}$ 2. $4\overline{)65}$ 3. $3\overline{)35}$ 4. $3\overline{)64}$ 5. $4\overline{)48}$

6. $2\overline{)17}$ 7. $2\overline{)29}$ 8. $4\overline{)45}$ 9. $5\overline{)68}$ 10. $4\overline{)79}$

11. $2\overline{)91}$ 12. $5\overline{)64}$ 13. $2\overline{)69}$ 14. $4\overline{)88}$ 15. $3\overline{)55}$

16. $3\overline{)47}$ 17. $5\overline{)86}$ 18. $4\overline{)66}$ 19. $2\overline{)36}$ 20. $5\overline{)48}$

Set B **For use after page 333**

Find the sums.

1. 2.4 + 3.5
2. 4.7 + 2.8
3. 82.6 + 11.3
4. 27.4 + 36.8
5. 64.5 + 27.5
6. 7.2 + 1.8
7. 65.3 + 26.1
8. 73.6 + 21.8
9. 26.2 + 45.9
10. 30.8 + 9.5
11. 4.8 + 7.6
12. 16.3 + 42.9
13. 65.2 + 28.8
14. 16.8 + 14.2
15. 59.4 + 27.7

Set C **For use after page 335**

Find the differences.

1. 8.6 − 5.1
2. 6.0 − 4.7
3. 25.2 − 1.9
4. 64.1 − 29.4
5. 40.6 − 28.4
6. 26.2 − 14.1
7. 8.0 − 7.4
8. 11.1 − 5.6
9. 98.4 − 39.3
10. 41.2 − 26.5

Table of Measures

Metric System		Customary System	
Length			
1 centimeter (cm)	10 millimeters (mm)	1 foot (ft)	12 inches (in.)
1 decimeter (dm)	100 millimeters (mm) 10 centimeters (cm)	1 yard (yd)	36 inches (in.) 3 feet (ft)
1 meter (m)	1,000 millimeters (mm) 100 centimeters (cm) 10 decimeters (dm)	1 mile (m)	5,280 feet (ft) 1,760 yards (yd)
1 kilometer (km)	1,000 meters (m)		
Area			
1 square meter (m^2)	100 square decimeters (dm^2) 10,000 square centimeters (cm^2)	1 square foot (ft^2)	144 square inches ($in.^2$)
Volume			
1 cubic decimeter (dm^3)	1,000 cubic centimeters (cm^3) 1 liter (L)	1 cubic foot (ft^3)	1,728 cubic inches ($in.^3$)
Capacity			
		1 cup (c)	8 fluid ounces (fl oz)
		1 pint (pt)	16 fluid ounces (fl oz) 2 cups (c)
1 teaspoon	5 milliliters (mL)	1 quart (qt)	32 fluid ounces (fl oz) 4 cups (c) 2 pints (pt)
1 tablespoon	12.5 milliliters (mL)		
1 liter (L)	1,000 milliliters (mL) 1,000 cubic centimeters (cm^3) 1 cubic decimeter (dm^3) 4 metric cups	1 gallon (gal)	128 fluid ounces (fl oz) 16 cups (c) 8 pints (pt) 4 quarts (qt)
Weight			
1 gram (g)	1,000 milligrams (mg)	1 pound (lb)	16 ounces (oz)
1 kilogram (kg)	1,000 grams (g)		
Time			
1 minute (min)	60 seconds (s)	1 year (yr)	365 days 52 weeks 12 months
1 hour (h)	60 minutes (min)		
1 day (d)	24 hours (h)	1 decade	10 years
1 week (w)	7 days (d)	1 century	100 years
1 month (mo)	about 4 weeks		

Glossary

a.m. A way to indicate the times from 12:00 midnight to 12:00 noon.

addend One of the numbers to be added.

Example: $\begin{array}{r} 3 \\ +5 \\ \hline 8 \end{array}$ addends

addition An operation that gives the total number when you put together two or more numbers.

angle Two rays from a single point.

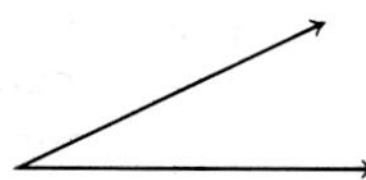

area The measure of a region, expressed in square units.

associative (grouping) principle When adding (or multiplying) three or more numbers, the grouping of the addends (or factors) can be changed and the sum (or product) is the same.

Examples: $2 + (8 + 6) = (2 + 8) + 6$
$3 \times (4 \times 2) = (3 \times 4) \times 2$

calendar A chart that shows months, days, and dates.

centimeter (cm) A unit of length in the metric system. 100 centimeters equal 1 meter.

1 centimeter

circle A plane figure in which all the points are the same distance from a point called the center.

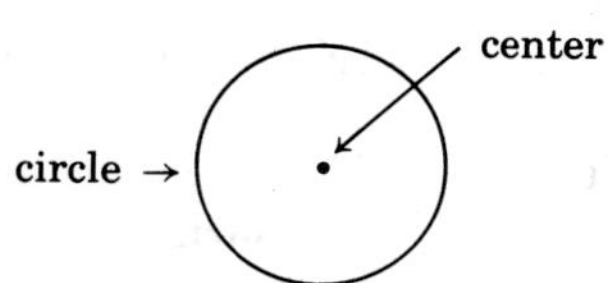

commutative (order) principle When adding (or multiplying) two or more numbers, the order of the addends (or factors) can be changed and the sum (or product) is the same.

Examples: $4 \times 5 = 5 + 4$
$2 \times 3 = 3 \times 2$

congruent figures Figures that have the same size and shape.

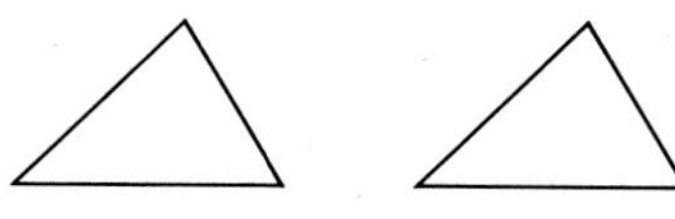

congruent triangles

coordinates Number pairs used in graphing.

cube A space figure that has squares for all of its faces.

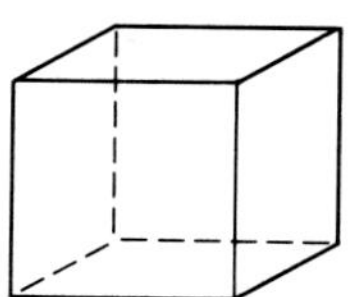

cup (c) A unit for measuring liquids. 1 quart equals 4 cups.

cylinder A space figure that has a circle for a face.

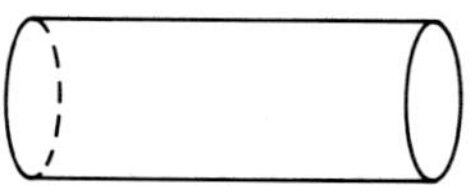

cylinder

decimal A number that shows tenths by using a decimal point.

3.2 ← decimal
↑
decimal point

degree Celsius (°C) A unit for measuring temperature in the metric system.

degree Fahrenheit (°F) A unit for measuring temperature in the customary system of measurement.

difference The number obtained by subtracting one number from another.

digits The symbols used to write numerals: 0, 1, 2, 3, 4, 5, 6, 7, 8, and 9.

dividend A number to be divided.

$7\overline{)28}$ with quotient 4 ← dividend

division An operation that tells how many sets or how many in each set.

divisor The number by which a dividend is divided.

divisor → $7\overline{)28}$ with quotient 4

END An instruction in a computer program that tells the computer to stop.

equation A number sentence involving the use of the equality symbol.

Examples: $9 + 2 = 11$
$8 - 4 = 4$

equivalent fractions Fractions that name the same amount.

Example: $\frac{1}{2}$ and $\frac{2}{4}$

estimate To find an answer that is close to the exact answer.

even number A whole number that has 0, 2, 4, 6, or 8 in the ones' place.

factors Numbers that are multiplied together to form a product.

Example: $6 \times 7 = 42$
↑ ↑
factors

flowchart A chart that shows a step-by-step way of doing something.

foot (ft) A unit for measuring length. 1 foot equals 12 inches.

fraction A number that expresses parts of a whole or a set.

Example: $\frac{3}{4}$

gallon (gal) A unit of liquid measure. 1 gallon equals 4 quarts.

gram (g) The basic unit for measuring weight in the metric system. A paper clip weighs about 1 gram.

graph A picture that shows information in an organized way.

greater than The relationship of one number being larger than another number.

Example: $6 > 5$, read "6 is greater than 5"

inch (in.) A unit for measuring length. 12 inches equal 1 foot.

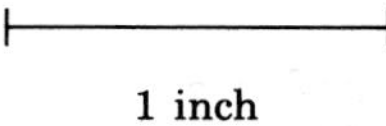

kilogram (kg) A unit of weight in the metric system. 1 kilogram is 1,000 grams.

kilometer (km) A unit of length in the metric system. 1 kilometer is 1,000 meters.

length The measure of distance from one end to the other end of an object.

less than The relationship of being smaller than another number.

Example: $5 < 6$, read "5 is less than 6"

line A straight path that is endless in both directions.

line of symmetry A line on which a figure can be folded so that the two parts fit exactly.

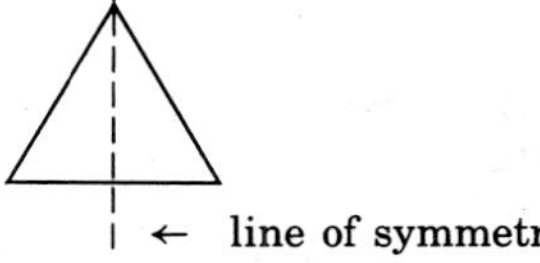

LIST A copy of the set of instructions that tells a computer what to do.

liter (L) A metric unit used to measure liquids. 1 liter equals 1,000 cubic centimeters.

measure A number indicating the relation between a given object and a suitable unit.

meter (m) A unit of length in the metric system. 1 meter is 100 centimeters.

mile (mi) A unit for measuring length. 1 mile equals 5,280 feet.

minus (−) Used to indicate the subtraction operation, as in $7 - 3 = 4$, read, "7 minus 3 equal 4."

mixed number A number that has a whole number part and a fractional part, such as $2\frac{3}{4}$.

multiplication An operation that combines two numbers, called factors, to give one number, called the product.

negative number A number that is less than zero.

number line A line that shows numbers in order.

Example: 7 8 9 10

number pair Two numbers that are used to give the location of a point on a graph.

Example: (3,2)

number sentence A way to express a relationship between numbers.

Examples: $3 + 5 = 8$
$6 \div 2 = 3$

numeral A symbol for a number.

odd number A whole number that has 1, 3, 5, 7, or 9 in the ones' place.

ordinal number A number that is used to tell order.

Example: first, fifth

ounce (oz) A unit for measuring weight. 16 ounces equal 1 pound.

p.m. A way to indicate the times from 12:00 noon to 12:00 midnight.

perimeter The distance around a figure.

pint (pt) A unit for measuring liquid. 2 pints equal 1 quart.

place value The value given to the place a digit occupies in a number.

Example: 3 5 6
hundreds' place
tens' place
ones' place

plane figures Figures that lie on a flat surface.

Examples:

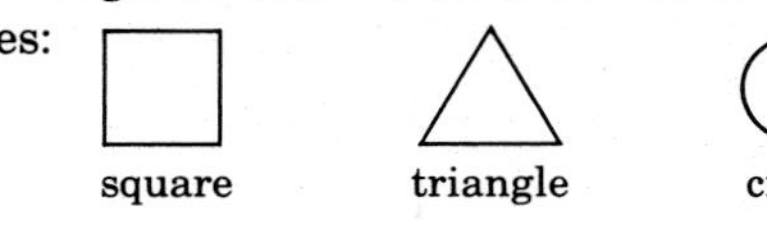

plus (+) Used to indicate the addition operation, as in 4 + 3 = 7, read, "4 plus 3 equal 7.

pound (lb) A unit for measuring weight. 1 pound equals 16 ounces.

PRINT An instruction in a computer program that tells the computer to print something.

product The result of the multiplication operation.

Example: 6 × 7 = 42 (↑ product)

program The set of instructions that tells a computer what to do.

quart (qt) A unit for measuring liquids. 1 quart equals 4 cups.

quotient The number (other than the remainder) that is the result of the division operation.

Examples: 45 ÷ 9 = 5 (↑ quotient)

$$\begin{array}{r} 6 \leftarrow \text{quotient} \\ 7\overline{)45} \\ -\ 42 \\ \hline 3 \end{array}$$

rectangle A plane figure with 4 sides and 4 right angles.

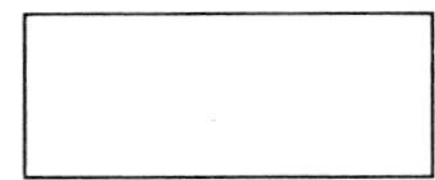

rectangular prism A space figure with six faces. It has the shape of a box.

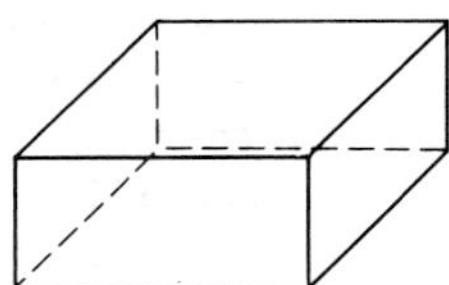

remainder The number less than the divisor that remains after the division process is completed.

Example:

$$\begin{array}{r} 6 \\ 7\overline{)47} \\ -\ 42 \\ \hline 5 \leftarrow \text{remainder} \end{array}$$

right angle An angle that has the same shape as the corner of a square.

Roman numerals Numerals used by the Romans.

Examples: I = 1, V = 5, VI = 6

rounding Replacing a number with a number that tells about how many.

Example: 23 rounded to the nearest 10 is 20.

RUN What appears on the video screen when a computer program is used.

segment A straight path from one point to another.

skip counting Counting by a number other than 1.

Example: 0 , 5 , 10 , 15
Skip counting by fives

space figure A figure that is not flat but that has volume.

Examples:

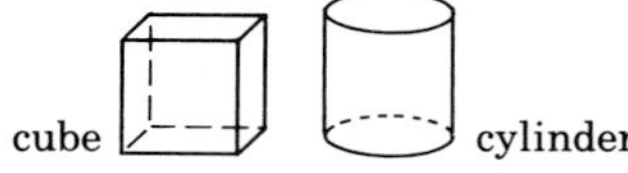

sphere A space figure that has the shape of a round ball.

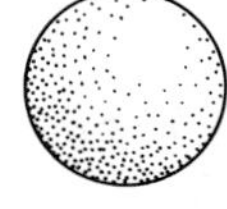

square A plane figure that has four equal sides and four equal corners.

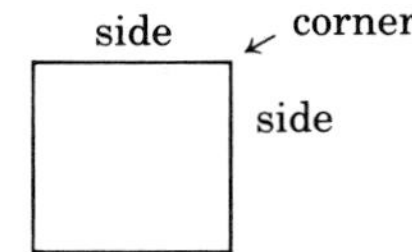

subtraction An operation that tells the difference between two numbers, or how many are left when some are taken away.

sum The number obtained by adding numbers.

Example:

$$\begin{array}{r} 3 \\ +\ 2 \\ \hline 5 \leftarrow \text{sum} \end{array}$$

times (×) Used to indicate the multiplication operation, as in 3 × 4 = 12, read, "3 times 4 equal 12."

trading To make a group of ten from one of the next highest place value, or one from ten of the next lowest place value.

Examples: one hundred can be traded for ten tens; ten ones can be traded for one ten.

triangle A plane figure with three segments as sides.

unit An amount or quantity used as a standard of measurement.

volume The number of units of space that a space figure holds.

yard (yd) A unit for measuring length. 1 yard equals 3 feet.

Index

A

B

C

D

E

F

N

O

P

Q

R

S